The NOLO *News—*

Our free magazine devoted [to] everyday legal & consume[r ...]

D1033270

To thank you for sending in the postage paid feedback card in the back of this book, you'll receive a free two-year subscription to the **NOLO** *News*—our quarterly magazine of legal, small business and consumer information. With each issue you get updates on important legal changes that affect you, helpful articles on everyday law, answers to your legal questions in Auntie Nolo's advice column, a complete Nolo catalog and, of course, our famous lawyer jokes.

Legal information online– 24 hours a day

Get instant access to the legal information you need 24 hours a day.

Visit a Nolo online self-help law center and you'll find:

- hundreds of helpful articles on a wide variety of topics
- selected chapters from Nolo books
- online seminars with our lawyer authors and other experts
- downloadable demos of Nolo software
- frequently asked questons about key legal issues
- our complete catalog and online ordering info
- our ever popular lawyer jokes and more.

Here's how to find us:

America Online Just use the key word Nolo.

On the **Internet** our World Wide Web address (URL) is: http://www.nolo.com.

Prodigy/CompuServe Use the Web Browsers on CompuServe or Prodigy to access Nolo's Web site on the Internet.

[...]ave [...]egal information. Because laws and legal procedures change often, we update our books regularly. To help keep you up-to-date we are extending this special upgrade offer. Cut out and mail the title portion of the cover of your old Nolo book and we'll give you 25% off the retail price of the NEW EDITION when you purchase directly from us. For details see the back of the book.

OUR NO-HASSLE GUARANTEE
We've created products we're proud of and think will serve you well. But if for any reason, anything you buy from **Nolo Press** does not meet your needs, we will refund your purchase price and pay for the cost of returning it to us by Priority Mail. No ifs, ands or buts.

NOLO PRESS
25 YEARS
LAW FOR ALL

How to Mediate Your Dispute

BY PETER LOVENHEIM

NOLO PRESS BERKELEY

YOUR RESPONSIBILITY WHEN USING A SELF-HELP LAW BOOK

We've done our best to give you useful and accurate information in this book. But laws and procedures change frequently and are subject to differing interpretations. If you want legal advice backed by a guarantee, see a lawyer. If you use this book, it's your responsibility to make sure that the facts and general advice contained in it are applicable to your situation.

KEEPING UP TO DATE

To keep its books up to date, Nolo Press issues new printings and new editions periodically. New printings reflect minor legal changes and technical corrections. New editions contain major legal changes, major text additions or major reorganizations. To find out if a later printing or edition of any Nolo book is available, call Nolo Press at 510-549-1976 or check the catalog in the *Nolo News*, our quarterly newspaper.

To stay current, follow the "Update" service in the *Nolo News*. You can get a free two-year subscription by sending us the registration card in the back of the book. In another effort to help you use Nolo's latest materials, we offer a 25% discount off the purchase of the new edition of your Nolo book when you turn in the cover of an earlier edition. (See the "Recycle Offer" in the back of the book.)

This book was last revised in: July 1996.

FIRST EDITION	JULY 1996
EDITOR	RALPH WARNER
MANUSCRIPT PREPARATION	STEPHANIE HAROLDE
COVER ART & DESIGN	LINDA WANCZYK
BOOK DESIGN	JACKIE MANCUSO
INDEX	SAYRE VAN YOUNG
PROOFREADER	ROBERT WELLS
PRINTING	DELTA LITHOGRAPH CO.

Lovenheim, Peter.
   How to mediate your dispute / Peter Lovenheim.
      p. cm.
   Includes index.
   ISBN 0-87337-329-4
    1. Dispute resolution (Law)–United States–Popular works.
   2. Compromise (Law)–United States–Popular works. I. Title.
KF9084.Z9L68 1996
347.73'9–dc20
[347.3079]   96-20977
                    CIP

Quantity sales: For information on bulk purchases or corporate premium sales, please contact the Special Sales department. For academic sales or textbook adoptions, ask for Academic Sales. 800-955-4775, Nolo Press, Inc., 950 Parker St., Berkeley, CA, 94710.

dedication

To my sister, Jane, and brother, Robert

acknowledgments

I appreciate the help of many people who shared information and ideas with me for this book: Sindy Cantor, Paul G. Charbonneau, Doneldon Dennis, Judge Roderic Duncan, Anne Hoyer, Anita Miller, Thomas VanStrydonck, Brian Johnson, Vicki Lewin, Helvi McClelland, Hugh McIsaac, Irina Novozhenets, Diane Nuemann, Peter Salem, John Sands, Michael Venditto, Scot Rasor and Judy Weiner.

I am especially grateful to the people at Nolo Press for their editorial assistance and good humor, particularly Jake Warner, Stephanie Harolde and Steve Elias. Also Thomas Jefferson, whose own experience with Nolo editors made my job a lot easier during the final drafts.

My thanks also to my wife, Marie, to my children, Sarah, Val and Ben, to my parents, June and Andrew Lovenheim, and to my brother, Robert Lovenheim, and my sister, Jane Glazer, for always asking me what chapter I was on and helping me keep at this book until it was done.

contents

one

What is mediation?

two

Selecting disputes for mediation

3 three

Where to take your dispute for mediation

4 four

Starting your mediation case

5 five

Selecting mediation services and mediators

6 six

Preparing for your mediation

7 seven

Inside the mediation session

 **eight**

Writing an agreement that works

 **nine**

If no agreement is reached: options available

10 ten

What to do if your mediation agreement doesn't work

11 eleven

Divorce mediation

12 twelve

Mediating business disputes

13 thirteen

Lawyers and legal research

appendix A

Sample mediation rules

appendix B

Standards of conduct
for mediators

appendix C

National and regional mediation
organizations and services

appendix D

Statewide mediation offices

Introduction

You have just been informed by your husband that he wants a divorce.

Almost daily your neighbor threatens to sue you for blocking his driveway.

You receive a stiff letter from a business claiming you are infringing its trademark and demanding $50,000 in damages.

Any of these situations—or a thousand others—are likely to send your blood pressure sky high. Why? The first word that is likely to come into your mind, of course, is court. And most likely, the second is lawyer. The litigation fever in this country—the often unthinking dash to lawyers and to court—is a symptom, I believe, of a society grown increasingly adversarial and violent, where ordinary people have lost the belief they can sit down together and reason out a solution to their own problems.

But every year, the millions of Americans who run to court, discover that the delays, costs and stresses of our legal system often leave them poorer and more frustrated than when they began. Many would agree with Judge Learned Hand, who said in an address to the New York Bar Association in 1926: "As a litigant, I should dread a lawsuit beyond almost anything else short of sickness and death."

Fortunately, there is now a way to resolve disputes that, compared to litigation, is often quicker, less expensive, more private, understandable and fair. It is called mediation.

Mediation is a process in which two or more people involved in a dispute come together to try to find a fair and workable solution to their problem. They do so with the help of a mediator, a neutral third person, trained in cooperative conflict resolution techniques.

Certainly the most efficient way to resolve any dispute is directly with the other person involved, by simply sitting down and talking it out. But if that's not possible, then for most of the disputes in your life, mediation will usually be the best alternative.

Mediation can be used to resolve most types of civil (non-criminal) disputes that traditionally would end up in court, such as those involving personal injuries, contracts, leases, employment and divorce. Mediators are also particularly good at resolving interpersonal disputes between neighbors, roommates, business partners, co-workers and friends.

Use of mediation as a means of resolving disputes has grown rapidly in the United States in recent years. Today there are nearly 400 tax-supported, community mediation centers, plus increasing numbers of all kinds of mediation organizations, programs and private dispute resolution companies. Wherever you live, you should be able today to find a mediator or mediation service to help with your dispute.

And in most cases, you will not need a lawyer to go to mediation. The rules of mediation are usually simple and straightforward. The preparation may take some time and thought, but normally is not complicated. The mediation itself will follow a simple procedure and will be conducted in plain English.

This book is designed help you understand how mediation works and how to do it well. Chapters 1-10 show the who, what, why, when and how of mediation, and will take you step-by-step through the process of mediating nearly any type or level of dispute.

Near the end of the book are two special chapters. Chapter 11, Divorce Mediation, shows how to mediate a divorce or relationship break-up (it applies to both married and unmarried couples) and covers money issues, such as division of marital property, and child issues, such as custody, visitation and support. Chapter 12, Mediating Business Disputes, shows how to mediate complex commercial disputes involving large sums of money, multiple parties and complicated technical issues.

The book does not cover mediation of disputes between labor and management. This aspect of mediation is governed by federal and state laws, and by the terms of union contracts. It is a special type of mediation and is not part of our discussion. Nor does the book cover multi-party environmental disputes or disputes arising in other specialized areas of public policy that, in fact, might be fruitfully resolved through the mediation process.

I have been involved in the mediation field for more than ten years, first as a mediator, then as a mediation company owner and administrator, and as a writer. In that time, I have seen the magic of mediation work time after time. I have seen people with seemingly insoluble problems come together with a skilled mediator, and after a remarkably short time, emerge with their problem settled. Mediation doesn't always succeed, of course, but most of the time it does. And when it does, it gives those who participate the valuable gifts of a fair and workable solution, an end to uncertainty and hostility and the ability to put a problem behind them so they can get on with their lives.

That's the magic of mediation as I know it. I hope this book will help you know it, too, and that mediation's benefits for you will be as great.

GUIDE TO ICONS USED IN THIS BOOK

 This icon lets you know where you can read more about the particular issue or topic discussed in the text.

 This is a caution to slow down and consider potential problems.

 This icon means that you may be able to skip some material that doesn't apply to your situation.

 This icon alerts you to a practical tip or good idea.

 This icon lets you know when you probably need the advice of a lawyer who specializes in landlord-tenant law.

O N E

What Is Mediation?

**THIS OVERVIEW CHAPTER IS DESIGNED FOR THE READER WHO IS
RELATIVELY NEW TO MEDIATION. Because most of the topics mentioned here
are discussed in greater depth later in the book, readers already familiar with
mediation may wish to skip or skim this material.**

A. What Is Mediation?

Mediation is a process in which two or more people involved in a dispute come
together to try to work out a solution to their problem with the help of a neutral
third person, called "the mediator." The mediator is normally trained in conflict
resolution, although the extent of this training can vary greatly. Unlike a judge or
an arbitrator, the mediator does not take sides or make decisions. The mediator's
job is to help the disputants evaluate their goals and options in order to find *their
own* solution.

1. MEDIATION IS NONCOERCIVE

The key to understanding mediation is to realize that it is noncoercive. This means that because the mediator has no authority to impose a decision, nothing will be decided unless both you and the other party agree to it. However, in the event you do arrive at a mutual agreement, its terms can easily be made legally binding. One way this is done is by writing the agreement in the form of an enforceable contract. (For more on how to write a mediation agreement, see Chapter 8, Writing an Agreement That Works.)

2. YOU DON'T GIVE UP RIGHTS WHEN YOU AGREE TO MEDIATE

Agreeing to mediate does not require you to give up any other legal rights. If mediation does not produce an agreement, you are free to pursue other remedies, such as binding arbitration or litigation. (For the difference between mediation and arbitration, see Section E, below.)

3. MEDIATION IS MORE LIKELY TO SUCCEED IN SOME SITUATIONS THAN IN OTHERS

You can mediate at any time during a dispute, whether or not a lawsuit has been filed. However, experience has shown that there are some times during the course of a dispute when it makes more sense to try mediation, either because you believe the other side is likely to agree to participate or because you think the chances for reaching a settlement are especially good. At these times, a case is said to be "ripe" for mediation. One of these times is normally at, or fairly close to, the beginning of a dispute, before each side's position has hardened. Another is after a lawsuit has been filed but before the parties have expended much time and money preparing for trial. At this point, each side may also be psychologically ready to compromise in order to avoid the possibility that a judge or jury will render a highly negative decision. For a similar reason, a third time is just before trial. For more information on determining when a case is "ripe" for mediation, see Chapter 4, Section A.

B. The Goals of Mediation

The primary goal of mediation is for all parties to a dispute to work out a solution they can live with and trust. In this sense, mediation is forward- not backward-looking. The goal is not truth-finding or law-imposing, but problem-solving. This is a far different approach than is followed in a court trial, where the judge or jury looks back to determine who was right and who was wrong by examining such issues as whether a law was broken or a contract breached.

Mediation also has some important secondary goals. Whether or not a dispute is fully resolved, the parties can benefit if any of these other goals are met:

- improved communication between the disputants;
- a better understanding of the other person's point of view;
- release of anger by meeting face-to-face with the person and having a chance to speak one's mind and be listened to;
- increased awareness of the strengths and weaknesses of one's position based on comments made in private by the mediator;

- recognition of hidden issues (such as personality traits) that may be involved in your dispute but about which you were not previously aware; and
- exposure to creative ideas for settlement suggested by the mediator.

WHY DO PEOPLE NEED TO MEDIATE?

Many disputes that come to mediation settle in just a few hours. It's fair to ask if the dispute was so obviously solvable, why did the disputants need to bother with mediation? Unfortunately, there are frequently barriers that prevent people from resolving disputes on their own. These commonly include an inability or unwillingness to communicate directly, a lack of trust in the other party and the absence of a safe private place in which to have a conversation. In addition, people who are caught up in a dispute often need help identifying creative ways to resolve it and sometimes to evaluate objectively both their own position and that of the other side.

In addition, the need for mediation—and its frequent success—has an important psychological dimension. Often, before people are willing to compromise and settle, they need the chance to say directly to the other person (ideally in front of an impartial person) how hurt they are, how inconvenienced they have been by the dispute, and how wronged they feel. It is difficult if not impossible for many people to get over these barriers on their own. This opportunity for what psychologists call "catharsis," is an important reason why mediation is so often needed, and often works so well.

C. What Types of Disputes Can Be Mediated?

Mediation is useful to resolve most kinds of civil (noncriminal) disputes that would otherwise go to court or arbitration, including those involving contracts, leases, small business ownership, employment and divorce. An unmarried couple separating and needing to divide valuable household items, two small businesses squabbling over customer lists and a recently divorcing couple trying to resolve child custody visitation issues are all examples of people who are good candidates to use mediation to try to resolve their disputes. Other types of disputes often settled through mediation include:

- consumer vs. merchant
- landlord vs. tenant
- employee vs. employer
- homeowner vs. contractor
- business partner vs. business partner.

Nonviolent criminal matters, such as claims of verbal or other personal harassment, can also be successfully mediated. In addition, good candidates for mediation include interpersonal disputes that may not rise to the level of a legal claim but are nonetheless important to the people involved. These include disputes involving:

- neighbor vs. neighbor
- roommate vs. roommate
- spouse vs. spouse
- employee vs. employee.

TO DETERMINE IF A PARTICULAR CASE IS APPROPRIATE FOR MEDIATION, see Chapter 2, Selecting Disputes for Mediation. See Chapter 11 for a full discussion of Divorce Mediation, and Chapter 12 for a full discussion of Business Mediation.

A BRIEF HISTORY OF MEDIATION

Mediation as a way of resolving disputes is unfamiliar to many Americans, but it is not new. People in Asian cultures have used this approach to solve legal and personal conflicts for thousands of years. Even in the U.S., mediation has a rich history, according to Jerold S. Auerbach, in his fascinating book *Justice Without Law?* (Oxford University Press, 1983). Auerbach points out that more than 350 years ago, in 1636, the Puritan founders of Dedham, a community located southwest of Boston, provided in their covenant for a system of informal mediation. And in New Netherland, Dutch colonists established a "Board of Nine Men" to serve as "friendly mediators and arbitrators." In colonial Virginia, the legislature noted the "excessive charges and great delays" of litigation and encouraged citizens to resolve disputes by other means. Later, beginning in the 1800s, Chinese immigrants on the West Coast, Scandinavian immigrants in the Midwest and Jewish immigrants in New York set up mediation boards to resolve disputes within their own communities.

D. The Advantages and Disadvantages of Mediation

As a dispute resolution process, mediation works extremely well in some contexts and less well in others. Let's briefly review these.

1. ADVANTAGES

Especially when compared to litigation as a way of resolving disputes, mediation offers the following advantages:

Swiftness: Mediations are usually scheduled within a few weeks or, at most, a couple of months, from the time of a request. Most mediation sessions last between a few hours and a day, depending on the type of case. In contrast, lawsuits often take many months or, more typically, years to resolve. In some large cities, it can take two or more years just to get a court date.

Confidentiality: Mediation sessions are private—there is no "public docket" as in court—so no one even needs to know that you have a dispute in the first place. Most things said in a court are available to the public, but everything said in mediation is confidential and with very few exceptions cannot legally be revealed outside the mediation or used later in a court of law. (For more about confidentiality in mediation, see Chapter 6, Preparing for Your Mediation.)

Low Cost: In many parts of the U.S., nonprofit community mediation centers provide quality services to handle relatively minor consumer, neighborhood, workplace and similar disputes, either free or for a small charge. Private dispute resolution companies, which typically mediate personal injury claims, business contract and employment disputes and other cases involving a substantial sum of money, are more expensive (some charge $200 or more per hour) but still offer services for fees that amount to a fraction of the cost of bringing a lawsuit. Similarly, couples who pay divorce mediators $100 or more an hour will often find they end up saving many thousands (and sometimes tens of thousands) of dollars as compared to what a litigated divorce would cost. (For more on the cost of mediation, see Section I, below.)

Fairness: In mediation, you tailor your own solution to the dispute according to your needs; legal precedents or the whim of a judge will not dictate the solution to your case. Best of all, if you don't think a settlement proposal is fair, you don't have to agree to it.

Flexibility: In mediation, you can raise any issues related to your dispute that you believe are important. For example, in divorce mediation, a couple may go beyond strictly legal issues of property and custody and include in their agreement matters that ordinarily wouldn't be part of what a judge would order, such as how each spouse will participate in extracurricular activities of their children, or visitation for the family dog. Similarly, disputes sometimes harbor undiscovered or undisclosed issues, and mediation offers the flexibility to ferret these out.

Success: Many independent mediators and mediation services report that in more than four out of five cases, the parties are able to settle all issues in dispute to their mutual satisfaction. As compared to court, where the losing party is almost always angry, this is success indeed.

Less Stressful: For many people, going to court is scary. You face hard-to-understand procedures, a win-lose scenario and the frustration of being dependent on a system whose practitioners speak a foreign language full of terms such as *motion in limine, order to show cause* and *res ipsa loquitur.* Mediation, by contrast, is informal, is conducted in English, and any solution must be agreed to by both parties.

2. DISADVANTAGES

Mediation is not appropriate for every dispute. In some situations, especially, it has disadvantages:

Noncoercive: The mediator does not have authority to impose a decision. Especially when going into a mediation where you are sure you are legally right and a judge would back your position, you take the risk that you will invest time, money and energy in the process only to find that, when it's over, your problem has not been resolved. Fortunately, this is usually not a big negative, since it's almost always clear within a day or two whether mediation is likely to work, and you can withdraw if it isn't.

Power Imbalance: If the other party has far more power than you—whether financial, intellectual, emotional or otherwise—you may be at a significant disadvantage in mediation, unless the mediator is willing and able to help you articulate your point of view and carefully evaluate any proposed settlement to be sure it is fair. For example, a person dissatisfied with the purchase of a home computer may find himself seated across the table from the computer store's district manager, who not only knows more about computers but has been trained extensively in negotiating techniques. Or a shy college student who works part-time and believes herself to have been sexually harassed by her employer may be at a serious disadvantage mediating with an older, more seasoned manager. For couples seeking to mediate their divorce, if one spouse has a long history of overpowering or intimidating the other, the imbalance of power can be an important consideration. (See Chapter 11, Divorce Mediation.)

Slippery Slope: Some people, including those who are extremely anxious, may be at considerable risk of internalizing the "settlement" goal of mediation and end up accepting an inappropriate agreement in order to appear cooperative.

Showing Your Hand: To mediate effectively you generally need to reveal enough about the strengths of your position to persuade the other side to compromise and settle. But if your case does not settle and there is later a need to litigate, in some circumstances, the information you revealed in mediation may help the other side plan a more effective defense. For more on deciding what information to reveal in mediation, see Chapter 6, Preparing for Your Mediation.

SOME COURT-ORDERED MEDIATIONS MAY BE COERCIVE

In a few court-sponsored mediation programs, judges have the power to order disputants to take part in mediation and, if a settlement is not reached, the mediator may recommend to the judge how the case should be decided. This type of mediation and the implications it holds for participants is examined in Chapter 6, Section C2, "Preparing for Your Presentation—If the Mediator Has the Legal Power to Influence the Decision," and also in Chapter 11, Section D11, "Divorce Mediation—If the Mediator Has Power to Recommend." In all other sections of this book, we assume the mediator follows the traditional role and does not have power to coerce.

E. Mediation Compared to Arbitration

People sometimes use the word "mediation" interchangeably with "arbitration," another popular method of dispute resolution. This is a mistake, since these procedures are very different.

1. THE GOAL OF MOST MEDIATION IS TO SEEK AGREEMENT

As we've noted, a mediator's job is to help the parties evaluate their goals and options in order to find their own solution, and once a solution is agreed upon, to help them write it down in the form of a binding legal contract. The mediator is usually trained in conflict resolution techniques but does not necessarily have expertise in the particular subject involved in the dispute.

2. THE GOAL OF ARBITRATION IS TO HAVE A NEUTRAL PERSON IMPOSE A SOLUTION

An arbitrator's job is to conduct a contested hearing between the parties, which normally involves hearing witnesses and considering evidence, and then, acting as a judge, to render a legally binding decision. The arbitrator (sometimes called "arbiter") is often an expert in the particular field involved in the dispute. Arbitration, which has long been used to resolve commercial and labor disputes, resembles a court hearing more than does mediation. The arbitrator's award is enforceable in court just like a judge's order.

3. MEDIATION, ARBITRATION AND LITIGATION COMPARED

While the list of available dispute resolution techniques is varied and also growing as new ones are developed to address specific needs—see Section F, below—mediation and arbitration remain the best-known and most commonly used alternatives to litigation. The following table compares mediation and arbitration with litigation.

COMPARISON OF FORMS OF DISPUTE RESOLUTION

PROCESS	MEDIATION	ARBITRATION	LITIGATION
Who decides?	Parties	Arbitrator	Judge
Who controls?	Parties	Arbitrators/attorneys	Court/attorneys
Procedure	Informal—a few rules are designed to protect confidentiality and let everyone speak and be heard	Agreed rules of procedure are followed	Formal and complicated rules abound
Time to schedule hearing	A few weeks	A few months	Two years or more
Cost to party	Nominal or low (business disputes can cost more)	Moderate	Substantial
Rules of evidence	None	Established but reasonably informal	Complex
Publicity	Private	Usually private	Public
Relations of parties	Cooperative effort may develop	Antagonistic	Antagonistic
Focus	Future	Past	Past
Method of negotiation	Compromise	Hard bargaining	Hard bargaining
Communication	Usually improved	Blocked	Blocked
Result	If successful, Win/Win	Win/Lose	Win/Lose
Compliance	Generally honored	Often resisted or appealed	Often resisted or appealed

Source: "Mediation and Prepaid Legal Plans," by Kenneth Cloke and Angus Strachan, *Mediation Quarterly*, No. 18, 1987, p. 94.

Above is adapted from the referenced table and includes material not appearing in the original.

F. Other Methods of Dispute Resolution

The growing popularity of mediation and arbitration has spawned variations of each that can be attractive options for certain types of cases. And, in addition, there are several other methods of dispute resolution, including negotiation, fact-finding, conciliation, mini-trials and private judging. Because someone in your dispute may raise the possibility of trying one of these, we'll briefly review them below. But before we do, let's introduce the term Alternative Dispute Resolution (often referred to as "ADR"). Since this term refers to mediation, arbitration and all other alternatives to litigation, it is extremely imprecise. Therefore, should you run into it, you will always want to determine what type of ADR is being discussed.

1. VARIATIONS ON MEDIATION

Variations on mediation include:

Mediation with a Recommendation: If mediation ends without a settlement but the parties respect and trust the mediator, they can ask the mediator to make a written recommendation as to how the dispute should be resolved. Assuming the mediator agrees to do this, the parties are then free to accept the recommendation or use it to further their own negotiations. (This is different from the authority some mediators have in a few states to recommend to a judge how cases should be decided if they do not settle in mediation. See the sidebar on "Coercive Mediation" in Section E, above.)

Med/Arb (pronounced "meed-arb"): The disputants consent to mediation but with the added provision that if mediation does not produce a settlement, then the mediator (or another neutral party) can act as arbitrator and make a binding decision. Med/arb gives assurance that, one way or the other, the dispute will be resolved: either a settlement will be reached or a decision will be arbitrated. For more on this process, see Chapter 9, Section C2.

2. VARIATIONS ON ARBITRATION

Variations on arbitration include:

"High-Low Arbitration": Like arbitration generally, this is a binding procedure, but to reduce the risk of an unacceptable award, the parties agree in advance to high and low limits on the arbitrator's authority. For a discussion of this procedure, see Chapter 9, Section C3.

Nonbinding (advisory) Arbitration: An advisory arbitration is conducted in the same way as a binding one, but by prior agreement the parties are not bound by the decision. If it's acceptable to both, they can jointly agree to it and be done. But if either doesn't accept it, they can simply use it to further their own negotiations. This technique is used when parties want the value of an independent opinion based on each side's best arguments but not the risk of getting a bad decision. (For more on arbitration, see Chapter 9, If No Agreement Is Reached: Options Available.)

3. OTHER TYPES OF ALTERNATE DISPUTE RESOLUTION

Now let's briefly consider several other common ways to resolve disputes:

Negotiation: In negotiation, the disputing parties talk directly to each other to try to reach an agreement. When it is successful, negotiation is usually the most efficient way of resolving a dispute because there is no cost or delay associated with the intervention of a third party. But if parties have trouble dealing with one another, negotiation may not work unless they hire agents, lawyers or other representatives to negotiate for them. (Mediation, it should be noted, often provides the needed structure and third-party help for parties who have trouble dealing with each other directly, thus reducing or eliminating the need for lawyers or other hired representatives.)

Conciliation: The conciliator's aim is not so much to resolve the dispute as to merely reduce tensions and get the parties talking. Parents often play the role of conciliator when their children are fighting. "I'm sure you two can work this out. How about something to eat while you sit and talk it over?" Conciliation is used fairly frequently in family and other interpersonal disputes, when a family member, friend or a member of the clergy is asked to try to help the parties solve a dispute.

Fact-Finding: When negotiations between the parties have reached an impasse, the parties may invite an independent "fact-finder"—often an expert in the field of the dispute—to analyze the issues (or sometimes just a single issue) and present findings of fact and recommendations for a solution. Fact-finding is most often used in labor disputes, although the process can easily be adapted to more general types of disputes. For example, if a construction dispute concerns a collapsed roof, the parties might agree to hire a physical engineer to examine the roof and report on what caused the collapse. The parties would then use the report to further their own negotiations.

Mini-Trial: This method is most often used in disputes between good-sized businesses. Typically, lawyers for each side are given the chance, within strict time limits (often half a day), to present their best case before top executives from both companies and a neutral advisor. The neutral advisor gives an advisory opinion to the executives, who then meet privately to negotiate a settlement based on what they've heard. For more on mini-trials, see Chapter 12, Mediating Business Disputes.

Private Judging: In about half the states, the law allows parties in noncriminal cases to try their case before a judge they jointly choose and pay for. The procedure, also known as "rent-a-judge," usually involves the disputants picking a retired judge or private attorney to render a decision in their case. In other states, a real judge appoints the private judge (sometimes called "referee"). Either way, the private judge usually has authority to decide the case as a real judge would. This procedure is most often used in cases such as those involving finances, patents, manufacturing or technical issues where the parties have an especially strong interest in protecting their privacy and being able to select a private judge with expertise in the particular field involved in the dispute, and where they can set their own hearing schedules and move quickly toward a decision. Most private dispute resolution companies that provide arbitration can also arrange for private judging.

G. Role of the Mediator

"To mediate" means "to go between" or "to be in the middle." This, literally, is what mediators do; they go between you and the other party to help you find a solution to your dispute. The mediator's role is not to be a judge, deciding who is innocent or who is guilty. Neither is it to give legal advice (even if the mediator happens to be a lawyer); nor to be a counselor or therapist. The mediator's sole function is to bring the disputants together to help them find a solution of their own making.

Exactly how the mediator does this may puzzle those who are not familiar with the process. Although each of us is, at times, a mediator—for example, department heads mediate between workers, parents mediate between children, friends mediate between friends—we probably would not attempt to sit in a room with total strangers and try to help them find a solution to a problem that has vexed them for months or years.

Our reservations about trying to do this would be well-founded. Although formal mediation involves a good deal of applied common sense, it also involves a lot more than just "getting folks together to talk about their problem." Done well, it features a mediator trained in successful conflict-resolution techniques who applies a multi-stage process efficiently designed to produce positive results. (For more on the stages of mediation, see Chapter 7, Inside the Mediation Session.) Employing her skills through the different stages of mediation, the mediator attempts to unfreeze the parties from their fixed positions, open them to the possibilities of creative solutions and finally to guide them to a mutually agreed-upon result.

To do this, she must motivate without manipulating, cajole without coercing and sometimes help create doubt where there was certainty. Or, put differently, the mediator must help both parties see the weaknesses as well as the strengths in their own positions, thus opening them up to the possibility of compromise.

In most disputes, the mediator has no power but the power to listen, persuade and inspire. These may not sound like strong tools, but used creatively, a good mediator can apply them to help the parties improve communication, change individual perceptions and eventually create trust where there was only suspicion, with the result that the disputants are able to arrive at their own mutually satisfactory agreement.

Specifically, the mediator works to help the parties:

- discover hidden issues involved in their case (people often obscure—or don't even understand—the real problems underlying a dispute)
- understand the difference between what they *want* and what they *need* (people make certain demands in a dispute—the payment of money, cutting down a tree, visiting children only on Tuesday—but these "wants" are not always the same as their broader needs for emotional and economic security, respect, recognition and preservation of important relationships; once identified, needs may often be easier to satisfy than wants)
- understand both the wants and needs of the other side (parties may discover that some of their "wants" overlap (avoidance of legal fees) and some "needs" do not conflict (economic security for one party, recognition and opportunity for the other)
- realistically consider the many possible solutions (mediators generate new ideas for settlement and act as neutral sounding boards as parties weigh the pros and cons of proposed terms of agreement).

H. Who Are the Mediators?

There may be as many as 50,000 people in the United States today who work full- or part-time as mediators. This estimate is necessarily rough, since there is no national registry for mediators. Included in the 50,000 figure are:

- a small but increasing number of career mediators who specialize in large, complex disputes involving business, construction, health care or the environment. Some of these mediators are employed by national dispute resolution companies; others work independently. (For the differences between dispute resolution companies, other mediation services and independent mediators, see Chapter 3, Where to Take Your Dispute for Mediation.)

- private mediators who specialize in divorce and family disputes, most of whom work independently or in small group practices. (For more on divorce mediators, see Chapter 11, Divorce Mediation.)

- a growing number of lawyers who mediate legal disputes part-time while they also practice law. Lawyer-mediators often work as independent contractors through local private dispute resolution companies.

- a large number of volunteers who mediate through the national network of about 400 tax-supported, community or court-approved mediation centers and programs.

- mediators, many of whom have backgrounds in social work, who work full-time in court-sponsored programs that mediate custody and visitation issues for divorcing couples. (See Chapter 11, Divorce Mediation.)

1. Training and Levels of Commitment to Mediation Vary Among Mediators

While the number of full-time career mediators is growing, most people in the field mediate only occasionally while pursuing other careers. Their level of commitment to mediation varies greatly, as does the extent of their training. It is not unusual, for example, to find that a volunteer nonlawyer mediator who helps at a community mediation center has received more extensive training than a lawyer who is paid to mediate through a court-connected program. What mediators earn varies widely, too. The volunteer may earn nothing or be paid very moderately ($35-$50 per mediation) while, at the other end of the pay scale, a career mediator in private practice who specializes in business disputes may charge as much as $200-$300 an hour.

2. Mediators Are Not Regulated by the Government

The mediation field is largely unregulated by state or federal law and therefore lacks universal standards of training and practice. And although this lack of structure results in disparities in the quality of service, fees and procedures, it has the advantage of keeping this relatively new field open to innovation and experimentation, as well as being reasonably accessible to those who want to enter. But as mediation becomes more widely used we can expect regulations to appear. For example, in states where legislatures have given judges authority to refer large numbers of cases for mediation, the courts are already setting minimum standards of training and experience for mediators who want to receive referrals. (For more about regulation of mediators, see Chapter 5, Selecting Mediation Services and Mediators.)

I. How Much Does Mediation Cost?

The cost of mediating varies greatly depending on the type of case and who does the mediating. In nearly all cases, however, mediating is far less expensive than going to court. Here is a quick overview of what you can expect to pay and a few examples of typical fees you might encounter in cases mediated in a mid-sized North American city:

Nonprofit community mediation centers. There are about 400 of these nonprofit centers around the country. They handle matters such as neighborhood disputes, minor criminal cases such as charges of harassment and disputes between landlords and tenants. Some centers are connected to local small claims courts to mediate small money disputes.

> **EXAMPLE OF NEIGHBORHOOD DISPUTE:** *A case in which three neighbors are involved in dispute over disruptive children.*
> *Typical length of mediation:*   *full-day*
> *Typical fees per party:*   *$10 filing fee (waived if financial hardship)*

Private, dispute resolution companies. These for-profit companies typically handle business and construction disputes, personal injury claims, employment matters and other large, complex cases. The private firms usually charge a set administrative fee plus an hourly rate for the mediator's time. Fees vary some-what with location: companies in New York, Los Angeles and other major cities may charge a $500 administrative fee per party plus $200 per hour per party. In medium-sized cities and small towns, expect fees to be reduced by about half. (Where cases involve more than two parties, the hourly fee per party is usually reduced by up to one-third.)

> **EXAMPLE OF PERSONAL INJURY CLAIM DISPUTE :** *A dispute over the value of injuries between a passenger in a car whose leg and spine were fractured when the driver hit a telephone pole, and the driver's insurance company.*
> *Typical length of mediation:*   *half-day*
> *Typical fees per party:*   *$600*

EXAMPLE OF BUSINESS CONTRACT DISPUTE: *A computer parts company sues Big Computer, Inc., for $5 million for rejecting parts, which it claims conformed to the contract. Just before the trial is to begin, the parties decide to try mediation.*

Typical length of mediation: *Four days.*

Typical fees per party: *$8,000.*

Divorce and family mediators. Though they specialize in divorce cases, these mediators also handle a variety of family-related problems, such as disputes between parents and children, siblings and extended family members. Divorce mediators, who often set up their own offices and practice on their own or in small groups, normally charge on a per couple basis anywhere from $60 up to $300 per hour, with a rate of $100 being typical. The higher rates apply in the larger cities.

EXAMPLE OF DIVORCE MEDIATION DISPUTE: *A divorcing couple with a house, two cars, bank accounts, pension plans and three minor children are trying to reach an agreement out of court as to the division of their property and the custody and visitation of their children.*

Typical length of mediation: *Six two-hour sessions over two months, plus five hours to prepare a written agreement.*

Typical cost for couple   *$2,215 (split 50-50)*

J. How Do Cases Get to Mediation?

Disputes come to mediation in several different ways. Most arrive voluntarily, with the mutual consent of the parties. But sometimes disputes must be mediated by order of a judge or are required by a state law or by the terms of a contract. Following is a brief look at the various paths to mediation.

1. VOLUNTARY MEDIATION

Most cases come to mediation when the people involved in a dispute agree to engage a mediator to try to help them resolve it. Usually, one party decides mediation might be a good idea and suggests it to the other or contacts a mediation service which in turn contacts the other side to propose mediation. Other times, an employer, trade group or other organization establishes a program for voluntary mediation that they promote to employees or members.

2. MANDATORY MEDIATION

Mandatory mediation means that the parties must attend a mediation session by contract or court order. It doesn't mean that they have to agree to anything.

There are a couple different types of mandatory, or required, mediation. One of these involves court-connected programs. In an effort to cut the flood of lawsuits and allow people the benefits of mediation, many states have passed laws that require you to mediate before you can take a case into the courtroom. For example, Florida residents who file lawsuits seeking $50,000 or less must go to mediation before they can proceed to trial. In Maine and several other states, small claims actions are routinely ordered to mediation. In California, if you want a divorce and have children you may be ordered by the court to mediate issues of child custody and visitation.

Another growing source of mandatory mediation involves the enforcement of business contracts that call for mediation in case of a dispute. With increasing frequency, this type of clause is contained in contracts people sign with their employers, banks, colleges and even gyms. For example, the author of this book signed a contract with Nolo Press, Inc., its publisher, which contains a dispute resolution clause. Under it, if a dispute arises and the author and publisher cannot resolve it by themselves in "a reasonable time," they must try mediation before either can file a lawsuit.

For more on the special issues raised by mandatory mediation, see Chapter 6, Preparing for Your Mediation.

K. How Many People Participate in the Mediation?

Everyone with an important stake in the outcome of a dispute should be invited to participate in its mediation. Often this is just two people, such as disputing business partners or divorcing spouses, but sometimes it is many people, as would be the case in a construction dispute involving a building's owner, architect, engineer, general contractor as well as sub-contractors, such as masons, plumbers, electricians and carpenters. Fortunately, mediation usually can accommodate as many people as necessary—often up to a dozen or more. In practice, if the group gets too large, sub-groups can be formed to be represented at the mediation by one person. Although how a mediation with more than two parties is conducted differs in small ways from the more traditional two-party mediation process covered in this book, the basic principles are the same and the information in this book should generally be applicable.

L. The Role of Lawyers in Mediation

In most mediations, having a lawyer directly participate with you is unnecessary. This is because you are trying to work out a solution to your problem with the other party, not trying to convince a judge or arbitrator of your point of view in a setting that puts a premium on knowing how to take advantage of lots of tricky procedural rules. Usually you will understand the problem and your own needs better than anyone else, including a lawyer. And since mediation rules are few and straightforward, and the entire proceeding is conducted in English, you don't ordinarily need someone with special training to figure out how to do it.

Lawyers *can* be helpful, however, to consult with before and after the mediation. If your case involves substantial property or legal rights, you may want to meet with a lawyer before the mediation to discuss the legal consequences of possible settlement terms. You may also want to condition your agreement to a settlement proposal on a lawyer's review afterwards, to be sure it does not impair your legal rights in any way you did not intend. For more on effectively using a lawyer or self-help law coach in mediation, see Chapter 6, Preparing for Your Mediation.

M. Where Are Mediations Held?

Not surprisingly, mediation is usually conducted in a conference room. Typically, the mediator sits at the head of a longish table and the disputants sit on either side, facing each other. Where the mediation conference room is located and what it looks like will vary greatly, depending somewhat on what type of mediator or mediation service you are working with.

For example, if your mediation has been arranged through one of about 400 tax-supported, community mediation centers, the session will likely be held at the center's offices, typically in a downtown office building or in space provided by a government agency. It will probably be a bare-bones conference room: pale green or yellow walls and a wobbly, wood-veneer table with folding metal chairs.

When mediations are arranged by private dispute resolution companies, the setting is usually plusher—often a suite of offices in a top drawer office building. Sometimes lawyer-mediators working on contract for these companies will conduct mediations in their own law firm's conference rooms. If the law firm or dispute resolution company is a big, prestigious one, you may find yourself seated in a high-backed, leather-upholstered chair facing the other party across a twelve-foot mahogany table.

Mediation programs run by local and state courts, such as Florida's Circuit Civil Mediation Program, may sometimes conduct mediations in conference rooms at the courthouse.

Private divorce mediators may work in downtown office buildings, suburban office parks or in their own homes. Their meeting rooms are designed to give couples a private and secure feeling. For example, rather than being "squared off" across a conference table as would be typical in a business mediation, a couple typically will be seated on a sofa, or in armchairs arranged around a coffee table.

DIFFERENCES BETWEEN MEDIATION ROOM AND COURTROOM

	MEDIATION ROOM	COURTROOM
Where parties sit	In mediation, the parties face each other directly, and the mediator sits at their level.	In a courtroom, the parties face the judge who sits up high on a bench.
Where witnesses sit	In mediation, witnesses are often unnecessary because you are not trying to prove anything; you are simply trying to solve a problem. If witnesses do attend to help explain or support your point of view, they will sit at the conference table alongside you.	In a courtroom, a prominent feature is the witness stand.
Where jury sits	In mediation, there is no jury because no one is making a decision in your case. Only the disputants will decide if they want to agree on a settlement.	In a courtroom, a large jury box is present.
Where spectators sit	In mediation, there are no spectators or press because the entire process is confidential.	In a courtroom, there are seats in the rear for members of the press and public spectators.
Where court reporter or recording device is located	In mediation, there is no reporter or recording device because what people say cannot be used in any later proceeding. Parties may take notes for their own use if they wish. The mediator may also take notes to help him or her keep track of the facts.	In a courtroom, a court reporter or tape recording device is usually located in the front of the courtroom, below and to the side of where the judge sits.
Where bailiff stands	In mediation no bailiff is needed.	Armed bailiff stands or sits in front of courtroom below and to the side of the judge.

When parties live a great distance apart and cannot travel to the same location, mediation sometimes can be conducted by telephone. This is rare but it does occur. The growing availability of low-cost visual-teleconferencing may encourage more long-distance mediation, particularly of business disputes.

N. The Rules of Mediation

Though mediation is much less formal than litigation and arbitration, it does have rules. Your mediator or mediation service should give you written rules well in advance of your first session. Read these and if you have any questions, contact the mediator or mediation service, or review them with a lawyer or law coach to be sure they are proper, because when you sign the "Agreement to Mediate" you will be pledging in writing to abide by the mediation rules.

Expect most sets of Mediation Rules to fill just a couple of pages as compared to a dozen or more pages for arbitration rules and whole volumes for court rules.

Typically, mediation rules cover the following:

- *matters of procedure*, including what forms you have to fill out to begin the mediation process and how the mediator will conduct the mediation (at the outset of the mediation session, the mediator will explain other rules, such as don't interrupt and don't threaten)
- *confidentiality*, stating that everyone involved in the mediation agrees to keep whatever is said confidential, and that the mediator will not disclose what was said in the mediation in any later court or arbitration proceeding (or more on confidentiality agreements, and how enforceable they are, see Chapter 6, Preparing for Your Mediation).
- *fees*, how much the parties will be charged and when fees need to be paid, and
- *liability*, usually exempting the mediator or mediation service from liability.

Mediation Rules are discussed further in Chapter 6, Preparing for Your Mediation. For sample Mediation Rules, see Appendix A.

O. How Long Does Mediation Take?

If the mediation rules permit (and most do), mediators will usually keep a mediation going as long as they and the parties believe progress is being made. If a mediation that begins at 9:00 a.m. produces quick results, the session may end at 11:00 a.m. But if the parties take longer to reach an agreement, the session may continue after a lunch break through the afternoon or longer. But some mediation programs—particularly those run by court systems—do impose time limits. A two-hour limit, with the option to continue another day if the mediation appears to be productive, is typical.

Even where rules allow mediation to continue indefinitely, many cases that go to mediation, such as consumer claims, small business disputes and auto accident claims, are resolved after a half-day or, at most, a full day of mediation. Multi-party cases last longer: add at least an hour of mediation time for each additional party. Major business disputes—such as complex contract and construction cases that involve many issues, parties and witnesses—may last several days or more.

Perhaps the major exception to the general rule that mediations last a relatively short time involves private divorce mediation. While some court-sponsored divorce mediation programs address only child custody issues in just one or two sessions, divorcing couples who choose private mediation often aim for a comprehensive settlement, including division of marital property and spousal maintenance, as well as child custody, visitation and support. Resolving all these issues generally requires half a dozen or more sessions spread over several weeks or months both because sticky emotional issues often must be dealt with and because the legal and practical issues can be complex. (See Chapter 11, Divorce Mediation.)

DON'T TRY TO HURRY MEDIATION. Given the uncertainty over how long your mediation will last, try to clear your calendar for the whole day so you will be able to stay as long as you need to. Or, put another way, if you drive to the mediation, park in a lot, not at a meter.

P. An Overview of the Six Stages of Mediation

Mediation is a multi-stage process designed to give the disputants time to speak and be listened to, to meet privately with the mediator and to work together toward a settlement. Mediation professionals differ as to whether mediation takes place in five, six or even seven stages. In this book we will split the difference and assume it occurs in six stages, as follows:

Stage 1: Mediator's Opening Statement: After the disputants are seated at the conference table, the mediator will sit at the head of the table, introduce everyone, review the goals and rules of the mediation and encourage each side to work cooperatively toward a settlement.

Stage 2: Disputants' Opening Statements: Each party in turn will be invited to tell, in their own words, what the dispute is about, how it has affected them and present some general ideas about how they would like to see it resolved. While one person is speaking, the other will not be allowed to interrupt.

Stage 3: Joint Discussion: At this point, the mediator may try to get the parties talking directly about what was said in opening statements. This is a time to identify and agree on what issues need to be addressed.

Stage 4: Private Caucuses: Often considered "the guts" of mediation, the private caucus is a chance for each party to meet individually and privately with the mediator to discuss the strengths and weaknesses of their positions, and new ideas for settlement. Typically, the mediator will ask one party to remain in the conference room with him while the other party waits in a nearby room or in the reception area. The mediator may caucus with each side just once, or several times back and forth, as needed.

Caucusing is used in most, but not all, mediations. It is commonly omitted, for example, in divorce mediation because, in the context of a breakdown in trust, which often occurs between divorcing couples, the mediator will prefer to keep the parties together to avoid paranoia—that is, anxiety about what the other spouse might tell the mediator in private. For the same reason, some community mediation centers do not use caucusing in cases involving interpersonal conflicts. For more on caucusing, see Chapter 7, Inside the Mediation Session, and Chapter 11, Divorce Mediation.

Stage 5: Joint Negotiation: After caucuses, the mediator may choose to bring the parties back together to negotiate directly whatever gaps remain in their positions.

Stage 6: Closure: This is the end of the mediation. If an agreement has been reached, the mediator may draft its main provisions as the parties listen. The mediator may ask each side to sign the written summary of agreement or suggest they take it to their lawyers for review. If no agreement was reached, the mediator will review whatever progress has been made and advise the disputants of their options, such as meeting again at a later date, going to arbitration or going to court.

The stages of mediation are discussed in more detail in Chapter 7, Inside the Mediation Session.

Selecting Disputes for Mediation

A Chinese proverb says: "A lawsuit breeds ten years of hatred." *The Chinese may be optimistic.*

Courts are always limited in the kinds of disputes they can hear: bankruptcy courts hear bankruptcy cases exclusively; family courts hear only divorce, adoption and other interpersonal disputes; and small claims courts are limited to small dollar disputes. Many other courts, such as those that deal with probate, patents and juvenile problems, have a similarly narrow focus.

Mediation, however, is not a court—it is a process—and, as such, it can be applied to nearly all kinds of disputes. It can be used to decide who will own the Sinai Peninsula or who will park their car on weekends in the driveway you share with your next-door neighbor. It can be used to determine how one computer company will compensate another for infringing operating system software or how your dry cleaner will compensate you for fraying the collars of your dress shirts. It can be used to determine if a shelter for the homeless can be operated by a church in a residential neighborhood in Atlanta or in whose home children should live after spouses divorce in Peoria.

The following two lists illustrate the variety of disputes regularly taken to mediation, and the differences in case mix between a typical community mediation center and a private dispute resolution company.

To decide if your dispute is one that you should try to mediate, consider the 14 factors we introduce in the following section. Seven of the factors tend to favor mediation (Sections A1-7) and seven do not (Sections B1-7). (Some of these factors are adapted from *A Student's Guide to Mediation and the Law,* by Nancy H. Rogers and Richard A. Salem (Matthew Bender, 1987).)

top 10

CASE TYPES HANDLED BY COMMUNITY DISPUTE RESOLUTION CENTERS—NEW YORK STATE, 1994-1995 (excludes matrimonial)

(Each of 41 counties in New York State has its own nonprofit, community mediation center.)

1. Personal Harassment
2. Breach of Contract
3. Interpersonal
4. Landlord/Tenant
5. Assault
6. Personal and Real Property
7. Juvenile Behavior
8. Criminal Mischief
9. Menacing Behavior and Neighborhood Noise
10. Fraud/Bad Check

top 10

CASE TYPES HANDLED BY RESOLUTE SYSTEMS, INC., IN 1994

(Resolute Systems, Inc., is a private, dispute resolution company based in Milwaukee, Wisconsin, with offices in five states.)

1. Personal Injury Claims (auto accident-related)
2. Contract
3. Construction
4. Product Liability
5. Employment
6. Professional Malpractice
7. Environmental
8. Real Estate
9. Property Damage
10. Health Care

A. Factors Favoring Mediation

The following factors apply to many kinds of disputes and highlight the advantages of mediation.

1. WHEN THE LAW CANNOT PROVIDE THE REMEDY YOU WANT

Although there are hundreds of thousands of laws on the books, many types of common disputes simply do not raise a legal claim that you can take to court. Disputes between family members and between neighbors are often of this type. Fortunately, mediation can be available to you even when courts are not. For example, two sisters who owned and ran a jewelry store disagreed about who should control different aspects of the business. If they could not come to terms, the business might fail. Yet there were no legal claims involved, just a dispute between partners, which mediation could very likely help settle. Similarly, when a suburban homeowner found that lights around his neighbor's driveway shone in his window at night, the law offered no solution, because no local ordinance regulated residential lighting, but the case could be mediated.

Even if there is a possible lawsuit, you may not want to bring it because of other factors. In the example above, for instance, the homeowner bothered by driveway lights could, in some states, sue his neighbor for nuisance (an interference with a person's right to enjoy her property). But the costs of doing so, in terms of legal fees, delay, publicity and damage to his relationship with the neighbor, would typically be out of proportion to the underlying problem. In mediation, however, the neighbors could sit down and probably work out an agreement quickly, cheaply and privately.

LOOKING UP THE LAW. It's often wise to research your legal rights and responsibilities. If you do not know whether the law might provide a remedy for your dispute, you should do some research or consult a lawyer. Often checking out the wording of a state law or local ordinance will provide great insight into how best to solve a dispute. (See Chapter 13, Lawyers and Legal Research.)

2. WHEN YOU WANT TO END A PROBLEM, NOT A RELATIONSHIP

Does your dispute involve another person with whom—either by choice or circumstance—you need to remain on good terms? This may include family members, co-workers, your landlord, neighbors or others with whom you have a continuing personal or business relationship. As compared to going to court, one of the advantages of mediation is its ability to resolve a dispute without destroying a relationship.

Face it—filing a lawsuit is almost always a hostile act. The common expressions "to be slapped with a lawsuit" or "hit with a lawsuit" convey the sense of combat and aggressiveness inherent in going to court. If you are the one doing the suing, you can be sure that whatever relationship you had with your adversary before papers were served will be worse afterwards. In part, this is because your attorney, motivated by the need to prove the other side's guilt or liability, will probably insist on using every means possible to show the other party in the worst possible light. From the lawyer's point of view, to do anything less could be malpractice. For example, even if you and the other party want to stay on speaking terms during a trial, your lawyers will likely forbid it, lest you reveal something to the other party that could jeopardize your case. Considering the hostility inherent in any lawsuit, Professor Jack Ethridge of Emory University Law School has written:

Litigation paralyzes people. It makes them enemies. It pits them not only against one another, but against the other's employed combatant. Often disputants lose control of the situation, finding themselves virtually powerless. They attach allegiance to their lawyer rather than to the fading recollection of a perhaps once worthwhile relationship.

Quoted in: "Mending Fences: Mediation in the Community," in Levin, et al. (eds.) *Dispute Resolution Devices in a Democratic Society*. (Final Report of the 1985 Chief Justice Earl Warren Conference on Advocacy in the United States.) The Rose Pound-American Trial Lawyers Foundation, Washington, D.C., 1985.

By contrast, mediation isn't about one side beating the other, but instead, about all parties reaching an agreed solution to a dispute. For example, unlike court, in mediation it would be inappropriate for one side to call a witness merely to establish the bad character of the other party. Similarly, in the written mediation agreement, there is no place for stating who was right and who was wrong; the agreement speaks only of who will do what and when in order to remedy the problem. It is this absence of fault-finding, plus the experience of working cooperatively toward settlement, that helps parties in mediation preserve or restore their relationship.

3. WHEN YOUR DISPUTE IS NO ONE ELSE'S BUSINESS—AND YOU WANT TO KEEP IT THAT WAY

As noted earlier, one of the drawbacks to having your dispute settled in court is that, by and large, everything said or submitted in connection with a lawsuit becomes publicly available. Only by a special order of a judge can information be "sealed" from public exposure. So whether your desire is to protect trade secrets or just to avoid washing your dirty laundry in public, your privacy will be substantially increased by resolving a dispute through mediation rather than through litigation.

If, for example, you were involved in a lawsuit against your employer based on your claim that you were sexually harassed, much of the background information both sides collect to try to blacken the reputation of the other would probably be available to the public. This would include not only what was said in court, but also what was revealed before trial in "discovery" proceedings, during which you may have had to answer very personal questions about your wages, work performance, associates and personal habits on and off the job. And your employer would likely have had to answer questions about the company's structure, ownership, profitability, employee relations and even whether lewd posters were hung on the men's room walls.

And don't assume your dispute won't be publicized. Newspaper and television reporters who cover the courts know where to find the information that will make an otherwise boring legal story come alive with interesting (usually embarrassing) personal details. And don't take this threat to your privacy lightly; every day the media—including trade journals and other specialist publications with a narrow focus—report on thousands of legal actions. For example, even if a sexual harassment claim against a trucking company wasn't reported in the daily newspapers, or on the TV news, it might be the subject of a big story in a magazine that covers the industry.

Mediation, by contrast, is a strictly private affair; there will be no stenographer or tape recorder. Mediators take an oath to protect the confidences entrusted to them. Many will even throw away their notes after the mediation session. And in some states, the confidentiality of mediation proceedings is additionally protected by so-called "privilege laws" that in most circumstances prevent a mediator from testifying in court (or arbitration) about what was said in mediation. (For more on confidentiality in mediation, see Chapter 6, Preparing for Your Mediation.)

AN EXCEPTION TO THE "CONFIDENTIALITY" RULE: If evidence of spousal or child abuse or other criminal behavior is disclosed in a mediation session, the mediator may be required by state law or the rules of the particular mediation service to stop the session and forward the evidence to authorities. This is one of the few exceptions to the general rule that everything said in mediation is confidential.

4. WHEN YOU WANT TO MINIMIZE COSTS

A Chinese proverb says, "Going to the law [court] is losing a cow for the sake of a cat." While this may sometimes be an exaggeration, it's undeniable that it occurs too often. And certainly, when going to court is likely to cost more than the dispute is worth, it makes sense to look for other ways to solve it.

Over 90% of your costs in bringing a civil (non criminal) lawsuit will likely be your lawyer's fees, which can range from $150 to $300 per hour and up. When you consider pre-trial preparation, including taking depositions and doing other discovery—many contested court cases eat up literally hundreds of hours of lawyer time for both sides. For example, a basic trademark dispute often costs each party more than $100,000 in legal fees, and it's all too common for spouses involved in contested divorce or child custody disputes to spend all the money they have, and then some.

By contrast, fees for using mediation services start at no charge at nonprofit community mediation centers (their operations are supported by tax dollars), and $500 or so at private dispute resolution companies handling consumer and business cases.

Mediation can especially save money for you as compared to having a lawyer charge you a contingency fee—where the lawyer doesn't charge by the hour but instead takes about 30%-40% of any amount you are awarded. Suppose, for example, you are hit by a telephone company's service truck and suffer several fairly serious injuries. If you sue the company and a jury awards you $100,000, your lawyer would take at least $30,000, leaving you, at most, $70,000. In addition to paying for your medical bills (or reimbursing your medical provider), you would need to subtract from that amount many more thousands of dollars for court fees, the costs of investigation and bringing physicians and other experts into court to testify. By contrast, if you can mediate the case without your lawyer's full participation, even if you settle for a little less, say $80,000, you will still end up with more than if you had sued. Not only will you be able to keep the 30% your lawyer would have taken, your actual costs will be much lower because expert witnesses often are not needed in mediation.

5. WHEN YOU WANT TO SETTLE YOUR DISPUTE PROMPTLY

"Our civil courts can be described as parking lots for civil litigation," Robert Coulson, former president of the American Arbitration Association, has correctly noted. A litigated case may be pending for two, three, four or five years before trial. Some 75,000 personal-injury cases backlogged in Chicago's Cook County Circuit Court took an average of 69 months to come to trial. While more than 90 percent of litigated disputes are settled before trial, settlement discussions often do not get serious until a trial date is near. This aspect of the law has not changed much since 1759 when the British statesman Edmund Burke observed, "The contending parties find themselves more effectively ruined by the delay than they could have been by the injustice of any decision."

Cases including large business, consumer, and public policy disputes that might take years to resolve in court can often be processed and settled within a few months in mediation. Even small consumer disputes that might take three months or so to resolve in small claims court can be disposed of far more quickly in mediation.

6. WHEN YOU WANT TO AVOID THE ESTABLISHMENT OF A LEGAL PRECEDENT

You may want to avoid a court ruling that would set an unfavorable precedent, particularly where the chances for a victory in court are slim and the consequences of an unfavorable decision are substantial. Suppose, for example, you and a group of neighbors want to stop a local manufacturing company from building a new factory on several acres of undeveloped, wooded land near your homes. You believe if you sue to block the company's plans you would have a small chance of winning under a state law designed to protect environmentally sensitive areas. However, if you lose in court, the judge's decision might set a legal precedent that would encourage other companies to build on many other environmentally sensitive areas. So, rather than risk the bad precedent, you decide to mediate with the manufacturing company in an effort to get them to abandon or at least modify their plans in order to minimize destruction of the woods.

7. When You Are Having Difficulty Initiating Negotiations, or Lack Negotiating Skills

Sometimes you may hope to negotiate a fair settlement to a dispute, but are just not able to get the attention of the other side to start the process. Maybe the other party is a large company or government agency that has a policy of not negotiating with individuals. In this situation, your formal offer to mediate—especially if it is made through a respected mediation service—may be enough to get their attention, especially if it carries with it the implied threat that if you are turned down, you might sue.

Similarly, if you fear you have poor negotiating skills or are intimidated by the other party, you might want to mediate because you believe the mediator's presence will allow you to negotiate in a safer environment and the mediator will help you get your points across clearly to the other side. In this sense, mediation often can serve as a structure for negotiation for parties who have trouble dealing with each other directly, thus reducing or eliminating the need for hired representatives. In addition, the mediator will see that neither party is threatened, browbeaten or intimidated.

IF YOU FEAR A FACE-TO-FACE ENCOUNTER WITH THE OTHER PARTY.
Occasionally, the other party—a former spouse or boss, for example—will
intimidate you to the point you can't effectively put two thoughts together, and
you will sensibly decide not to mediate. However, in other, less dire, situations,
there are steps you can take prior to mediation to help counter the effects of
intimidation and reassure you that mediation may still be a good choice. See
Chapter 6, Section F, and the material in Section C, below, concerning how to
deal with a power imbalance.

B. Factors Opposing Mediation

If some or all of the following factors apply to your case, bringing that case to
mediation may not be a good choice.

1. WHEN YOU WANT TO PROVE THE TRUTH OR SET A LEGAL PRECEDENT

If you are part of an advocacy group—one promoting environmental, women's
or immigrants' causes, for example—setting a legal precedent by winning an
important court case can help interpret or define the law according to your
group's point of view. But establishing a legal precedent cannot be done through
mediation, for several reasons. For one, mediation agreements do not establish
who is "right" or "wrong," but only what steps each party will take to resolve the
dispute. And second, because a mediated settlement is binding only on the
parties to that dispute, it does not establish a precedent. Another way of saying
this is that what is agreed to between parties in a mediation proceeding does not
affect the parties to any other dispute.

What this amounts to is that if there is a bad law—or prior court decisions—that you want overturned, or if you need publicly to prove the truth of something—for example, if you have been unfairly maligned in the local newspaper and want to clear your name—you may sensibly choose to do this through the courts rather than in mediation. On the other hand, one possible result from a mediation would be for an offending party to publicly apologize to the offended party.

2. WHEN YOU WANT TO GO FOR THE JACKPOT

If you are in the situation where you believe you can win a million dollar verdict against a big company (or even a small company with a big bank account or plenty of insurance), your choice should be a jury trial, not mediation. In mediation, chances are good you would achieve a settlement more quickly and therefore get your money sooner than you would by filing a lawsuit, but because of the tendency of disputants in mediation to compromise, you would be less likely to get big money. This is especially true if your legal action involves the realistic possibility that a jury might award you punitive damages (see "Punitive Damages" sidebar, below) or a significant amount of money for pain and suffering. Of course, it's also true that you could lose in court and recover nothing. A lawyer can advise you in advance of what your chances might be in court.

PUNITIVE DAMAGES DEFINED

Courts may sometimes award a person "punitive damages." This is payment over and above the value of actual losses or injuries, and even beyond compensation for "pain and suffering." Punitive damages get this name because their purpose is both to punish the defendant severely and, by so doing, to deter him and others from doing similar acts in the future. Punitive damages may be awarded when the defendant, in committing the wrong complained of, acted recklessly or deliberately and with malice, or intentionally disregarded the rights of others. In most states, punitive damages can be awarded in cases involving personal injuries, damage to property, false arrest or imprisonment, fraud and deceit, interference with employment or business relations, libel and slander, nuisances and interference with one's rights under the Constitution. Punitive damages are rarely, if ever, awarded in divorces or cases involving a breach of contract.

3. WHEN ONE PARTY REFUSES TO MEDIATE, OR IS ABSENT OR INCOMPETENT

"What is the sound of one party mediating?" Nothing, of course, which pretty much sums up what happens when only one party agrees to try mediation. For any one of several reasons, you may find that the other side has no desire to mediate:

- He may genuinely prefer litigation because he thinks he has a good chance to win in court.
- He may not perceive enough of an advantage in mediation to consider trying it.
- He may enjoy the dispute so much—or the prospect of beating you in court—he isn't in a hurry to end it. Or,
- He may dislike or fear you so much he doesn't want to be in the same room.

Nationally, about 30% of cases referred to mediation never reach the table because one party declines to participate. Some ways to try to overcome a party's reluctance to mediate are discussed in Chapter 4, Starting Your Mediation Case. Often a mediation service will actively work to bring the reluctant party into mediation. But if the other side persists in refusing to participate, there is little you can do about it. Perhaps at a later stage of the dispute, if his circumstances have changed so that mediation looks more attractive (his legal fees are getting too high, a court decision is inconclusive or he needs to end the dispute quickly), you can try to interest him in mediation again.

Similarly, if one or more parties to your dispute is physically unable to attend, then mediation most likely cannot take place. For example, if a party is in jail or out of the area for an extended period, then you cannot mediate. (However, as technology for video-teleconferencing improves, the practice of long-distance mediation will probably increase. Some divorce mediators already do a fair amount of telephone mediation with couples living in different cities.)

Mediation also assumes that both parties are rational and can participate in reasoned discussion and negotiation. If one party is mentally impaired or affected by alcohol or drug abuse, mediation will obviously not work.

A physical impairment such as a speech problem or an inability to speak English should normally be no bar to mediation, since it's usually possible to arrange for an interpreter or spokesperson.

4. WHEN THE DISPUTE INVOLVES A SERIOUS CRIME

Cases involving spousal or child abuse, or other serious criminal behavior, including murder, rape and armed robbery, do not belong in mediation. By law, crimes must be prosecuted by the authorities. But even beyond that, mediation requires that both parties be able to engage in rational and effective negotiation, and if one party has been the victim of criminal behavior, that party is likely to be too intimidated or fearful of reprisal to participate freely. In Massachusetts, for example, district attorneys are instructed that no crime for which the state would normally recommend a jail sentence should go to mediation.

On the other hand, minor criminal cases—for example, assault with no injury, personal harassment, as might occur among neighbors or co-workers, and minor property damage, where the major issue is how much money the offender should pay the victim—are often good candidates for mediation because the process allows parties to get at underlying attitudes and behaviors with the idea of heading off repeat problems. In many areas, these types of cases, which are often referred to mediation by prosecutors or judges to see if the parties can reach an agreement, make up a significant part of the caseload at community mediation centers.

5. WHEN YOU NEED A COURT ORDER TO PREVENT IMMEDIATE HARM

Your dispute could be a good candidate for mediation except that, by taking the time to mediate, you might suffer immediate personal or business harm. For example, if another company in the same field as your small manufacturing firm has copied your trademark and is advertising their competing product widely, and you need to stop them pronto before your customers become confused, the best way to accomplish this (expense aside) is by getting a court to issue a restraining order. Similarly, if town officials announce their intention to cut down all the maple trees lining your street by next Thursday, you obviously need to get a judge to issue a court order preventing (enjoining) them from wielding the ax until the case can be heard. Once you get the court order stopping the tree choppers, you may want to propose to the judge the case be put on hold while you try to resolve it through mediation.

6. WHEN YOUR CASE WOULD BE BETTER OFF IN SMALL CLAIMS COURT

For some disputes, you may be better off filing in small claims court rather than initiating mediation. The time it takes to get a small claims court case heard, the small fees involved and the fact you don't need a lawyer make the time and cost elements fairly comparable with mediation at a community mediation center. Small claims courts are particularly good at handling cases where the facts and the law are clear, and where each party's legal rights are plainly spelled out in writing, as in a lease or other contract. Many disputes between landlords and tenants involving nonpayment of rent or return of security deposits, for example, are routinely handled in small claims court. The maximum amount for which you can sue in small claims court varies from state to state. In most states, it's between $2,500 and $5,000.

But small claims judges—like most other judges—have neither the time nor the authority to help disputing parties resolve personal differences, with the result that interpersonal disputes often are not successfully resolved in small claims court. In addition, often overbusy small claims courts are not usually good at dealing with complicated fact situations that can take a long time to sort out, such as what the general contractor told the homeowner's spouse about whether the electrician or the plumber would move the electrical jacks before installing the radiant heaters, and who should pay for the delay.

In addition, small claims court offers no privacy from the public or the press, meaning that even small disputes can sometimes be blown way out of proportion.

YOU MAY BE ABLE TO TAKE ADVANTAGE OF THE TREND TO DOVETAIL MEDIATION AND SMALL CLAIMS COURT. Maine, Washington, D.C., parts of California, Oregon and Connecticut, among others, have programs where you are encouraged or required to attempt to mediate small claims disputes as part of a two-step process. If mediation doesn't result in a solution the dispute is then quickly heard and resolved by a small claims court judge. For more on small claims court, see *Everybody's Guide to Small Claims Court,* **by Ralph Warner (Nolo Press).**

SHOULD YOU MEDIATE?

FACTORS FAVORING MEDIATION	FACTORS OPPOSING MEDIATION
No legal remedy	Wanting test case
Preserving a relationship	Wanting jackpot
Maintaining privacy	Party refuses, is absent or incompetent
Avoiding high fees	Serious crime
Avoiding delays	Need court order to prevent harm
Avoiding legal precedent	Better off in small claims court
Unable to negotiate	Real court victory is assured

7. WHEN THE OTHER PARTY'S POSITION IS SO WEAK THAT YOU CAN EASILY WIN IN REGULAR COURT OR ARBITRATION

Few disputes are so clear-cut that either side can confidently predict that going to court will get them what they want. Even if they win, the costs and attorneys' fees are likely to make it a pyrrhic victory. But occasionally, it will clearly pay off to go to court. If you find yourself in such a situation, it does not make sense to mediate, as long as the dispute presents no other important concerns, such as preserving a family, business or social relationship, and you are willing to tolerate the delays, loss of privacy and other drawbacks of a lawsuit. You might as well take a route that will get you a decision 100% in your favor. Arbitration can also provide this type of absolute victory if the other side is willing—or required—to arbitrate.

C. The Question of Power Imbalance

Unlike the other factors that tend to favor or oppose mediation discussed earlier in this chapter, what mediators call "power imbalance" concerns not the facts of a dispute, but the people involved in it. It is worth taking a moment to consider this issue as you decide whether or not to mediate.

Power imbalance occurs when one party in a dispute is significantly stronger than the other in terms of knowledge (financial, legal or technical, for example), negotiating skills or emotional strength. Sitting down for face-to-face mediation with the contractor who you believe did a lousy job of sealing your driveway would not be a problem for most people, but what if the other party is the senior vice-president of a huge company, or your boss or the dean of your college? Should you really attempt to mediate a dispute where the other person may be far more powerful than you are?

Most mediators are concerned about the issue of power imbalance but are of different minds as to how to handle it. Some quickly advise not to attempt mediation with a too-powerful person on the theory that it is like taking a lamb to slaughter (with you as the lamb). Others are a bit more relaxed, saying that fears about lambs being slaughtered are exaggerated and that the presence of an experienced mediator normally offers ample protection for the weaker party. They point out, too, that for a variety of reasons, the alternatives to mediation (doing nothing, direct negotiations, litigation) may create worse barriers or problems.

I favor the latter view and believe that under the right circumstances, you can mediate effectively with just about any one. Many mediators will take an active, interventionist approach and do their best to ensure that any agreement they oversee is not blatantly unfair to one of the parties. This practice is especially common in divorce mediation, discussed in Chapter 11, Divorce Mediation. (For a discussion about how to identify and select a mediator who will take an active role when you fear a power imbalance, see Chapter 5, Selecting Mediation Services and Mediators, and Chapter 11, Divorce Mediation.)

In addition, here are some other constructive steps you can take to help prevent being overwhelmed by a powerful opponent:

- Prepare in advance, by carefully identifying your goals, preparing your presentation strategy and gathering evidence, as discussed in Chapter 6, Preparing for Your Mediation.
- Bring someone along—a friend, adviser or lawyer—who can provide moral, practical or legal support during the course of the session.
- Plan to leave the mediation if you don't like the way it's shaping up. In most cases, mediation is completely voluntary. If you don't like the direction it's taking, you are under no obligation to stay. (However, if you are going to mediation because a state law, court rule or contract provision requires it, you may need to remain in attendance for at least one complete session.)
- Sign nothing until it's checked. Refuse to make any final agreement until you have had it checked by your lawyer or other adviser. (See Chapter 8, Writing an Agreement That Works, for how to set this up in advance.)

THREE

Where to Take Your Dispute for Mediation

"He who avoids entering into litigation [and seeks a friendly settlement] rids himself of hatred, robbery, and perjury."

—PIRKE AVOT (ETHICS OF THE FATHERS)

DIVORCE AND FAMILY MEDIATION, AND HOW TO FIND A MEDIATOR, are discussed in Chapter 11.

When it's time to file a court case, detailed rules govern which court is appropriate. By contrast, in mediation you will often be free to choose where to have your case mediated. Depending on where you live and what kind of dispute you are involved in, there may be several mediators or mediation services available. Incidentally, for simplicity's sake, we will often use the term "mediation service" to refer to all kinds of mediation centers, companies, programs and organizations.

A. Choosing a Mediator or Mediation Service

There is no rule about when, and by whom, a mediator or mediation service gets chosen. Much depends on the circumstances of each particular dispute. This section considers various circumstances that may apply to your dispute and suggests when and how you can select the mediator, or participate in the selection. (Specific questions to ask when selecting a mediation service or independent mediator are addressed in Chapter 5, Selecting Mediation Services and Mediators.)

1. WHO GETS TO CHOOSE THE MEDIATOR?

To answer the question of who gets to choose the mediator or mediation service, it's best to ask and answer another question: How do cases get to mediation? Some get there because a contract requires it (see Section 1D, below) or a judge orders it (see Section 1E, below), but most get there simply because one party thinks it would be a good idea to try mediation and initiates a contact with a mediator or mediation service. Assuming this contact leads to a mediation taking place, it's obviously the initiating party who has done the most to select the mediator or mediation service (although, as we'll see, depending on the type of mediation, the other party will also have a major say in the process).

Here are a few common situations showing how a mediator or mediation service may come to be selected.

A. MEDIATION IS YOUR IDEA AND YOU AND THE OTHER PARTY ARE ON SPEAKING TERMS

Assuming you and the other party are talking to each other, it makes sense to approach this person directly and suggest mediation. But be prepared for the possibility that the other side may not know much about mediation, and you'll need to explain patiently what it is, how it works and why you think it's worth a try. To help allay any understandable suspicion about an unfamiliar procedure, you may want to give him or her a copy of this book, or other written material that explains mediation.

If the other party is willing to mediate, an excellent way to select a mediator or mediation service is for the two of you to cooperatively research mediators and mediation services in your area. Once you settle on a good one, you can then jointly make the contact. If you are not working together quite that smoothly, one alternative that can work well is for one of you to do the research and draw up a short list of possible mediator or mediation services, with the other getting to pick which one to use.

NAMING THE MEDIATION PLAYERS

Different types of mediators and mediation services go by different names.

Community Mediation Center: A tax-supported service that handles cases involving harassment and other minor criminal matters, small consumer claims and neighborhood disputes

Private Dispute Resolution Company: A privately-owned business that handles cases such as business contract disputes, personal injury claims, construction disputes and employment disputes. Mediation may be done by staff mediators or by outside judges and lawyers or others who act as independent contractors for the mediation company.

Independent Mediators in Private Practice: Individuals who mediate full- or part-time on their own rather than on the staff of a center, company or other mediation service. Many divorce mediators work as independents, as do some mediators with a specialty in large, complex business disputes.

Court-sponsored Mediation Programs: These programs are sponsored and paid for by state or local courts and usually handle a particular type of case, such as minor criminal matters, small claims disputes or divorce and family mediation, particularly involving issues of custody and child support. Most cases are sent to mediation under a provision of court rules or by a judge's orders.

Divorce Mediators: Specialists who handle only divorce and family disputes. Most work independently or in small group practices. See Chapter 11, Divorce Mediation.

SOME TYPES OF CONTRACTS SPECIFY THE MEDIATOR. Occasionally, contracts, including those used by some securities brokers, insurance companies and other businesses, specify which mediation service you must use. (See Section A1, below, and Chapter 12, Section C1.)

B. MEDIATION IS YOUR IDEA BUT YOU AND THE OTHER PARTY ARE NOT SPEAKING

By the time one party to a dispute is considering mediation, the parties are often no longer communicating. With little or no trust between you, it may be difficult for you to convince the other side to mediate. Especially if he is unfamiliar with the process, he is likely to suspect mediation is just a scheme or gimmick to help you get the better of him. And because he is already angry at you, he is unlikely to be persuaded by your arguments as to why mediation is a good idea. As the saying goes, in a dispute *"If one side proposes, the other opposes."*

A common way to deal with the problem of an uncooperative party is for you to contact a mediation service and let the service try to sell mediation to the other party. For example, if you were to contact a private dispute resolution company, the company would typically ask you for some information about your case and then send the other party a letter explaining their services and inviting him to mediate. If the other side fails to respond, the company would follow up with phone calls to try to secure his agreement to participate. For more on how a mediation service works to persuade a party to mediate, see Chapter 4, Starting Your Mediation Case.

C. YOU HAVE BEEN ASKED TO PARTICIPATE IN A MEDIATION INITIATED BY THE OTHER PARTY

If the other party has contacted you to suggest mediation, or a mediation service has contacted you at the request of the other side, what should you do? If you think your dispute is appropriate for mediation (see Chapter 2, Selecting Disputes for Mediation), you'll want to agree to mediate. But just because you think mediation is a good idea doesn't obligate you to use the mediation service the other side selected. Check it out to be sure it meets your goals and can provide the quality services you want. Take a look at their brochure; if they have a local office, try to make time to visit it. Also, think about any lawyers or others you might know with links to the local mediation community and call them for an opinion.

You may also want to investigate alternatives. For example, by calling a court clerk, reference librarian or chamber of commerce, you may learn about a highly regarded local mediation service you might prefer to use. There can be all sorts of reasons why this might be true. For example, the other party may have contacted the American Arbitration Association, but when you look at their rules, you find they will only give you a list of five names from which to select a mediator. A locally-owned, private dispute resolution company, on the other hand, will send you their whole roster of 15 possible mediators. (See Chapter 5, Selecting Mediation Services and Mediators, for more on selecting a particular mediator.) You may prefer the bigger selection, or there may be a particular retired judge on the local company's roster whom you would like to use as your mediator and who works exclusively with that company. Fees, location, reputation for quality—any of these can be legitimate reasons for preferring a mediation service other than the one the other side initially has suggested. If so, call or write the other party and explain your preference for the other mediation service. Chances are, as long as you are agreeable to mediate and the mediation service you want is competent and neutral, the other party will agree to switch.

D. YOU SIGNED A CONTRACT REQUIRING YOU TO MEDIATE

You may have signed a contract that requires you to mediate. A typical dispute resolution clause in such a contract would read:

> **If a dispute arises out of the terms of this contract, the parties agree that before either one files a lawsuit, they will attempt in good faith to resolve the dispute through non-binding mediation.**

To see if your contract contains such a clause, look near the end of the contract for a section labeled "Dispute Resolution," "Mediation" or sometimes, erroneously, "Arbitration."

If your clause is like the one above, you and the other party are free to choose any mediator or mediation service you want. But some clauses name the mediation service you must use. Construction contracts and consumer contracts, such as those with banks and real estate companies, are fairly likely to do this. Such a clause might read:

> **If a dispute arises out of this contract, the parties agree to try to settle it by mediation through Settlement Consultants International, Inc., of Dallas, Texas.**

If you and the other side both want to use a mediation service other than the one named in the contract, you can agree to do so in writing. This will, in effect, amend the contract. But if you can't both agree on an alternative, you are required to use the named service. Exceptions would occur only for some very good reason, such as that the service has changed its business focus and no longer has mediators available who are qualified to handle your type of case, or the mediation needs to be held at a distant location where the service does not operate or a personal, business, or financial connection between the service and you or the other side makes the service unable to be impartial in your dispute. (For more on possible conflicts of interest in choosing a mediation service, see Chapter 5, Section A, "Ten Questions to Ask a Mediation Service.")

E. YOU ARE ORDERED TO MEDIATE BY A JUDGE

Today many state courts have the power to prevent a case from going to trial until the parties first try mediation. This is particularly true for disputes involving child custody and visitation and small claims, but can apply to other types of civil cases as well. For example, in some states, a judge has the power to divert (order) any civil case asking for damages up to a specific level (often between $25,000 and $100,000) to mediation. If you have been ordered by a judge to mediate, the order may name the mediation service you have to use. It might be an internal mediation program run by the court itself, or an outside mediation company or center, such as a nonprofit community mediation center. For example, in some cities, neighbor disputes and minor assault cases routinely are referred to publicly-funded community mediation centers. The order might read:

> By Order of the District Court you are hereby notified that you must contact, within 30 days, the Center for Dispute Settlement to arrange a Mediation session in this matter before further proceedings may be scheduled in this Court.

Some Texas courts maintain a roster of mediators and assign them at random as cases arise:

> MEDIATION ORDER: This case is appropriate for mediation pursuant to Section 154.001 et. seq. of the Texas Civil Practice and Remedies Code. Michael J. Venditto is appointed mediator in the above case and all counsel are directed to contact the mediator to arrange the logistics of mediation within seven days from the date of this Order.

If a judge tells you where to go for mediation, or who your mediator will be, you won't have a lot of choice. But if you strongly prefer a different mediation service, it won't hurt to explain why and ask the judge to reconsider her order. Less often, a judge may refer the parties to a list of mediation services that the court has deemed "qualified" and leave it up to the parties and their lawyers to agree on which one to use.

2. GOALS IN SELECTING A MEDIATOR OR MEDIATION SERVICE

When selecting a mediator or mediation service, you should normally have the following goals in mind.

A. GETTING THE OTHER PARTY TO THE TABLE

You can't mediate anything without the other side's participation. Therefore, if the other party is reluctant to mediate, one key issue in selecting a mediator or mediation service is to choose one that will be able to get that party to the table. A prominent private dispute resolution company, for instance, that prints lots of reassuring materials (including testimonials from satisfied clients) and has its own offices, might be more convincing than a small, local mediation service run by a couple of mediators without much name recognition.

If you have reason to think the other party will be reluctant to mediate, you should initiate your case with a mediation service—such as a mediation center, company, program or organization—rather than with an independent mediator in private practice. Most of these mediation services have "case managers" on staff whose job it is to educate the parties to a dispute about how mediation works and persuade them to participate. Independent mediators, on the other hand, are less suited for this task. They don't usually have the staff to sell mediation and will be reluctant to do it themselves, fearing that doing so can compromise their own neutrality.

B. CHOOSING A QUALITY MEDIATOR

The success of your mediation may well be determined by the skills your mediator brings to the table. Mediator skills include both *process skills*—the ability to conduct a mediation effectively—and *subject-matter knowledge*—an understanding of the issues in dispute, sometimes including technical issues, if they will be important to resolving the case. Of the two, process skills are usually the more important, but this can also depend on the particular facts of the case.

In complex cases, such as business disputes involving multiple issues and many parties, both types of skills are usually necessary. For example, a software licensing dispute might include many different parties (an author, software publisher, distributing company, a primary licensee and various secondary licensees) as well as complex legal issues involving copyrights and patents, publishing and distribution contracts and the emerging field of software licensing. For this case to be efficiently and successfully mediated, you would probably want a mediator with the process skills to handle a multi-party case and the subject-matter knowledge to handle the complex legal and technical issues involved in the dispute.

In Chapter 5, Selecting Mediation Services and Mediators, we will discuss how to select a particular mediator who has the right combination of skills for your case, but at this point—if you are selecting a mediation service, your immediate goal should be to identify services whose mediators have the types of process skills and subject-matter knowledge you need. What kind of mediation service is likely to be able to supply you with this kind of mediator? The best bet is a private dispute resolution company. A full-time, independent mediator in private practice who specializes in this type of dispute would also likely have the needed combination of skills.

C. GETTING GOOD VALUE FOR YOUR MONEY

Obviously you will want to pay the least money necessary for the services you need. If your mediation service will be a community mediation center or a court-connected program, cost is not an issue because most of these services will be available free or for a nominal fee.

But if you will be using a private dispute resolution company or an independent mediator in private practice, it makes sense to shop for price as well as quality of services. For example, you may like one mediator whose name appears on the list of a local private dispute resolution company. The company quotes you a per hour cost for using this mediator of $125 per hour for each of two parties to the dispute, or a total of $250 an hour. But if this same mediator also works privately, you may be able to hire her directly—without going through the company—at a much lower rate, say $150 per hour, or just $75 per side.

Typically, the smaller a case, the more you will need to be careful that the cost of the mediation doesn't consume a significant part of what you hope to gain. On the other hand, if your dispute involves a business contract for auto parts worth $8 million, it may matter very little what the mediation costs—a few thousand dollars either way won't seem significant if you can get your case resolved without paying the much higher costs and attorneys' fees inherent in going to court.

B. The Various Types of Mediators and Mediation Services

Following is a brief description of the various types of mediator or mediation services available today in many communities, the kinds of cases each is most experienced in handling and a quick description of the backgrounds and skill levels of the people who actually do the mediating. Section D of this chapter provides additional discussion of which types of disputes fit best with which types of mediation services.

I. COMMUNITY MEDIATION CENTERS

Community mediation centers are, for the most part, independent, nonprofit organizations that receive funds from state and local governments. Services, which are usually available to anyone in the community, are generally provided for free or at low cost (perhaps $25). These centers have been found to be an extremely cost-effective way of resolving relatively minor cases (such as neighbor disputes, small consumer claims and minor criminal charges such as harassment) that often get lost in, or otherwise are not well served by, the local courts and criminal justice system.

There are about 400 of these centers nationwide. They are called by various names—such as "dispute resolution center," "neighborhood justice center" and "center for dispute settlement." To find out if there is a center in your community, check in the telephone Yellow Pages under "mediation," or try the general information number at city hall, or at the local bar association. If this doesn't produce results, contact the National Association for Community Mediation, 1726 M St., NW, Suite 500, Washington, DC 20036 (202) 467-6226.

Community mediation centers typically have a no-frills "public service" look. This works just fine, since all you need for a successful mediation is a quiet room, a table with a few chairs and a good mediator. Indeed, the modest look may help disputants relax—you know you're not paying for circular stairways or Persian carpets.

Many cases heard at the centers are referred there by judges, police and social service agencies. But these days, especially when it comes to small consumer claims and disputes between neighbors and between landlords and tenants, the centers are also seeing lots of cases brought to them directly by disputants.

Most community mediation centers are designed to be accessible and helpful. You can walk into them with many different kinds of disputes and they will be able to accommodate you. For example, most centers are prepared to handle disputes involving charges of assault without injury, personal harassment, consumer claims, disputes between spouses, housing disputes, neighborhood disputes and disputes among co-workers. (See table in Chapter 2, "Top Ten Case Types, Handled by Community Dispute Resolution Centers—New York State, 1994-1995.")

Some centers have also developed special mediation programs to meet local needs. For example, disputes between roommates may be a common occurrence in a college town, but, in rural areas, centers may specialize in mediating disputes between farmers and food storage companies or bankers, as well as disputes between mobile home park owners and tenants.

2. WHO ARE THE MEDIATORS AT COMMUNITY MEDIATION CENTERS?

A distinguishing feature of community mediation centers is that most of their cases are usually mediated by trained community volunteers. Some centers may pay mediators a small stipend. The Justice Center of Atlanta, for example, pays its mediators $15 a case; others centers may pay up to $30 or $40. But the bulk of the work is done on a volunteer basis.

Volunteer mediators bring a diversity of experience to their work. In New York, for example, more than 2,400 citizens over the last 20 years have completed the required 25-hour training program plus apprenticeship to serve at the state's network of 62 county-based community mediation centers. They come from a variety of professional and work backgrounds: teaching, social work, law, business, parenting and homemaking and journalism, among others. Most mediators are college-educated, with an average of 3.5 years of mediation experience. Their median age is 46 years.

In Massachusetts, about 700 mediators serve at nearly 30 community mediation centers. A statewide study found them to be, on average, "more white, more female, somewhat better off financially, (with) more formal education and somewhat older" than the general population.

Most of the state laws that establish community mediation centers set minimum standards for training of the mediators who work there. New York's program of 25 classroom hours plus a supervised period of apprenticeship is typical. Indeed, many people who consider making a career of mediation start out at their local community mediation center specifically to take the free or low-cost state-sponsored training, thus using the community center as a stepping-stone for their own careers.

Most community mediation centers do not give the parties much choice in who their mediator will be. Instead, the case manager will consider various factors, such as subject matter and complexity of the case and which mediators are available and haven't heard a case lately, and then assign a mediator from the pool of volunteers available. But sometimes you can choose your mediator, or at least influence the assignment. For information on how to request a particular mediator and how to evaluate the mediator assigned, see Chapter 5, Selecting Mediation Services and Mediators.

In general, volunteer mediators at community mediation centers are trained and excel at handling interpersonal disputes, particularly those without major financial issues. This includes many painful types of disputes that never get handled well in court, such as arguments between neighbors over shared driveways, barking dogs or late-night pool parties, claims by a couple that the man's ex-girlfriend or the woman's ex-boyfriend is harassing them and small consumer claims having to do with cars, dry cleaners, magazine subscription sales, and the like.

THE OLD WOMAN AND THE FAST CAR: A TYPICAL COMMUNITY CENTER MEDIATION

In Delaware County, Pennsylvania, an elderly woman was at the end of her rope when she called the Community Dispute Settlement Center. She complained of a young couple next door who came and went at all hours of the night in a high-performance Porsche, with motor roaring and radio blaring. So intimidated was she by her neighbors that she asked for police protection at the mediation (a center staff member assured her it wouldn't be necessary).

At an evening mediation session, the woman and the young couple reached a settlement. The couple agreed to operate the Porsche quietly while in their driveway or on their street (not shifting above second gear, and with the radio off, for example) and the woman agreed to call the couple at their home or offices (they exchanged phone numbers) if she had further complaints. The woman was so relieved, she later told the mediation center's staff, "I didn't believe in miracles until the night of my mediation."

Adapted from Anne Richan, "Developing and Funding Community Dispute Settlement Programs," *Mediation Quarterly*, No. 5, 1984, p. 86.

3. Private Dispute Resolution Companies

Private dispute resolution is a growth industry. An increasing number of for-profit firms now compete to mediate cases such as contract disputes between businesses, construction cases, employment disputes involving wrongful discrimination and termination and disputed insurance claims arising out of auto accidents and other mishaps. (See table in Chapter 2, "Top Ten Case Types, Handled by Resolute Systems, Inc., 1994, a Private Dispute Resolution Company.")

The primary functions of a private dispute resolution company are:
- to provide a panel of trained and experienced mediators
- to provide a way to get all parties to agree to participate in mediation
- to administer the mediation, including all paperwork, scheduling and billing, and
- to follow-up with the parties after mediation if further dispute resolution services are needed.

There are hundreds of private dispute resolution firms. Some operate at the national level, with offices in major cities, while others are mid-sized or smaller firms that operate regionally or locally. The biggest national outfit is Judicial Arbitration & Mediation Services/Endispute, Inc., headquartered in Irvine, California. Known in the industry as "JAMS/ENDISPUTE," this company has about 30 offices nationwide and generates nearly $50 million in annual sales.

Other national firms include Resolute Systems, Inc., headquartered in Milwaukee, Wisconsin, and U.S. Arbitration & Mediation, Inc., in Des Moines, Iowa. The American Arbitration Association, Inc., in New York, New York, and Arbitration Forums, Inc., in Tampa, Florida, are well-established nonprofit corporations that handle many of the same kinds of large, complex disputes as the newer, for-profit companies.

Fees at most of the private firms generally start at a minimum of about $500 per party for a half-day mediation session. Costs can rise to thousands of dollars, depending on the complexity of the case and the length of time needed to resolve it.

For a list of some of the larger national and regional private dispute resolution firms, see Appendix C.

PRIVATE MEDIATION: WHAT DOES IT COST?

Most private mediation firms charge a combination of administrative fees for opening and managing a case, and hourly fees for the time a mediator spends preparing for mediation by reviewing papers submitted by the parties and actually conducting the mediation. Some firms want a "filing fee" paid when a case is submitted; others will accept full payment after the mediation is completed. Listed below are fees charged by some of the larger national and regional firms in early 1996. (These fees assume a two-party dispute and an expected half-day or full-day of mediation.)

Judicial Arbitration & Mediation Services Inc. (Irvine, CA)
Administrative Fee: $125 per party
Hourly Fee: $125-$250 per party

U.S. Arbitration & Mediation, Inc. (Des Moines, IA)
Administrative Fee: $50-175 per party
Hourly Fee: $50-$125 per party

Resolute Systems, Inc. (Milwaukee, WI)
Administrative Fee: $125 per party
Hourly Fee: $125-$150 per party

Settlement Consultants International, Inc. (Dallas, TX)
Administrative Fee: $200 fee paid by initiating party
Hourly Fee: $180 split by parties

4. WHO ARE THE PRIVATE DISPUTE FIRM MEDIATORS?

Most of the larger private firms, and many of the smaller ones, maintain a list of people available to mediate disputes, usually referred to as "mediation panels." The panel is simply a list or roster of mediators available through that firm. Most panel members are former judges and practicing attorneys, or others with expertise in subjects such as engineering, health care, construction and land-use. Panel members are usually not employees of the company, but work as independent contractors. But the bigger companies' panels sometimes also include "career mediators" who have advanced mediation training and experience and who mediate full-time.

In addition to the mediators available on a company's panel, you will also find that, at some smaller companies, the owners or staff members are them-selves mediators who are available to handle cases. For example, two or three mediators may have gotten together to form a local dispute resolution company. They run the business, mediate some of the cases and assign the rest of the cases to members of their panel of outside mediators. (For more on why, when choosing a mediator, it is sometimes advantageous to choose a staff member over a member of the panel, see Chapter 5, Section B1.)

Some popular members of a company's panel may be selected to mediate weekly, or a couple times a month; others may be selected just a few times a year. Mediators may be exclusive to one company, or they may appear on the panels of several companies. It all depends on how much they are in demand and whether any particular company is able to generate enough business to sign up mediators to work with that company exclusively. For example, some of the retired judges on panels maintained by California-based Judicial Arbitration & Mediation Service, Inc. ("JAMS") work only for that firm. If you want one of these judges to mediate your case, you have to go to JAMS. But a lawyer with mediation training in a mid-size city may appear on the panels of several local or regional companies, none of which keeps him busy enough to warrant an exclusive relationship.

Companies may have just one panel of mediators that is made available to everyone who wants to mediate or they may have several panels organized by the subject area of the mediators' specialty. For example, a company active in a number of different types of mediation may have a Negligence Panel composed of lawyers and judges familiar with accident claims; a Health Care Panel com-posed of health-care lawyers, physicians and hospital administrators; and a Construction Panel composed of construction lawyers, engineers, architects, builders and contractors of various specialties.

Private firms can differ hugely in terms of how much training and skill their mediators have. At one extreme they often provide the most highly-skilled career mediators. Yet, paradoxically, it is also in these firms where you are fairly likely to run into problems with inexperienced mediators. This often results from the penchant of these firms to hire big-name judges who have recently retired. Judges with little background or training in mediation may believe their role is just to "knock people's heads together" until they settle, as they did when they were on the bench. Similarly, you may encounter a lawyer-mediator with great specialized knowledge and reputation in a particular area of the law—but who is similarly untrained and inexperienced in mediation. (For information on how to check on and evaluate the credentials of mediators, see Chapter 5, Selecting Mediation Services and Mediators.)

5. INDEPENDENT MEDIATORS IN PRIVATE PRACTICE

Independent mediators in private practice work on their own, unaffiliated with private dispute resolution companies or other mediation providers. Whether they practice locally or nationally, independent mediators set their own fees, handle their own paperwork, keep their own schedules and often develop and use their own rules. Fees range from $100 - $300 an hour for independent mediators who work at the local level and handle a general variety of cases, to $2,000 - $5,000 a day for those who operate nationally and specialize in large, complex disputes in areas such as business and construction. Some local mediators will use a sliding fee scale based on size and complexity of the case, the parties' ability to pay and how much the mediator wants the work.

It's wise to consider using an independent mediator when you don't need or want to pay for the extra services that a mediation service typically provides—perhaps all parties readily agree to mediate and you're willing to set up the date, time and place yourself. As discussed in Section A2A, above, one big limitation to using an independent mediator is that she will usually not want to get involved trying to persuade reluctant parties to mediate. So, if you anticipate any reluctance on the part of the other side to mediate, you should probably choose a mediation service rather than an independent mediator.

You also should consider using an independent mediator when your case will require a mediator highly knowledgeable in a particular field. For example, if you are involved in a complicated construction dispute, an independent mediator who specializes in this type of case can bring to the table a great deal of knowledge about construction law and practices and also experience in working out creative settlements in these types of cases.

To find an independent mediator with a specialty in your field, inquire among lawyers or business owners who work in the area of that specialty. For example, if your case involves a construction dispute, a local lawyer who specializes in construction litigation is likely to have access to a list of independent mediators, both locally and nationally, who specialize in construction cases. A lawyer who specializes in health care—as well as the president of the local medical society—may have names of mediators who handle medical disputes. Similarly, if your dispute involves a particular area of business—printing, scrap metal or injection molding, for example—state or national offices of trade groups representing these fields may have lists of mediators with those specialties. You may also get help in locating independent mediators qualified to handle your case from the various mediator professional groups listed in Appendix C.

6. WHO ARE THE INDEPENDENT MEDIATORS IN PRIVATE PRACTICE?

Some independents are full-time, career mediators with advanced training and a specialty in large, complex cases, such as those involving business ownership, construction, intellectual property, environmental or public policy. Many of these full-time independent mediators work in just one city or region, while others, who are widely recognized, travel extensively, mediating cases within their specialty all over North America. Independent mediators include most of those who specialize in family and divorce cases. Mediators with this specialty are discussed in Chapter 11, Divorce Mediation.

Other independent mediators work only part-time; for their primary income, they rely on some other profession or occupation, such as law, business or social work. Some of these people have been well-trained and make pretty good mediators, but also among this part-time group you will find people who have done nothing to prepare beyond participating in a few one-day mediation seminars and are primarily looking for what they see as an easy way to make a buck. To distinguish skilled, part-time independent mediators from the unskilled "have business card, will mediate" crowd, check on what kind of training they have received, how experienced they are and what their reputation is among mediators and other professionals familiar with their services. (See Chapter 5, Selecting Mediation Services and Mediators.)

INDEPENDENT MEDIATOR OR PRIVATE COMPANY?

Commonly, independent mediators are also on the panels of dispute resolution companies: this allows the mediator to get extra assignments, while the company gains by having a panel member who may attract business to the firm. If the opportunity arises, should you hire the independent mediator on your own or go through the company?

For example, in your local Yellow Pages, you see these two listings:

Nancy Neutral
Attorney-Mediator
Business and Legal Disputes
555 Main Place
Flagstaff, AZ 80808
(xxx) xxx-xxxx

Flagstaff Mediation Associates, Inc.
Experienced Mediators for
Family-Business-Legal Disputes
123 Elm Drive
Flagstaff, AZ 80810
(xxx) xxx-xxxx

You call Flagstaff and see Nancy's name on its panel. When knowledgeable business and legal people you check with speak well of Nancy, you decide to hire her to mediate your dispute. Your question is, should you hire Nancy as an independent at $125/hour, or go through Flagstaff, where her services would cost $200 per hour plus an administrative fee.

To arrive at a decision, answer these questions:
1. Are you pretty sure the other party is willing to mediate?
2. Are you really certain Nancy has the knowledge and skills to handle your case?

If both answers are "yes," avoid Flagstaff's overhead and just hire Nancy. If either answer is "no," use Flagstaff because:

1. An independent mediator will not want to "sell" a reluctant party to participate in mediation. Persuading a reluctant party to mediate is a job best handled by a mediation service that has a case manager on staff; it's part of what you pay the service to do.
2. A well-run mediation service will know the abilities and strengths of its panel members. They may suggest someone who they believe is better-suited than Nancy to mediate your dispute.

7. COURT-CONNECTED MEDIATION PROGRAMS

State trial courts all over the country are initiating mediation programs in order to reduce their caseloads and operating costs, and perhaps because they see mediation as a better way to resolve some types of disputes. These are programs that handle many different types of civil (non-criminal) cases. Typically, under these programs, before people who file lawsuits are allowed to proceed with their cases, they are either required or strongly encouraged to try mediation. States with broad court-referral programs include Florida, Texas, Minnesota, Michigan, California, New Hampshire, Utah and Georgia, but nearly every state today has some kind of court-connected mediation program. A number of other states require that parties receiᵃve a written notice about the availability of mediation, but do not require them to pursue it.

In some states, the court itself provides the parties with conference rooms and mediators. In others, judges or court clerks simply instruct the parties to pick a mediator from a list of "qualified" mediators or to go out and find their own mediator.

If your case is already in court, call the clerk of the court to find out if there is a mediation program available, or ask your attorney to check on this. If your case is not in court, a court-based program is not currently an option.

DON'T FILE A COURT CASE JUST TO BE REFERRED TO MEDIATION.
You normally do not want to incur the hostility, fees and delays inherent in filing a lawsuit just to have access to a court-connected mediation program. But if the other party adamantly declines to negotiate or mediate, meaning you must either sue or forget about pursuing your case, you may want to go ahead with an eye towards asking the judge to refer your dispute to a court-connected mediation program. For more on this option, see Chapter 4.

8. WHO ARE THE COURT-CONNECTED MEDIATORS?

Typically, mediators in programs run by the courts are practicing lawyers who volunteer or are paid a small stipend for occasionally mediating cases. These lawyers probably have had some minimal mediation training but most do not handle enough cases to develop really good skills. In Philadelphia, for example, parties in cases with less than $50,000 in dispute can try a new mediation program run by the local trial court. All mediators must be lawyers; the court pays the lawyers $350 per day and provides a brief training of two to three hours. (Most professional mediator training programs run 25-40 hours. For more on mediator training, see Chapter 5, Selecting Mediation Services and Mediators.) On the other hand, Florida courts run an extensive mediation program for all civil cases and require substantial training for their lawyer-mediators.

If the court refers parties to other local mediation services rather than trying to run the whole program itself, things may be better. In some situations, you may even have your pick of anyone in the local mediation field, including panels of mediators put together by private firms as well as independent mediators. In some states, you can even use a non-lawyer mediator in a court-connected program. For example, under a new Wisconsin law, a judge can appoint as mediator "any person who the judge believes has the ability and skills necessary to bring the parties together in settlement." (Wis. Stat. Sec. 802.12(2)(c).)

9. PROSECUTORS' MEDIATION PROGRAMS

Mediation programs established by local public prosecutors or district attorneys are often fairly similar to those established by courts. But unlike court programs, which usually focus on civil disputes, prosecutor programs are designed to resolve minor criminal complaints without prosecution.

In Cleveland, for example, when a citizen files a criminal complaint against someone, she may have an opportunity to mediate. The program applies to "non-serious" crimes, such as those involving theft of property valued at less than $300, telephone harassment and personal menacing without an allegation of use of a weapon or threat of serious bodily harm. Particularly if the parties have some kind of ongoing relationship such as being neighbors or co-workers, the complainant may be encouraged to take the dispute to the Cleveland Prosecutor's Mediation Program. The program is voluntary and is available at no charge. When a case is referred, the mediation program sends the other party a letter stating "You are notified to appear" for mediation. Though participation is not legally required, the program's director, Cornell P. Carter explains, "If a party refuses to mediate, the case will be reconsidered by the prosecutor for possible legal action. If there is evidence (to support the criminal allegation) and no cooperation (by the responding party), the case may be more likely to be prosecuted."

About 3,000 cases are mediated each year. Sessions last about 45-60 minutes. When successful, agreements often call for parties to pay damages, or return property or avoid contacting each other. Nearly nine of ten cases result in a written settlement with no need for corrective follow-up within the next four weeks, a period the program's directors consider meaningful given that many of the parties are in ongoing relationships.

10. WHO ARE THE MEDIATORS AT PROSECUTOR MEDIATION PROGRAMS?

Programs around the country will differ as to staffing, but typically the mediators will be either full-time court employees with backgrounds in social services or criminal justice, or part-time mediators with legal backgrounds. At the Cleveland Program, mediations are conducted both by full-time professionals and by law students, who receive about 20 hours of initial training plus monthly in-service sessions that cover developments in the dispute resolution field and advanced techniques for handling various types of cases and parties. The law students, who are paid modestly, typically mediate about four cases a night.

Mediators who work at this type of program are generally handling a high volume of cases, most of which present intense personal grievances. If they are able to continue mediating these kinds of cases successfully for more than a few months, they probably have developed a pretty good skill level and are delivering a quality service under difficult circumstances.

II. SPECIALIZED MEDIATION SERVICES

As mediation gains in popularity, some specialized groups, including business trade organizations and religious groups, have begun to develop their own networks of mediation services. For information on mediation services that specialize in business disputes, see Section 13, below. Chapter 12, Mediating Business Disputes, also covers this subject. The following are a few of the other types of specialized programs available:

- *Institute for Christian Conciliation.* If you would like your dispute mediated based on Christian biblical principles of conflict resolution, you may want to contact the Institute for Christian Conciliation, a national group with members and affiliated organizations around the country. The Institute trains and certifies its own mediators, which include people from many professional and work backgrounds, including lawyers, mental health counselors, clergy, homemakers and business people. Mediation, arbitration and med-arb (see Chapter 1, Section F) are among the services available. For information, contact: Institute for Christian Conciliation, 1537 Avenue D, Suite 352, Billings, MT 59102 (406) 256-1583.

- *Jewish Conciliation Board of America.* This organization provides dispute resolution services, including mediation, to the Jewish community. To help resolve disputes involving parents and children, financial matters, marital conflicts and other issues, the Board will convene an impartial panel of experts from the rabbinical, business, legal and mental health communities. Services are offered in both English and Russian. This organization primarily serves residents of the New York City area, but may be able to make referrals to other organizations around the country. For information, contact the Board at 120 West 57th Street, New York, NY 10019 (212) 425-5051, ext. 3202.

- *Lesbian and Gay Community Services Center Mediation Program.* This program helps gay men and lesbians resolve conflicts outside the court system, including relationship breakups, child custody and visitation issues and organizational disputes. Mediators include lawyers, mental health professionals, teachers, activists and health care workers. Disputants are asked to pay a nominal administrative fee, but no one is denied services due to inability to pay. For those seeking lesbian/gay mediation services outside the New York City area, the Mediation Service can provide referrals nationally. For more information, contact the Mediation Service at 208 West 13th St., New York, NY 10011 (212) 620-7310, ext. 321.

- *Asian Pacific American Dispute Resolution Center.* This organization provides mediation and conciliation services in Asian Pacific languages, including Chinese, Korean, Japanese, Vietnamese and Tagalog (Philippines). The Center handles ethnic disputes as well as domestic, housing, neighborhood, employment and business conflicts, and matters involving race relations. Disputants are asked to pay nominal processing and hourly fees, but fees are waived for those unable to pay. The Center primarily serves Los Angeles County, but can assist those outside the area by conducting telephone mediation and by making referrals nationally to mediators or translators fluent in Asian Pacific languages. For information, contact the Center at 1010 South Flower Street, Suite 301, Los Angeles, CA 90015, (213) 747-9943.

12. FEDERAL AND STATE GOVERNMENT MEDIATION PROGRAMS

Lots of federal and state agencies are trying mediation programs as a way to improve services and reduce administrative and litigation costs. If you have a dispute with a government agency (or a dispute with a private party that a government agency is supposed to handle), it makes sense these days to ask if mediation is available. For example, at the federal level, if you file a workplace discrimination claim with the Equal Employment Opportunities Commission, you may be able to resolve it through a mediation program run in several cities by that agency. Or, if you are a farmer, and a bank has foreclosed on your mortgage, you might be able to mediate through the Farmer-Lender Mediation Program run by the Farmers Home Administration. At the state level, in Wisconsin, for example, if the government denies your request to open a landfill or run a hazardous waste treatment facility, you can ask for mediation and the government must provide the names and qualifications of possible mediators. (Wisc. Stat. Section 144.445.)

13. TRADE AND PROFESSIONAL GROUP MEDIATION PROGRAMS

Some trade groups and professional organizations, such as realtors and lawyers, have created specialized programs to try to mediate their own disputes. For example, lawyers in some cities and states have set up mediation programs to handle fee disputes with clients. And the National Association of Realtors has set up the Homebuyer-Homeseller Dispute Resolution System, a program currently offered in nearly two dozen states that mediates disputes that develop after home sales.

Beware. Although they have the advantage of being free or very lost-cost, programs established by trade groups at least in part to reduce the number of lawsuits against members are not really neutral. The mediators are themselves often members of the trade or professional group and their training may have included a bias in favor of working out solutions favored by the organization. Nevertheless, even though you understand the problems, you may wish to try mediating with one of these groups. After all, you can always withdraw if you believe the process is unfair. For example, let's say you hired a real estate sales agent to handle the sale of your home, but now believe the agent disclosed confidential information about your negotiating position to a prospective buyer, thus resulting in a lower offer for your home. After asking for a specific dollar amount and being turned down, you agree to mediate the dispute through a program run by the local real estate board. Under the program, the board pays supposedly neutral local real estate agents a small stipend to sit as mediators. Can a realtor-mediator really be neutral as between you and your former agent? Probably not. But since the process is free to you and the Realtor has no authority to impose a decision you don't agree to, it may be worth a try. Also, some trade groups want their mediators to be pro-consumer in order to head off any potentially bad publicity directed at their group as a whole. In other words, the mediator may try to push for a settlement in your favor to keep you from contacting "60 Minutes."

C. How to Locate a Good Mediator

Throughout this chapter, we provide much general information that should be useful if you want to find a mediator. Here we supplement it with some additional tips.

1. YOUR OWN PRIVATE INFORMATION NETWORK

No matter where you are or what kind of dispute you face you should be able to pick up the phone and quickly get useful information about how to find a quality mediator. For example, depending on the specifics of your dispute, a local woman's organization, gay-lesbian organization or business trade group (or their key members) may be able to make a knowledgeable referral. Lawyers are often another excellent source of referrals. Even if you are "Josephine Citizen" with few professional contacts, you probably know someone who knows a decent lawyer (your Uncle Herman's wife?) and that lawyer, in turn, may know just the independent mediator or mediation center to help you.

Try making a short list of the people you know who are in the best position to advise you about a mediator or to refer you to someone who can. You may end up calling your son's financial advisor or your daughter's minister. But so what? If you get results, that's all that matters.

2. STATE AND NATIONAL ORGANIZATIONS, DIRECTORIES, LISTS, ETC.

There are lots of state and national groups you can contact for help in locating mediators and mediation services. The Academy of Family Mediators, for example, will provide lists of divorce and family mediators in your area who meet their membership standards. (See Chapter 11, Divorce Mediation.) For contact information on this and other national groups, see Appendix C. Also, many states now have government-sponsored offices (California, New Jersey, Ohio and Texas, to name a few) that keep track of mediation programs within their states. For contact information, see the list of "Statewide Mediation Offices" in Appendix D. *The Directory of Dispute Resolution*, an expensive ($99), privately published listing of thousands of lawyers, retired judges and others who describe themselves as mediators (credentials are not verified by the publisher) may also be of some help. It's available at many law libraries and large public libraries, or contact the publisher: Martindale-Hubbell, Inc., 121 Chanlon Road, New Providence, NJ 07974, (800) 526-4902.

3. Bar Association Listings

Your local bar association—the professional organization of lawyers—may keep a list of lawyers available who act as mediators and provide names to the public without a fee. Beware, though, that most bar associations will just tell you the name of the next person on the list, and not evaluate or comment on the person's skill level. Also, lots of busy, in-demand mediators won't bother to list with the bar. In addition, the national office of the American Bar Association publishes the "Dispute Resolution Program Directory," a nationwide listing of community mediation centers and other mediation services. Check for the book at law libraries and some public libraries, or you can order it ($60, plus $3.99 shipping and handling) from: American Bar Association, Section of Dispute Resolution, 740 15th St., NW Washington, DC 20005, (202) 662-1680, World Wide Web (http://www.abanet.org).

4. Yellow Pages

Check under "mediation" or "dispute resolution" or, if all else fails, "arbitration." Most mediation services, as well as independent mediators in private practice, will have some kind of brochure to send you with descriptive information about their services.

SUMMARY—WHO ARE THE MEDIATORS?

	COMMUNITY MEDIATION CENTER	PRIVATE DISPUTE RESOLUTION COMPANY	COURT CONNECTED MEDIATION PROGRAM	INDEPENDENT MEDIATORS IN PRIVATE PRACTICE
Regular Occupation/ Work Background	Teacher Social worker Lawyer Parent/Homemaker Business	Lawyer Retired Judge Business Engineer Career Mediator with specialty	Lawyer Social Work Criminal Justice System	Lawyer Business Career Mediator with specialty Career Mediator specializing in divorce (see Chapter 11)
Earnings (per hour)	$0 - $40	$100 - $300	$0 - $150, depending if court pays mediators (or uses volunteers) or parties are free to hire mediators from private sector	$75 - $300
Training	Required by state law or court rule, usually 25-40 hours (some mediators with prior experience may qualify under state law or court rules without additional training)	Varies with company policy; most require some education in the field and knowledge of subject areas in dispute, but others may be lax on training	Varies with court rules; may be extensive or minimum	Varies with commitment of individual mediator; full-time career mediators may have advanced training; a practicing lawyer who mediates only occasionally may have little or no training
Mediates How Often?	Part-time	Mostly part-time as chosen by parties from company panel; a few may work full-time	Full-time or part-time	Some who make mediation a career work full-time; most are part-time

D. Common Types of Disputes and Where They Can Best Be Mediated

Certain types of disputes are best mediated with particular types of mediation services. For example, a community mediation center would be an excellent place for neighbors to take a dispute over a shared driveway. Mediators at the center probably have loads of experience handling driveway and other neighbor-to-neighbor disputes, and, because it is tax-supported, the center can handle the case for free or a nominal fee, which is important because you likely don't want to be paying a lot of money to resolve a dispute that probably is more of a nuisance than a business matter. On the other hand, if you have a business partnership termination dispute, you probably do not want to go to a community mediation center because the mediators there are unlikely to have much experience with business cases. Instead, you should use a private dispute resolution company or an independent mediator in private practice who has experience handling such cases. You'll pay a fee for this service, but by shopping around you can find a mediator who will handle the case for a reasonable amount that is not out of line compared to the amount of money at stake. (For more on checking on a mediation fees, see Chapter 5, Section A4.)

Section B described the various types of mediators and mediation services. Below we discuss various categories of disputes and recommend the type of mediation provider you should call, as a general rule.

Assault, petty harassment: If you are involved (as alleged victim or alleged perpetrator) in minor criminal matters such as assault, harassment, petty larceny, trespass or vandalism, mediation may be available through either of two forums.

If a criminal complaint has not yet been made, you can take the dispute to the local community mediation center (if there is one). Many community mediation centers have lots of experience handling minor criminal cases, so the volunteer mediators there are experienced with these typical kinds of cases. If the other party is reluctant to mediate, the center will try to persuade him or her to participate. If the parties can reach a mediated settlement (payment of money, promise to keep apart, apology, etc.), there may be no need to go ahead with a criminal complaint.

If a criminal complaint has already been filed, you can still ask the prosecutor to refer the case to the community mediation center—unless your community has a Prosecutor's (District Attorney's) Mediation Program, in which case the prosecutor would refer the case there.

Contract disputes: Resolving disputes involving business contracts, particularly between two businesses, is an area in which mediation can really shine. This type of case can be expensive, time-consuming and, because of the large stakes involved, often frightening to take to court. By contrast, mediation offers an efficient, private way to work out a settlement. Private dispute resolution companies, as well as independent mediators who specialize in small business and contract mediation, are the best choices to handle these kinds of disputes. For more information, see Chapter 12, Mediating Business Disputes.

Construction disputes: These involve all sorts of disputes arising out of residential, commercial and sometimes public building projects. Construction disputes are well-suited to mediation, as they often involve complex issues, large sums of money and multiple parties, such as owners, general contractors, architects, engineers and sub-contractors. Often, if mediation is begun fairly quickly and results in a settlement, the job can be finished reasonably promptly, with lots of money saved. Private dispute resolution companies with mediators knowledgeable about construction practices, or independent mediators who specialize in this area, are the best choices for these cases.

Consumer complaints: These typically include demands for reimbursement for unacceptable goods or services, or sometimes a request to redo or fix substandard work. Complaints against auto repair shops and dry cleaners are common, as well as against in-home contractors such as roofers, plumbers and carpenters. If the amount of money you are seeking is not terribly large, say under $10,000, a community mediation center is your best choice, because their services are provided free or at nominal cost and the mediators will be experienced in handling these types of small-money consumer matters, particularly the parts of these disputes that often involve interpersonal issues rather than just financial ones.

For larger sums, we recommend a private dispute resolution company. Compared with the volunteer mediators at a community mediation center, the private company's mediators are likely to be more knowledgeable about the contract and financial issues involved in these larger disputes, and probably better able to help the parties create financial arrangements to settle the matter. Private companies' fees, starting at about $500 per side, are not out of line for cases above $10,000 or so.

Divorce and family disputes: Most divorce mediators work independently or in small private practices. If you can afford their fees—which often include a sliding scale depending on your income—they are the best choice. If not, some community mediation centers have mediators with specialized divorce training available for free or at very low fees. In addition, many states now require mediation of divorce-related issues such as child custody and visitation, and have court-sponsored programs to provide this service. For more on these court-sponsored mediation programs, as well as using independent divorce mediators in private practice, See Chapter 11, Divorce Mediation.

Employer/Employee: These include disputes over money owed in salary, unused vacation and sick leave; claims of discrimination based on sex, race, age, etc.; and claims of sexual harassment and wrongful termination. As long as the case is big enough to warrant the fee, I would take these cases to a private dispute resolution company, or to an independent mediator in private practice who specializes in the area. (Some big employers offer in-house mediation programs where co-workers trained as mediators try to resolve such disputes at an early stage. These are generally fine to try as a first resort. For more on businesses' in-house mediation programs, see Chapter 12, Section G3.)

With so many state and federal laws now addressing relations in the workplace, it is important to use a mediator who is knowledgeable about the often complicated legal aspects of employment relations. So even though the amount in dispute might be relatively small, I don't think a community mediation center is the place to go because, in general, most of the mediators there are not going to have a good handle on the various laws possibly involved. (Some state and federal agencies that monitor discrimination in the workplace, such as state departments of labor and the federal Equal Employment Opportunity Commission (EEOC), run their own mediation programs. Contact these offices locally to see if a program is available in your area.)

Environmental disputes: These include disputes about how land, waterways and other natural resources are affected by development, as well as location of waste disposal facilities and clean-up of toxic materials. These cases often involve multiple parties and technical or scientific issues. Private dispute resolution companies with mediators knowledgeable in these areas, and independent mediators who specialize in environmental issues, are usually the best choice for these disputes. For very large cases, there are some national organizations that specialize in environmental dispute resolution. (For contact information, see Appendix C, National and Regional Mediation Organizations and Services.)

Interpersonal disputes between former friends or acquaintances: This includes disputes involving former friends, roommates, lovers and others with close personal relationships. Claims often involve money, disputed ownership of property or one person having damaged or destroyed the other's belongings. If keeping costs low is a factor, use a community mediation center. They are very experienced at handling these types of cases and may even have mediators available who have developed specialties in some of these areas, such as disputes involving roommates or unmarried couples, or gay and lesbian couples. On the other hand, if you can afford the fees, an independent mediator in private practice who specializes in divorce and family mediation would also be a good choice. Though your dispute may not specifically involve divorce or even a traditional family, these divorce and family mediators have much experience handling emotionally charged interpersonal disputes and the sometimes complicated financial and property issues involved. For more on how to locate a divorce and family mediator in private practice, see Chapter 11, Divorce Mediation.

Intra-family disputes: This includes disputes between spouses, siblings or relatives concerning such things as inappropriate behavior, monetary disputes and inheritances. Especially if little money is involved, most of these disputes can be handled adequately at a community mediation center, for little or no cost. If more complex business and financial matters are involved, a private dispute resolution company or independent divorce and family mediator will probably bring a higher skill level to the mediation. Certainly, if the dispute affects the running of a good-sized family-owned business or a large inheritance, the private company or independent mediator is definitely preferable.

Landlord/Tenant: This includes issues such as the landlord's failure to make repairs or return a security deposit, and the failure of the tenant to adhere to occupancy rules. For disputes involving your own apartment or other residence a community mediation center will usually be the best choice because of the low cost and their experience handling these types of issues. In some areas, you may even find community mediation centers with specialized landlord/tenant dispute resolution programs. However, if you are the owner or tenant of commercial property, where complicated lease issues and significant amounts of money are at stake, mediators at a private dispute resolution company will have more experience and expertise in the subject matter.

Neighbor disputes: Nationally, nearly one-fourth of cases at community mediation centers involve neighborhood disputes concerning such things as damaged property, noise, view-blocking trees, shared driveways, barking dogs and the behavior of young people. The community center is the best place to take such a case. The mediators who see these kinds of cases day in and day out have lots of experience helping structure workable solutions.

Public policy disputes: These disputes include all kinds of issues, from zoning and road construction, to school rules and tax rates. To handle them well, a mediator needs special skills, as they often involve multiple interest groups, tight deadlines, press coverage, technical issues and the possibility of political interference. Private dispute resolution companies—and some community mediation centers—may have mediators with experience in these types of often tense multi-party mediations. There are also national organizations that specialize in providing mediators for large, complex public policy disputes.

Small business ownership disputes: These include situations in which co-owners (partners and stockholders) are unable to agree on how to run a business, or where one wants to buy out the other, or one has died and the survivors must cope with the deceased's inheritors. A private dispute resolution company or independent mediator specializing in business disputes is usually the best choice to handle these cases. See also Chapter 12, Mediating Business Disputes.

The following table summarizes the recommendations discussed above.

COMMON TYPES OF DISPUTES AND WHERE
THEY CAN BEST BE MEDIATED

CASE TYPE	BEST CHOICE	FEES
Assault, Harassment	Community Mediation Center	$0 - $50 Sliding Scale
Contract Dispute	Dispute Resolution Company	$90 -$200/hour per party
Construction	Dispute Resolution Company	$90 -$200/hour per party
Consumer Complaint	Community Mediation Center	$0 - $50 Sliding Scale
Divorce	Private Divorce Mediator	$80 - $400/hour per couple; sliding scale sometimes available
Employment	Dispute Resolution Company	$90 - $200/hour per party
Environmental	Dispute Resolution Company	$90 - $200/hour per party
Interpersonal	Community Mediation Center	$0 - $50 Sliding Scale
Intra-Family	Private Family Mediator	$50 - $125/hour
Landlord vs. Tenant	Community Mediation Center for residential	$0 - $50 Sliding Scale
Neighbor vs. Neighbor	Community Mediation Center	$0 - $50 Sliding Scale
Public Policy	Dispute Resolution Company	$90 -$200/hour per party
Small Business Ownership	Dispute Resolution Company	$90 -$200/hour per party

REASON	OTHER CHOICES
Low cost; experience mediating these disputes; subject matter expertise	Court-run or prosecutor's program, or private company if large sums involved
Experience mediating these cases; subject matter expertise	Independent mediator with this specialty
Experience mediating these cases; subject matter expertise	Independent mediator with this specialty
Low cost; experience mediating these cases; subject matter expertise	Private company if $5,000 or more involved
Experience mediating these cases; subject matter expertise	Community Mediation Center for cost-savings
Experience mediating these cases; subject matter expertise	Independent mediator with this specialty
Experience mediating these cases; subject matter expertise	Independent mediator with this specialty
Low cost; experience mediating these cases; subject matter expertise	Private Divorce and Family Mediator
Low cost; experience mediating these cases; subject matter expertise	Private Divorce and Family Mediator
Low cost; experience mediating these cases; subject matter expertise	Private company, if commercial lease issues are involved
Low cost; experience mediating these cases; subject matter expertise	Independent mediator with this specialty if case justifies mediator fees
Experience mediating these cases; subject matter expertise	Community Mediation Center, especially senior staff mediators
Experience mediating these cases; subject matter expertise	If owners are family members, Divorce and Family Mediator with financial expertise

FOUR

Starting Your Mediation Case

This chapter discusses when and how to begin your mediation. For the most part, I assume you will be the person initiating the effort to mediate, which means it will be up to you to start the process with a mediator or mediation service.

WHEN MEDIATION IS REQUIRED: If you have been ordered to mediate by a court or other agency, as part of a court-connected mediation program, or are required to mediate under the terms of a contract, many issues discussed in this chapter, such as when and how to start your case, will obviously not apply, and it makes sense to skip or skim them. However, if under the court order or contract terms you have the right to participate in selecting your mediator or mediation service, then the information in Section E, "Starting Your Case with a Mediator or Mediation Service," will still be useful.

A. When Is a Case Ready for Mediation?

In theory, mediation can occur at any point in a dispute. The fact that a court case has been filed, or even that a trial is about to begin, makes no difference—if both parties agree, you can always mediate.

As a general rule, however, the sooner you can bring a fresh dispute to mediation, the better. Not only can an early mediation mean a quick end to uncertainty and anxiety (especially when litigation has begun or is seriously threatened), but it also can mean significant savings of money, time and energy. Paradoxically, disputes can sometimes be brought to mediation too early. This can occur when people are still extremely angry (some mediators inelegantly refer to this as "the frothing at the mouth stage") and thus not yet ready to participate in a rational discussion. Mediation can also be premature when one party does not yet have enough information to know what, or how much, he should settle for, such as would be true in the case of an automobile accident, when doctors have not yet determined if a person's injuries will cause a permanent disability.

Here are several factors that should help you decide if your case is ripe for mediation.

1. YOU HAVE TRIED—WITHOUT SUCCESS—TO SETTLE THE DISPUTE BY TALKING DIRECTLY WITH THE OTHER SIDE

Direct negotiation between disputing parties is the most efficient way to resolve most disputes. Not only do one-on-one negotiations save time, they eliminate the expense and delay of getting third parties involved (including mediators). So, step one is to contact the other party to see if you can negotiate a settlement. If you have not tried to settle your dispute directly with your opponent, it is probably too soon to mediate. For example, if you hired a contractor to put a new roof on your house and now the roof leaks, it makes sense to call the contractor to try to resolve the problem before calling a mediation service.

2. Emotions Have Had at Least Some Time to Cool

Emotions run high in many disputes, even those over seemingly dry business matters. As mentioned, although mediation is well-suited to accommodate people with strong emotions, there may be an initial period when one party, or even both parties, are so angry that rational discussion is difficult, if not impossible. If you recognize that your dispute has resulted in your feeling intensely angry, hurt or even full of rage, it is often best to cool off a little before trying to mediate. Similarly, if you recognize these emotions in the other party, it may be easier to get him to mediate constructively if you slow things down enough so that his emotions have a chance to cool.

3. You Have Enough Information About Your Case to Know Approximately What You Want to Settle For

In order to mediate intelligently, you need enough information about your dispute to know how to settle it to your advantage. Sorting out all the facts that underlie a dispute can take time. In legal terms, the period of investigation is called "discovery." For example, a boundary dispute with a neighbor really can't be mediated until a survey is completed. A period of delay will also be advantageous if you want to do some legal research yourself or get the opinion of a lawyer about the important legal issues in your dispute or how a judge or jury would be likely to value it.

B. When It Can Be Too Late to Mediate

It's fairly common for disputants to wait too long to begin mediation. In the jargon of mediators, their case has become "overripe." The usual result of trying to bring an overripe case to mediation is either that one side will refuse to participate or, if the mediation occurs, it will fail to produce a settlement.

Your dispute may be overripe if any of the following factors apply:

- *Preparations for trial have proceeded too far.* Once the other party has invested heavily in preparing for trial—in terms of legal fees, time and effort—he may be much less willing to settle for anything less than what he imagines as full court "victory." By comparison, if mediation is suggested at an earlier stage of a dispute, he may be more open to methods of resolution such as mediation, which will put the hassle behind him without his needing to file a court action or take the case to trial.

- *The people personally involved in the dispute no longer control it.* Another situation in which a dispute is "overripe," or hard to mediate, occurs when the original disputants—who might have been willing to mediate—lose control of their own decision-making. This can occur when lawyers—especially those who charge by the hour—become intensely involved and strongly advocate fighting it out in court. In a business, it can happen when senior managers or owners take a dispute away from lower-level employees who might have been more likely to settle it.

EXAMPLE: *Peter, the sales manager of a parts manufacturer, and Rosamund, the purchasing agent for a manufacturer, get into a dispute over the quality (or lack thereof) of certain parts Peter's company has delivered to Rosamund. These two have been doing business together for years, and though they disagree about this job, they normally work things out so as to not jeopardize their mutually-beneficial relationship. As long as they can keep in sight the mutual advantage of continuing to do business together, chances are a mediator can help them solve their immediate dispute. But if the matter gets "bumped upstairs" to their respective bosses or company lawyers, each side's position may harden. Now, instead of being motivated to compromise so as to make future business dealings possible, both companies may make it a priority to try and beat the other out of as much money as possible.*

SOMETIMES HAVING A MORE OBJECTIVE PERSON HANDLE A DISPUTE IS BENEFICIAL. If the original disputants feel extremely bitter towards one another or have dug deep bargaining positions, they may find it difficult to mediate successfully. By contrast, a manager or lawyer may take a more dispassionate view and be willing to work out a reasonable settlement in mediation.

- *Emotional links among disputants are "dead."* Some types of disputes involving close interpersonal relationships between friends, spouses, and relatives are particularly likely to become overripe and thus unlikely to go to mediation. This occurs when hurt feelings have been allowed to fester so long that the parties would rather live with them than to risk opening up the entire dispute to try and settle it. For example, a brother and sister fighting bitterly over their mother's estate may be open to trying to resolve the dispute through mediation for a couple of months (or maybe even a year after the mother's death). But if a couple of years pass with grievances still unresolved, the positive feelings they once had for each other may be so "dead" that neither feels any motivation to resuscitate them through mediation. In short, one or both of them would rather stay passively angry than to risk inflaming the old wounds to resolve the underlying dispute.

C. The Best Times to Start Mediation

Unless you know for a fact that the other party is willing to mediate, start by assuming she will be at least a somewhat reluctant participant, if for no other reason than she may be prone to oppose anything you propose. One excellent way to increase the chances of her agreeing to mediate, is to try to time your proposal to mediate so that the other side is most likely to say "yes." This may be less difficult than you think. In the course of any dispute, there are usually events, such as a fact-finding hearing or court appearance, that promise to be expensive or scary or where the results are highly uncertain. It follows that a proposal to mediate just before one of these events is slated to occur may be especially appealing to the other side.

Let's look more closely at a couple of situations where a dispute may be most ripe for mediation.

1. If Your Dispute Is Not Yet in Litigation

If your dispute has not yet resulted in a court filing or other formal action, you can often successfully get the other party to mediate by presenting mediation as a way to avoid this eventuality. For example, if your dispute involves an employment-related claim against your employer, which is scheduled for a fact-finding hearing under your company's internal grievance procedure, your proposal to mediate shortly before the hearing date may be welcomed as a way to possibly settle your claim before it escalates.

Similarly, if your dispute is with a small company you know is negotiating to sell out or go public, the owners may be eager to clear up all possible disputes rather than risk being sued at what they see as a very critical time.

With smaller disputes, particularly, you can oftentimes make mediation more appealing to the other party by proposing it at one of those predictable times during the year when many people like to get disputes out of the way. One of these is the end of the year. Many mediators find, for example, that early December is one of their busiest periods; people want a clean slate for the new year (and may be motivated by the approaching Christmas season to try to make peace). Therefore, a good time to invite a person to mediation would be in the late fall, when the likelihood of having the dispute resolved before the holidays would be an inducement.

Similarly, you can propose mediation just before some personal event in the other party's life that may put him in a mood to "clear the air." It's hard to know exactly what events will trigger such a mood in another person, but common ones include an upcoming marriage, birthday, birth of a child, anniversary, change in employment or even a visit from a relative.

2. IF YOUR CASE IS IN LITIGATION

If your dispute has already resulted in a lawsuit, it can make sense to push for mediation just before an expensive or otherwise unpleasant stage of this litigation is scheduled to occur. For example, you might propose mediation just before the other side has scheduled the deposition of a physician or other expensive expert witness. Similarly, you might suggest mediation just before the deadline for exchanging sensitive documents, or before an important pre-trial motion (for example, one considering whether key evidence will be admissible at trial). Sometimes it's even possible to head off a fast-approaching trial date by proposing a last ditch effort to mediate, since many judges agree to delay (continue) the trial to give mediation a chance.

TIME-LINE OF STRATEGIC POINTS TO INITIATE MEDIATION

before lawsuit filed ....> date when answer due ....> before deposition... ....> before document exchange ....> before pre-trial conference ....> before trial date

D. How to Propose Mediation

Mediation doesn't just occur—usually one party proposes it. It's then up to the second party to say yes or no. As noted earlier, exceptions occur when a judge or government agency orders parties to mediate and when parties go to mediation because their dispute arises out of a contract that requires them to mediate before going to court. (See Chapter 3, Where to Take Your Dispute for Mediation.) Here we present a strategy for how you can propose mediation in a way that will have the best chance of getting the other party to agree to participate.

I. STRATEGY: INVITE THE OTHER PARTY TO MEDIATE (BUT DON'T TRY TO SELL MEDIATION)

You may be tempted to call the other party to urge her to join you in mediation. This might work if you and she have a history of trust and goodwill that remains at least somewhat intact. Realistically, of course, this is unlikely, since most people in a dispute that they can't resolve by the normal give-and-take, or negotiation, distrust each other. The result is: if you propose mediation directly to the other party, she may suspect you of trying to trick her in some way and be strongly predisposed to say no.

One big exception to this general rule is when the other party has had experience with mediation and already knows it is an efficient and non-threatening way to resolve disputes. For example, this might be the situation if you propose mediation to a home repair contractor who you know is a member of a builder's trade group that has actively supported the creation of a community mediation center in your city.

The best way to keep distrust from getting in the way of your desire to mediate is normally for a mediation service to extend the invitation to mediate. For one thing, they have lots of experience in knowing what to say and when to say it. After all, a mediation company or organization that can't convince people to mediate won't stay in business long. This holds true even for the nonprofit, community mediation centers; they must conduct a large number of mediations to justify continued support from the public agencies that fund them.

**MANY INDEPENDENT MEDIATORS PREFER NOT TO "SELL" A PARTY
ON MEDIATING. As discussed in more detail in Chapter 3, Where to Take
Your Dispute for Mediation, many independent mediators prefer not to try to
talk people into mediating, in part because most of them don't have trained staff
to do the job. And they are reluctant to do it themselves, fearing that by doing
so, they risk their neutrality. For this reason, if you fear the other party may be
reluctant to mediate, you are better off using a mediation service rather than an
independent mediator.**

Is it best for you to refrain altogether from broaching the subject of mediation with the other side, and instead just contact the mediation service? This may
be tempting, but it overlooks another important fact of human behavior: people
don't like to be surprised. Think of it this way: If you call a mediation service
without telling the other party, she may be extremely suspicious of your having
initiated a process without her knowledge. For example: she might jump to the
conclusion that you have said negative things about her or that you have "influence" with the particular mediation service. Or, if she is unfamiliar with mediation, she may even accuse you of plotting to bypass her legal rights.

2. NOTIFY YOUR OPPONENT BY MAIL

Writing a short, polite letter is usually the best way to notify another party that
you want to mediate and will be contacting a mediation service. (An exception to
this general rule might occur if you and the other side have had such a close
relationship in the past that, despite your dispute, even a friendly letter would
seem too formal.) Why is a letter usually better than a phone call? In writing,
you can simply state that you want to mediate, with no need to discuss the
merits of the dispute. Personal contact, such as a phone call, is much trickier,
because you or the other party may be tempted to argue about either the merits
of mediation or of your case, exactly the sort of interaction you probably want to
avoid at this stage of your dispute.

Your letter should inform the other side of your desire to mediate without saying anything that is likely to trigger a defensive response. Here are some suggestions that should help:

1. State that you would like to try mediation and list some reasons why. (You can use any or all of these phrases; see the sample letter below.)

"If mediation works, we can both save a lot of time and aggravation and a fortune in legal fees"

" Mediation is quick, inexpensive, understandable, and we can do it without lawyers"

"Mediation carries no risk because the mediator is neutral and has no power to impose a decision on us"

2. Do not try to persuade the other person to mediate. Leave it up to the mediation service to do the selling.

3. Do not presume to say what the other person thinks or wants. For example, it's fine to say, "I want to mediate because I believe mediation is an excellent way to solve disputes." But it's a mistake to say, "You probably don't know much about mediation" or "I doubt you will agree to this...." A good way to steer clear of this problem is simply to avoid using the word "you."

4. Never threaten the other person. For example do not write, "If you don't agree to mediation, I will have no recourse but to commence a lawsuit."

5. State clearly that you have no personal connection with the mediation service that you have chosen other than contacting them for the purposes of this mediation. The other party may not believe this, but at least you will have raised the issue and stated the facts. If you want, you can state that if the other person is willing to mediate but wants to investigate another mediation service, you would be open to that.

6. Let the other person know he will be contacted by the mediation service so he will not be surprised when that happens.

7. Let the other person know that you are using this book and that you are willing to provide him/her with a copy so that you can both be on the "same page" regarding mediation. Or, if the cost of the book is a problem, see whether it is available in your local public library. The point is, the more proactive you are in getting this information into the other person's hands, the more likely it is that your mediation will take place and succeed.

The following example illustrates how to put the writing tips discussed above together.

EXAMPLE: *Mike and Ron are co-owners of Big Slice Pizza, Inc., a restaurant. For some time, they have had serious arguments over various issues of running their business, including pricing meals and dealing with employees. Each owns half the company. If they can't work out their differences or decide who will buy the other out, the business may fail. They have had several conversations in an effort to directly negotiate a settlement, without success. Mike has read several books on dispute resolution and believes the time is right to mediate. After some investigation, he has identified a local private dispute resolution company, Settle It Now, Inc., as a good mediation service to handle the case. Mike and Ron have never discussed mediation and Mike doesn't know if Ron will be willing to give mediation a try. So, to start the process, Mike writes the following letter to Ron:*

October 24, 1997

Dear Ron:

I am writing to let you know that I have given our situation at Big Slice Pizza a lot of thought and have decided that one way we can both try to get this thing resolved without spending a huge amount of time and a fortune on lawyers is to try mediation.

I have read that mediation is a simple and straightforward way for people to try to work out a solution to many different kinds of disputes. As I understand it, mediation is quick, we don't need lawyers, it's fairly inexpensive and no decisions or actions can be imposed on either of us unless we both freely agree. For starters, we don't need to make any commitment short of showing up and sitting down with a neutral third person who will try to help us work out a solution. I'm willing to give it a try if you are.

As a first step, I've asked Settle It Now, Inc., a private dispute resolution company here in town, to send you some information about their service. I don't have any personal connection with this company; they just seem to have experience working with businesses like ours. If for any reason you don't like Settle It Now, I'm open to your suggestions for another mediation service for us to use.

Incidentally, I am using a book published by Nolo Press called Mediate Your Dispute, by Peter Lovenheim. I find it very helpful, and if you would like your own copy I will be happy to find you one. If both of us are using the same resource it may help this entire matter go more smoothly.

Yours,

Mike

E. Starting Your Case With a Mediator or Mediation Service

To initiate your case with a mediator or mediation service, you normally contact them and complete a one- or two-page "submission" or "intake" form. Some services may charge you an up-front filing fee to open and begin processing your case; others charge no fee until all parties to the dispute have agreed to mediate and a date for the mediation is scheduled. (For more on the range of fees charged by different types of mediation services, see Chapter 3.) Below I discuss some of the forms you will probably need to complete and some choices you may face as you start your case.

1. COMPLETING THE "SUBMISSION TO MEDIATION" FORM

When you call a mediation service, you will typically be asked to complete a short information sheet called "Submission to Mediation," or something similar. Most offices will take the information over the phone, or you can ask them to mail the form to you. It shouldn't take more than a few minutes to complete.

The submission form requests basic information about your case, such as names and addresses of the parties, attorneys (if any), what type of case it is, whether a lawsuit has been filed and what solution you are seeking. If you call an independent mediator, such as one specializing in business disputes, where the mediator himself will handle the dispute if both sides agree to participate, the initial contact may be less bureaucratic.

The information you put on the Submission Form will not normally be considered confidential by the mediation service and may be communicated to the other side for purposes of getting him to mediate. Typically, the mediation service will use your information in two ways:

- to the extent it's relevant, as part of the letter it sends to the other party inviting him to participate, and
- if the other party is slow to agree, as part of follow-up phone calls to try to persuade him to mediate.

> ### WHAT'S IN A NAME?—"CLAIMANT" "RESPONDENT" "INITIATOR" "DISPUTANT"
>
> Some mediation services—particularly community mediation centers—call the person who submits a case the "claimant" and the other person the "respondent." This can create a problem when both sides feel they have something to complain about, with the "respondent" taking offense at being cast in what sounds like a defensive role. For this reason, some services avoid the term "claimant" by calling the party that initiated the case the "submitting party" or the "initiator," but most still refer to the other party as "respondent."

2. DESCRIBING YOUR DISPUTE

To avoid revealing any sensitive information to the other party, and also to avoid saying anything that would make him reluctant to mediate, it is usually best to describe your dispute in a fairly general and non-inflammatory way. Let's look at how to do this in the context of the types of questions you are likely to be asked on the "Submission to Mediation" form.

A. "WHAT IS THE NATURE OF THE DISPUTE?"

Here you want to state the very broad outlines of your dispute. After all, the mediation service doesn't know if you have a claim against an insurance company for injuries you received in a motorcycle accident, a dispute with your employer about conditions at work or an argument with your neighbor about his tree roots ruining your driveway.

When describing your dispute, it's best to use ordinary—not legal—words, since the mediation service's case manager may refer to your terminology when she asks the other side to agree to mediate. For example, if your dispute is with your landscape gardener because the shrubbery that was guaranteed for three years died after three months, instead of describing this as "breach of contract," it's better to write "dissatisfaction with shrubbery plantings." In addition to the fact that plain words are easier to understand, another good reason to prefer them is that they are less likely to trigger a "litigation response," with the other party charging off to a lawyer to counter your legal claim and, as a result, very possibly being talked out of mediating.

Or, suppose your dispute is with the local newspaper over how you were identified in a news story. It's best to describe it on the mediation intake form as a "problem with how I was identified by the *Mt. Pleasant News* in a story that appeared on January 3, 1996 (page B-1)," rather by describing it as a case of "libel and defamation of character."

B. "WHAT REMEDY IS SOUGHT?"

When describing the result you wish to achieve, your best bet is to be straight-forward. These statements are all fine, assuming the dispute involves money or property:

- "Return of the following property" (include a list with clear descriptions), or
- "Fair payment for my injuries suffered on 1/7/96," or
- "My job at Racafrax International back."

If your case involves how someone is behaving toward you or your family, it's particularly important to be diplomatic about what you write so as not to anger or affront the other person, with the likely result that he rejects your proposal to mediate outright or runs to his lawyer. For example, if you are complaining about a neighbor who drives dangerously on your street, you might say "Remedy sought: Mr. Adams to drive carefully on Hickory St." However, it would be a mistake to say, "that Mr. Adams stop speeding [or driving recklessly]…so he doesn't run over my kids."

Perhaps it will help you modulate your tone if you imagine yourself as Mr. Adams for a moment. You receive a call from a mediation service's case manager telling you a neighbor is seriously concerned about your driving so badly you are likely to run over his children. What would your response be? Chances are you would tell the mediation service and your neighbor to go shove it, which, of course, is exactly why it's best to be non-threatening and non-accusatory.

C. "WHAT AMOUNT OF MONEY IS BEING ASKED FOR (IF ANY)?"

How much money, if any, do you really want the other side to pay you? Unlike in litigation (and sometimes even negotiation), where it's common to establish a "strong bargaining position" by claiming a much higher amount than you really want—sometimes by a factor of ten or more—in mediation, it's usually wise to claim an amount much closer to what you really want. Remember, your first hurdle is to get the other side to agree to mediate. If a demand for money appears too outrageous, it's likely to be counterproductive to this aim, with the other person either going straight to a lawyer or taking the position, "We're so far apart there's no point in mediating because we'll never bridge the gap."

Some people worry that by being reasonable in mediation they will give up their right to go for the jackpot in court if the mediation fails. Not to worry. The fact you asked for less in the mediation will not be admissible in any later court action. This is because statements made in the course of settlement attempts cannot later be used against the party making them.

D. "SHOULD ADDITIONAL PARTIES BE CONTACTED?"

Your Submission Form may ask if there are additional parties whom the mediation service should contact. This is an important question. To be successful, mediation needs to be inclusive—that is, everyone with a significant stake in the outcome of the dispute should be invited to participate. An agreement that excludes an important stakeholder will be of little value if that person is in a position to undermine it. For example, assume you are a real estate agent who lost a commission because your clients backed out of a signed purchase offer for a new home after cracks were found in the chimney, even though your clients' offer was not contingent on an engineer's inspection. Legally, your clients might be obligated to buy the house, but to avoid the cost, delays and damage to your relations with your clients, you instead would like to get the case to mediation to see if the deal can be put back together—maybe by you, the seller's agent, and the sellers all contributing some money towards repairing the chimney. But for this to work, you will need at the mediation not only your former clients, but also the sellers' agent and the seller.

E. "WHAT TYPE OF DISPUTE RESOLUTION DO YOU WANT?"

The Submission Form may also ask what type of dispute resolution services or help you want. This is because some mediation services offer half a dozen or more varieties. In Chapter 1, What is Mediation?, we briefly define and discuss the major non-court alternatives. Please review that list if you are unsure whether mediation is your best choice.

Chances are you'll prefer mediation. But you may also want to consider one or more of the other possibilities. Indicating a preference for one type of dispute resolution does not prevent you from changing your mind later; your initial preference, however, will determine what the mediation service says in its introductory letter to your opponent.

WHAT IS "BINDING" MEDIATION?

Mediation is, by definition, non-binding, but some mediation services may ask, on their Submission Form, if you want "binding" or "non-binding" mediation. What they mean is: if you settle your case in mediation, do you want the mediator to write the terms of the settlement in the form of a legally-binding contract so it will be enforceable in court? Otherwise, the settlement just expresses the parties' intentions, and is not legally enforceable.

Some mediation services offer this option, and others do not. In most cases, you should choose the binding option. If the other party reneges on the settlement, you can go to court to have the agreement enforced as a contract. For more on writing your mediation agreement as a binding contract, see Chapter 8, Writing an Agreement That Works.

F. Securing an Agreement to Mediate

The mediation service will normally start by sending the other party a form letter asking her to agree to mediate, with telephone follow-up if there isn't an affirmative response. (For more on how to select a particular mediation service, see Chapter 5, Selecting Mediation Services and Mediators.)

If you and the other party are required to mediate under the terms of a contract or court order, the other party has no legal choice but to mediate. Even so, he or she may still foot-drag or try to avoid it. In this situation, the mediation service should be particularly persistent by sending letters and making repeat phone calls to set a firm date for the mediation. (If you show up and the other side doesn't, at least you've fulfilled your obligation under the contract or court order and can go on to pursue other legal remedies.)

IF YOU ANTICIPATE NO PROBLEM SECURING THE OTHER SIDE'S AGREEMENT to mediate, skip to Chapter 5, Selecting Mediation Services and Mediators.

If the other side fails to respond to—or otherwise resists—your offer to mediate, it will be the job of your mediation service to try to change the other side's initial reaction of "no" into "yes." In the rest of this section, we will look at how this is typically done.

1. WHY PEOPLE RESIST MEDIATION

Sometimes a person may have a good reason to resist mediation. For example, if she is likely to win a substantial victory in court, and if she has the money and time to see the case through, mediation—which often results in a compromise settlement—may not be to her advantage. (See Chapter 2, Sections A and B, which review factors favoring and opposing mediation.) More often, however, people decline to mediate for one of the following reasons:

- *Unfamiliarity:* Although mediation is gaining in popularity, a majority of Americans still do not understand how it works. For many, it is easier to say "no" to mediation than to bother learning about something new.
- *To be proved right:* The other side may not want the potential compromise solution mediation has to offer. Instead, he may want the chance to fight it out in court so, as he imagines it, he can be declared "the winner."
- *Because a lawyer advises against it:* A lawyer who is hostile towards mediation—or simply wants to collect a larger fee—may tell the other party something like this: "Mediation isn't for you. Ignore it. If the guy's serious, he'll file a lawsuit and then we'll deal with it."
- *The mediation process is threatening:* Cooperative problem-solving can be intimidating to those who have never been exposed to it. Some people just plain don't like any process that requires them actually to sit down with the other side and try to work out a solution. Others may fear that somehow they will be talked into giving up important rights as part of a procedure they don't understand.

2. HOW A MEDIATION SERVICE WORKS TO OVERCOME RESISTANCE

The initial letter and supporting materials that a typical mediation service will send to the other party will likely emphasize the benefits of mediation, stating the advantages in terms of low cost, privacy and speed. Letters from private dispute resolution firms often go on to point out the high quality of the people on their mediation panels, their "user-friendliness" and competitive pricing.

Some community mediation centers go beyond this "soft-sell" approach. In an effort to get people to the table, they sometimes play up their affiliations with courts or government agencies, coming fairly close to making a subtle threat that negative consequences may result from a failure to mediate.

For example, if your dispute came to a community mediation center or to a court-connected mediation program on referral from the local prosecutor, the letter to your opponent may say something like this: "District Attorney Sullivan has referred this dispute to our center in hopes it can be mediated." The implied threat is: "If you don't go to mediation, you might annoy the district attorney." Some centers even dress up their letter with case captions in imitation of court papers apparently to confuse the recipient into thinking the letter is a court notice.

> In the Matter of the Mediation between
> Steven Gordon, Claimant and
> Joseph Klein, Respondent,
> Case No. C-177-89

This sort of hard-sell approach seems to work. In a U.S. Department of Justice study, four out of five cases referred by judges for voluntary mediation actually were mediated.

RESPONDENT'S NOTE. Don't be intimidated by a tough contact letter. If you are the recipient of a heavy-handed contact letter, there is no reason to be pressured into doing something you don't want to do. Unless a contract or court order requires you to mediate, you are under no obligation to do so. Whether you choose to mediate should depend on how you assess what is in your own best interest, and should have little to do with whether a mediation service's letter is enticing or intimidating. (See Chapter 2, Sections A and B, for a discussion of factors that favor and oppose using mediation.)

If the mediation service gets no response from the other party to its initial letter within a week or two, the staff person—often called "case manager" or "case coordinator"—will usually follow up with a phone call (or series of phone calls) to answer the other side's questions about mediation and review mediation's potential benefits. If the side declines to participate based on a lawyer's advice, the staff person may ask permission to call the lawyer directly to be sure the lawyer understands mediation.

How successful a case manager is likely to be in overcoming a person's resistance to mediation will depend on the facts of your case, the other party's personality and the case manager's own skills. For example, some of the better private dispute resolution companies have very well-trained case managers who are quite skilled at turning a party's "no" (about mediating) into a "yes." On average, I'd say if the other side's first reaction to a proposal to mediate is "no," there's still about a 25%-33% chance that a good case manager can get him to agree to participate. If the other side's initial response is "I don't think so" or "maybe," then the chances of getting him to the table are probably up around 60%-75%.

3. Working Out an Agreement to Mediate

After proposing mediation, you should expect to hear within a week or two from your mediation service with the results of their contact with the other side. If not, call to check on your case. Often, politely reminding the person whose job it is to set up the mediation (again, often called the "case manager") that you are eager to get into mediation may help motivate her to work on your case.

Hopefully, before long, the case manager will report good news: the other side is willing and ready to mediate. If so, you can now select a mediator and schedule the mediation. (See Chapter 5, Selecting Mediation Services and Mediators.)

More likely, however, the case manager may report that the other party's response is a pretty firm "maybe." Here is a short list of what the other party is most likely to have said:

- I might mediate, but only if you pay all the fees, since it was your idea, or
- I might mediate, but only with a certain mediator, or
- I might mediate, but I want to limit (or expand) the issues to be discussed, or
- I might mediate but I want to use a different mediation service, or
- I won't mediate but might consider another type of dispute resolution such as binding arbitration, to get the dispute over with, or
- I need more time to think about it [or, investigate my case, or talk to my lawyer, or take care of personal business ("I'll think about it seriously after my daughter's wedding.")].

This type of conditional response may seem disappointing. In fact, it's positive, since it means you and the other side—with the help of the mediation service—are now negotiating on how to go about resolving your dispute. Chances are excellent that a competent case manager will be able to successfully guide you and the other party through these preliminary negotiations so that mediation can take place.

Depending on the other side's position, here is a chart setting out some typical strategies you and/or the case manager might adopt in response:

IF THE OTHER PARTY SAYS	YOU CAN RESPOND
Might mediate, but won't pay any fees	Especially if fees are low, as would be the case in many community mediation centers, you offer to pay them all, deciding that it's worth it to get on with the mediation. You each agree to pay own fees, but during the mediation you can discuss splitting them differently; You will pay your own and his administrative (start up) fee, but you'll split the hourly fees; You'll pay all the fees up to some fixed amount after which you each pay half.
Might mediate, but only with certain mediator	If you can accept his choice, fine. If not, suggest that you each submit a short list of preferred mediators from the service's panel. If you both name the same person, that person will be selected. Suggest that the case manager appoint an available mediator on the basis of skills, knowledge and availability. Suggest that the case manager propose three possible mediators, with you and the other side each having the power to eliminate one.
Might mediate but wants different mediation service or independent mediator	First find out why. If fees are a problem, the service you chose may be willing to lower them. If fees aren't an issue, consider whether he gains any personal advantage with the other service. Often, the answer is "no," since after all, a mediator has no power to decide your case. If so, you might want to switch to secure his participation If you don't like the mediation service he has proposed, suggest a couple of different possibilities, leaving the final choice up to him.
Might mediate but wants to limit or expand issues	Usually there's no harm in agreeing to this so long as the list of issues is not either: 1. So limited that important issues can't be reached 2. So long and diffuse that the mediation will become unfocused

IF THE OTHER PARTY SAYS	YOU CAN RESPOND
Won't mediate but might go to binding arbitration. (See definitions of the various types of arbitration in Chapter 1.)	If you have proposed mediation in the first place, it may be because you don't want a result imposed on you, in which case you won't want to agree to binding arbitration. One response would be to ask if he would agree to Advisory (non-binding) Arbitration. He might agree because though this procedure does not impose a binding result, it does give each side a chance to present their best arguments andthen provides both sides with a written evaluation which may form the basis for a quick settlement. Another possibility is to agree to mediation where, if no agreement is reached, the mediator will give a written recommendation to the parties. (Again, see definitions, Chapter 1.) Though the session itself is a mediation, the written recommendation at the end may appeal to his desire for a third party to say how the case should be resolved.
Wants more time to think it over; investigate, talk to a lawyer, or to take care of personal business	A delay may be okay if more investigation really is needed, emotions need to cool or personal schedules require it; but it's usually sensible to press for a reasonable deadline by which to begin mediation. If you agree to a delay, will the other side commit to a deadline? If there is an immediate problem, will the other side agree to mediate or negotiate an interim solution? (For example, he won't plant any more trees that interfere with your view until mediation occurs.)

Mediation services vary in how long they will keep trying to get a reluctant party to agree to mediate. Community mediation centers, with limited funding and staff, may make just one or two follow-up calls to the other party before marking your case "party refuses to mediate" and closing the file. Private dispute resolution companies, on the other hand, may keep a case manager working much longer to try to bring a dispute to mediation. They are highly motivated to do so because private firms generate most of their income from hourly fees charged during actual mediation. Independent mediators in private practice, as noted earlier, generally prefer not to get involved in trying to persuade a reluctant party to mediate because in doing so they risk losing their neutrality and thus their potential effectiveness as mediators, and also because it takes a lot of time for which they won't be compensated if the case never gets to the table. Faced with strong reluctance from the other side, an independent mediator would probably tell you, "Look, the other side doesn't seem ready to mediate. If he changes his mind, let me know and I'll be glad to handle the case, but I can't 'sell' him on the process; it's inconsistent with my role as a neutral."

4. OPTIONS IF THE OTHER PARTY REFUSES TO MEDIATE

If the other party refuses to mediate but you don't want to take "no" for an answer, there are a few tactics you can still try to get her to reconsider. Start by remembering that, as discussed in Section C, above, there are strategic times in every dispute when a person is likely to be more inclined to mediate than others—for example, just before or after a lawsuit has been filed. Next, consider when the next "strategic point" will occur and prepare to reintroduce your proposal to mediate then.

If no obvious "strategic points" are soon upcoming, you may want to try to create one. For example, if no lawsuit has been filed in your case, you can threaten to file one. One way to do this is to have a lawyer prepare the summons and complaint (if your case can be taken to small claims court, you can prepare the papers yourself) and send them to the other party with a letter stating that if he refuses to mediate you will file them. Be cautious with this approach, however, because not only will you likely incur legal expenses to prepare the paperwork, but the lawyer may persuade you to undertake more aggressive legal action than you originally had intended. And there is also the danger that your actions will be thought to be so aggressive that the other party will sue you first.

If you do file a lawsuit, but still want to mediate, tell the judge (or have your lawyer do it if you are represented) that you would prefer to try to resolve the dispute through mediation. (In a few courts, your case may even be automatically sent to mediation.) Many judges will be glad to get your case off their docket and strongly suggest to the other party that she try mediation. Sometimes the judge will even go a step further and refer you both to a local mediation service. In this context, it will often be difficult for the other side to resist the judge's suggestion—after all, if she does, it will be the same judge who hears the case.

There are some obvious disadvantages to this tactic, however. One is that you have to pay court filing fees, which may amount to several hundred dollars, plus an attorney's fee (unless you represent yourself). Another is that even if the other party agrees to mediate, he may not do so in good faith since he is mediating under duress. And then there is the possibility that a contested court case can result in both parties becoming too angry to mediate. Still, if you are intent on going to mediation, this tactic might get you there.

A variation on this tactic can also be used in disputes involving minor criminal offenses. Let's assume, for example, you are troubled by excessive noise from a neighbor's house, and your neighbor has refused your invitation to mediate. At this point, you can file a complaint about the noise with the police, and tell the responding officer, or the prosecutor if you get that far, that you would like to mediate. There is a good chance the police will be delighted to divert the case from the criminal justice system to a court-connected mediation program or community mediation center. Now, when the mediation program contacts your neighbor, the letter will state the dispute has been referred by the police. Your chances of getting your neighbor to mediation should markedly improve.

5

Selecting Mediation Services and Mediators

The information in this chapter will help you:

- select a mediation service and then select a *particular* mediator from a service's panel, or
- pick an independent mediator in private practice. The special issues involved in selecting a divorce mediator are discussed in Chapter 11, Divorce Mediation. Chapter 4, Starting Your Mediation Case, helps you decide whether a mediation service or an independent mediator is most appropriate for your type of dispute and circumstances.

A. **10 Questions to Ask a Mediation Service**

IF YOU HAVE DECIDED TO USE AN INDEPENDENT MEDIATOR, SKIP AHEAD TO SECTION B2.

When you have located one or more mediation services you think you might want to use, the next step is to call them directly and ask for a descriptive brochure. Nearly all services have a brochure. After you look it over, call them again to ask as many of the following questions as are applicable to your case. The information you receive should be sufficient to help you decide if it is the right kind of service to handle your case.

1. HOW EXTENSIVE IS THE CASE MANAGEMENT?

"Case management" is industry jargon for getting a reluctant party to mediate, and then helping both parties deal with such matters as:

- selecting a particular mediator from a service's panel
- agreeing on a date for the session, and
- agreeing on how fees will be split.

If the other party is reluctant to mediate, the skills of a mediation service's case managers will be the key to getting the other party to the table. Obviously, in this situation, you'll want to know the following information: How will they work to get the other side to agree to mediate? Will they contact the other side by letter only, or will they followup with phone calls? How long will they keep at it? Some services close files after an arbitrary time or charge a processing fee to keep a case open. Others will keep working on a case for a very long time without a fee in hopes of finally getting both sides to agree to mediate. Compare answers to these questions with the discussion in Chapter 4, Section F, about how different mediation services persuade reluctant parties to mediate.

2. WHO ARE THE MEDIATORS?

Ask about the type of people on the mediation service's panel to be sure there will be mediators to choose from who are competent to handle your case. Refer to Section C, below, about training, skill levels and style of mediators.

For example, does the service use only retired judges? Only lawyers? Or do they have a mix of mediators, including some full-time career mediators? Are their mediators trained? Who trains them? Is the training minimal (they read a pamphlet and watch a videotape) or extensive (25-40 hours)? How many cases a year does a typical member of their panel mediate: just a few, or dozens? For how long have most of them been mediating?

Do they have mediators available with special areas of knowledge and expertise (if applicable to your case) such as engineers (mechanical, electrical, civil), physicians, business people, real estate experts, family therapy and juvenile matters?

3. HOW WILL THE MEDIATOR BE CHOSEN?

Many private dispute resolution companies will allow the parties to jointly select a mediator from their panel, while most community mediation centers will simply a assign a mediator to your case. Does the mediation service you are considering give you the opportunity to pick? If so, what process is used? (For a discussion of advantages and disadvantages of the various selection processes, see Section B1, below.)

4. ARE THE FEES REASONABLE?

Is there a published fee schedule? If so, ask to see it. If you are the one initiating mediation, do you have to pay a filing fee simply to have the case opened? Or are fees due only if the mediation service is successful in getting the other side to agree to mediate, and then from both sides equally? What if your dispute settles before mediation, will you owe them a fee? (If no filing fee was charged, a closing fee is not unreasonable if the mediation service did substantial work on your case before it settled.) Is there a rescheduling fee if the mediation is scheduled but something comes up and you have to change the date? (Again, not unreasonable if the fee bears some relation to the amount of administrative work that has to be done to reschedule the case.)

5. Can I Mediate Without Legal Representation?

You can handle most mediations without having a lawyer represent you, and most mediation services will not require you to bring a lawyer. A few, however, may have policies on this. It's worthwhile to find out at the start whether there is any problem if you come with or without a lawyer. Sometimes having legal advice available during mediation is a good idea; the pros and cons of bringing a lawyer with you to mediation or even having one available to consult with by telephone during the session are discussed more fully in Chapter 6, Preparing for Your Mediation.

6. Are There Written Rules?

Though mediation is a relatively informal process, a good mediation service will have written rules and procedures, since doing so avoids needless disputes about the process itself. Even independent mediators in private practice—including those who handle divorce and family matters—will usually have a set of written rules or procedures for the parties to follow. Ask to see the mediation rules. Are they in plain English so you can understand them without needing a lawyer to interpret? Do they cover procedures to be followed before, during and immediately after your case? A Sample set of mediation rules appears in Appendix A.

7. How Will Confidentiality Be Protected?

Will your confidentiality be protected by this mediation service? How? For example, is the confidentiality of the mediation process merely part of the rules or is it emphasized by requiring the parties to sign a separate Confidentiality Agreement that specifies exactly what the parties and the mediator are promising to keep confidential? Can you see a copy of their standard Confidentiality Agreement? (Compare with sample confidentiality agreement in Chapter 6, Preparing for Your Mediation.)

8. HOW CONVENIENT WILL THE PROCESS BE?

Are you dealing with a "user-friendly" mediation service that will treat you like a valued customer? For example, if you need your mediation scheduled after work hours or on a weekend, will they do it? And where are mediations held? If their offices are highly inconvenient for you, will they arrange another location? If so, is there an extra fee? How quickly could they schedule your mediation if both you and the other party were ready to start? A day or two? A week or two? It shouldn't take much longer than that.

9. CAN I GET REFERENCES?

Are there past users of this mediation service whom you can contact? Most services will start by saying their client list is confidential (that's appropriate—you'll probably want your name kept confidential, too). Still, you can often press them a little to see if they will call one or two former customers and ask if you can call to talk—not about the details of their case—but about the process and their experience using the mediation service.

10. ARE THERE ANY CONFLICTS OF INTEREST?

Does the mediation service have any conflicts of interest with you or the other side that would prevent it from handling your case in an impartial manner? For example, are any relatives or business partners of you or another party connected in some way with the mediation service, for example, as employees, officers or directors? Or does the mediation service have an ongoing contract with the other side—as it might with a bank, brokerage firm or insurance company—to mediate a large volume of cases? If so, are the individual mediators on the service's panel aware of this arrangement and, if they are, can the service satisfy you that the arrangement does not in any way encourage the mediators to push for settlements favorable to the other side? It's the mediation service's duty to be aware of and disclose any potential conflicts of interest to you, but it doesn't hurt to ask a few questions of your own to uncover problems early on.

B. Methods of Selecting a Mediator

As discussed in Chapter 3, the method by which you select your mediator will depend, in part, on what type of mediator or mediation service you are working with. Against this background, this section looks at several common methods of selection.

ONE MEDIATOR IS USUALLY ENOUGH. Some people who are new to mediation assume it's a good idea to have more than one mediator handle a case. But experienced mediators are generally well able to handle cases by themselves, and usually prefer to work alone. Using a second or third mediator not only increases costs and makes a case more difficult to schedule, it can also complicate the process if it involves mixing different mediation styles. (But note that in some large, complex cases with many parties, a team of two mediators sometimes can be useful especially if one is knowledgeable about the technical issues in dispute, and both can spend time interacting with all the parties. For more on using a co-mediation team, see Section C2, below, and Chapter 12, Section A1.)

1. SELECTING FROM A MEDIATION SERVICE'S PANEL

As we saw in Chapter 3, mediation services often maintain panels (lists of 10 to 20 names) of mediators available to handle their cases. Private dispute resolution companies typically invite the parties to select for their case one mediator from the panel. At community mediation centers, on the other hand, the staff often appoints the mediator who will handle a case. The following describes the various ways a mediator may be selected or appointed for your case from a service's panel. (Later in this chapter, we will look at how to investigate mediators so you can decide which mediator to select if you have the opportunity to do so.)

   a. By Appointment: At some community mediation centers, the staff will simply appoint a mediator for you from their panel without asking for your input. Many court-connected mediation programs also run this way.

   Typically, the case manager will look over the file to determine if your case presents any special requirements for a mediator, such as speaking a foreign language, or ability or knowledge in a technical field. If you think your case needs a mediator with special ability, make this request to the staff. If so, the case manager will pick someone from their panel who has these qualifications. You could also request a mediator of a particular ethnicity or gender if you could reasonably show that this would help facilitate your mediation. For example, if two African-Americans or two gay people involved in an interpersonal dispute felt strongly they could only discuss the intricacies of their dispute with someone with a similar background, many mediation services would honor the request if they have the desired type of mediator available.

   If the case presents no special mediator needs, the case manager will assign someone from the panel, either at random or in rotation, in an effort to give all mediators on the panel a chance to handle cases. Before making the assignment, the case manager will probably call the mediator to ask if there are any reasons he should not be assigned the case, such as a conflict of interest or scheduling problem.

   Despite the fact that it may appear as if the case manager's selection of a mediator is final, you do not always have to accept this person. If you can show a valid reason for rejecting the mediator—an overlooked conflict of interest, for example, where the mediator has a family, social or business connection with you or the other party—the mediation service will make a new assignment. But if your only reason for objecting is that you don't like people of the mediator's race, ethnicity or sex, the mediation service is unlikely to honor your request.

b. Striking-Out Names: This method has traditionally been used by the American Arbitration Association and other organizations serving the labor field, and is used today by some private dispute resolution companies. In the "strike-out" method, each party is sent a list of mediators and asked to strike (cross out) the names of mediators they do not want. You don't have to give a reason for striking a name—it can be because you know the person and think he would not be a good mediator, or just because you don't like his name. From the names remaining, the case manager will appoint a mediator.

c. Ranking by Preference: In this process, you are asked to rank in order of preference the four or five people on the list who you would most like to have mediate your case. The case manager then appoints the one ranked highest by both parties. This method is favored by some of the better private dispute resolution firms because it is "friendly" to customers, in that it gives both parties some measure of control over mediator selection. On the other hand, this process can be more cumbersome than others, since the names you and the other side select may not overlap and you may have to repeat the process.

d. Combining the Strike-Out and Ranking by Preference Methods. Some mediation services combine the "strike-out" and "rank by preference" methods. Following this approach, you may be presented with a list of ten or so mediators' names, with the following instructions:

"Line out any names that are unacceptable and rank the remaining in order of preference with #1 representing the most preferred. Subject to availability, the most mutually acceptable mediator will be selected."

STAFF MEDIATOR VS. OUTSIDE MEDIATOR. At some mediation services, staff members are themselves mediators who handle cases as well as help run the business. In my experience, staffers are often more experienced and skillful mediators than are many of the part-time mediators on the service's panel, and other things being equal, you may wish to choose one.

2. SELECTING AN INDEPENDENT MEDIATOR

If yours is a small business or other special dispute for which you and the other party prefer to select an independent mediator in private practice, how you make the selection will depend, in part, on how well you are getting along. For example, if you and the other party are on relatively good terms, you could both make calls to find a few possible independent mediators and then jointly interview them—either in person or by conference call—to decide which one you want to use. (For information on locating independent mediators with the skills and subject knowledge you need, see Chapter 3, Where to Take Your Dispute for Mediation.)

More typically, you and the other party may prefer to work cooperatively, but with less direct contact. For example, if you and your business partner are breaking up, you might agree that one of you will identify three independent mediators who have a specialty in disputes involving small business. The other can then check out all three and choose the one to mediate your case.

C. More About Mediators

Later in this chapter (Section D), we will look at how to investigate prospective mediators. But first, it will be helpful to consider how prospective mediators might measure up based on criteria, such as skill level, subject-matter knowledge, style and philosophy. With this information, you will better know what to look for and what questions to ask as you conduct your investigation.

1. SKILL LEVEL

Here we mean a mediator's ability to effectively conduct a high quality mediation. (See Chapter 7, Inside the Mediation Session, to learn more about what this involves.) Generally, a mediator's skill level reflects both his training and experience, plus the mediator's own intuitive peacemaking abilities. While you can't easily measure a mediator's intuitive ability, you can learn whether she's been well trained and has adequate experience. Therefore, if you are selecting a mediator from the panel of a mediation service or from among independent mediators in private practice, the first two questions to ask are: who among these mediators has been well-trained, and how much experience has each had? Obviously, there can be a big difference between a mediator who had just four hours or even four days training and someone who has studied mediation skills for several years.

Checking on a mediator's skill level is important when you understand that some people who call themselves mediators have had little or no training or experience. This is particularly likely to be true of recently retired judges, lawyers and other professionals who assume they need do little more than put the word "mediator" on their business card. They wrongly believe their prominence in the community or skills in other areas are substitutes for never having bothered actually to learn how to mediate.

A. TRAINING

Most good, basic mediator training programs involve between 25-40 hours of classroom time and include lectures, demonstrations, videos and role-plays. Topics covered include the psychology of human conflict and conflict resolution, negotiation theory, laws of mediation and confidentiality, mediator ethics and the practical steps involved in conducting a classic six-stage mediation session.

These days many colleges and universities offer degree programs in conflict resolution, but because they focus more on theory than development of practical skills, some of these academic studies are not necessarily relevant to an individual's actual mediation ability. I wouldn't favor a particular mediator simply because she had such a degree, nor would I rate one lower because she lacked it.

As mediation has grown in popularity, mediator training has become a good-sized industry involving community mediation centers, private dispute resolution companies and a growing number of independent trainers who travel around the country giving training seminars. Training quality varies with the quality of the trainer, the sponsoring organization and the group of people being trained. But, again, if the mediator you are investigating attended a training program of 25 hours or more, you can probably assume—regardless of the specific training organization—that the course adequately covered the basics.

Beyond the basic 25-40 hour programs, mediators who specialize will often have participated in advanced training programs. For example, a divorce mediator may have taken a program established by the Academy of Family Mediators. (See Chapter 11, Divorce Mediation.) Similarly, mediators serious about specializing in areas such as construction, health care, business and intellectual property will often have taken further training in these fields.

B. EXPERIENCE

It takes practice to mediate well. This is not to say that a person who has successfully completed a mediator training course could not do a good job for you in her first time out, but all things being equal, it makes sense to pick a mediator who has some experience.

Some people mediate full-time and have handled hundreds of cases; others—such as practicing attorneys whose names appear on mediation panels—may have only mediated two cases in the last three years. Those are the extremes, of course. In between, there are many well-trained people who mediate with some regularity; even mediating one case a month will let a person build up her skills over time.

In addition to paying attention to how much general experience a mediator has, it can make sense to find out how much experience the mediator has had with cases like yours. For example, if yours is a complicated interpersonal dispute with your wife's former husband who turns out now to be a colleague of yours at work, you will want a mediator who has considerable experience handling interpersonal disputes. A mediator who has handled 200 cases, but nearly all of them cut-and-dried claims for money between auto accident victims and insurance companies, may be a poor choice to handle a case such as yours.

Similarly, the skills required to mediate a case with multiple parties are different from those required to mediate a simple two-party case. When a mediator is dealing with three, four, five or six or more parties, aspects of mediation that are relatively simple with two parties—like maintaining order and keeping the discussion moving forward—became much more complicated. If your case involves multiple parties, you should select a mediator who has had experience with these kinds of cases.

TAKE A LOOK AT MEDIATOR SETTLEMENT RATES, IF AVAILABLE. Some mediation services keep statistics on settlement rates for each mediator on their panel. For example, "Joe Doaks mediated 17 small business disputes last year, and of those, 12 settled either at the session or within a short time afterward." While settlement rates are no guarantee that a mediator will be able to settle your case, it can be a useful indicator of experience and skill level.

C. CERTIFICATION AND LICENSING

If a mediator says he is "certified," what, if anything, does this say about his skill or experience level? Not much. Generally, certification means only that a person has received a certificate from a mediation training program confirming he was trained—not that he is skilled or likely to do a good job in your case. Unfortunately, certification also does not mean a person has lots of mediation experience; nor does it normally require any continuing education, advanced training or minimum level of practice.

"Licensing" involves a government agency empowering a person to do something (such as practicing medicine or law) that they would otherwise be prohibited from doing. Presently, there is no licensing requirement for mediators, so no mediator should claim a license. Some people advocate licensing mediators because they think it would help protect consumers against unqualified practitioners. Others oppose licensing, which would probably be based on test results or minimum educational requirements, because they say it would squeeze out of the field some of the most talented people who, though they may lack advanced degrees, have natural skills as mediators. The debate goes on. Eventually, some states probably will enact some sort of licensing requirements.

MEDIATOR ETHICS

One way to tell if a prospective mediator is serious about being a mediator is to see if he or she is familiar with the ethical standards of the field. Three groups which together represent a large number of active mediators—The Society of Professionals in Dispute Resolution, the American Arbitration Association and the American Bar Association—have jointly published the "Standards of Conduct for Mediators." Excerpts appear below. (For full text, see Appendix B.)

1. Self-Determination: A mediator shall recognize that mediation is based on the principle of self-determination by the parties.

2. Impartiality: A mediator shall conduct the mediation in an impartial manner.

3. Conflicts of Interest: A mediator shall disclose all actual and potential conflicts of interest reasonably known to the mediator.

4. Competence: A mediator shall mediate only when the mediator has the necessary qualifications to satisfy the reasonable expectations of the parties.

5. Confidentiality: A mediator shall maintain the reasonable expectations of the parties with regard to confidentiality.

6. Quality of Process: A mediator shall conduct the mediation fairly, diligently and in a manner consistent with the principle of self-determination by the parties.

7. Advertising and Solicitation: A mediator shall be truthful in advertising and solicitation for mediation.

8. Fees: A mediator shall fully disclose and explain the basis of compensation, fees and charges to the parties.

D. PROFESSIONAL AFFILIATIONS

Another way to try to evaluate a mediator is by asking if she belongs to any professional mediator organizations. Because most professional groups have no fixed requirements for membership, other than payment of dues, membership by itself won't tell you how skilled a mediator is. However, if a person is willing to pay for memberships in two or three professional groups, it suggests (but certainly doesn't guarantee) she wants to keep up with developments in the field, and interact with other mediators at meetings and conventions.

One mediation group, the Society of Professionals in Dispute Resolution, does have an additional membership requirement. This national organization, with about 3,500 members, requires full members to have at least three years' substantial experience as a mediator or arbitrator (or as a teacher of these disciplines or an employee of a mediation service). Associate members have less than three years' experience. But since the Society accepts new members without checking their statements of experience, I wouldn't assume that a member of this group was truly experienced. This and other professional mediator groups are listed in Appendix C.

(The Academy of Family Mediators, which has membership standards for those who practice in the area of divorce and family mediation, is discussed in Chapter 11, Divorce Mediation.)

2. SUBJECT-MATTER KNOWLEDGE

For some types of cases, such as small claims, simple contract matters or neighborhood disputes, any well-trained, experienced mediator should be able to handle the problem adequately. But for more involved cases, you will usually be better off with a mediator with specialized knowledge of the issues and options in that particular type of dispute. For example, if your case is against a bank over the way finance charges were levied on an overdue portion of a commercial real estate mortgage, it will be helpful to have a mediator who starts with a basic understanding of the financial aspects of the dispute. This way you don't have to spend the beginning of your mediation educating the mediator. Similarly, if your dispute involves the break-up of a small business partnership, you should look for a mediator who is experienced in helping small businesses arrive at creative solutions. Subject areas in which mediators often specialize include:

- divorce and family (see Chapter 11)
- business (see Chapter 12)
- construction (see Chapter 12)
- intellectual property (patents, trademark and copyright) (see Chapter 12).

The case manager at your mediation service can tell you which, if any, of their panel members are up to speed in the subject area of your dispute. If you are considering an independent mediator, ask whether the subject of your dispute is among his areas of specialty and, if not, if he knows any other independent mediators who work in this area.

Two alternatives to selecting a mediator with subject-matter knowledge consist of using either a co-mediation team or one mediator aided by a technical expert.

With a co-mediation team, you can choose one mediator with strong mediation process skills and a second mediator with specific knowledge of the subject. Co-mediation teams are especially good with large, multi-party cases; the extra mediator can meet in private caucus (see Chapter 7) with some parties while the first mediator meets with the others. But a co-mediation team is likely to be nearly twice as expensive as using a single mediator.

The other option, which is less expensive, is to use one mediator but to put at his disposal a non-mediator who is an expert in the subject area of the dispute. The expert can be chosen jointly by the parties or by the mediator himself and is available to the mediator to help him understand the issues and to suggest possible solutions. For example, if your dispute involves a building project where the basement flooded during construction, you can hire a good general mediator and back her up with a civil engineer with a specialty in subsurface construction issues. The mediator can consult with the engineer as needed during the mediation. You and the other side would pay the engineer only for the time he was involved—much less, probably, than paying for a full-time co-mediator.

3. MEDIATOR'S STYLE AND PHILOSOPHY

In selecting a mediator, ask yourself what exactly you want your mediator to do. This may seem an odd question. After all, like most disputants, you want the mediator to help resolve your dispute. But in doing this, realize that mediators have different philosophies and take different approaches to their work, and that these differences will be reflected in how they conduct their cases. For a variety of reasons, you may want to work with one type of mediator, but not another.

A. FACILITATIVE OR EVALUATIVE?

Some mediators are traditional, almost "purist," in their approach to mediating. They see their role as "facilitators" whose primary job it is to be good and patient listeners who can accurately and sensitively carry messages back and forth between the parties, help the parties see the strengths and weaknesses of each side's position and think expansively about ideas for settlement. These mediators will not tell the parties what a case is "worth" or how they think it might be settled.

"Evaluative" mediators, on the other hand, will take a more direct, or "activist," approach. For example, they might tell the parties how they think a judge or jury would decide a case, and they may propose concrete settlement proposals for the parties to consider.

Do you want a mediator who is more "facilitative" or one whose style is to plunge in and propose a specific resolution? In many cases, it won't matter; either type will do a good job. But in some cases, you may sensibly have a preference. For example, many business executives seem to favor evaluative mediators, since the executives themselves are used to weighing alternatives and making decisions, and often have little patience with long drawn-out proceedings. On the other hand, if your dispute concerns a more interpersonal problem—such as a painful feud with a relative or long-term friend or neighbor—you may want a mediator who will be patient enough to help you arrive at your own solution, not one who will presume to suggest how you should resolve the case.

If you are selecting a mediator from a mediation service's panel, discuss your preference with the case manager, who will be familiar with different mediation styles. Since the terms "facilitative" and "evaluative" are not universally used, you may need to describe the type of mediator you want either as one who will be actively appraise the case and propose solutions, or one who will refrain from giving an opinion and instead focus on helping you and the other party communicate and work toward finding your own solutions.

B. WILLING TO MAKE A SPECIFIC RECOMMENDATION?

Going a step farther, you might want a mediator who, if your case appears unlikely to settle, will make a recommendation as to how you and the other side might resolve it. Since this would be appropriate only if the mediation appears to have failed, the recommendation is entirely different than when the mediator uses his or her evaluative skills to help advance a mediation that still has a chance of succeeding. See Chapter 9, Section A2, for more on asking a mediator to make a recommendation.

If you think you and the other party might want your mediator to make a written recommendation in the event you are unable to reach a settlement, tell the case manager and she can help steer you toward members of the panel who might be willing to do it if it becomes necessary.

C. WILLING TO INTERVENE TO PROTECT THE WEAKER PARTY?

In some disputes, there is definitely a person who, for any one of a variety of reasons—a poor education, language difficulty or an emotional fragility—may be intimidated by the other into accepting an unfair settlement.

In general, a mediator has no duty to protect the interests of a weaker party; it is just not part of his job. Indeed, the rules of some mediation programs even spell this out. Reflecting this orthodox view, many mediators will never intervene to help a weaker party, even if he is about to agree to what seems like an unfair solution. In Minnesota, for example, a mediated settlement agreement cannot be binding—that is, enforced by the courts—unless the parties were advised in writing that the mediator "has no duty to protect their interests." (Minn. Stat. 572.35.)

Nevertheless, there are times when some mediators will intervene to protect a weaker party. If they see the parties headed down a road that might lead one party to agree to a settlement that the mediator sees as grossly unfair or likely to cause more problems later, some mediators will step in and at least warn the person of the dangers posed by the agreement he is about to make.

If you want a mediator who will be willing to intervene to steer you away from making a bad deal, discuss this preference with the case manager or the independent mediator. Even if you end up choosing a mediator who says he will not intervene—perhaps you choose him because you like his other qualities so much—at least you will know what you can expect.

For information on other ways weaker parties can protect themselves in mediation, such as by careful preparation and bringing a friend, adviser or lawyer to the mediation, see Chapter 2, Section C, "The Question of Power Imbalance."

D. IMPARTIALITY

You want your mediator to be impartial as between you and the other party. The concern over bias is not so great as it might be with an arbitrator or judge who has the power to impose a decision (except where a mediator has authority to make a recommendation to a judge—see Chapter 11), but it's nevertheless real, since a biased mediator could steer you toward settlement terms tilted in the other side's favor. As the "Standards of Conduct for Mediators" state, "the concept of mediator impartiality is central to the mediation process." (See Appendix B, Standard No. 2.)

What would constitute bias or partiality? It can be any relationship, experience or set of beliefs that might cause the mediator to favor one side over the other. For example, you probably would not want a mediator who has a social, family or business relationship with the other party, or a lawyer-mediator who works in the same law firm as the one that represents the other party on this or other cases.

There are other types of biases you may wish to consider. For instance, if you are a tenant in a landlord-tenant dispute, you may have qualms about a mediator who is a landlord. Or, if you are a homeowner mediating against a contractor, a contractor mediator may be suspect in your eyes. Although you should feel free to raise these types of concerns with the case manager or mediator, also remember that a mediator with a good grasp of the subject matter can often work much more efficiently, and that such a person often will come from one side of the dispute or the other. On balance, the most sensible approach is to assess the mediator's character rather than worry about these types of side issues—especially since you, rather than the mediator, are in control of the final decision.

The best source of information about possible mediator bias is your case manager or, if you are using an independent mediator, the mediator himself.

WORRY LESS ABOUT BIAS IN SMALL DISPUTES. If your dispute is with a neighbor over a tree or with the dry cleaner over a damaged suit, and you are confident you can hold your own regardless of a mediator's possible bias, you won't want to bother with too much investigation.

DON'T WORRY TOO MUCH ABOUT A LAWYER-MEDIATOR'S LEGAL BACKGROUND. Can lawyer-mediators who, in their law practice, tend to represent mostly plaintiffs or mostly defendants, be neutral as mediators? Generally, I find that lawyer-mediators who are otherwise well-trained and experienced can take off their other professional hats and be impartial as mediators (but the same cannot be said if they are acting as decision-making arbitrators). In fact, sometimes having a mediator who as a lawyer usually represents the other side's point of view can be to your advantage. This is because he will be especially perceptive of the weaknesses in the other side's case and therefore can be especially effective at moving the other party off his original position.

E. MEDIATOR'S PERSONALITY

You may be spending many hours in private and sensitive discussion with your mediator. It follows that, if possible, you'll want to select a mediator with whom you feel personally comfortable. Working with a mediator can be a little like working with a music teacher, or therapist, or clergyman—if you don't connect with the person on an intuitive level, you're better off picking someone else.

Of course, your case may be too small to care much about this, or you may just not get the chance to meet any mediators before you have to make a selection. But if as part of the selection process you do get the chance to meet or even to talk on the phone with a mediator, consider your reaction to him or her on a personal level. Or occasionally you may be able to form an opinion without even talking to him: one disputant, asked by a mediation service to select from a panel of mediators, recognized one of them from the mediator's appearance on televised fund-raising auctions for the local public television station. She couldn't quite put her finger on it, but something about the person made her feel uneasy. Wisely, she did not select him as the mediator.

D. Five Ways to Investigate Prospective Mediators

As you now know if you've read previous sections of this chapter, if your case is important to you, it's often helpful to find out more about a prospective mediator, whether that person is listed on a mediation service's panel or is an independent mediator in private practice.

1. INTERVIEW CASE MANAGER AT MEDIATION SERVICE

If you are using a mediation service that allows you to have a say in who will mediate your case, a big part of what you're paying for is the case manager's availability to help arrange your mediation by a competent mediator. (If you will be using an independent mediator, there will be no case manager, so you will have to get this information on your own. See Subsection 5, below, about interviewing the mediator directly.) It usually makes sense to ask the case manager for information about each prospective mediator according to the criteria discussed in the previous section:

Skill Level
- training
- experience
- professional affiliations.

Subject-Matter Knowledge:
(if applicable to your case).

Style and Philosophy
- facilitative or evaluative?
- willing to make specific recommendation?
- willing to intervene to protect weaker party?
- impartial?

2. Ask for a Resume

Many mediation services will provide you with a one- or two-line statement about each mediator listed on the panel, often including what degrees the mediator holds and where she is currently employed. Obviously, this doesn't tell you much. To get more information, you can often request to see the more detailed resume for mediators who interest you. The resume should do a good job of outlining the mediator's professional background. It may even reveal possible conflicts of interest of which you were unaware.

3. Request References

You can learn a lot about a mediator's style and demeanor from others who have used her, particularly in a dispute similar to your own. Some mediation services and independent mediators may hesitate to provide names of past users on the ground that doing so violates these people's privacy. In practice, however, most satisfied users of mediation will be glad to discuss their experience as long as no confidential information about their case is disclosed. So, when you ask for references for a particular mediator, explain you just want to discuss briefly how the mediator conducted the mediation and that you aren't interested in any details of that case. With this understanding, the case manager will likely call a past user and ask if his name can be given for purposes of a short reference call.

4. Talk to Professionals Who Know the Mediator

Another way to learn about mediators is to ask others in your local dispute resolution community. For example, if one panel member in whom you are interested is a lawyer, you may be able to get a knowledgeable opinion by calling another lawyer you know. Even if that lawyer doesn't know the mediator, he will probably know someone who does. But as with any personal evaluation, you'll want to evaluate both what is said and who says it. For example, if your brother-in-law is the lawyer you talk to and he has often proved to be a blundering fool, you'll probably want to check out anything he says about the mediator with others.

5. Interview the Mediator

When you can't get the information you want about a mediator from the sources listed above, one good approach is to go to the source and talk to the mediator himself.

If you are using a mediation service, ask the case manager to arrange a phone or face-to-face interview with one or two of their panel members. The case manager should be willing to cooperate, but will probably want to invite the other side to participate in the interview so as not to compromise the prospective mediator's neutrality by having a private conversation with just one party.

If you are hiring an independent mediator, either you or the other party will probably have made the initial contact. Most independent mediators will engage in a brief initial conversation about their practice with whoever contacts them. But, if you or the other party wants to have an in-depth interview about the mediator's background, philosophy and possible approach to handling your case, she will almost surely suggest that all parties participate in the conversation. Again, the realistic concern is that a private conversation between a mediator and either party to a dispute may jeopardize the mediator's neutrality—or at least the appearance of his neutrality.

Probably the best way to do an in-depth interview with an independent mediator is to ask the mediator to arrange a conference call during which you and the other party can do the interview together. A joint, face-to-face meeting can sometimes be arranged, but because this requires a greater time commitment from the mediator before he has been retained, it usually is done only in larger cases where the mediator's fee—if he were selected—would be substantial, such as when a mediation is expected to last for several days or a number of sessions.

Preparing for Your Mediation

This chapter will concentrate on things you can do to prepare for your mediation session. While mediation isn't nearly as complicated or exacting a process as a full-scale court trial, there are still many things you can do to improve your chances of achieving a positive result. How much preparation you need will often depend both on the facts of the dispute and how significant it is to you. A small consumer dispute worth a couple of hundred dollars, for example, is unlikely to require nearly as much preparation as a work-related sexual harassment claim involving a lot of money and, possibly, affecting your future career.

Preparing for mediation normally involves these steps:

- reviewing the mediation rules
- gathering documents and other items you want to present in the mediation
- determining if anyone should attend the mediation with you and, if so, making the necessary arrangements
- clearly identifying your goals, including both what you hope to achieve and the minimum you will accept, and
- writing a memorandum to the mediator outlining your version of the facts and issues involved in the dispute.

CHAPTER 7, INSIDE THE MEDIATION SESSION, shows you how to make your opening statement and deal with other stages of the actual mediation session.

A. Reviewing Mediation Rules and Other Forms

Begin your preparation by thoroughly reading the rules and regulations that will govern your mediation. Most will appear in a set of written Mediation Rules prepared by the mediator or mediation service. Other important information may be found in two additional forms you may receive: the "Notice of Mediation" and the "Agreement to Mediate."

1. THE MEDIATION RULES

Nearly all mediators and mediation services will send you a set of rules. If yours has not, call and request one.

Mediation rules cover things like when and how fees are to be paid, actual procedures to be followed during the mediation and the degree to which the mediation proceeding will be considered and kept confidential. (For more on confidentiality, see Section A3, below.) Fortunately, mediation rules are usually just a few pages long and almost always written in plain English. (Sample Mediation Rules appear in Appendix A.)

Because mediation rules don't vary much from place to place, chances are good yours will cover the following points:

a. Sending Notices. If you need to notify the mediator or the other party of something—for example, you plan to bring someone with special expertise—the rules may say what notification method you must use. For example, can you call on the telephone or do you have to send a fax or letter? Can the letter be by regular mail, or must it be certified? Do copies have to be sent to the other parties to the mediation?

IT'S WISE TO LEAVE A PAPER TRAIL FOR IMPORTANT MESSAGES. If the rules do not tell you how to send an important notice to the mediator or the other party, be safe and always leave a paper trail. For example, if you use the telephone or e-mail, be sure to follow-up with a fax or letter.

b. Pre-Mediation Memorandum. This is a written statement you prepare that educates the mediator about your version of the facts and issues involved in your dispute. The rules should tell you whether or not you will be required (or allowed) to submit a memorandum before the mediation. If so, should you send it to the mediation service, or directly to the mediator? Must a copy be sent to the other side? If so, how many days before the mediation? (For more on preparing a Memorandum, see Section E, below.)

c. Mediation Procedures. How will the actual mediation be conducted? Will the mediator hold only "joint sessions," where everyone meets together? Or does the mediator also reserve the right to have private "caucuses," separate meetings with each party? Caucuses are common in most types of mediation, but less frequent in divorce and family mediation. (For more on caucuses, see Chapter 7, Inside the Mediation Session.) Knowing whether caucuses will be used can help you plan your presentation strategy. For example, if you have an idea of how your dispute could be settled, you might want to try it out on the mediator during private caucus before introducing it at a joint session. But if you know you won't be having caucuses, then you will have to give some thought as to how and when to present the idea to the other side directly.

d. Restrictions on Presenting Documents, Testimony and Other Evidence. In mediation, strict courtroom rules of evidence do not apply. This makes sense, since, after all, the mediator is not a judge but simply a person trying to help the parties reach an agreement. Nevertheless, because parties sometimes want to offer testimony from witnesses, or present or refer to documents or other written reports or information (lawyers call these "exhibits"), mediation rules typically address this issue. Some leave it up to the mediator to decide what sort of outside information is and is not appropriate, while others set more definite rules. (For more on different types of evidence, see Section D, below.)

e. Use of Lawyer, Law Coach or Friend. It's uncommon to bring lawyers to mediations involving small consumer disputes and interpersonal matters, but more common to have them involved in business disputes and cases involving complex legal issues. Mediation rules will usually tell you if there are any restrictions on bringing a lawyer or other adviser or friend to the mediation. (For more on bringing a lawyer to mediation, see Section H, below.)

f. Deadlines. The rules will probably subject you to various deadlines, such as:

- a deadline for submitting a written memorandum to the mediator prior to the mediation. Often, the memorandum will be due at the mediator's office seven or 14 days prior to the date set for your mediation. (See Section E, below.)

- a deadline for rescheduling or canceling the mediation without a fee. Mediation services may charge anywhere from $50 to $250 for canceling or rescheduling less than 24 or 48 hours before the date of the session (the amount depends on how hefty their regular fees are).

- a date by which you must notify the other side if you plan to bring an "expert" witness, such as a physician or accident investigator, to your mediation session. Since this requirement is designed to give the other side time to find his own expert, it's common to set this deadline at least a week—but more often two weeks—before the date of the mediation.

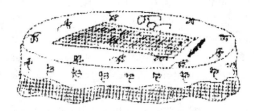

2. "NOTICE OF MEDIATION" AND THE "AGREEMENT TO MEDIATE"

After your mediation has been scheduled, you will likely receive from the mediator or mediation service a document called a "Notice of Mediation" (sometimes "Hearing Notice") confirming the date, time and place of your mediation. Be sure the date, time and place for your session is as you agreed, or if you had not agreed on a date, that the date assigned is convenient for you. If it is not, promptly request a new date.

THERE IS FLEXIBILITY IN SCHEDULING A MEDIATION. Typically, a mediation service will schedule your mediation within a few weeks or a month after a mediator has been selected. Unlike in court, where scheduling is at the convenience of the judge and civil servants, in mediation your case can be scheduled at the convenience of the parties and the mediator. This is especially true if you are using an independent mediator or private dispute resolution company and therefore paying enough to be treated as a good customer. So, if you're not a "morning person" and don't want to mediate before noon, and if Tuesday afternoons are inconvenient because that's when you attend your daughter's Suzuki violin lesson, tell the case manager you're only available on afternoons other than Tuesdays. Assuming the other party's schedule permits, your request will probably be accommodated.

You may also receive and be asked to sign an "Agreement to Mediate." The purpose of the Agreement is simply to commit the parties in writing to mediate their case in good faith, to follow the rules and to pay the fees. Check it carefully to be sure your name is spelled correctly, your dispute is accurately described and the mediator assigned is one whom you have agreed to use (if you were permitted to select, as discussed in Chapter 5, Selecting Mediation Services and Mediators). Also, be sure the fees are as you agreed.

You will also want to check to see if there is a confidentiality provision. If not, the Agreement should refer to the mediation rules, which should contain a statement about confidentiality. (See Section A/3, just below.)

3. Confidentiality of Mediation

During a mediation, you may want to make deeply personal statements or share confidential information. How confident can you be that what you say will be kept confidential? For example, if you're a business owner mediating a claim of sexual harassment with a former employee, you might be tempted to share information about exciting new products the company is about to introduce, to encourage the person to settle and take a new job with your company. Or in a case involving your own business partner where the two of you are trying to rebuild trust and save the company, you may be called on to acknowledge your own past mishandling of company finances or business opportunities. (Disclosing secrets can be an especially relevant issue in divorce cases. For more on confidentiality in divorce and family mediation, see Chapter 11, Section C5.)

Can something you said in mediation be introduced as evidence in a later court trial if your dispute does not settle in mediation? Even if your case doesn't wind up in court, what's to stop the other party or the mediator herself from telling someone (a friend, relative, your boss, the newspaper) something embarrassing or damaging that you said during the mediation?

It should be obvious that a high level of confidentiality is essential to mediation. Without it, many people would sensibly not agree to mediate (and certainly would not want to confide in the mediator). Accordingly, as the practice of mediation has grown, so too has the web of legal and ethical protections designed to make mediation as confidential as possible.

A. MEDIATION RULES FREQUENTLY REQUIRE CONFIDENTIALITY

Provisions in most mediation rules require the mediator and the parties to keep private everything said during the session. These rules also frequently provide that if the case ends up in court, neither party may call the mediator to testify about what was said in the mediation. Unfortunately, the consequences of breaching these rules—particularly by the disputants themselves—are murky. For example, there's really no practical way for you to prevent the other party from telling his neighbor or brother-in-law what went on during your mediation.

B. MEDIATOR'S ETHICS REQUIRE CONFIDENTIALITY IN MOST SITUATIONS

Ethical rules that most mediators apply to their activities usually require that a mediator "maintain the reasonable expectations of the parties with regard to confidentiality." (See the full text of "Standards of Conduct for Mediators,"

No. V, Appendix B.) Note, however, that mediation is not a licensed profession, so there are few professional sanctions for breaching these ethics, which therefore function more as guidelines than true professional standards.

C. SOME STATE LAWS PREVENT MEDIATORS FROM BEING CALLED TO TESTIFY IN COURT

Laws in some states specifically prevent a mediator from being called to testify in court (or arbitration) about what was said in mediation. But these so-called "privilege laws" vary greatly in terms of what they cover, and many apply only to mediators working in specific types of programs. In Illinois, for example, a law making "any communication" during mediation confidential, only applies to mediations conducted by non-profit organizations that provide mediation services at no charge. (Chapter 710 Illinois Compiled Stat. Sec. 20/8 (1994).)

D. FEDERAL AND STATE RULES OF EVIDENCE OFTEN ARE USED TO KEEP COMMUNICATIONS MADE IN THE COURSE OF MEDIATION OUT OF COURT

Federal Rule of Evidence 408 and comparable laws in most states make settlement offers, responses to them, as well as general settlement discussions confidential and thus not admissible in court (or arbitration) for the purpose of proving the validity or value of a claim. These laws have generally been interpreted to exclude much of what is said in mediation from later court or arbitration proceedings.

EXAMPLE: *Jim broke his back and leg when he fell on a rotted stair at a restaurant. Jim and the insurance company for the restaurant went to mediation. During mediation, Jim offered to settle if the insurance company would pay him $40,000 for his injuries, but the insurance company refused and the mediation ended without a settlement. Now, Jim is suing the insurance company and asking a jury to award him $100,000. Under the state law that is comparable to Federal Evidence Rule 408, the insurance company may not tell the jury that during settlement discussions in mediation Jim was willing to settle for less than half that amount.*

By contrast, sometimes federal and state laws *require* people in helping professions (such as therapists, social workers and often *mediators*) to report information they learn about felonies, family abuse and other serious crimes that have been, or are about to be, committed. This means that in most states if you tell your mediator you have physically abused your own child, the mediator may be under a legal duty—despite all the confidentiality provisions of mediation—to report this to local child protection authorities. Similarly, if you tell the mediator you are planning to kill your husband—and if the mediator believes you really will do it—he may be obligated to report this to the police.

IF YOU HAVE COMMITTED A SERIOUS CRIME. Admitting to a serious crime during mediation could be legally foolish. If you have committed a crime you fear may come out in mediation, see a lawyer before proceeding further.

So how confidential is mediation? From a practical viewpoint, confidentiality has not been much of a problem in mediation. Generally, you can safely rely on most mediators to keep quiet about what happens in your mediation. But if someone—such as the other party—decides to disclose what is said in a mediation, there's very little to be done about it. The best advice is: if you have a secret that you don't want known, don't spill it in mediation.

To check on specific confidentiality provisions that may apply to your mediation, check the Rules, the Agreement to Mediate and any other documents you receive. If you have particular concerns about confidentiality based on the discussion above, ask the case manager at the mediator service or the independent mediator directly, or a lawyer, to tell you what specific laws, if any, on confidentiality apply to your case in your state.

B. Determining Your Goals for the Mediation

Start by reminding yourself that the purpose of mediation is not to prove who is legally right, or to establish the truth of the situation or to sell your point of view. The only purpose is to find a solution that you and the other party both find acceptable. Unlike a lawsuit, where the legal rules governing who wins and who loses are both well-established and fairly strict, mediation rules allow lots of flexibility.

> **EXAMPLE 1:** *House painter Tom painted the interior of homeowner Sally's house but was not paid for his labor. Tom sues Sally. The law would normally require Sally to pay Tom according to the terms of their contract—unless, of course, Tom had seriously breached the contract. In court, Tom's goal would be clearly to prove that the contract had been carried out and to get a judgment for the money owed. In other words, Tom's goal is to establish what happened in the past and then rely on the law to reward him appropriately.*

> **EXAMPLE 2:** *Same circumstances, but now Tom and Sally decide to mediate. Here they face an entirely different situation, since no law or set of procedures defines or limits the results. Their goals in mediation can include what the law would allow, but they can also deal with much broader issues. For example, Sally, who believes that parts of the job weren't done well, may agree to pay Tom the money he claims is owed only if he does some of the work over, or differently. Or, Tom might agree that Sally need only pay him a portion of what he has asked for, but also help find Tom other jobs, or promise to provide employment for Tom's hard-to-employ brother-in-law. Or, Tom and Sally might agree that Tom should be paid 100% of what he is owed, but over a period of months, instead of immediately. Or maybe even that some of the payment will be cash and the rest services (for example, If Sally owns a car repair garage, she might agree to repair Tom's truck).*

In other words, in mediation, your goals are essentially forward-looking—what will work best for both of you—and the results you will accept are neither as obvious nor as limited as they would be in court.

Just below, we will look at several methods designed to help you identify what your goals might be in mediation. Following discussion of each method, there is a short exercise to help you apply the method to your particular dispute. Although completing the exercises below will take a few minutes, doing so will be worth your time.

First, briefly describe the nature of your dispute: (You may have already done this on the Submission to Mediation form. See Chapter 4, Section E.)

1. USING THE LAW AS A MEDIATION BENCHMARK

The most likely solution a court would impose on your dispute is one way to define or limit your mediation goals. Although this legal benchmark may turn out to be a less imaginative or less efficient solution than you and the other party end up devising, it shouldn't be ignored. For example, if you were injured in a car accident and are preparing to mediate with the company that insures the at-fault driver, it would be helpful to know what a judge or jury in your area would be likely to award for your injuries. For example, if your case went to court, would it most likely be worth $10,000 or $100,000, or nothing at all? To find the answer, you may need to consult briefly with a lawyer. (See Chapter 13, Lawyers and Legal Research, for information on how to find a reliable and experienced one.) Some lawyers will provide this type of information as part of an initial consultation for which they don't charge a fee. Generally, however, it's a poor idea to try to get good advice for nothing. Better to pay a lawyer fairly for an opinion or any other help you may need. Not only is this approach honest, it's also practical. If you pay the lawyer, he or she will have less motive to try and sell you something you may not need (such as talking you out of mediation and into a lawsuit).

Once you find a good lawyer, lay out the facts of your case and ask, "If this case went to court, how much would I be likely to get?" Also with the help of the lawyer, consider how long the legal process would take, what you would have to pay for court costs and other expenses and how much of your award would go to the lawyer.

Of course, lawsuits involving auto accidents aren't the only area where the likely result in court may provide a useful benchmark to examine your mediation goals. For example, if your dispute involves a contract, how much would you be likely to recover if you sued for breach of contract? Or if your dispute involves a neighbor's garage that you believe extends a few feet onto your property, it will be helpful to know the likely remedies a judge might apply as part of preparing for mediation.

EVALUATING THE LEGAL STATUS OF A CASE CAN BE TRICKY—you may want to hire a self-help law coach. If you think you will need more than one consultation with a lawyer to help you figure out what your case is worth, to help you prepare for mediation in other ways or to be available for consultation during your mediation, consider using a self-help law coach. A law coach is a lawyer who does not represent you in your case but who is willing to provide you legal advice as you handle the case on your own. The coach should charge you a fee only for the time you consult with him and should help you educate yourself so as to do as much as possible on your own. Some lawyers are willing to coach self-helpers; others are not. (For more on finding and using a self-help law coach, see Chapter 13, Lawyers and Legal Research.)

IDENTIFYING GOALS

EXERCISE #1	USING THE LAW AS A BENCHMARK

Describe here what court remedies might be available in your dispute. _____

_____

_____

_____

Assuming your dispute involves money, how much do you estimate a judge or jury might award to you? _____

_____

_____

How much might it cost, in legal fees, court costs and other expenses to obtain such an award? (Lawyers usually charge either by the hour ($150 an hour and up) or on a contingency basis (often 30% to 40% of any verdict or settlement).) _____

_____

_____

_____

2. CONSULTING WITH EXPERTS

Experts in various fields can provide useful information and opinions to help you identify your mediation goals. For example, if you and your business partner are coming to mediation to dissolve your partnership, an accountant with training in business valuation and/or a broker who specializes in selling businesses could provide you with valuable information as to how much the business is worth, either sold as one entity or carved up in different ways. Or if your dispute is with a person or business in a particular field—electrician, gardener, tile layer—it might make sense to find another person in the same field to ask for an impartial opinion about the validity of your complaint and creative ideas on how to resolve it.

HOW TO OVERCOME PROFESSIONAL COURTESY. Occasionally a professional will be reluctant to consult with you once she realizes you have a claim against another person in the same profession. You can probably lessen these concerns by explaining that you are mediating with the other professional to try to work out a settlement; you aren't taking the other person to court. If you have trouble finding a practitioner with whom to consult, think about who else is expert in that area. For example, if you can't find an electrician to evaluate problems with a wiring job, try someone who teaches in that field—possibly at a local trade school or union-sponsored accreditation program.

Depending on the type of dispute in which you are involved, there will be a variety of experts you can consult concerning possible goals and likely outcomes. Here are just a few who are often consulted as part of preparing for mediation:

ACCOUNTANT OR BUSINESS BROKER   Often useful to deal with problems concerning the break-up of a small business. For example, you might want to know, "What is the value of my partner's share of this business? Can I afford to buy her out over time? What is the fair value of the stock options her husband holds?"

BUILDER OR SKILLED TRADES PERSON   Can be extremely valuable in helping you decide when a contract having to do with building or repair has been properly carried out and, if it hasn't, how this breach should be valued and/or remedied. For example, if a carpenter you hired to redo your stairs botched the design for the handrail and newel post, one question might be, should a reasonably skilled carpenter have been able to follow the rough drawings you supplied? And another question would involve how the problem could sensibly be fixed and at what cost.

ARCHITECT   Can provide a second opinion as to the quality of another architect's work, whether too many or too few drawings had been made in response to your original request, and whether fees charged were fair based on local practice. For example, if an architect charged you for a preliminary sketch you thought was part of her bid, you might ask if that is normal. You might also want suggestions as to ways you might be able to work out a compromise with the architect without paying the whole fee.

PROSECUTORS   Though they generally won't give legal advice, prosecutors (also called district attorneys) sometimes will tell you what procedures they would typically follow in a given situation, or how they recently responded to a similar situation. For example, you might want to ask, if I were to file charges against a local nightclub for violating the noise ordinance, how would the prosecutor respond? Have there been other cases recently where nightclubs have been forced to take steps to lower or muffle noise?

ACOUSTICS EXPERT   Can be helpful in suggesting a range of practical solutions to a variety of noise situations. For example, you might want to ask, what are some ways I can deal with noise from a restaurant, or from a neighbor who has frequent late parties, and how much would it cost? And how can I establish the level of noise about which I'm complaining? What kind of noise-measuring equipment can I use?

CITY OFFICIAL   Local government employees will sometimes be willing to advise you in the areas they help regulate, such as zoning, trash collection, roads, property mainte-nance and the like.

IDENTIFYING GOALS

EXERCISE #2   **EXPERT CONSULTATION**

What, if any, information or opinions have you obtained from experts in fields relevant to your dispute about the strength of your position and different ways it might be resolved?

_____

_____

_____

3. Time-Line Analysis

Often a useful way to help identify goals for mediation is to examine your dispute in terms of time—past, present and future. This approach can help you understand your dispute from different perspectives and can prompt you to think of a range of possible remedies that might satisfy your needs.

EXAMPLE: *An office secretary is so emotionally stressed by her boss's manic-depressive behavior, that she quits and threatens the company with a harassment lawsuit. Now, however, she's out of a job and is worried about her chances of finding a new one. Before filing her lawsuit, she agrees to mediate with her former boss. How does it help to see the secretary's goals as part of a time sequence?*

- *Past:* To deal with what happened in the past (the boss's inappropriate behavior), the secretary might want cash compensation for her mental suffering and a written apology from the boss.
- *Present:* To deal with the fact that she is currently without income, the secretary might want a consulting position with the company for several months to cover living expenses while she looks for a new job. In addition, she might want temporary use of a company desk, phone and fax to help with her job search (or the company can rent space for her elsewhere).
- *Future:* To be sure that the past incident and resulting dispute will not affect her future employability if someday she must look for a new job, removal from her personnel file of critical material and a favorable job reference.

IDENTIFYING GOALS

EXERCISE #3	TIME-LINE ANALYSIS

In the spaces below, list goals for resolving your dispute that relate to the three time periods:

Your goals related to coping with what's happened in the past _____

_____

_____

_____

Your goals related to dealing with ongoing problems in the present _____

_____

_____

Your goals related to coping with or avoiding future effects of the dispute _____

_____

_____

4. WANTS VS. NEEDS ANALYSIS

Another way to look at your mediation goals is to do what's often called a "wants vs. needs analysis." People in the midst of a dispute generally think they know what they want: "I want my job back with full pay," or "I want the money you owe me for the work I did," or "I want your dog to keep quiet and let me sleep." But as a long-time participant in the mediation field, I've learned that what people say they want is not necessarily the same as what they really need. The truth is that people's needs are often different from, and easier to satisfy than, their wants.

Consider a simple dispute between two neighbors:

Ted wants to erect a six-foot solid wood fence between his backyard and Joan's, a plan that Joan opposes for aesthetic reasons. Ted's desire (want) for a fence reflects a need for privacy. But privacy can be achieved in many ways. A hedge, a stone wall or perhaps even a porch or patio screen can also provide privacy. If Ted and Joan can see past Ted's wants (a fence) and focus on his needs (privacy), they may be able to think of alternative ways of ending the dispute in a mutually acceptable way.

When you focus on your dispute, it will help if you first think of your wants as the positions you've staked out in your last phone call or impassioned letter to the other party—for example, a sum of money, the right to live in a rental house or getting your old job back.

Your real needs may be harder to identify. To help you do it, here is a short list of common human needs:

- emotional and economic security
- respect and self-esteem
- recognition
- vindication
- protecting your reputation
- avoiding needless expense, aggravation or stress
- preserving stability and predictability in your life
- removing the uncertainty caused by a dispute
- keeping your options open for the future.

One very common, but sometimes overlooked, need that is involved in many disputes is to maintain a relationship. You may need or want to have a long-term relationship with one or more people involved in your dispute, such as a customer, boss, co-worker, fellow church-member, sibling, parent, relative, friend or the parent of your child's playmate. For example, if your father in his will left management of the family business to you and your sister and now the two of you are in a dispute, you need to resolve this in a way that doesn't make you into each other's enemies, or you and your respective families risk losing something far more valuable than the business itself.

Fortunately, if maintaining a relationship is one of your needs, mediation probably offers the best chance to meet this need while resolving your dispute. Compared with taking your dispute into court, where the very process of creating a winner and loser will probably weaken or destroy any underlying relationship, mediation offers the disputants the relationship-enhancing opportunity of working together to solve their mutual problem.

Wants and needs are both legitimate goals to pursue in mediation. It's fine to get your wants met, but it's important not to lose sight of your needs as well. Some apparently simple disputes (such as our example of the neighbors and the privacy fence) can be resolved only when the disputants understand what basic human needs underlie their demands. Certainly, by being aware of both your wants and your needs, you enhance your chances of crafting goals for your mediation that are likely to result in a long-term solution.

It is also useful to try to identify the other party's wants and needs and then compare them with your own. (See the exercise below.) You may even discover, for example, that some overlap (avoidance of legal fees, protecting reputations, working together in the future) and that others don't necessarily conflict (economic security for the one; recognition for the other). This information can provide a more realistic sense of possible outcomes for your mediation.

As the Rolling Stones once said, "You can't always get what you want. . . but if you try sometime, you just might find, you'll get what you need."

IDENTIFYING GOALS

EXERCISE #4 | **WANTS VS. NEEDS ANALYSIS**

1. List your stated wants. (What is it you have been telling people on the other side you want out of this dispute?) _____
   _____
   _____

2. List the economic, emotional, relational and other needs that underlie your stated wants in this dispute. (See above list of common needs.) _____
   _____
   _____

3. What are the other party's wants? (Do the best you can with this one. One good place to start is with any formal written or oral demand or offer to settle the other side has made.) _____
   _____
   _____

4. What do you think are some of the other party's important underlying needs?
   _____
   _____

5. Comparison of Mutual Wants and Needs

   In the table below, list your own and the other party's wants and needs.

What I Want	What I Need	Other Party's Wants	Other Party's Needs

   Are any needs—yours and the other side's—the same? _____
   _____

   Can any of the other party's needs be satisfied without harm or cost to you? _____

   _____
   _____

   Can you think of solutions to your dispute that might satisfy most of both side's needs?
   _____
   _____
   _____
   _____

WHAT DOES BENJAMIN NEED?

My son, Benjamin, two years old at the time of this writing, sometimes will cry when his mother and I leave the house. He's crying because he wants us to stay. But what are Benjamin's needs? Although he can't yet articulate them for himself, I think Benjamin needs:

- Emotional security, someone with whom he feels protected, a person who he knows cares for him, and with whom he can cuddle and feel loved.
- Responsible care, someone to help keep him safe, to make sure he doesn't pull any lamps over on his head or tumble down the stairs (or, if he does, to give him needed care and comfort). Ben also likes his lunch on time and a good nap afterwards.
- Playful companionship, someone with whom he can play, take a walk, sing, talk and learn.

There is probably only one way Benjamin's wants can truly be satisfied, and that's by Mom and Dad staying home. Nevertheless, responsible and loving baby-sitters, relatives or grandparents can do a good job meeting his underlying needs.

5. Determining Your "No More Compromise" Line

Once you have identified your goals, your next step is to determine the minimum for which you would be willing to settle. I call this your "no more compromise" line.

Having a no more compromise line is important because mediation is a fluid, ever-changing process where compromise is encouraged. While it is normally in everyone's interest to allow the mediation to establish a mood that is conciliatory and collaborative, you will also want something firm to hold onto—some way to be sure that no matter what clever, or complicated or perhaps even completely unexpected solution is proposed, it really meets your minimum goals. Another way of saying this is that you want to guard against being bamboozled into agreeing to something you'll later regret.

One way to determine your no more compromise line is to take all the information you have gathered as part of the written exercise above and then consider what would be 1) the best possible outcome, 2) an adequate outcome, and 3) the minimum acceptable outcome. The last one is your no more compromise line.

EXAMPLE: *Assume Edna was hired to do some interior painting at a private home. The contract called for Edna to do $5,000 worth of painting, but as the work began, the homeowner kept insisting on small changes that took extra time and required a different kind of paint. Then, when just over half the work was done, the homeowner criticized Edna's work and refused to pay. Edna disagreed that her work was substandard and asked for full payment. After several acrimonious conversations, Edna and the homeowner agreed to mediate.*

After checking with a friend who is a lawyer, discussing the situation with a couple of other painters and doing both a Time-Line (Exercise Part B3) and Wants vs. Needs analysis (Exercise Part B4), Edna identified the following as major goals:

Money: Payment of $3,000 for work completed, plus $750 for extra labor and materials needed when the homeowner changed the original plans and asked to have part of the work done differently; be allowed to finish job and be paid balance of $2,000 as per contract.

Future Work: Be allowed to bid on painting for Phase II of homeowner's remodeling plan later in year.

Reputation and Future Opportunities: Maintain good professional reputation so this problem does not hurt word-of-mouth referrals.

Relational Needs: Avoid major feud with homeowner as we each belong to same church and know lots of the same people.

In considering each of the above goals, Edna might next break them down as follows according to "best," "adequate" and "minimum acceptable" results.

Best Possible Outcome: I get paid $3,750 immediately for work already done; be allowed to finish job with no further hassle (maybe half the money up-front and written agreement with the homeowner on how exactly he wants the new work done); chance to bid on Phase II; and the homeowner to acknowledge that the work I've done is of high quality and be willing to recommend to others who may call for a reference, and also to end this mess in a friendly way so when we see each other at church it's not awkward or uncomfortable.

Adequate Outcome: I get paid $3,000 immediately for work done, I'm allowed to finish the job (maybe half the money up-front and written agreement on how exactly he wants the new work done); and a chance to bid on Phase II (if I decide after the mediation I am willing to do more work for this person). We agree not to badmouth each other in the future.

Minimum Acceptable Outcome (No More Compromise Line): I get paid $3,000 immediately for work done. We agree not to badmouth each other in the future.

As noted, mediation is a fluid and changing process, and it is possible that a solution may emerge that does not exactly meet Edna's no more compromise line. For example, in the dispute just discussed, suppose the homeowner adamantly refuses to pay anything for the work Edna did based on his claim that she used the wrong color. However, because Edna otherwise did excellent work, he will agree to pay her promptly if she redoes the painting (the prep wouldn't have to be redone) and to hire her for the much bigger job of painting the interior of the office section at a new factory he owns. Painting at the factory would be done during the coming winter, Edna's slow season, and she would receive a generous up-front deposit. If the factory painting goes well, she would stand to make $15,000—way more than the $3,000 in immediate cash she had identified as her no more compromise line. Obviously, in this case, Edna may choose to change her no more compromise line and consider doing the required repainting.

But it's important to realize that the fact Edna may ultimately choose to change her no more compromise line doesn't mean that it was wasted effort to determine it in the first place. Not only will having a no more compromise line in mind during the mediation process provide her with a clear and thoughtful measurement against which to evaluate any new proposal, it will act as a useful brake on any tendency she might have to too quickly agree on a solution that doesn't really meet her needs.

C. Who Are You Trying to Persuade?

Before you plan what you are going to say in mediation, it is important to understand who you will be trying to persuade. In this section, we will consider this important question in two contexts: first, for the great majority of mediations, where the mediator has no formal power to influence the final decision, and second, in Section 2, below, for those special mediations where, by law, the mediator does have the power to recommend a final decision.

1. TYPICAL CASE WHERE MEDIATOR HAS NO SPECIAL POWER

In most mediations, you "play" to two audiences: the first, and most important, is the other party; the second is the mediator. The reason the other party is by far your more important audience is that she, not the mediator, is the decision-maker. This, of course, is the opposite of the situation in court, or arbitration, where the neutral person (the judge or arbitrator) makes the decisions.

It's extremely important that you grasp this crucial point: the mediator is not a judge. Every day I see one or both parties to a mediation make the mistake of presenting their case to the mediator as if she was wearing a black robe and sitting at the front of a courtroom. Far better to focus your strategy on trying to persuade the other side to agree to an acceptable resolution of your dispute. (Of course, if you have trouble confronting the other party directly, it's okay to face the mediator and focus your attention on him or her, as long as you understand in reality it is the other side who ultimately you are trying to persuade.)

But although the other party is your real critical audience, you also need to address the mediator for different reasons. First, if the mediator clearly understands your points, he may be able to help the other party do likewise, should there be a private caucus. Second, as part of the caucus process, your mediator may share with the other party his or her impressions of you and your case. If the mediator grasps the strength of your position and advises the other party that you would make a strong adversary in a lawsuit or arbitration, this might encourage the other side to agree to a compromise settlement.

2. IF THE MEDIATOR HAS THE LEGAL POWER TO INFLUENCE THE DECISION

Although fairly unusual, in some states, in a few situations when judges refer cases to mediation, mediators do have at least some legal authority to influence the decision. This usually occurs when a case does not settle and the mediator has the power to recommend a solution to a judge. In California, for example, where the law requires divorcing couples to mediate issues of child custody and support, California Family Code Sec. 3183 allows the mediator to recommend how the Superior Court judge should decide these issues if the parties can't settle them themselves. (For more on court-sponsored divorce mediation where the mediator has power to recommend a decision, see Chapter 11, Section D11.) Similarly, in a small claims mediation program in Michigan, when mediation does not resolve a dispute, the mediator may send a report about the case to the judge who will preside over the trial.

An even more obvious situation when the mediator needs to be convinced occurs in the hybrid process known as "med-arb" where the parties agree to mediation by a person who will become an arbitrator if the case does not settle. Since the mediator can ultimately impose a decision, you'll want to be as convincing as possible. (For more on Med-Arb, see Chapter 1, Section E.)

CHECK THE MEDIATION RULES TO SEE IF YOUR MEDIATOR WILL HAVE AUTHORITY TO RECOMMEND A DECISION. Although it's somewhat unusual that mediators have power to recommend or influence a decision, it's still a good idea to check the mediation rules provided by the mediator or mediation service to see what, if any, powers your mediator has if your case does not settle. If necessary, contact the case manager or other administrator involved in arranging your mediation, or the mediator directly if you are using an independent mediator.

D. Gathering Information to Bring to the Mediation

"Objection, hearsay!" shouts the prosecutor, rising to her feet.

The young woman on the witness stand has just said the defendant's cousin told her the defendant was nowhere near the victim's apartment on the night of the robbery.

"But, Your Honor, the statement is offered only to show the witness's relationship to the defendant's cousin," interjects the defense attorney.

"Objection sustained," rules the judge.

Courtroom drama like this is good fun for movie and TV watchers and much less fun for law students, who have to learn all the intricate technical rules of evidence that underlie it. Fortunately, you don't have to learn to think like a lawyer.

1. LEGAL RULES OF EVIDENCE DO NOT APPLY

In mediation, the legal rules of evidence do not apply; each of the disputants is expected to speak using ordinary English, and no issue will be ruled irrelevant or immaterial or otherwise banned for some technical reason, such as its being hearsay. In short, pretty much anything is grist for the mediation mill.

Because no evidence is excluded, you might think this would make mediations go on endlessly. Just the opposite is true. With no hypertechnical objections to evidence and continuous wrangles before a judge to contend with, the parties say what they want, show what they want and usually, with the mediator's help, fairly quickly move on to try and craft a mutually acceptable solution.

When preparing for the mediation, the question to ask about anything you want to use in the mediation to make your points is not, "Will it be admissible under the technical rules of courtroom evidence?" or "Will it make a judge or jury decide in my favor?" but instead:

- "Will it help me tell my side of the story in a clear and persuasive way?"

- "Will it help educate the other party in a situation where her position on an issue is based on a mistake or misperception?"
- "Will it help establish the extent of any losses or injuries I've suffered?"
- "Will it help the other side and me arrive at a settlement by showing how fair and workable a particular plan might be, or by showing the likelihood of my winning in court (or arbitration) if we don't settle?"

On a strategic level, bringing evidence to the mediation can increase your bargaining strength by showing the other party you have a strong case. It says, in effect, "You should settle with me in mediation, because if I am forced to take you to court, a judge will take evidence like this seriously and I may win." (But sometimes you may want to hold back evidence so as not to show your complete hand in case your dispute does later go to court. For more on this, see Section D4, below.)

Generally, the best time to present your evidence is at the beginning of the mediation when you make your opening statement. As discussed further in the next chapter, you should normally use your opening statement to tell, in plain English, how your dispute arose and how it has affected you. As you speak, you will want to show the other party and the mediator whatever evidence best supports the points you are making. You are normally free to bring to the table almost anything and anybody that will help you present and support your case. This can include:

- witnesses or letters from witnesses
- photographs
- drawings
- maps
- tape recordings
- medical bills
- pay stubs
- receipts
- apartment or condominium rules
- repair estimates
- letters from friends and neighbors, and more.

As long as the particular item will really help demonstrate the fairness of your position or help establish the reasonableness of your proposed solution, you can and should be creative. Here are some examples:

- At a California mediation program that handles disputes about noise from barking dogs, owners often bring in the offending beast, especially if it's relatively benign-looking. (This strategy assumes people will tolerate more barking from a dog they know than a dog they have never met.)
- A man who wanted to show that his basement was damaged by water pouring off his neighbor's roof brought photographs, taken during a rainstorm, of the neighbor's gutter angled at his house and water running onto his basement wall. He also brought photos of his water-filled cellar.
- When the owner of an auto repair shop wanted to show why a customer should have clearly understood that he was expected to pay a storage fee for unclaimed engine parts, he took an 8-foot by 4-foot sign off the front of his building and brought it to the mediation. The sign said, "Storage Fee: $1 per day after 30 days."
- When the co-owner of a "quick print" printing business wanted to illustrate what he claimed was irrational behavior by his partner, he brought to the mediation copies of memos from the partner that contained disjointed, contradictory and ranting statements.

2. FOUR KINDS OF EVIDENCE

To present your position in mediation in a clear, persuasive way, you should focus on bringing the types of evidence generally considered most persuasive. Much of this is just common sense. An invoice documenting how much you paid to fix your car, for example, will almost surely be more persuasive than your handwritten notes recounting the transaction after the fact. Following are examples of four types of evidence ranked according to how persuasive they normally are considered to be:

a. Real or Demonstrative Evidence: Sometimes called "the thing itself." For example, the BB gun you claim your neighbor's child used to shoot your dog; the shutter with bubbled paint you claim the painter forgot to prime; the suit from the cleaners, with bleach stains. If you can bring in the physical item that the dispute is about and its condition tends to support your position, it normally has a powerful affect on getting others to understand a problem from your point of view. (See sidebar regarding bassoon.)

b. Live Testimony by a Witness With Knowledge of the Facts: In legal lingo, sometimes called "viva voce" (the living voice)—for example, in a dispute with an insurance company having to do with whether a faulty wiring system might have caused a fire in your home, testimony of one of the firefighters who responded to your "911" call and who saw that the problem came from a short in your wiring system would surely be highly effective.

c. Documentary Evidence: There are four important kinds of documentary (written or printed) evidence.

- *Public Records:* Government documents carry much weight because of their official status. For example, they commonly include the report the police wrote about your accident or complaint; copies of your town ordinance (usually available from the local public library or law clerk) showing allowable noise levels in your community; a brochure distributed by the city explaining rules for putting trash in front of your house.

- *Business Records:* Unless contradicted, a record routinely made in the ordinary course of business is usually considered to be reliable. Common examples include a hospital's or doctor's medical report; your receipt for a purchase at a hardware store; the organization chart drawn by your company's personnel department showing who is supposed to report to whom; the rules of your apartment building issued by the building manager when you signed your lease, and the lease itself.

- *Photographs, Maps, and Other Written or Printed Materials That Have a High Likelihood of Authenticity:* Obviously, these are more believable if the maps or other materials come from reputable companies, or if something else about them helps show their authenticity. For example, if the photos have a date of printing on the back (ask the developer to date the paper on the back so you can prove they are current photos), it helps show they were taken before that date.

"YOU SHOULD HAVE BROUGHT THE BASSOON"

A college music student, injured in a car accident, sustained damage to her shoulder muscles. This was especially troublesome as she was a bassoonist and hoped to play professionally as well as teach. But with the shoulder injuries she could barely hold the bassoon in proper playing position for more than a few minutes at a time before the pain forced her to stop. Among other things, she sought money from the other motorist's insurance company for lost future wages if she remained unable to play her instrument.

At the mediation, she described the bassoon, how it rests against the shoulder, and the importance of strong shoulder muscles to hold it. After a mediation session that lasted eight hours, the case finally settled and the woman got a reasonable amount of money for her lost ability to play. After the mediation, the mediator confided to the music student, "If you'd really wanted to show the insurance people how hard it is to hold your instrument, you should have brought the bassoon. If you had, I think we would have been out of here hours ago."

SOMETIMES YOUR OWN PHOTOGRAPHS CAN BE CONVINCING EVIDENCE. Your own photos of the matter in dispute (an ugly fence, for example), can often be a big help. But be sure to take them from the point of view that matters most to you. In one case, for example, a homeowner complained of a junked car parked on his neighbor's lot. He brought to the mediation color photos of the old, rusted car that he had taken from his kitchen window, the one from which he had to look at the car every day.

- *Private writings:* These include written statements from family, colleagues or neighbors about your dispute, such as a neighbor's written statement that, "Yes, the Gallaghers' dog barks at all hours of the night." Although these writings carry less weight than other types of evidence because the writers are not present at the mediation, they can still be very effective. And you can make them more persuasive if the writers will have them notarized, proving that they really wrote them. Alternatively, writers might provide daytime phone numbers so the other party can call if verification—or additional explanations—would help.

d. *Expert Testimony:* This includes a witness such as a doctor, auto mechanic, or carpenter—anyone who, by training or experience, has special knowledge in a field and who has agreed to render an opinion on some important aspect of the dispute. When the mediator has no special knowledge of the subject in dispute (say a major engine repair or replacing a bearing wall with a header), this kind of witness can be especially helpful, since the better informed the mediator is about the subject of the dispute, the more creative he can be in helping the parties reach an acceptable solution. (For more on expert witnesses, see Section G2, below.)

3. CHECKLIST OF EVIDENCE

Now let's get more specific and look at several common types of disputes, and examples of the kinds of evidence that would be most helpful for you to bring to mediation for each case. (Evidence that may be helpful in divorce mediation is covered in Chapter 11, Divorce Mediation.) Though the list below is organized by type of dispute, you should at least skim through the whole list since you never can tell what will spark a good idea for kinds of evidence to bring in your case.

THE PROBLEM	GOOD EVIDENCE TO BRING
Harassment	
Your ex-boyfriend grabbed, pushed and threatened you in public. You feared for your safety and called the police. Though refusing to drop the criminal charges, you agreed to try to mediate some of the interpersonal issues	The police report on the incident; a notarized statement from a friend who was with you and who saw the incident; a notarized statement from your current roommate who has heard your ex-boyfriend telephone repeatedly, late at night; a letter from your doctor stating how the past incidents of harassment you reported to him and fear of future ones have affected you (loss of sleep, anxiety, difficulty concentrating at work).
Personal Injury	
While backing out of your driveway one morning on your way to work, a car traveling ten miles per hour over the speed limit struck the rear of your car. You sustained injuries to your back, neck and upper chest.	Photographs showing your injuries; the police report saying the other driver was at fault; a live witness or a notarized statement from a witness who can affirm that you were not at fault for the accident; a doctor's report describing the extent of your injuries; all your medical bills; a written statement from your employer showing wages lost due to absence from work; a copy of your own health insurance company statements showing medical expenses not covered by insurance.
Property Damage	
During a high wind, a neighbor's tree fell onto your house, damaging the roof, wall and windows on the upper story. There is some dispute not only about the value of the damage, but whether your roof and windows were already in disrepair before the tree hit.	Photographs of the damaged areas of your home before and after the incident; actual repair bills or estimates from two contractors who specialize in home repair; a police report (if you had called the police) affirming your version of events; a statement from your insurance carrier stating or affirming cost of repairs.

THE PROBLEM	GOOD EVIDENCE TO BRING
Business Contract Dispute	
Your company received a contract to make one million widgets, but half way through the job the buyer told you to change the sizes, and then later refused all shipments. They owe money for the work already done	A copy of the original contract and specifications for manufacture of widgets; subsequent memos from the buyer changing the specifications; handwritten log entries by your assembly supervisor attesting to the quality of widgets as they came off the line; bills of lading for shipment of widgets to the buyer.
Neighborhood Noise	
A noisy neighbor who throws noisy parties and keeps a noisy dog, is driving you crazy.	Tape recordings of the neighbor's dog barking, and of the rock band that played at the neighbor's most recent backyard party (recorded from your bedroom window); a written, notarized statement from other neighbors about the level of noise; a copy of the page from the town ordinance stating the legal limits of acceptable noise in residential areas during evening hours; a report on the decibel level reading by an acoustics expert.
Landlord/Tenant	
Despite repeated requests, the landlord has refused to repair the stairway leading to the basement in your apartment. Every time you go down there to check your things in storage, you believe you are risking your life.	A photograph showing the dangerous condition caused by rotted boards on the stairs; a sample rotted board; a copy of your lease stating the landlord's duty to repair; a copy of a report by a city housing inspector responding to your complaint.
Employment Dispute	
Two day's after your 55th birthday, you were summarily dismissed from your office job. You believe your boss's negative attitude toward older workers was the primary reason.	The termination letter from your boss; copy of your employment contract; copies of state and federal laws prohibiting discrimination in the workplace based on age; a copy of the company manual stating same; one or more co-workers as live witnesses to affirm that the the boss had made unflattering remarks concerning your age; an internal company memo written by your boss disparaging the value of older workers.

4. SHOULD YOU DISCLOSE ALL YOUR EVIDENCE IN MEDIATION?

Assuming you believe certain information will help with your mediation, should you plan to disclose all of it? Or, is it wise to hold some of it back, in case the dispute ends up in arbitration or court? As a general rule, your best strategy is to use all persuasive information and evidence at the mediation so as to enhance your chances of achieving a satisfactory result. Also, there is a real-world possibility that if you don't disclose it, and mediation proves unsuccessful, by the time your case gets to arbitration or trial, the evidence you held back may have lost some of its ability to convince. This could occur because the other party has used the pretrial "discovery" process to ask you about it or has found out about it through his own investigations and, either way, has prepared ways to counter it. And of course, if a live witness is involved, that person may have died, changed his mind or moved away.

However, there are situations where it may be wise to hold back evidence in mediation, particularly if disclosing it would be unlikely to move your dispute toward settlement but would surely help the other side in litigation later. For example, if your claim is against a manufacturer for making an unsafe product and someone from the company has leaked you an internal memorandum showing the company knew the product was unsafe, you might want to keep it secret on the chance your case does not settle and goes to trial where you can use it to undercut the company's legal position. Disclosing it now would allow the company plenty of time to prepare a defense against it. If your case involves an issue of this importance, you should probably get some advice from a lawyer or law coach about what evidence to disclose in mediation.

You may also choose not to divulge some evidence because of the reaction it would trigger from the other side. For example, say your claim is for wrongful termination against a former employer. You have evidence your boss occasionally used drugs at work, but you know she in turn has evidence about an affair you had with a woman you were supervising which you hope won't be revealed. In this case, maybe you shouldn't cast the first stone.

If you are hesitant about divulging evidence, talk to your lawyer or a self-help law coach you hire to help with your mediation. (See Section G in this chapter and Chapter 13, Lawyers and Legal Research.) Or, you can go into mediation and during private caucus ask the mediator how he thinks the other side might react if you had a particular piece of evidence and were to reveal it at mediation, or later at a trial or arbitration. The mediator might give you an educated opinion based on his understanding of the case and of the other side's position, and you can make your decision accordingly.

E. The Pre-Mediation Memorandum

A Pre-Mediation Memorandum briefly outlines the facts and issues of your dispute in order to educate the mediator about the case before the mediation begins. Most mediation providers handling cases involving substantial money, property or legal issues, require or encourage submission of a Memorandum. Community mediation centers, on the other hand, often do not allow them because many of their cases concern neighborhood and small claims matters where the facts are not complex and parties might not have the training or resources to prepare a Memorandum. Whether you must submit a Pre-Mediation Memorandum is normally governed by the Mediation Rules being used in your case, although occasionally, it may be included in your Notice of Mediation or the Agreement to Mediate.

If you have not been told whether you must submit such a Memorandum, check the rules and the Notice of Mediation, or ask the mediation service or independent mediator. If the opportunity is available, it is almost always worthwhile to take advantage of it. Do this even in small disputes, sensibly adjusting the size and complexity of the memo to the size of the dispute.

1. PURPOSE OF THE MEMORANDUM

The purpose of the Memorandum is to educate the mediator in advance about the basic facts and issues that will be addressed in your case. The Memorandum can be especially useful if the dispute involves legal or technical issues. If such issues are involved in your case, you should attach to the Memorandum copies of the legal statutes, technical papers or contracts involved, with relevant sections highlighted. This will allow the mediator to review matters beforehand and so be "up to speed" when the mediation begins. This, in turn, will save you time and, if you're paying by the hour, money, as well.

2. WHEN, AND TO WHOM, TO SUBMIT THE MEMORANDUM

Typically, where mediation rules require or allow a Pre-Mediation Memorandum, the parties may submit it any time up to a week or ten days before the mediation. Submission is normally made directly to the mediator. For example, the Commercial Mediation Rules of the American Arbitration Association provide:

> At least ten days prior to the first scheduled mediation session, each party shall provide the mediator with a brief memorandum setting forth its position with regard to the issues that need to be resolved.

> **— (RULE 9, "IDENTIFICATION OF MATTERS IN DISPUTE")**

Most commonly, but not always, only the mediator sees your Memorandum. Even if, in this situation, there is no danger of intemperate language inflaming the other party, you'll create the best impression with the mediator if you state your position as calmly and objectively as possible. Under some mediation rules, disputants are required to exchange copies of their Memoranda. If so, be especially careful to write your Memorandum in neutral, non-inflammatory language. Mud-slinging or being needlessly accusatory may trigger an equally nasty reply from the other side and also cause the mediator to question the credibility of your other statements. Most importantly, being highly accusative is counter-productive to the whole idea of mediation and gets in the way of arriving at a settlement.

DON'T EXCHANGE MEMORANDA IF IT ISN'T REQUIRED. If the rules are silent as to whether or not you have to exchange Memoranda, I recommend that you don't. While you do want to educate the mediator, there is normally no sense in showing the other side exactly how you intend to present and support your point of view before your session even begins. Write at the top of yours that you are submitting it in confidence to the mediator and do not intend it to be seen by anyone else.

Note that if you do exchange Memoranda with the other party, their contents would be subject to the Mediation Rules on confidentiality. Under most sets of rules, the other party would not be able to use the information in your Memorandum against you in any other proceeding, such as an arbitration or trial. (For more on confidentiality, see Section A3.)

3. CONTENT AND FORM OF THE MEMORANDUM

A good Memorandum is brief, usually just a few pages in length, unless it concerns a very large and complex case. (Remember, if you are paying hourly fees for your mediation, this will usually include the time a mediator spends reviewing materials before the session.) The Memorandum should give the mediator a sense of what the dispute is about and highlight any technical issues that may need some advance study. Again, since your mediator isn't a judge with the power to decide anything, nothing can be gained by arguing your points in detail or including lengthy legal-sounding discourses. (If you have a lawyer who will prepare and submit the Memorandum for you, be sure she understands the purposes of the Memorandum and ask her to keep it informal and short; you won't want to pay the lawyer for a court-style Memorandum or brief.)

Think of your Memorandum as a terrific chance to make a good first impression on the mediator. (See Section C1.) Present your information clearly and with some passion, but without sounding strident or unreasonable. Don't lie or overstate your case. As one mediator put it, "If I find I can't have confidence in what one of the parties says to me, if I have to be skeptical—then just as a human being, my heart won't be in it and it becomes that much more difficult as a professional to do my best for that person."

There is no official format to follow in preparing the Memorandum. I recommend that you type or print your memo on plain white 8½" x 11" paper and cover the following points:

A. A BRIEF STATEMENT OF THE FACTS NOT IN DISPUTE

Begin by giving the mediator a quick overview of what your dispute is about, starting with the undisputed facts. For example, "ABC Manufacturing Company makes wood furniture for residential and commercial customers. From 1992-1997 (May), I was employed at ABC as a lathe operator. My immediate supervisor was Mr. Gene Dowl. On May 3, Mr. Dowl informed me in writing that I was being terminated in ten days because of 'sloppy work.'"

SAMPLE FIRST PAGE | **PRE-MEDIATION MEMORANDUM**

Date: July 2, 1997

To: Michael Mediator

From: John Smith

Re: John Smith vs. ABC Manufacturing Co.

Mediation Scheduled on July 14, 1997, at 10 a.m. at office of Mediation First, Inc.

This Memorandum is submitted to provide you with the basic facts and issues involved in this dispute.

In accordance with the mediation rules, I am submitting this Memorandum to you in confidence and request that it not be seen by any of the other parties in this dispute. [Or, if the mediation rules require an exchange of memos: I am also sending a copy of this Memorandum today to Mr. Gene Dowl of ABC Manufacturing Co.]

1. Facts Not in Dispute

ABC Manufacturing Company makes wood furniture for residential and commercial customers. From 1992-1997 (May), I was employed at ABC as a lathe operator. My immediate supervisor was Mr. Gene Dowl. On May 3, Mr. Dowl informed me in writing that I was being terminated in ten days because of "sloppy work" (see letter enclosed).

B. STATE WHAT ISSUES ARE IN DISPUTE

Clearly explain what the dispute is about. For example, "When I asked Mr. Dowl the next day after I got my letter of termination what he meant by my work being 'sloppy,' he said I made too many errors on the Royal Oak account (1,000 lots of sculpted chair legs). I know this is not the real reason, sin•ce my work is always good and I wasn't sloppy on the Royal Oak job. The real reason is that he overheard me in the lunchroom talking with other employees about how we didn't like working with the cheaper wood the company has been buying and how it's unsafe to make furniture with wood that could easily crack and break.

I think I was fired to keep me from talking about this problem and maybe some of it leaking outside the company to the media."

After you have explained what the dispute is about from your point of view, don't go on and provide a series of arguments and justifications as to why you are in the right and the other party is a dishonest noodle brain. Again, the purpose of your memo is simply to tell the mediator what your dispute is about, not to convince her that you are right.

C. STATE WHAT RESULT YOU WANT FROM THE MEDIATION

State in general terms what you hope to achieve from the mediation. For example, "I am coming to mediation because I want my job back at ABC. I am willing to sue over this if I have to but I am willing to try to work out a settlement as long as I get my job back with no penalties, and if Mr. Dowl is no longer my supervisor." There is no need to go into great detail or to disclose your no more compromise line (see Section B5).

D. INCLUDE COPIES OF KEY DOCUMENTS

To help the mediator prepare for your case, include copies of any documents that you think the mediator should read and study before the first session. These might include: laws, court decisions, contracts, company rules and insurance policies. Use a yellow marker or similarly readable highlighter to mark the important provisions.

F. Who Should Attend the Mediation

Will you attend the mediation alone, or are there people whom you should plan to have with you? This section discusses why and under what circumstances you may want to have others, such as a witness, a friendly supporter or a lawyer, accompany you.

1. DECISIONMAKERS MUST ATTEND

It is essential that each disputing party be represented at the mediation by a person with authority to agree to a settlement. Obviously, if this is your personal dispute, you are that person. But in disputes involving businesses or public entities, it's not always clear who has the power to say "yes." It's important to find this out before the mediation begins. You don't want to spend many hours working in good faith toward a solution to a dispute, only to find at the last minute that the other side cannot seize the moment and agree, because its representatives lack the authority to make an agreement. In fact, if another person at the mediation table says he does not have authority to make a settlement on behalf of whatever company or organization he represents—and during the course of the mediation cannot easily reach someone who does—I would be hesitant to continue. If the person assures you that his or her recommendations are routinely accepted by the powers that be, then you may wish to proceed—assuming you feel comfortable with the explanation. However, if you are unable to get such an assurance, it makes very little sense to continue. If you are mediating because of a contractual provision or court order, you can take the position that the other side has not met the requirement because of the failure to send someone with the authority to reach an agreement.

> **EXAMPLE:** *Richard Wagner, a claims representative of the Racafrax Insurance Company, comes to the mediation of a personal injury claim with authority to settle only for an amount up to $10,000. He does not inform the other parties or the mediator of this limitation. After several hard-working hours, everyone— including Richard Wagner—decides that a fair settlement would be $15,000. Only now does Wagner reveal that he cannot agree because he lacks the authority. The mediation must adjourn with the dispute at least temporarily unresolved while the claim rep goes to consult with his supervisor.*

IF YOU DON'T HAVE ULTIMATE AUTHORITY, be sure you are in close touch with someone who does. If you are coming to mediation as a representative of a large organization or company, be sure that you are given adequate authority. If not, at least arrange for a decision-maker to be available by telephone during the time the mediation is expected to last (including a home telephone number in case the mediation extends after normal working hours).

2. PEOPLE EMOTIONALLY INVOLVED IN THE DISPUTE

If your dispute involves a group entity, such as a business, non-profit organization, club or government agency, think about whether particular people in your organization have such a strong emotional involvement in the dispute that they might find it hard to agree to a rational settlement. If so, that person is too emotionally involved to negotiate rationally, and it's often best that they not attend the mediation, unless they are in a position to thwart or subvert a mediated settlement, in which case their presence is probably essential.

EXAMPLE: *A large computer maker and a small parts-supplier were involved in a contract dispute about the quality of manufactured parts. At first, the decision-makers for each company (the VP of the parts supplier and regional manager of the computer maker) planned to come to mediation alone to try to work out a settlement that might involve not only solving the problem but paving the way so that the two companies could do business together in the future. But in this case, a strong personal distrust had developed between the computer maker's director of engineering and the parts-maker's chief engineer. The president of the parts supplier realized that if the antagonism between these two men was not resolved, either would be in a position to sabotage future relations. Therefore, she suggested that both of them be at the mediation—even though they were not decision-makers—in order to have their say in the presence of the mediator and each other and get things off their chests face-to-face. Hopefully, once the air had been cleared, both companies could confidently work out a settlement that involved future contracts.*

3. WITNESSES

In most mediations, disputants are permitted to bring any witnesses they wish. In the rare situations where there are restrictions on witnesses, they will normally be found in the mediation rules.

A. PURPOSE OF WITNESSES

The purpose of bringing a witness is primarily to support your version of the facts and your point of view as to what a reasonable solution might be. This is in contrast to a court trial, where a witness's role is to try to convince a judge or jury of the truth of something. For example, if your complaint involves a neighbor who keeps a rusted car in his front yard, you might bring as a witness another neighbor to confirm the unsightly condition of the car for the purpose of helping the other side see that it really is an eyesore that bothers more than just you.

Because a mediation is run very differently from a court trial, you normally do not ask questions of your witness. Instead, the mediator simply invites the witness to tell what he or she knows about the dispute. The mediator and the other party may then ask your witness questions to clarify one or more points, but the process looks and feels far more like a conversation than a cross-examination at trial.

If you plan to bring a witness, take some time to prepare the person. Review with your witness the points you would like him to cover when he speaks, and be sure that what he has to say will, in fact, support your point of view. Also, explain to your witness that a mediation is not an adversary proceeding, and that the mediator is there not as a judge but as someone trained to help facilitate a settlement. This information should help your witness to avoid presenting himself as too angry or strident.

Although a good witness can help you arrive at a good mediation settlement, there can be downsides to bringing witnesses. Even if your witness is not an "expert" and so does not charge you a fee (see the next section), witnesses usually slow down the mediation, thus increasing the per hour fees for the mediator. In addition, no matter how much time you spend preparing your witness, you still cannot be sure what he or she will say if the mediator or the other party asks a question that you did not anticipate. The witness could even end up saying something that undermines your position. For example, if the neighbor ends up saying that although the rusted car in your neighbor's yard isn't pretty, it's not really as much of a neighborhood problem as the two old pick-ups you park on the street, you will hardly have gained much. Also, by bringing witnesses you risk making the other party feel "ganged up" on, which could cause him to be even more rigid and uncompromising in his position, thus reducing the chances for a settlement.

IN A NEIGHBOR DISPUTE, BE SURE YOUR WITNESS IS REALLY YOUR SUPPORTER. Talk to the neighbor whom you plan to bring as a witness about other possible issues the other side might raise, since these rather regularly come up in mediation. Find out if the neighbor will generally support your broader perspective.

One possibility is to consider whether an alternative way of presenting evidence might accomplish the same thing a witness would but without the possibility of delay, risk and cost. One way is to get a written statement from the witness (notarized if possible) and offer it instead of the live testimony. Since you are only using the witness to try to better explain your position and convince the other side that you can prove it if necessary, you don't lose that much by using the statement instead of the person. Also, if you don't like what the witness says, you don't have to use it at all. For example, instead of bringing a neighbor to support your complaint about another neighbor's rusted car, you might bring a notarized statement from the witness to that effect, and also include some color photographs of the car taken from different angles. The persuasive value of various kinds of evidence is discussed in Section D2.

B. EXPERT WITNESSES

As noted, expert witnesses, such as doctors, accountants, investigators and others, can effectively support your point of view and show that you would have a strong case if you were to take your dispute to court or arbitration. This type of witness can be extremely valuable in situations where a major issue is the dollar value of an economic loss, but of little or no value in neighbor type disputes where convincing someone to change their conduct is the main issue. For example, if your claim is against an insurance company for injuries involved in a car accident, you can bring your doctor to talk about the extent of your injuries and how they affect your ability to work. (But in this situation it is much more common just to bring a written report from the doctor. This saves a lot of money because you don't have to pay the doctor for her time attending the mediation nor the mediator for her time to sit and listen to the doctor.) If you do plan to bring an expert witness, check your mediation rules to see if they require you to notify the other party so he has the opportunity to bring his own expert if he wishes. (See Section D2.)

EYEWITNESS VS. EXPERT WITNESS: KEEPING THE TWO STRAIGHT

An eyewitness is someone who can talk about what he actually has seen or otherwise experienced firsthand. An expert witness is someone who is regarded as qualified, either by careful study or experience, to give an opinion about the facts of a dispute. But these labels can sometimes be confusing. For example, there are "eyewitnesses" who may happen to be experts, and then there are true "expert witnesses." Suppose you have a dispute with a neighbor who, you believe, keeps unsafe play equipment in his backyard which creates an attractive hazard for your children. As a witness, you may bring a third neighbor who has seen the play equipment, shares your concern about safety and who also happens to be a family physician; her testimony as a witness will be especially effective because she is a physician. However, the way the legal system categorizes people, she is not a true "expert witness," such as an engineer or safety expert you hire strictly for her expertise about child safety and who has no personal involvement in the case.

Though expert witnesses can be persuasive, they can also be very expensive, since many charge $200-$500 per hour. Therefore, if you have suffered an injury, bringing a physician to your mediation as an expert witness may cost thousands of dollars. A good alternative is often to obtain a copy of your medical records, along with a letter from a doctor detailing his opinion of your injuries. In court, the doctor's letter would probably not be acceptable evidence (because the doctor is not available to be cross-examined), but in mediation, where there are no formal rules of evidence, it is convenient, cost-effective, and welcome.

C. SHOULD YOUR WITNESS BECOME A PARTY TO THE MEDIATION?

In some disputes, it might be better to ask a person you would consider bringing as a witness to join you as a party to the mediation. For example, if you were a tenant in an apartment building and had agreed to mediate a dispute with your landlord over poor trash collection in the parking lot, your first impulse might be to bring other tenants to your mediation as witnesses to confirm your story about the trash problem. It may be better, however, to ask them if they want to join you as parties.

One reason for this is that a mediated agreement only applies to the parties in a dispute, not witnesses. Thus, if your mediation agreement said, in effect, "The landlord agrees that rent can be withheld unless parking lot dumpsters are emptied once a week," this might be a good agreement for you, but it would not let the other nonparty tenants in this situation withhold their rent. A better way would be to sign any willing tenants on to the case as "co-claimants." Then they could come to the mediation as parties (or, if the group was too large, they could designate you to represent them) and share in the benefits of the mediated agreement. Their participation as co-claimants would also give you added bargaining power at the mediation, and possibly help you achieve more favorable settlement terms.

D. CHARACTER WITNESSES NOT NEEDED IN MEDIATION

In a courtroom, a witness may be called to testify about a party's character. The purpose of this is to show, by evidence of past acts or reputation, that a party is likely either to be telling the truth or to be lying. In mediation, where the ultimate goal is not to find the truth but to find a solution, there is no need for character witnesses. Similarly, the other party's vices and bad reputation are not at issue. Furthermore, there is in mediation an underlying assumption that both sides have come to the table in good faith to work together toward finding a fair and workable solution. To bring in a witness with no knowledge of the dispute but merely to speak ill of the other party or to show that the other party has a reputation for lying would, in effect, challenge the other party's good faith. This could poison the cooperative atmosphere necessary for mediation to succeed.

4. SUPPORTIVE FRIEND OR RELATIVE

When you come to mediation, you sit face-to-face across the table from the other person (or persons) involved in your dispute. For some shy or easily dominated people, this face-to-face encounter can be intimidating, even though mediation is informal and many mediators will help assure that neither party gets steam-rollered by an aggressive adversary. (For more on mediators' willingness to intervene to block an unfair agreement, see Chapter 5, Section C3.) This problem typically occurs when the disputants were in a personal relationship such as a marriage or living-together relationship and one of them was far less forceful or dominant, but it isn't limited to domestic situations. It could also involve co-workers, neighbors or friends. A similar problem can occur when a person doesn't speak well in front of other people, has a speech problem or is not fluent in English or whatever other language the mediation will be conducted in.

Any significant power imbalance—no matter what causes it—not only threatens the position of the weaker person, it also affects the entire mediation process. For example, many people who perceive themselves at a disadvantage are extremely reluctant to agree to anything, even a fair solution.

If any of these circumstances apply to you, consider bringing a friend or relative to the mediation to support you and, if necessary, to help articulate your point of view during the mediation. This not only allows you to prepare and plan together, but also lets you appoint your friend as the keeper of your no more compromise line. (See Section B5.)

Your "helper" can be a friend or relative, or a lawyer or other professional such as a teacher, social worker or member of the clergy. (For a discussion of the role of lawyers in mediation, see next section.) But be careful not to let your "helper" become your advocate. Even if the mediator permits it, this would most likely make the other party more defensive and reduce the chances for a settlement.

WITH A LITTLE HELP FROM MOM AND SISTER . . .

Rebecca, a college student, had worked extremely hard as a part-time advertising salesperson for a magazine and was disputing the amount of commissions she was paid. Only 18, Rebecca felt shy and intimidated by the prospect of facing the publication's advertising director. To help counter this, she brought her older sister and mother with her to the mediation.

Rebecca still did most of the talking, but her family was there to remind her of points she wanted to make, of dates that escaped her mind, and to put in a few words now and then about the extent of her work on the magazine's behalf.

Thus supported, Rebecca was able to represent herself adequately in the mediation and to agree with the magazine ad director on what both considered to be a fair settlement.

G. Using a Lawyer in Mediation

Nearly all mediation rules give you the right, if you wish, to bring a lawyer to the mediation. In most instances, I don't recommend that you do so, since mediation is a process that most people can safely use without lawyers.

1. Lawyers Can Be Counterproductive to the Mediation Process

Usually, for mediation to be most effective, disputants need to deal with each other directly, to air their differences, learn to perceive the dispute from each other's point of view and work together to find a resolution. Against this background, the presence of a lawyer, especially one trained to function in the more adversarial atmosphere of the courtroom, can sometimes be self-defeating, especially in interpersonal disputes involving family, friends, neighbors or business colleagues where preservation of the underlying relationship is a goal. This is particularly likely if a disputant lets the lawyer do most of the talking for him. Bringing and relying on the help of a lawyer is likely to be less of a problem in disputes between strangers over money or property.

As compared to court, there is much less for lawyers to do at a mediation. For example, there is no need to object to evidence, or lead witnesses through testimony or give a closing summation to a jury. After all, nothing will be decided unless you agree. Problems are particularly likely to develop if a lawyer doesn't have confidence in the mediation process, and tries to turn it into an adversarial battle.

2. When Your Lawyer Should Attend

There are some circumstances in which you probably should have your lawyer attend the mediation, such as:

- When complex legal issues are involved and it would be impractical to conduct the mediation without a ready source of legal advice. For example, a dispute between a town government and a building contractor where any settlement would have to take into account the company's compliance with complicated provisions of local building codes.
- When substantial amounts of money or property are involved. For example, if your dispute concerns a claim of sexual harassment against your former boss and you are seeking $200,000 in settlement.
- When you lack self-confidence, are intimated by the other party or need help articulating your position. Bringing a lawyer is one remedy for a "power imbalance," but, as discussed above, this problem can often also be solved by bringing a strong-minded friend or other adviser. In any situation like this, you will have to weigh the benefits versus the costs of bringing a lawyer. If a lawyer will charge $200 an hour to represent you, is the dispute big enough to justify that expense? How long might the mediation last? Could you get as good (or better) help by bringing someone else?

If you do want to bring a lawyer, try to use one who is experienced in mediation and supports its methods and goals. She will be more likely to understand that the lawyer's role in mediation is not to be an aggressive advocate, but to help the client present her case, evaluate possible solutions and work cooperatively toward a settlement. (For more on finding a lawyer to work with in mediation, see Chapter 13, Lawyers and Legal Research.)

Be sure to work out in advance what your lawyer's fee will be for attending the mediation. Many lawyers charge one hourly rate for office work and another, higher rate for time spent in court. In my view, it is not appropriate for the lawyer to charge you the court rate for attending mediation because the lawyer's role is so much different and less demanding in mediation than it would be in court. A rate somewhere between the "office rate" and the "court rate" would probably be fair.

ASK YOUR LAWYER TO STAY IN THE BACKGROUND. If your lawyer does come to the mediation, she doesn't need to play a lead role. One good approach is to have her sit quietly and listen. Occasionally, you can have a private conference to be sure all the points about which you are concerned get discussed, and that you are considering all of the legal implications of various proposed settlement terms.

3. Consulting With a Lawyer Before, During and After the Mediation

If you feel you need formal legal help with your mediation, or simply the assurance that your legal information or conclusions are accurate, often the best way to use a lawyer is as a consultant or information specialist. Under this model, the lawyer becomes your law coach, providing helpful insights into the more technical legal aspects of your dispute before, during or even after your mediation sessions.

Before the mediation: Consult with your lawyer about the issues in dispute. In order to use the law as a benchmark in determining your goals (Section B1, above), ask about the likely result if your case went to trial or arbitration. This should help you arrive at your no more compromise line. (Section B5.) For example, in a personal injury case, a lawyer can give you a pretty accurate high and low guestimate as to how much a judge or jury might be expected to award for your type of injuries. Or in a case where you believe someone plagiarized an article you wrote, a lawyer could advise on what effect settling with the other side might have on your ability to stop others from plagiarizing the same work.

During the mediation: You can have a lawyer more or less on call and break off during the session to telephone the lawyer for help on a particular point. For example, in a business mediation, if you and the other owner of your company are moving toward a settlement where you will buy her out, you can take a break to call your lawyer and ask about the personal tax consequences of various ways of structuring the buy-out.

After the mediation: Successful mediation doesn't have to result in an agreement on all the details, but rather can provide a sound framework for an agreement. Your lawyer can help later with hashing out the final details. Even if you do reach a detailed agreement, you can condition it on your lawyer's approval. One way is to have the mediator insert a clause stating that the agreement will take effect one week after it is signed, unless either party objects in writing before that date. During that week, have your lawyer review the agreement to be sure it says what you want it to say and that it does not impair your legal rights in any way you did not intend. If you want your written agreement to have the binding effect of a contract, ask your lawyer to be sure it is written in the correct form of a contract. (For more on conditioning an agreement on your lawyer's review and drafting an agreement in the form of a contract, see Chapter 8, Writing an Agreement That Works.)

SEVEN

Inside the Mediation Session

The bailiff bangs three times and says, "All Rise! This Court is now in session, The Honorable Thomas A. Watson presiding! You may now be seated."

That is how a typical courtroom hearing begins. Mediation begins differently.

"Hello. Are you Elizabeth Ferraro? Are you Richard Rafferty? I'm Tom Watson, the mediator. Will you both follow me into the conference room, please?"

The mediator's low-key opening sets a tone of sensible informality that will continue throughout the proceedings. But it is also a little deceiving, because it is such a casual overture to the compelling drama about to unfold. By comparison, what happens most days in a rule-bound trial court, is boring. The key to understanding why mediation can be so dramatic is to remember that you have not turned your dispute over to lawyer intermediaries; instead, in the mediation session, you and the other side—your former business partner, your annoying neighbor, the boss who fired you—will be the principal players. In just a few moments you will be nose-to-nose across a conference table, with the chance to say what is on your mind, to wrangle over the issues and, hopefully, together with your adversary, to arrive at a solution.

This chapter examines the six stages of a typical mediation session. For each we discuss what is really likely to be happening and how you can use this information to make your mediation as successful as possible.

A. The Six Stages of a Typical Mediation Session

Mediation is a process that usually moves from one fairly-defined stage to the next, giving the disputants time to speak and be listened to, sometimes to meet privately with the mediator, and finally, to work together to find a solution to their dispute. For example, if you were mediating a dispute over noise with the upstairs neighbor in your co-op apartment building, the mediation would begin with the mediator explaining the purposes of mediation and the procedures to be followed. Then, you and your neighbor would each be invited to make an opening statement to explain what the dispute is about from your point of view. A short joint discussion might follow, during which the mediator reviews the issues raised by you both and helps you decide in what order they will be discussed. After you have each expressed your point of view, the mediator will likely ask to meet with each of you privately to confidentially discuss your positions on the issues and how you see the problem being solved. After shuttling back and forth to conduct several rounds of these private meetings (called "caucuses"), the mediator might call you back together to try to work out the details of a settlement in another joint discussion. Finally, if both of you agree to the same settlement terms, the mediator will outline the agreement, read it to you for your approval and declare the mediation closed.

Exactly how many stages is a mediation session divided into? Even mediators differ; some see five stages, while others see six, or even seven. As you have doubtless gathered from the heading of this subsection, we divide the process into six stages, as follows:

1. Mediator's Opening Statement
2. Disputants' Opening Statements
3. Joint Discussion
4. Caucus
5. Joint Negotiations
6. Closure.

Exceptions to the six-stage process usually involve omission of Stage Four, the private meeting or "caucus" between the mediator and each of the parties. Divorce and family mediators, particularly, are likely to omit the caucus, preferring instead to keep family members together in order to help them jointly rebuild at least a measure of trust. (See Chapter 11, Divorce Mediation.) Some community mediation centers also do not use the caucus when cases involve interpersonal disputes, fearing that separate meetings may cause one or both sides to worry that the mediator is being unfairly influenced by the other.

B. Before the Mediation Begins

In Chapter 1, What is Mediation?, we discussed the various types of facilities in which mediations are held and how long mediation sessions typically last. Here, we start by assuming you are about to enter the mediation room.

1. WHERE TO SIT IN THE MEDIATION ROOM

Typically, the mediator will come to greet you and the other parties in a waiting area. He will introduce himself to everyone and then escort all of you together to the conference room or other room where the mediation will be held. He does it this way to protect his image of neutrality. If the mediator brought one side into the room before the others, the party entering last might wonder if the first-arriving party had said anything to influence or prejudice the mediator.

Once in the conference room, the mediator will invite you to take a seat at the table. (See sidebar, below.)

There is no strategic advantage in trying to jockey for table position; the mediator usually knows where he wants you to sit and, much like a host at a dinner party, will direct you to a seat. A typical seating plan would place you at one side of a rectangular table, the other party directly across, and the mediator at the head. If a lawyer or witness is with you, she will normally be seated next to you, or perhaps just behind you if there isn't room for everyone to fit at the table. If for some reason you are uncomfortable with the seating arrangement, speak up and the mediator will often be willing to accommodate you.

THE GREAT MEDIATION TABLE DEBATE

Exactly what is the perfect shape for a mediation table? Believe it or not, this is a subject that mediators debate vigorously in the pages of professional journals. Some prefer a rectangular table because they believe its resemblance to a typical boardroom table inspires confidence in the mediation process; others dislike the rectangular table because they think its straight lines encourage hard and inflexible bargaining. Some like a square table on the theory that its four equal sides suggest equality among the parties. Round tables also have their proponents. Paul G. Charbonneau, director of Maine's Court Mediation Service, observes: "Our mediations are held in conference rooms in old courthouses. We prefer round tables because it's more collaborative and less adversarial than having people sitting across from each other at a rectangular table. But really, the success of mediation doesn't rise or fall on the shape of the table." In fact, some mediators prefer no table at all, and instead like to have the disputants sit in upholstered armchairs or on a comfortable sofa facing the mediator.

The mediation table debate is taken seriously enough that some mediation centers will have available several rooms of varying size and furniture arrangements. The mediator can choose which he or she prefers to use in a particular case.

ADVANTAGES OF SITTING BY THE DOOR. If you think your mediation has any chance of becoming physically threatening (an extremely rare occurrence), take a seat on the side of the table nearest the door so you can easily leave the room without having to pass the person by whom you feel threatened.

2. WHAT THE MEDIATOR KNOWS ABOUT YOU

If you submitted a Pre-Mediation Memorandum (see Chapter 6, Section E), the mediator will open your session already knowing the basic facts and issues in dispute. And assuming the Memorandum highlighted any technical issues involved, such as relevant government regulations, construction practices or aspects of employment law, the mediator may have spent some time familiarizing himself with these matters.

If Pre-Mediation Memoranda were not submitted, however, the mediator will likely open the session knowing nothing more about your dispute than what you and the other party put on the submission form. (See Chapter 4, Section E.) For example, at many community mediation centers Memoranda are not prepared because many of the disputes concern neighborhood and small claims matters where the facts are not complex and parties might not have the training or resources to prepare one. If your case was referred by a judge or prosecutor, the mediator probably would know that, but not a great deal more, unless your dispute involved a call to the police, in which case a copy of the police report may be in the mediator's file.

3. SIX COMMANDMENTS FOR SUCCESSFUL MEDIATION

As your mediation session is about to begin, consider six simple ideas which can help make your mediation successful. Some of these relate to the exercises for determining your goals discussed in Chapter 6, Preparing for Your Mediation, and some are just common sense.

1ST COMMANDMENT: LET GO OF THE PAST/LOOK TO THE FUTURE

The law and courts usually look back to see who was right and who was wrong. By contrast, mediation looks forward to the future. In mediation, the important question for you and the other party is: How can we work out a solution that will benefit both of us? To find that solution, at some point in your mediation you and the other party will need to let go of the wrongs and hurts of the past and focus instead on the future.

2ND COMMANDMENT: FOCUS ON YOUR NEEDS, NOT YOUR WANTS

As we discussed earlier (Chapter 6, Section B4), in mediation you have the opportunity to satisfy not only your wants, but also your underlying needs or interests, such as emotional and economic security, respect and self-esteem, recognition, vindication and protecting your reputation. Fortunately, meeting your needs is often easier to do than satisfying your wants or your technical legal rights.

3RD COMMANDMENT:
FOCUS ON YOUR NEEDS, NOT YOUR LEGAL RIGHTS

As we discussed in Chapter 6, Section B1, mediation often uses the law as a benchmark when deciding how a particular dispute might be resolved. While the law may appear to favor you over the other disputant, you might be wise to let go of that point in a mediation. For instance, assume the law gives you the legal right to be noisy at your house until 10:00 p.m. and you fully take advantage of it. If you end up mediating with a neighbor who believes you are being unreasonable, you may be far better off compromising than standing on your rights and creating a resentful and potentially retaliatory neighbor. In this kind of situation it is important to examine what you really need rather than insist on what you are legally entitled to.

4TH COMMANDMENT: BE PREPARED TO SHARE RESPONSIBILITY

There are few disputes where one side is completely right and the other side is completely wrong. Even if the other party is mostly wrong, if you can own up to your small part of the problem, you will make it possible for the other side to save face and make important concessions to you. If you can go even farther, and accept the other side's view of where you went wrong, this can do a lot to move the mediation ahead. If you refuse to take any responsibility, however, the other side may be unwilling to compromise.

KEEP IN MIND THE AWESOME POWER OF A SINCERE APOLOGY.
Sometimes when disputes get all wrapped up in issues of money and rights and demands for this and that, we lose sight of the human element. As you go into mediation, keep in mind the power of a simple but sincere apology for your part in the dispute. In the right case, it can go a long way toward helping the other party reach the point where he is ready to settle the dispute by reasonable compromise.

5TH COMMANDMENT: PRESERVE NEEDED RELATIONSHIPS

Mediation gives you the chance to deal with your dispute while still maintaining a civil relationship with the other party, whether it is a relative, friend, business colleague or neighbor. So if your dispute involves a person with whom you want to—or need to—maintain a relationship, take advantage of the reasonably pleasant atmosphere of mediation to solve your immediate dispute without destroying the relationship. That means speaking respectfully and politely to the other person, and accommodating her needs as far as possible.

6TH COMMANDMENT: BE FLEXIBLE

As opposed to court, the ability to be flexible is one of the advantages of mediation. But to really take advantage of this freedom from technical rules, you yourself must be flexible. Recognize that from the minute your session starts, you won't know exactly where the discussion will go, what offers may be made or what hidden issues will emerge. If you have prepared adequately so that you know your goals and "no more compromise line" (see Chapter 6, Section B5), you should feel secure enough to consider any novel ideas and creative solutions proposed by the other side or by the mediator.

C. Stage One: The Mediator's Opening Statement

As a mediation sessions begins, the mediator usually has no need to get the disputants' attention because no one is speaking. You and the other party will probably be sitting silently, across the table from one another, waiting for the mediator to explain what will happen next.

The first lines in the mediation drama are known as the "Opening Statement." It is almost always a short speech, usually delivered without notes, through which the mediator will try to demystify the proceeding for you by describing, in simple terms, the procedures and rules of mediation. Listen carefully so you'll understand exactly how things will proceed. Do this even if you have participated in mediation sessions before, as this is where any variations from normal mediation rules will be explained. When the mediator finishes, you will normally have a chance to ask any questions.

1. Sample Opening Statement

The opening statement below is adapted from those typically delivered by a mediator at a community mediation center. But no matter what the mediation setting, this is essentially the statement you will hear. In this case example, the parties are neighbors who have come voluntarily to a community mediation center to try to resolve a dispute involving noise, among other problems. Neither has brought an attorney. The mediator is a volunteer.

Introduces Self: "Good morning, my name is Tom Watson. I'm the mediator who has been assigned to your case." (Or, if you selected the mediator, "I'm pleased you selected me as the mediator to hear this case.")

Introduces Parties: "Before we go any farther, I want to make sure I have everyone's correct name and address. On my left is Elizabeth Ferraro of 112 Bristol Ave. And on my right is Mr. Richard Rafferty, 644 Eastbrooke Drive. Mr. Rafferty, the witness you have brought with you is Mr. Robert Medden of 206 Savannah Boulevard."

Commends Parties: "I would like to start by commending each of you for choosing mediation as a way to resolve your dispute. By doing so, you have given yourselves the opportunity to solve this problem in a cooperative, rather than an adversarial, way and with greater flexibility, speed and privacy than you would likely have in court."

States Goal: "This community mediation center is a nonprofit organization set up to help people in our town resolve their disputes." (Or, if you are using a private dispute resolution company, "Reliable Mediation, Inc., is a private company that provides quality dispute resolution services to the business community.") "Our goal is to help you find a solution to your problem that will be fair to both of you and workable in the long run. Our experience is that disputants who work in good faith during the mediation have a very high success rate in reaching an agreement and sticking to it. My job is to help you do this."

Explains Mediator's Role: "As a mediator, I have been trained and certified by this center to handle disputes such as yours. I have no authority to render a decision or to recommend one to a judge. I can't send anyone to jail or impose any fines. My only job is to help you find your own solution to this dispute.

"I am completely neutral. I don't know either of you, and I know very little about your dispute except its general nature as you described it on your submission forms. (Rules of this community mediation center did not allow disputants to submit a Pre-Mediation Memorandum. If they had, the mediator would know more about the case and the positions of the parties and refer at this point to the Memos and the fact that he had read them. See Chapter 6, Section E.)

No Time Pressure: "One of the advantages of mediation is that we are under no time pressure. This room is available to us for as long as we want it, and I am prepared to stay here as long as our effort appears to be productive. If, as we go along, you want to take a break, just let me know and we'll do that." (Some mediating programs, particularly those run by court systems, do impose time limits. See Chapter 1, Section O.)

Explains Procedure: "We'll begin today by having each of you make an opening statement to tell us what this dispute is all about from your point of view.

"Ms. Ferraro, you were the one who initiated mediation, so you will go first, and then Mr. Rafferty will have his turn. While one of you is speaking, the other one will absolutely not be allowed to interrupt. If you need to make notes to remind yourself of comments you want to make later, there are pads and pencils on the table for you to use.

"While each of you is speaking, you may notice me taking notes. If I write something, it doesn't mean I agree or disagree with what has been said. I am taking notes just to help keep track of the facts of the case."

Use of Evidence: "While you are speaking, you can show us anything in the way of evidence you have brought with you, such as bills, letters, photographs or whatever. The purpose of evidence is to help us understand your side of this dispute. The technical rules of evidence followed in court are not followed here, so I am willing to look at anything you want to show me. The other person will be able to look at it, too."

Discussion Stage: "After the opening statements, we will begin to discuss the issues in dispute, and hear from any witnesses you have brought today. During this discussion phase, you can each say whatever you like, but I will not allow any uncivil language or swearing."

Caucusing: "At some point, I may want to talk to each of you separately in what is called a caucus. If that happens, I will ask one of you to leave the room while I speak with the other. Everything you tell me in a caucus I will keep confidential and not tell the other side, unless you give me specific permission to do so. If I spend longer in caucus with one of you than the other, it doesn't mean I am partial to one side, it just means it may be taking me a little longer to understand all the facts and the options available."

Confidentiality: "You have both signed a pledge to keep everything said and revealed in this session confidential." (This pledge would appear in the "Agreement to Mediate" both parties signed before the mediation. See Chapter 6, Section A.) "I have taken a similar pledge to keep secret everything you say or show me. In fact, when this mediation is over, I will even throw away my notes." (At community mediation centers it is a common practice for mediators to destroy their notes after a case concludes. Private mediators handling business disputes would more often keep their notes in case the parties wanted to come back into mediation to address related disputes.) "The mediation center considers this rule of confidentiality the most important rule of mediation and expects each of you to uphold it strictly."

Consent Agreement: "As I said, our goal today is to find a solution to your dispute that both of you feel is fair and workable in the long run. If we can find such a solution, I will help you write it up in the form of what we call a 'Consent Agreement.'" (See Chapter 8, Writing an Agreement That Works.) "This will be an official document you both will sign and we will have notarized. It will be a binding contract and may be legally enforceable in court." (In disputes involving large sums of money, property or legal rights, the parties will often want a lawyer or business advisor to review an agreement before signing. (See Chapter 8, Section E.) Especially in this situation, the agreement reached in mediation may not be the final, detailed agreement between the parties, but just provide a solid basis for further negotiations.)

Questions? "Now, before we begin with your opening statements, are there any questions? If not, then Ms. Ferraro, let's begin with you. Please tell us what this case is all about."

2. UNDERSTANDING THE MEDIATOR'S STRATEGY

Besides explaining the mediation process, your mediator will use his Opening Statement to help achieve his first and perhaps most important goal: to gain control of the mediation.

The mediator has temporary control just by virtue of making his opening statement, but that is not the same as earning the trust of both you and the other party. He knows his temporary control can be lost if it is not reinforced. For example, if one party calls the other a rotten liar, things can quickly get out of hand; the other person might leave, or take a punch at the other, or more likely, make the same type of accusation, with the result that a shouting match ensues and nothing is accomplished.

Only by gaining and keeping control can the mediator keep the mediation on track and moving forward. So, from the moment he meets you, everything your mediator says and does is designed with this goal in mind. He did it when he met you in the waiting room, by presenting a neat appearance and speaking politely and respectfully. And he will try to do it during his opening statement, by speaking confidently, answering your questions fully and otherwise demonstrating that he is intelligent, knowledgeable and unbiased—in short, someone in whom you can and should place your trust.

3. WEAPONS CHECK

At some community mediation centers (but not at private mediation companies handling business disputes), particularly those that handle disputes involving assault and harassment, the mediator may follow his opening statement with a "weapons check." (If the mediation is held in a courthouse or other public facility, weapons checks may have been done when the parties entered the building.) He will ask if any of the parties are carrying weapons and, if they are, that they be removed from the room and checked with the receptionist or other staff member. The parties may then be required to sign a statement affirming they are unarmed. Whether or not this procedure is effective is open to debate.

D. Stage Two: The Disputants' Opening Statements

After the mediator's Opening Statement, it will be time for the disputants themselves to speak. Each will have a turn to make an opening statement. Typically, the party who initiated the mediation speaks first.

I. HOW TO MAKE YOUR OPENING STATEMENT

This is your chance, finally and without interruption, to tell the other party and the mediator your view of the dispute. Consider how delicious this opportunity is: even if you have previously tried and failed to negotiate a settlement, you probably never had the chance to tell your side of the story without being interrupted. Even if you had taken your case to court instead of mediation, chances are that you would be constrained by court rules to limit your testimony to the narrow legal issues in dispute, and even so would probably be interrupted by objections from opposing counsel.

But now in mediation, the floor is yours. No one will stop you (unless you just ramble on too long). No one will object or try to twist your words. If the other party does try to say something, the mediator will quickly remind him to let you make your presentation without interruption.

(If witnesses are in attendance, some mediators may ask them to leave the room during the disputants' opening statements so their views are not influenced by what the disputants say. They will be asked to return later to speak.)

Here are some guidelines for making your opening statement.

A. SPEAK TO THE MEDIATOR

Stay seated, use a conversational tone and speak directly to the mediator. Unless the mediator invites you to use first names, address the mediator and the other parties as Mr. or Ms. (Later, if the mediation is going well, you may begin speaking directly to the other party, and using a first name.) Addressing your remarks to the mediator has at least two benefits: it helps you keep calm by avoiding having to look directly at the other party and also helps establish a rapport between you and the mediator. Of course, if the other party is a member of your family or a former close friend, if you are able to do so you should look at them as you speak.

B. START FROM THE END, NOT THE BEGINNING, OF YOUR STORY

Your task in your opening statement is to tell the mediator and the other side what the dispute looks like from your point of view and how it has affected you. The best and simplest way to do this is to start with the end of the story—that is, to explain the event that triggered the mediation. If this was a loud party or a dog bite or a fender bender, start with that, so the mediator has the crucial information as to what the dispute is about. Then go back and fill in important preliminary facts that help the mediator understand how your dispute developed.

Before I demonstrate how to make an opening statement, here is a brief summary of three cases we will follow through this chapter in an effort to make what follows seem as real as possible:

Case 1—The Noisy Neighbor. This is a neighbor dispute involving Ms. Ferraro, who is complaining of noise from late evening pool parties hosted by her backyard neighbor, Mr. Rafferty. Ms. Ferraro, who initiated the mediation, will make her opening statement first.

Case 2—The Missing Security Deposit. Ms. Sherman leased space in her office park to United Tea Bags, Inc., a company that sells tea wholesale to local restaurants. The company has moved out of the space but Ms. Sherman has refused to return a security deposit because of damage she claims the company's employees did to the offices before they left. Mr. Nehru, the owner of United Tea Bags, will make the first opening statement.

Case 3—Business Owners Fall Out. The third dispute concerns ownership of a small business. Mike Woo and Ted McDonald are co-owners of Big Slice Pizza, Inc., a restaurant. They have had a falling out over various issues of running the business, including pricing and employee relations. Each owns half the company. They have come to mediation either to work out their differences or to decide who will buy the other out. Mike will make his opening statement first. (This same case example was used earlier to illustrate how one disputant can propose mediation to the other. See Chapter 4, Section D2.)

OPENING STATEMENT FOR NEIGHBOR DISPUTE: *Ms. Ferraro: [Starts with the end of her story "I'm here today because my backyard neighbor, Mr. Rafferty, keeps me up at night with noise from his parties. [Now tells her story chronologically.] The trouble began in July of 1996. Before then, the neighborhood was very quiet. I could sleep with the windows open and never be disturbed by noise. But that summer is when I first started being woken up at night by noise from parties that Mr. Rafferty had at his backyard pool. Our houses back up to each other."*

OPENING STATEMENT FOR LEASE DISPUTE: *Mr. Nehru: [Starts with the end of his story.] "I'm here because my company, United Tea Bags, Inc., rented space from Ms. Sherman. After we vacated the building last month, she didn't return our security deposit, which, according to our written agreement, was refundable. [Now tells story chronologically.] Our company represents several nationally-known tea manufacturers and sells tea bags by the case to restaurants, hotels and some convenience stores. A couple of years ago we were looking for local office space and met Jane Sherman who had space to rent in the Four Corners Office Park."*

OPENING STATEMENT FOR BUSINESS OWNERSHIP DISPUTE:
Mike Woo: [Starts with the end of his story.] "We're here today to resolve—one way or the other—a problem between Ted McDonald and me that has been

growing for nearly three years. We've either got to figure out how to run our restaurant together, or one of us has to buy out the other. [Now tells story chronologically.] I started Big Slice Pizza by myself in January of 1993. We were doing okay, and then my brother-in-law introduced me to Ted McDonald, who was looking for a new business to get involved in. We didn't know each other at all, but he seemed capable and was really eager, and frankly, I was a little overwhelmed to be starting up this business on my own. So I sold him 25% and later another 25% of the stock, so that we owned the business 50-50. That's when our troubles began."

C. USE DATES CAREFULLY

As you tell your story, be prepared to explain the dates when important events happened as accurately as possible. This will help the mediator place everything that happened in correct historical order. (If you submitted a Pre-Mediation Memorandum, you have already begun this process.)

NEIGHBOR DISPUTE: *Ms. Ferraro: "The first time I was woken up by noise from a pool party was one night around the middle of July 1996 at about 2 a.m. I remember the incident because the next morning I had to be up at 6 a.m. for an early flight to Chicago for business."*

Or, looking again at the lease dispute:

LEASE DISPUTE: *Mr. Nehru: "We signed a lease for 1,800 square feet of office space in Ms. Sherman's building to begin on January 1, 1994, and run for two years, until December 31, 1996. We left the premises on schedule the morning of December 31st by 5:00 p.m."*

Mike's recollection of his problems with Ted in the pizza business are keyed to an important date:

BUSINESS OWNERSHIP DISPUTE: *Mike: "I signed over 50% of the stock to Ted around October 12, 1993—I remember the date because it was right around Columbus Day and we had a big special on deep-dish Sicilian-style pizza. The next night was when we had our first big argument in front of the employees."*

Showing the mediator you can be reasonably accurate with dates is also a good way of demonstrating to the mediator and the other side that you will be reliable when relating other information, too. Later on, this can be a big help in arriving at a settlement, since the other party is likely to be more forthcoming if she believes you are trustworthy enough to do what you promise.

D. DISPLAY EVIDENCE AS YOU TELL YOUR STORY

To help illustrate and support your point of view as you tell your story to the mediator, you may want to present photographs, receipts, medical reports and other evidence. (See Chapter 6, Section D.) A display of compelling evidence may also prompt the other side to change his position, or will at least show him you have the evidence necessary to take your case to court or arbitration if a settlement isn't arrived at in mediation.

But it's important to realize that, unlike in court, where evidence is used to prove the truth of one's claim and must be qualified under highly technical rules, in mediation, almost any evidence can be presented, but is meant only to be explanatory or persuasive. As a result, you can be much more playful and inventive with the things you choose to bring as evidence.

THINK TWICE BEFORE PRESENTING EVIDENCE LIKELY TO ANGER OR EMBARRASS THE OTHER PARTY. Since your goal is to solve the problem, not win a court case, it's counterproductive to present evidence likely to harden the other party's position, making it less likely he will be willing to settle. For example, in the neighbor dispute, Ms. Ferraro, the neighbor complaining of loud pool parties, might have found bits of roll-your-own cigarette paper that wafted onto her lawn. She may believe this is evidence that her neighbor and his guests have been using marijuana, but it would be a mistake to introduce this at the mediation. It is not relevant to the noise dispute, and if she accuses her neighbor of drug use he is likely to take offense (particularly if it were not true), possibly ruining any chance she had for working out a settlement.

Display your evidence as it comes up in your story, rather than all at once at the beginning or at the end. For example:

NEIGHBOR DISPUTE: *Ms. Ferraro: "I tape-recorded what I often hear from my bedroom window when Mr. Rafferty has one of his loud, work-night parties. The recording on this cassette I brought today was made from a tape-recorder placed on the ledge of my bedroom window at 1:30 a.m. on a weekday morning in July. I am playing it at the same loudness that I hear when trying to get to sleep. You can clearly make out the shouting and the loud music." [With permission of mediator, she now plays a segment from the tape.]*

LEASE DISPUTE: *Mr. Nehru: "Here's a copy of my company's lease with Ms. Sherman, and here's a copy of my letter to her written two months after we vacated the building, requesting the prompt return of the security deposit."*

BUSINESS OWNERSHIP DISPUTE: *Mike: "We've been unable to keep any chief cook employed in our restaurant for more than six months at a time because they always end up having problems with Ted. Here are resignation letters from two of them where they clearly state they are leaving because they find it too difficult to work with him" [displays resignation letters].*

The mediator will look at any documents and other evidence you present and then pass them to the other side to view. But since the floor is still yours, the other party will usually not be allowed to comment or ask questions at this time. Similarly, in order not to disturb your presentation, the mediator will likely hold major questions or comments about your evidence until later.

E. DO NOT CONCLUDE YOUR OPENING STATEMENT WITH A DEMAND

When you have finished explaining your version of the dispute, stop talking. Resist the urge to conclude with a strong demand, such as, "I insist Mr. Rafferty not have any guests in his backyard after 10 p.m. or I will be calling the police each time."

Not only does making a demand or proposing a solution at this stage risk needlessly annoying the other party, it also locks you into a settlement demand you may wish to change later. (See Chapter 6, Section B5.) Better to first find out what the other side wants and what he is willing to give up. For example, you may learn during the other side's opening statement that you could have asked for more and gotten it in exchange for something you would not mind giving up. Only after you have a good idea of the other party's position does it make sense to present your no more compromise line or anything close to it.

IF YOUR MEDIATOR HAS AUTHORITY TO RECOMMEND TO A JUDGE HOW YOUR CASE SHOULD BE DECIDED. Obviously, if the mediator really has the power to influence how your dispute is decided, you will want not only to impress him or her as a reasonable person but also to persuade him or her that your point of view is correct. Starting with your opening statement, you will want to direct your persuasive efforts simultaneously at the other party—in hopes that you can reach a favorable settlement—and at the mediator as a potential decision-maker. (See Chapter 6, Section C2.)

F. WHAT TO DO IF YOUR LAWYER IS PRESENT

As discussed in Chapter 6, Section G, unless a case involves complicated legal issues, or lots of money, it's usually not a good idea to bring a lawyer to mediation. If you do decide to bring a lawyer to your mediation, you will probably want to do most of the talking yourself and have the lawyer advise you about the legal implications of various proposed settlement terms. Or, if your case raises complicated legal issues, you could have the lawyer share the opening statement with you. You would start by stating the facts of the dispute; then, the lawyer could present the legal theory on which you base your position. Finally, you could explain how the dispute has affected you personally.

HOW TO RELATE TO YOUR MEDIATOR

In theory, what your mediator thinks of you as a person should not affect how he does his job. The mediator is, after all, acting as a skilled intermediary, not a judge. Personal likes or dislikes should not affect the performance of his duties. But mediators, like the rest of us, may sometimes be influenced in their work by their personal impressions of the disputants. If the mediator comes to see one side as more reasonable and reliable than the other, she may try to move the other party's position in that direction. Another way of saying this is that, given a choice, you want the position you present to be viewed by the mediator as being the more reasonable of the two.

As one mediator put it, "If I know a party is himself making a good-faith effort to find a solution, I'm motivated to use my powers of persuasion [with the other side] to help that party. But if a party isn't being straight with me and I have to be skeptical about what he's saying, then as a human being my heart may not be in it to help move [the other side]."

The best way to impress on the mediator that you are rational, flexible, and forward thinking is to show that you are reliable with the facts—particularly if the other side is given to exaggerate or omit things. It will also help if you demonstrate that you understand there are two sides to the dispute, are focused on the future and open to fair settlement. "As far as I'm concerned," you might say, "our respective versions of history aren't really important. I'm here to talk solutions, and am open to any ideas that might work."

G. UNDERSTANDING WHAT YOUR MEDIATOR IS DOING

While you are making your opening statement, you may have the feeling that no one outside your family and closest friends has ever listened to you quite as attentively as your mediator. If so, the mediator is doing a good job demonstrating that she cares about both the facts of your problem and your emotional reaction to it. This is called "empathic listening," an important skill your mediator uses to help build your trust in her and thus help her maintain control of the mediation.

The skilled mediator listens not only to what you are saying, but pays attention to the subtle signs that communicate how you are feeling. As part of doing this, she will normally turn towards you, listen with full attention, but not interrupt. In short, with her eyes, facial expression and other body language, she lets you know she cares about you and your problem, and that you are being heard.

DON'T DISMISS YOUR MEDIATOR AS A PHONY. Much as some people are put off by therapists, occasionally people have a negative reaction to a mediator's effort to convey her interest and concern. Here is my advice: Give the process a chance. Over several decades, mediators have collaborated to develop a style that works. Although occasionally a mediator will come across as being just a little too sincere, it's my experience that the great majority do have an honest desire to help people solve problems.

Although the mediator's primary job is to listen while you speak, she should also be ready to help you tell your story. For example, if like many disputants under the pressure of making a statement, you stumble on one or more details of your story or mix up names or dates, the mediator should ask the questions necessary to get the whole picture. One way to do this is to summarize what you have covered, thus giving you a chance to hear what you have said and make any needed corrections or additional points.

Some of the devices the mediator may use to make sure you have told your story completely include:

- *Helping questions:* These are "stage prompts" the mediator may use to help you get the facts straight. For example, "Excuse me, Ms. Ferraro, let me be sure I understand. Did that event happen in August, before you called the police?"

- *Open-ended questions:* The mediator may interrupt to ask a neutral, open-ended question designed to remind you of a part of your story that may prove important but that you may have forgotten to tell. For example, "Ms. Ferraro, do you often need to get up for work very early in the morning?" These questions can also be used to probe for important underlying issues that neither party has remembered, or chosen, to discuss. For example, "Have you and Mr. Rafferty ever had any conversation that was not about the noise problem?" or, "Mr. Nehru, did you and Ms. Sherman ever talk about renewing your lease?"

- *Echoing and summarizing:* By repeating back to you in her own words what she has heard you say, the mediator both assures herself she has understood the facts of your story and gives you the chance to correct any misstatements you may have made. Example:

NEIGHBOR DISPUTE: *Mediator: "OK, Ms. Ferraro, let me see if I understand what you are telling us about your dispute with Mr. Rafferty. Since he opened his backyard pool last July, you have been disturbed from your sleep at least one night each week by loud noise from parties held at his home." [The mediator summarizes the major facts of Ms. Ferraro's story.]*

Ms. Ferraro: "Yes, that's the situation."

2. WHAT YOU SHOULD DO: THE OTHER SIDE'S OPENING STATEMENT

Along with the mediator, your primary task while the other party makes his opening statement is to listen carefully. If you do, you will often hear things about your dispute you did not know, such as a fact you weren't aware of or the other party's emotional reaction to your conduct. As you listen, think about whether you are being given any clue as to the type of settlement the other party might accept.

A. DO NOT INTERRUPT

Keeping quiet and calm may often not be easy, especially if the other party is prone to exaggeration or just plain lying. Perhaps it will be easier to refrain from interrupting if you remember two things. First, you're not in court, where the judge has the power to make a decision based on misinformation. Second, the mediator will have lots of experience dealing with people who exaggerate or lie. And the more outrageously the other party engages in this type of behavior, the faster the mediator is likely to figure it out and make the adjustments. Make a note of the statement that upsets you and raise it later if it still seems important.

B. LISTEN FOR "WANTS" VS. "NEEDS"

In the previous chapter on preparing for mediation, we noted that in determining your goals for mediation it is important to understand the difference between your "wants" and "needs" as well as the wants and needs of the other party. (See Chapter 6, Section B4.) Your wants are the positions you've staked out—for example, a demand for a sum of money, the right to live in a rental house or to get your old job back. Your needs are your underlying interests, such as emotional and economic security, respect and recognition, avoiding needless expense, aggravation or stress and maintaining important relationships. As we noted, people's needs are often different from, and easier to satisfy than, their wants.

When the other party makes his opening statement, try to differentiate between his wants and needs. For example, he may insist he wants to be president of the company; what he "needs," however, is power and recognition. Or, a bank officer may demand (want) that you pay a loan back immediately, but what the bank "needs" is to make a profit and protect its assets. Even if you agree to pay the loan back gradually, it can achieve this.

Obviously the point of trying to distinguish between wants and needs is simple. If you can see past the other side's stated "wants" and focus on his "needs," you may be able to think of alternative ways of satisfying him and ending your dispute in a mutually satisfactory way.

C. TRY TO UNCOVER BARGAINING CHIPS AND OPPORTUNITIES

By listening carefully to the other party's opening statement, you may also discover some bargaining chips you didn't know you had. He may, for example, refer to a problem or dispute separate from the one you are discussing. Your first reaction may be to get angry, because you are now faced with another "unfair" accusation. This would be a mistake. Far better to treat the new subject as an opportunity. For example, you may find that the new issue involves something you can easily eliminate or control, and therefore is a perfect trade for an issue you care more about. In short, you've picked up a bargaining chip that may be useful later in the mediation.

> **NEIGHBOR DISPUTE:** *Mr. Rafferty: "You know, I would like to feel I can enjoy my own yard without having neighbors rushing to call the cops the second things get a little loud. And if she's so concerned about being a good neighbor, why doesn't she keep her dog on a leash like she's supposed to, and out of everyone's trash?" [Possible bargaining chips for Ms. Ferraro include a promise not to call police without advance warning, and a promise to leash her dog, which obviously annoys Mr. Rafferty.]*

LEASE DISPUTE: Ms. Sherman: *"I have no interest in withholding a tenant's security deposit if I'm not entitled to it. It doesn't do me any good to have my former tenants running around this town bad-mouthing me."* [Here, a possible bargaining chip for Mr. Nehru might be to promise not to discuss the dispute with other business owners.]

BUSINESS OWNERSHIP DISPUTE: Ted: *"I thought when we got into this business I could help out my sister's husband by buying our imported cheese from him. But because of all the problems between Mike and me our business has been extremely uneven—do you know how embarrassing it is to continually place and then cancel cheese orders from my own brother-in-law? Instead of helping him out I've actually ended up costing him money!"* [As Ted reveals a sense of duty to help his brother-in-law, a possible bargaining chip for Mike in trying to get Ted to sell him back his stock in the restaurant would be an agreement to have the restaurant continue to buy imported cheese from Ted's brother-in-law.]

E. Stage Three: Discussion

After opening statements are concluded, your mediator will likely move the mediation into a discussion stage, during which you and the other party can start talking directly to each other. The take-off point for the discussion is often a comment one disputant wants to make on something the other said during the opening statement.

NEIGHBOR DISPUTE: Ms. Ferraro: *"Mr. Rafferty, I don't know where you got the idea that I have a reputation in the neighborhood for being a complainer, but I can tell you that's just not true. I'm a quiet person and mind my own business. Since I moved into my house five years ago, you are the first person who has given me any reason to complain about anything."*

There is a tendency for things to get out of hand during these early stages of discussion, and so the mediator will be working hard to stay in control. He may remind disputants about not using uncivil language and will discourage character attacks. Instead, he will try to help the disputants discuss in general terms the various issues in dispute.

Beginning at this stage and continuing through to the conclusion, your mediator will likely use one or more of the following common mediator techniques to control and advance the mediation. These include:

- *Investigation:* In searching for the facts behind the dispute, sometimes the mediator finds information the disputant did not want to give, or demonstrates potential holes in a disputant's point of view. For example, in a dispute over property rights, by examining a plat map brought by one of the disputants, the mediator may discover an error in measurement that casts new light on the position of the complaining party.

- *Demonstration of empathy:* By showing a willingness to hear and discuss matters of concern to the disputants, even if not technically relevant to the dispute, the mediator builds trust and helps engender a cooperative attitude. For example, in a case where the president of a subsidiary of a large conglomerate terminated an employee, the mediator listened patiently as both the president and the former employee complained about heavy-handed tactics used by the parent company.

- *Persuasion:* Slowly at the beginning, and then more intensively as the session progresses, the mediator may encourage disputants to embrace one or more possible terms for settlement. During private caucus, for example, the mediator may say, "John, I can't tell you what to do, but I really think this plan will satisfy many of the needs you've expressed." You are more likely to see the technique used by a mediator who has a more active ("evaluative") approach to mediation, as opposed to a mediator who sees her role as simply facilitating the parties' ability to arrive at their own agreement. (For more on mediator styles and philosophy, see Chapter 5, Section C3.)

- *Distraction:* The mediator may try to relieve tension during the session by use of humor, anecdotes, or just switching to other issues. "You know," the mediator might say, "this reminds me of a story...."

- *Invention:* If no workable options for settlement emerge from the disputants, then during the later stages of the session the mediator may propose some of his own creation. As with "persuasion," you are more likely to see this technique from a mediator who takes an active approach to her work.

1. How the Mediator Organizes the Issues

Once things are on a fairly even keel, your mediator may attempt to put the issues in some kind of order. A common practice is to tackle the easiest ones first in order to build up the disputants' confidence in the mediation process and in their own ability to address their dispute in a reasonable and productive way.

> **LEASE DISPUTE:** *Mediator: "Well, from everything you two have told me, it does seem clear we need to focus on this question of whether United Tea should be re-paid the $7,000 left as security with Ms. Sherman's real estate firm. Ms. Sherman says employees of United Tea damaged the reception area of the office, and therefore some or all of the deposit should be used for cleaning and repairs. Before we talk about that, however, let's see if you both can agree about the condition in which United Tea left the other rooms in the space it rented."*

Somewhat paradoxically, this is a time for both narrowing and broadening the issues in dispute. On the one hand, your mediator will try to narrow the number of issues in dispute. For example, she may probe to see if any complaints discussed in the opening statements can be dismissed because they are no longer relevant or were based on misinformation. (If so, it will be easier now to focus on the other issues.) On the other hand, the mediator will probe to see if any of the issues raised need to be broadened to include underlying issues—such as hidden interpersonal conflicts—not disclosed by the parties.

2. How the Mediator Looks for Hidden Issues

Often, disputants do not reveal to the mediator an important issue in their dispute, either because they do not want to or because they honestly do not recognize it. In disputes between business partners, for example, it is often easier for the parties to focus on "nuts and bolts" business matters like sales, profits and control of decision-making than it is to examine underlying personal issues such as personal habits and styles, career goals, personal financial needs, self-image, recognition outside the company, pride or the fact that they honestly can't stand their partner. By gentle questioning and careful listening, a skilled mediator can often find clues to underlying issues even when the parties will not or cannot raise them. For example, in one dispute between two co-authors of an Italian cookbook over who owned several key recipes, it didn't take long for the mediator to figure out that one side needed money and the other side had money. Even though the parties were convinced they were arguing about the principal of who developed the secret recipe for killer garlic bread, it turned out that a little cash moving from one to the other made the problem disappear. In neighborhood disputes, particularly, there are often hidden issues. For example, in our neighborhood case, if Mr. Rafferty (who hosts the pool parties) hadn't mentioned the concern he has with Ms. Ferraro's unleashed dog in his opening statement, the problem nevertheless might have been festering in the background, waiting for a skilled mediator to discover through active listening—Mediator: "Is there anything else you want to say?" "Tell me about the rest of your relationship as neighbors"—and then help the disputants arrive at a settlement.

3. YOUR CHANCE TO QUESTION THE OTHER SIDE

While the other party tells his version of the dispute in his opening statement, you will probably feel he has failed to answer some questions that have been troubling you. Although as a general rule in mediation, your strategy should be to use your opportunity to tell the story from your point of view and not worry too much about the other side's "misstatements," you may have important questions. If so, this is the time to ask them.

Some mediators may skip the question-asking stage. When both opening statements are complete, most mediators will ask if either party has questions or wants to clarify any point. But because some mediators may skip this "Discussion" stage, be prepared to speak up if you want to ask questions.

NEIGHBOR DISPUTE: *Ms. Ferraro: "There are a couple of things I don't understand, Mr. Rafferty—when I called your home to complain about the noise, why didn't you show me the courtesy of taking the call yourself and talking with me about the problem of a few out-of-control guests? Instead, you let one of your guests handle it. If you didn't want me to call the police, I don't see why you did this*

"Also, what kind of schedule do you generally keep at your house? I'm not sure why you use the pool so often after 10 p.m. on week nights. I'm just curious about this."

Finally, listen carefully to the other party. Just as you did during his opening statement, try to discern from the discussion what his real needs are and what he is seeking from mediation. (See Chapter 6, Section B4.)

FINDING THE REAL ISSUES

Two equal partners in an advertising agency were at an impasse over how to run their business. Their immediate problem was they often argued about daily business details, even though each recognized intellectually that the other added considerable value to the business. They came to mediation seeking a plan to reorganize the business so they could both keep working in the company, but with less strife. After opening statements, the mediator invited the parties to begin a joint discussion. She listened carefully to see what kinds of questions each partner might raise. Amidst comments back and forth about problems of day-to-day operations, one of the partners asked, "If we're going to restructure the company, I want to be able to give some of my stock to my kids."

To the mediator, this was an interesting comment; the partners were talking about day-to-day operations and then one of them out of the blue talks about passing on stock to his children. Could it be that one was more interested in being an investor and stockholder and the other more interested in actually managing the business? As it turned out, this was exactly the situation. After several lengthy mediation sessions, the one partner emerged as the firms' new Chief Executive Officer responsible for day-to-day operations, and the other took the roles of secretary-treasurer and part-time paid creative consultant working three days per week.

4. CALLING WITNESSES

As we noted earlier, in most mediations there is no need for witnesses. The facts may be in dispute, but proving them is not nearly as important in mediation as it is in court. Again, remember that your goal is to find a solution. However, there are some situations where a witness's attendance will be helpful, such as when the other party denies crucial facts and the mediation isn't likely to make progress until they are established. For example, you may need to establish the cause of an electrical fire in your home (witness: consulting electrician) or the seriousness of injuries you received in an automobile accident (witness: physician). Or, as in our Neighbor Dispute, a friend or neighbor of one of the parties may have a useful perspective to share. However, as noted in Chapter 6, Section G2, you do not always need to bring a "live" witness; in some instances a letter, memo or report from the person will do the job. If you have any of these documents, you should present them as you tell your story in your opening statement.

If witnesses are present at your mediation, the mediator will likely ask to hear from them early in the Discussion Stage. Most likely, the mediator asked the witnesses to wait outside the room during opening statements. He will now call them back in and, in the presence of both parties, invite them to tell what they know about the dispute. As the disputants were allowed to make their opening statements without interruption, so the witnesses are given a chance to say what they came to say:

NEIGHBOR DISPUTE: *Mr. Rafferty's Witness: "I was at the party in July where Mr. Rafferty's neighbor says she called to complain about the noise and that people were rude to her. But you should have heard how nasty she was when she called and some of the language she used. I'm not going to repeat it here. If she'd asked us nicely to turn down the music we would have. But when someone starts off by calling you a bleep, well, forget it. The point is that most of the folks at the party— we all work together—are not the kind of people who would purposely disturb someone. She's got the wrong idea about us."*

If you have any questions of the witnesses, you can ask them directly. The mediator may ask a few questions, too. After that, the mediator will dismiss the witnesses and probably tell them they can go home. Witnesses in mediation are seldom recalled because the rest of the session focuses exclusively on the disputants and possible solutions to their problem.

F. Stage Four: The Caucus

At this point in the session, your mediator will likely take advantage of one of mediation's most distinctive features: the private caucus.

LEASE DISPUTE: *Mediator: "I would like to meet now with Mr. Nehru for a private caucus. Ms. Sherman, would you mind stepping into the waiting room, and I'll come and get you when we're done?" [Ms. Sherman leaves the room.]*

1. PURPOSE AND PROCEDURE

The caucus is a private meeting between you and the mediator, during which the mediator can talk with you more informally and candidly than he could in the presence of the other side. It is often considered "the guts" of the mediation process, since it's where most of the business of working out a settlement usually gets done. During her caucus with each side, the mediator may discuss the strengths and weaknesses of your position and the other party's position, and float new ideas for settlement. The mediator may caucus with each of the parties just once, or several times back and forth.

As discussed earlier, most mediators and mediation services use caucuses, but there are notable exceptions. These are principally in divorce and some community mediations, on the theory that the disputants are likely to be so distrustful of each other that it is better to keep them together so they always know what each is saying to the mediator. (See Chapter 11, Divorce Mediation.) If caucuses will be used in your mediation, this will probably be noted in the mediation rules you receive prior to the mediation.

To begin caucusing, the mediator will ask one party to leave the room and wait in the reception area while he or she meets alone with the other party. Or, the mediator may ask one party to move into a second conference room, and the mediator will shuttle back and forth from one room to the other, meeting separately with each side. If an extra conference room is available, the latter approach is often more convenient because the parties don't have to keep moving in and out of one room.

During caucus, your mediator may assume a more relaxed posture, taking off his jacket and rolling up his shirt sleeves. And he may step over the line of strict impartiality just a little, to tell you he genuinely sympathizes with your predicament and hopes a solution can be found. By openly empathizing with the parties, the mediator continues to win their trust and solidify his control over the mediation.

> **NEIGHBOR DISPUTE:** *Mediator to Ms. Ferraro: "Well, I can see you've been under tremendous stress because of this situation. I really hope we can find a positive way out of this for you so that you can get some sleep."*

2. CONFIDENTIALITY

Confidentiality of the caucus is important to the success of mediation, because otherwise you wouldn't feel free to confide in the mediator. The general rule is that the mediator may not repeat anything you say in caucus to the other side unless you expressly okay it. For example, if the mediator is using the caucus to try to help you craft a compromise offer, the background chat won't be communicated to the other side, but—with your permission—the offer will be. If the mediator has not made this policy clear in his opening statement or when he announces the first caucus, ask what the policy will be so you are clear about it before the caucus begins.

Typically, the mediator will caucus with each side several times during the course of mediation. In a relatively simple two-party mediation—for example, involving an auto accident or dispute between two business people—it would be typical for a mediator to caucus two or three times with each side during a half-day mediation. A mediation that lasts a full day may involve three to five caucuses with each side. But there is no rule on this. The frequency of caucusing depends entirely on the mediator's style and assessment of whether the caucusing process is moving the parties closer to settlement.

3. RESPONDING TO MEDIATOR'S QUESTIONS

Although the mediator may sympathize with your point of view during the caucus, it's also likely that he will challenge your attitudes and positions. He may also probe to find additional facts about your story in any effort to reveal your underlying interests, and through them, your no more compromise line. He may even point out some weaknesses or holes in your story in order to create some doubt in your mind and help you bring your expectations in line with reality. He will not, however, ridicule or find fault with your past behavior.

Another task the mediator will undertake is to translate what he thinks the other side is trying to tell you into language you can more easily understand. For example, if the other party spoke mostly in jargon or euphemisms, the mediator during caucus may tell you in plain words what he understands the person to be saying.

> **BUSINESS OWNERSHIP DISPUTE:** *Mediator, in caucus, to Ted: "Ted, I think what I've heard Mike say this morning is that he doesn't think it's possible for him to remain in business with you any longer, but he is willing to sell his share for a reasonable price or, in the alternative, buy yours."*

Finally, the mediator is almost sure to challenge you to think of new options for settlement that might satisfy both you and the other side. Often, people in disputes get stuck in their thinking and can only focus on a couple of possible courses of action. But a good mediator will push you to stretch your thinking in new directions to see if some new choices might emerge.

BUSINESS OWNERSHIP DISPUTE: *Mediator, in caucus, to Ted: "Just as an exercise, let's see how many different ways of dividing or breaking up this business we can think of. Can you help me come up with a list of ten different ways?"*

The following are among the questions a mediator is likely to ask you during caucus to help get you thinking both realistically and creatively:

- Being practical, how would you really like to see this dispute resolved?
- What will you do if you can't reach an agreement?
- How much time and money are you likely to spend in this dispute if it's not settled as part of this mediation and you end up in court?
- If you were in the other person's shoes, how would you feel?
- If you were in the other person's shoes, what sort of solution would you propose?
- What are some ways of settling this dispute that would be fair to you and to the other side?
- Can you think of a solution to which you and the other side might agree?
- How would it feel to walk away today with this whole matter settled?

Perhaps the most important questions the mediator may ask during caucus are those beginning with "What if…?"—in other words, posing to you the terms of a hypothetical settlement: "What if the other side did X, would you do Y?"

NEIGHBOR DISPUTE: *Mediator: "Ms. Ferraro, what if Mr. Rafferty agreed to turn off the stereo and radio around 10:00 o'clock and move all his parties indoors after 11:00? How would you react to that?"*

LEASE DISPUTE: *Mediator: "Mr. Nehru, what if Ms. Sherman were to give you a check today for half the amount of the security deposit. Would you be willing to walk away from this whole dispute and call it even?"*

To take full advantage of the caucus, do your best to respond openly and honestly to your mediator's questions. And if there is some issue about which you have not been able to be entirely truthful in the presence of the other side, tell your mediator the full story during caucus.

BUSINESS OWNERSHIP DISPUTE: *Ted to Mediator: "Dealing with people is something I've never been good at. It's possible that some of the employees just found me too aggressive or hard-nosed to work with, and I can accept that. I think if I got into another business of some kind, I would not want to be responsible for managing anyone. Maybe I should be looking at a profession or other situation where I won't need a lot of employees."*

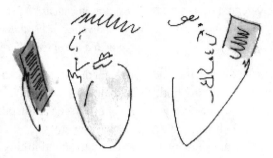

4. HOW THE MEDIATOR HELPS YOU RETHINK YOUR POSITION

To help you arrive at a solution to your dispute, your mediator has to get each party to change his or her position (or simply to see that their positions don't really conflict). One important way he will do this is to plant seeds of doubt about the correctness or wisdom of the positions both you and the other side expressed in your Opening Statements. His questions directed to you will be designed to make you wonder if you are being realistic about your case. Expect questions along these lines:

- Do you think someone who didn't know you would see you as being entirely without fault in this dispute?
- If this case went to trial, is it realistic to think a jury would find the other side 100% at fault?
- (To Ms. Ferraro in the neighbor dispute): "I know when you bought your house Mr. Rafferty was not living behind you, but when you moved in, did you know the house behind you had an outdoor pool fairly near your house?"
- (To Mr. Nehru in the lease dispute): "According to the strict wording of the lease you signed for this office space, it is the landlord, isn't it, who decides how much of the security deposit should be returned?"
- (To Mike in the business ownership dispute): "I know you feel Ted's involvement has prevented the pizza restaurant from being successful, but before you started the restaurant, did you ever run a business successfully on your own?"

5. How the Mediator Plays "Agent of Reality"

Your mediator may also play the "agent of reality." In this role, the mediator will point out the likely consequences of holding firm to your present position. Mediators usually do this by asking questions rather than making statements. Expect to hear questions from your mediator, such as:

- If the other side were to agree to your last proposal, how workable do you think that plan would be in the long run?
- How much will not reaching an agreement today cost you?
- (To Mr. Nehru in the lease dispute): "What happens when customers, job applicants and others go to your former office address and can't find you?"
- (To Ms. Ferraro in the neighbor dispute): "If Mr. Rafferty sold his house tomorrow, do you think the new owners might use their pool on warm evenings?"

One possible response to your mediator's efforts to give a reality check is to get angry. After all, the mediator is asking you questions you don't want to answer or giving you feedback you don't want to hear. A more positive response is to accept and take advantage of your mediator's role as "agent of reality." After all, the mediator has loads more experience in settling disputes than you do, and her feedback, whether in the form of questions or advice, is likely to be sensible.

One good approach is to come right out and ask your mediator for a reality check: "Am I on solid ground here? Is there some aspect of this problem I'm not seeing clearly?"

6. How the Mediator Creates Settlement Options

An important part of the mediator's job is to help you think of new ways to resolve your dispute. People caught up in a conflict often get stuck seeing it from only one perspective. Ask your mediator, "Are there possible ways of solving this mess that I'm not thinking of?"

Good mediators are skilled at creating new options. Here are some techniques your mediator may use:

a. Compromise. It's a simple and obvious approach, but if the mediator has won the trust of the both parties, she may be able to settle a dispute merely by encouraging each to move a little toward the middle.

> *Mediator to Ms. Ferraro: "Closing up his pool at 10 p.m. is a little early for Mr. Rafferty, and keeping it open on weeknights until midnight is clearly too late for you. Could we compromise and say on weeknights the pool will close at 11 p.m.?"*

b. Apology. The mediator will persuade one party to provide a verbal or written apology to the other for past conduct. This is most often effective in disputes involving an interpersonal relationship, particularly where there was a power imbalance between the parties, such as between a large corporation and an individual employee. It also can be effective in a dispute between neighbors.

> *Mediator to Mr. Rafferty: "Ms. Ferraro might be more willing to agree to a reasonable compromise if you would offer her a sincere apology for the some of the things your friends said to her when she called your house."*

c. Make an Exception. One party agrees to make an exception to its normal policy, with the understanding that it will not apply to other people who were not involved in the mediation, and that the terms of the settlement will be kept confidential. This can work well where one party is willing to bend the rules in order to get a settlement but does not want to face similar actions from other potential disputants. For example, a utility company facing a complaint from a homeowner over location of its poles and wires might be willing to move the poles to settle this case, as long as other homeowners are not told about it.

d. Go Beyond the Contract. In order to create a "win-win" solution for both sides, the parties agree to create additional benefits for each other—or "expand the pie"—by doing things that were never planned in their original contract. (See the sidebar "Expanding the Pie," for an example.)

This technique can also be applied to situations where there is no formal contract. In our Neighborhood Dispute case, for example, Mr. Rafferty might be able to "expand the pie" by occasionally inviting Ms. Ferraro and her boyfriend to use his pool.

e. Staged Agreement. This method, which involves reaching a comprehensive settlement by a series of small steps, can create a sense of security among parties who initially do not trust each other. For example, "Egypt will remove its troops from the west bank of the Suez Canal and Israel will remove its troops from the east bank; after both of those things happen, Egypt will pull back its armor from the Mediterranean coast off Sinai, and Israel will pull back its armor 20 miles from the same coast."

Or, to take an example closer to home: "Mr. Rafferty will begin immediately to close his pool each weekday by 11 p.m. If, for a period of 30 days starting today, Ms. Ferraro is not disturbed after 11 p.m. on weeknights by noise from Ms. Rafferty's pool, Ms. Ferraro will agree not to call police in the event she is again disturbed by noise, but instead will in the first instance call Mr. Rafferty directly to inform him of the problem."

"EXPANDING THE PIE"

A small metal binding company was hired by a large defense contractor to make parts for a new armored vehicle. The small company made the parts, but the big company rejected them, saying they did not conform to the contract. Executives of the small company thought the parts were just fine, and were angry. Not only had they spent a lot of money to make the parts, but now they were losing a major customer. Feeling cheated, the small company sued the big company for $6 million. After many months, the two firms agreed to mediate. A private dispute resolution company provided a mediator with a background in contract law and engineering.

At the mediation, the small company was represented by its president and its lawyer. The big company sent a vice-president, a lawyer and an engineer.

After several sessions over a two-week period, the two companies were just $200,000 away from a settlement. Then the mediator proposed a solution: the big company would give the small company a new contract to make a different type of part. If the parts were made correctly, the profit for the small company would be in excess of $200,000.

Executives of both firms wrote thank you notes to the mediator, who effectively had helped them "expand the pie."

f. Interim Agreement. The parties agree to try something for a few weeks or months and to meet again at a future date to evaluate the results. A divorcing couple, for example, who cannot agree on a visitation schedule for the non-custodial parent, may agree to try a plan for six months, and then meet again with the mediator to evaluate how it is working for each of them and their children.

> *Mediator to Mr. Rafferty: "I don't think Ms. Ferraro is ready yet to give up her right to call the police. She's been too disturbed too often. What we need is to re-build some trust between you. If we can agree that you will try to control the noise from your pool for, say, three weeks, and then we'll meet again to see how it went, that experience may allow us to move ahead to a permanent agreement. Would you be willing to try it?"*

g. Partial Settlement. The parties settle what they are able to now and leave the rest for later. Although similar to the interim agreement strategy, here the disputants make a partial settlement and decide to put the rest of their dispute "on hold" for a while. They agree that during the holding period they will not file lawsuits and will treat each other civilly. Later, they will meet with the mediator again to see if circumstances or their positions have changed in a way that might allow them to resolve the rest of the dispute.

> *Mediator to Ms. Ferraro and Mr. Rafferty: "I'm glad we've been able to work out today this matter of noise from Mr. Rafferty's pool. Unfortunately, the matter involving Ms. Ferraro's dog raises some issues that are going to take more time to resolve, and we have agreed to meet again in two weeks to discuss them further. In the meantime, Mr. Rafferty you have agreed not to call Animal Control if you find Ms. Ferraro's dog loose in your yard, and Ms. Ferraro, you have agreed to try to restrain your dog from wandering in the neighborhood as best you are able."*

7. LETTING THE MEDIATOR NEGOTIATE FOR YOU

Mediators are trained to help people settle disputes. When a settlement occurs, the mediator has succeeded. When no solution is arrived at, the mediator has failed. Understanding this bit of mediator psychology is extremely important, since it also means that you understand that, during your session, the mediator has a strong personal interest in getting a settlement. Take advantage of this by letting him negotiate for you.

Here's how it can work. Assume you are Mr. Nehru in our lease dispute. You want at least $6,000 of the $7,000 security back from Ms. Sherman, the landlord. During caucus, tell your mediator you want $6,000 and that's it. No ifs, ands or buts.

> **LEASE DISPUTE:** *Mr. Nehru to Mediator: "Look, I appreciate all your suggestions and will concede my people may have spilled some tea on the rug. Ms. Sherman can keep $1,000 for damages but I want $6,000 back and I'm not leaving here with less. And I hope you will clearly tell her that!"*

Would you really not leave the mediation with less than $6,000? Maybe yes, maybe no. For the moment, you can keep that to yourself. But now, $6,000 is the message you want to send to the other side, and if you're wise, you'll let the mediator carry it for you. Since you know the mediator wants badly to settle your case, it follows that if she is convinced your position is both reasonable and firm, then she will also see that to get a settlement, she will have to persuade the other side to pay you $6,000—or something very close to it.

In short, when the mediator next caucuses with the landlord, you want her to express your demand in clear and unequivocal terms. Here is how it might go:

> **LEASE DISPUTE:** *Mediator to Ms. Sherman: "Well, I've talked with Mr. Nehru and I'm glad to say we've got some movement on the damage issue. Although he's not conceding liability, he is willing to pay up to $1,000 for damages; is that something you can live with?"*

You can also use your mediator to "float trial settlement balloons" by posing your own "What if…" questions. For example, in a dispute between two neighboring business people over one company's "unsightly new sign," you might say to the mediator, "What if I were to repaint the sign in more muted colors?" Earlier in the mediation, when the other side was present, you may not have wanted to propose a settlement idea like this for fear of looking weak or too eager to settle, but during caucus you can try the idea out on the mediator. If the mediator thinks it holds promise, chances are he will be willing to present it to the other side as if it were his idea and not yours.

LEASE DISPUTE: *Mr. Nehru to Mediator: "When you meet with Ms. Sherman again, ask her what she'd think of a package deal like this: She keeps the full damage deposit of $3,500, returns to me the $3,500 security, my people pick up the samples she's got in storage, and she agrees to post our company's new address in her office lobby for the next six months. Don't say directly that I'm proposing this, but just kind of float the idea and see what her reaction is."*

In this way, Mr. Nehru, has just proposed a comprehensive settlement package to Ms. Sherman, but Ms. Sherman may choose to believe it was the mediator's suggestion, not Mr. Nehru's idea. Moreover, the proposal will be presented to her by the mediator—whom she has come to trust, respect and regard as impartial—thus increasing the chances she will give it favorable consideration.

G. Stage Five: More Joint Negotiations

At any point during the caucus process, your mediator may conclude that it is likely to be more productive to bring the parties back into one room for another round of discussions with everyone present.

I. PURPOSES AND PROCEDURES FOR JOINT NEGOTIATIONS

If your mediation is making progress, it should begin to show now. After the honest exchanges with the mediator during caucuses, disputants by this stage should be focused on a narrower range of forward-looking issues. As you and the other party search for a workable settlement, your relationship will usually begin to change. For example, your negotiation styles typically will have become less competitive and more collaborative.

In addition, the parties' perceptions of each other are typically more realistic. Mediator Anne Richan, in her article "Developing and Funding Community Dispute Settlement Programs," (*Mediation Quarterly,* No. 5, 1984), has compared the final stages of a successful mediation to "watching a wall come down brick by brick, as the disputants confront each other with all the things that have been bothering them and discover that the other is not an inhuman tormentor." Indeed, mediators often notice at this stage that disputants start using each other's first names.

If you and the other side are able to conduct your own negotiations, the mediator at this point may be quiet and just follow the conversation, adding a suggestion or word of caution as necessary. If not, he may be an active orchestrator of your negotiations, proposing new ideas for settlement and using information he learned in caucus to cue you when changes in bargaining positions might be helpful. If needed, he may call another round of caucuses, or perhaps caucus with just one of you again. All the while, the mediator will be listening carefully to be sure that:

1. The negotiations stay focused on the real issues in dispute.

LEASE DISPUTE: *Mediator to Mr. Nehru and Ms. Sherman: "The question you're discussing—how efficient the Postal Service is at forwarding business mail—is interesting, but not within our ability to influence. Let's stay focused on the things we can do something about."*

2. The parties are willing to confront any new issues that have arisen during the mediation that are sufficiently important so that they need to be addressed before a settlement can be reached.

NEIGHBOR DISPUTE: *Mediator to Mr. Rafferty: "This fence we've been talking about that separates your backyard from Ms. Ferraro's yard—did you just mention something about it protruding onto your property? Is that an issue we need to look at today?"*

3. The negotiations do not head towards an unworkable settlement. This is a settlement that the mediator believes is pretty sure to fall apart later. A settlement would be unworkable, for example, if it would require a party to do something unlawful or something that is likely to be beyond his power to deliver. For instance, in a mediation between a company and a former employee, where the issue is wrongful termination, the company owner—overeager to resolve the dispute—might offer to find the former employee a new job at another firm. It's a nice offer, but probably unworkable. The company owner can try to find the person a new job, but except in unusual circumstances, she can't guarantee it. A good mediator would discourage the parties from making this agreement. A more sensible solution might be to try to find the employee a suitable new job, but to compensate her up to a certain dollar figure if the new job is not forthcoming.

2. WILL THE MEDIATOR BLOCK AN UNFAIR SETTLEMENT?

Some, but by no means all, mediators will intervene to discourage the parties from settling their dispute on terms that the mediator believes are clearly unfair to one side. In divorce mediation, particularly where one spouse appears to be overpowering the other psychologically or in terms of financial knowledge, many mediators will intervene against what they see as a highly one-sided settlement. (See Chapter 11, Sections C and E2C(vi).) Most mediators will also intervene against unfair settlements in disputes involving children. Indeed, in California, where the law requires divorcing parents to try to reach agreements about child custody and visitation through mediation, rules require such intervention. "If the mediator's professional opinion is that a proposed agreement of the parties does not promote the best interest of the child, the mediator should inform the parties of this opinion and its basis." (Uniform Standards of Practice for Court Connected Child Custody Mediation for the State of California, (c)(2).) In addition, under some circumstances, California mediators are required to tell a judge that a proposed agreement would be harmful to a child.

But in non-family disputes, particularly business disputes, most mediators do not see their role as protecting one side or the other. Therefore, you should not rely on the mediator to protect you from making a bad bargain. Or put more bluntly, it's up to you to protect yourself. As discussed in Chapter 8, Section E, in some situations, you may want to do this by having a lawyer or other adviser review any settlement agreement before you sign.

3. How the Mediator Can Help You Change Your Negotiating Position

Suppose now that something you learn during the mediation causes you to want to modify your position. You fear you will lose face if you announce a major change in front of the other side. A better approach is to use the mediator to help you communicate the change. For example, in our Neighbor Dispute case, Ms. Ferraro had been insisting all along that her neighbor, Mr. Rafferty, adhere to strict "quiet hours" as set down by the Town's noise code. But late in the mediation she realizes it may be to her advantage to be a little more flexible in order to strike a deal with Mr. Rafferty. For example, because she usually stays at her boyfriend's on weekends, she may be unworried about noise after the weekend noise curfew, but because she often has to get up early would love it if things could quiet down even earlier during the week.

NEIGHBOR DISPUTE: *Ms. Ferraro: "Well, the mediator has convinced me that the 'quiet hours' in the town's noise code that was written 80 years ago are a little unrealistic on Friday and Saturday evenings, so I'm not going to insist that you follow that law to the letter on weekends, but...."*

IT CAN MAKE SENSE TO MAKE THE MEDIATOR A SCAPEGOAT. Although it may seem unfair, it can actually work well to blame last-minute changes of position on the mediator. ("The mediator's really pushing me on this and I'm just going to let him have his way. . .") He can take it; it's part of the job. More positively, you can do as Ms. Ferraro just did and credit the change in your position to the persuasive powers of the mediator.

4. Consult by Phone With Outside Advisers, If Needed

As noted in Chapter 6, Preparing for Your Mediation, in some types of disputes it can be helpful to have a lawyer, law coach or other advisor on "stand-by" during your mediation to consult with by telephone as needed. If you do have an advisor on-call, it is at this point in the mediation that you may want to check in with him or her to advise you on some of the fine points under discussion. For example, in our Business Ownership dispute, Ted McDonald, who is considering accepting a cash buy-out offer for his stock from his partner, Mike Woo, may want to step out of the mediation to call his accountant and review the basics of this plan to see what the tax consequences might be.

Mike to Mediator: "I need to take a break at this point. You know, I didn't really expect us to be talking today about a cash buy-out of my stock, but since we are, before we go further I'd like to run the idea by my accountant. There may be more or less beneficial ways to structure it from a tax point of view. I think I can probably reach him at his office. Is there a phone available where I can make a private call?"

In addition, for disputes that involve lots of money or important legal rights, the parties should condition their agreement on a more thorough review of the legal, tax and business consequences by their respective lawyers and other business advisers. But for now, getting at least an initial opinion from his accountant will probably be enough to help Ted decide whether he should continue negotiating a possible cash buy-out of his stock. For more on having your agreement reviewed before signing, see Chapter 8, Section E.

H. Stage Six: Closure

The final stage of mediation occurs when an agreement is reached that resolves the dispute. In fact, there are several steps in this final process: first the mediator announces the agreement, then she reviews the terms with the parties, and then (sometimes) the parties sign the agreement or initial the draft of an agreement. By contrast, if an agreement is not reached, the mediator announces this fact and ends the session. (For useful things you can do if your dispute does not settle in mediation, see Chapter 9, If No Agreement is Reached: Options Available.)

1. MEDIATOR ANNOUNCES AGREEMENT

"Closure" in mediation occurs at the moment you and the other side say "yes" to a proposed agreement. Mediation sessions tend to speed up as this point nears. By now, disputants are speaking directly to each other and probably using first names. Everyone is intimately familiar with the issues and so a kind of shorthand language typically develops that helps move the discussion along quickly. The mediator is also more direct in proposing refinements to possible terms of settlement.

Your mediator will also be listening carefully to detect the first instance when a package of terms for settlement emerges from your negotiations. When this occurs, he will seize the moment by stopping the discussion and reviewing with the parties the tentative terms of settlement.

NEIGHBOR DISPUTE: *Mediator: "Ms. Ferraro, Mr. Rafferty, if I'm hearing you both correctly, I think you have reached agreement on all the major issues. I've tried to write them down in a very rough format. Let me read them to you and you tell me if I have it straight:*

"On the noise issue, Mr. Rafferty is willing to turn off any amplified sound, including stereos and radios, in his backyard by 10 p.m. on weeknights and by midnight on weekends, and will encourage his guests not to use the pool after 10:45 on weeknights and midnight on weekends. In the rare event this isn't humanly possible, he will insist that they conduct themselves quietly.

"Ms. Ferraro, you will agree to call Mr. Rafferty directly, before calling the police, if you are disturbed again at night.

"On the dog issue, Mr. Rafferty would agree to call Ms. Ferraro directly, before calling police or animal control officers, if he thinks her dog has disturbed his trash barrels, soiled his lawn, or in any other way disturbed his property. For her part, Ms. Ferraro has agreed to buy Mr. Rafferty one dog-proof trash container; if replacement or additional containers are needed, Mr. Rafferty agrees to buy these at his own expense."

LEASE DISPUTE: *Mediator: "I'm pleased to tell you both that in caucus each of you has told me you will agree to the same settlement terms. These include: 1) Ms. Sherman will return to United Tea $4,000, keeping $3,000 to cover damage to the office space, 2) United Tea employees may have access to the building next Thursday and Friday to remove product samples left in storage, 3) Ms. Sherman will post, in the building's lobby, a prominent notice showing United Tea's new address and phone, for a period of six months, and 4) none of the parties nor their employees will discuss with anyone outside their respective companies the nature of this dispute or the terms of its settlement."*

BUSINESS OWNERSHIP DISPUTE: *Mediator: "Mike, Ted, I believe we have an agreement here. Ted, you have agreed to sell all of your stock in Big Slice Pizza, Inc., back to the company in exchange for an immediate lump-sum payment of $70,000, plus 8% of company gross revenues in the next fiscal year beginning October 1. Mike, you have agreed to lend the company $50,000 to allow it to make the cash payment to Ted. You have also agreed to prepare a contract to Ted's satisfaction under which Big Slice Pizza will agree for a period of three years beginning October 1 to buy all its imported cheese at market rates as quoted weekly in the 'Cheese World' price sheet from Pure Cheese, Inc., a company owned by Ted's brother-in-law."*

Although the mediators in these three disputes may be acting as if these are the final agreements, in fact they are probably still testing the terms to see if both parties really agree, and that they hold reasonable promise of being workable in the long run. They are also trying to recall everything said during the mediation to be sure there were no underlying issues that may have been forgotten that would threaten the agreement.

2. EVALUATING THE SETTLEMENT TERMS

Before the mediation goes further, carefully evaluate how satisfied you would be with the tentative terms of settlement. Just because the agreement has been announced, don't be bulldozed into a quick acceptance. If the mediator didn't get it right, or even if she did and you have second thoughts, say so. One good way to deal with doubts or worries is to request a caucus with the mediator to give yourself a chance to talk over the proposed terms and get his assessment of how they would affect you.

In our Neighbor Dispute, for example, if you are Ms. Ferraro, are you really willing to tolerate some noise from Mr. Rafferty's home until 11 p.m. if the radio and stereo are turned off earlier? If the agreement isn't kept and you are awakened at 2 a.m., are you willing to take the trouble of reaching Mr. Rafferty on the phone rather than just calling the police? And if your dog does disturb Mr. Rafferty's trash, are you willing to clean it up as intimated by the agreement?

**NEVER AGREE TO THINGS YOU ARE NOT REALLY WILLING TO DO
OR THAT MIGHT BE TOO DIFFICULT TO PERFORM. If the proposed terms
don't look favorable or realistic enough, this is the time to say so. Don't wait until
the agreement is in writing and everyone is standing around waiting for you to
sign your name. At that point, the compulsion to sign may be too great, and you
might end up signing an agreement you don't believe in.**

**If you feel you need a face-saving excuse to change your mind about some of
the settlement terms, you can:**

- **blame it on the mediator ("I didn't understand that this is what the mediator
  was proposing")**
- **say you need to review it with your lawyer (see Chapter 8, Section E)**
- **say you need to review it with another adviser, such as an accountant, member
  of the clergy or trusted friend.**

When the mediator hears you and the other side both say "okay," he will
seize the moment.

"Then we have agreement," he says.

Closure.

3. REQUEST AGREEMENT BE REVIEWED BEFORE SIGNING

It is always a good idea to put your mediation agreement in writing. And it's
absolutely essential to do this if the terms are fairly complicated, as would be the
case in most business ownership, child custody and employment disputes. A
good written agreement:

- clarifies the decisions, intentions and future behavior of the parties
- provides a permanent record of your agreement
- exposes issues that might be overlooked if not for the discipline of putting
  them in writing

- encourages compliance with the agreement because, as a practical matter, only a written agreement can be enforced.

For more on the importance of written agreements, see Chapter 8, Writing an Agreement That Works.

In some minor consumer cases or interpersonal disputes, like the Neighbor Dispute we have examined, your mediator may offer to draft the agreement while you wait, and you and the other party can both sign it before you leave. But in many other cases, it will take some time and work by both parties and possibly their lawyers or advisors to get the language of an agreement just the way both sides want it. For example, an agreement over who can use a trademark would need to be prepared in a way that complies with U.S. Patent & Trademark Office rules. And if an agreement between businesses involves potentially serious tax consequences, you would want a tax advisor to review it. Similarly, If your dispute involved business contracts, property, legal rights or similar matters, you should probably not sign the agreement until you have it reviewed by a lawyer, law-coach or other business advisor. You may already have interrupted your mediation to consult by telephone with a lawyer or other business adviser (see Section G4), but at this point you will be looking for a more thorough and formal review of all the terms of the agreement.

Tell the mediator and the other party you are pleased you've reached an agreement and it looks fine to you, but you want a couple of days to have it reviewed. You are entirely within your rights to do so. The mediator will probably respond to your request by suggesting that he write an outline of the main terms of the agreement, giving each of you a copy and retaining the original. In the next chapter, we will discuss how your mediated agreement should be structured and drafted, how to have it reviewed by an advisor, what happens if you want to change it and when and where you should sign it.

EIGHT

8

Writing an Agreement That Works

Assuming you reach a full or partial settlement of your mediated dispute, your next step is to put your agreement into writing. In this chapter, we will examine how and when the agreement gets written, the form it should take and some specific suggestions on content.

IF YOU DO NOT REACH A SETTLEMENT IN MEDIATION, YOU CAN SKIP THIS CHAPTER AND GO TO THE NEXT.

A. The Importance of Written Agreements

When a mediation agreement has finally been reached, it's fairly common for the participants to be worn out and just want to go home. Patience. You have one more major task—you need to put your agreement in writing. Even if your dispute was a major, complicated one and advisers need to work out the details, you should still at least put an outline of it in writing.

I. FOUR KEY REASONS TO CREATE A WRITTEN AGREEMENT

An agreement that spells out in writing the decisions, intentions and future behavior of the parties provides four important advantages:

- *It creates a permanent record.* A written agreement creates a permanent record should you or the other party remember parts of the agreement differently. Anyone who has ever referred back to a lease, contract or other written agreement knows just how tricky memory can be. I, for one, have occasionally been genuinely surprised to see that some of the details of a written contract differed from my recollection.

- *It exposes overlooked issues.* Putting the terms of your agreement into writing can help uncover issues or details you may have overlooked during the mediation session. For example, if an auto shop agrees to redo the body work on your car, it may not be until you start writing the agreement that you realize you didn't discuss whether the auto shop will lend you a car while the work is being done. Or, if your business partner agrees to buy out your share of the business with 32 equal monthly payments, you may overlook a detail, like how much interest will be charged if a payment is late, until you attempt to reduce the agreement to writing.

- *It encourages compliance.* When settlement terms are put in writing and signed in the presence of a mediator, disputants are far more likely to comply with them than if the agreement is left unwritten. It is customary for the mediator also to sign the agreement, a gesture which I think encourages the parties to keep their word.

- *It allows the agreement to be enforced.* Mediation agreements are difficult, and often impossible, to enforce unless they are in writing. Think about it. If the other side disputes that a certain agreement was reached, how would you prove it had been? Your first thought might be to rely on the mediator. Think again; the mediator will probably be prevented from testifying by rules guaranteeing the confidentiality of what occurred during the session. Realistically, to make your agreement enforceable by a court, should that be necessary, it will have to be in writing. (For more about making agreements legally enforceable, see Section D, below.)

2. Simple Disputes: Draft and Sign the Agreement Before You Leave the Mediation Session

If you've reached a settlement in your mediation, it's a mistake to leave the room with the intention of returning another time to draft and sign the agreement unless the agreement is so complex that it can't possibly be prepared on the spot. And even where this is the case, it's best to mutually prepare an outline of all key points. Delay is doubly dangerous. Not only does it give the other side time to have second thoughts and possibly even be persuaded by others who were not even at the session—such as friends and relatives—that the agreement is not in his or her best interest, but it also allows time for each party's memory to play tricks.

In simple cases, such as those heard at community mediation centers involving neighborhood disputes or claims for relatively small dollar amounts, the mediator will typically draft the agreement in the parties' presence, then read it aloud to be sure the language is acceptable to both sides. Often, several drafts will be needed before the wording is to everyone's satisfaction. The mediator will then usually either enter her handwritten draft in a word processor herself or get a secretary to help, while the parties wait in the mediation room or the reception area.

KEEP COOL IN THE PRESENCE OF THE OTHER PARTY. If the mediator leaves you alone with the other party while your agreement is being typed, sit quietly or make small talk about the weather, but don't discuss the dispute or the terms of settlement. If you do, you risk saying something that might cause the other person to change his mind.

3. COMPLEX DISPUTES: DRAFT AND SIGN AN OUTLINE OF YOUR AGREEMENT BEFORE YOU LEAVE THE MEDIATION SESSION

In large, complex cases, things often realistically can't be wrapped up on the same day an agreement is reached. For good reasons, lawyers, accountants or other advisers usually must review language and work on the details. Still, it's a mistake to leave the mediation without anything in writing. Here the best approach is for the parties to draft and sign a summary or outline of the agreement, covering all essential points, before they leave. While this type of preliminary agreement is normally not legally enforceable, it will tend to preserve the fruits of the mediation because of the human tendency not to renege on agreements put in writing. (For a sample of this kind of summary agreement, see Section C.) If for some reason, such as the lateness of the hour or schedule conflicts, the mediator or the other party wants to skip this step, it's up to you to insist that at least the most important points be covered in writing.

4. ACTIVELY PARTICIPATE IN WRITING YOUR AGREEMENT

Whether your case is large or small, take an active role in helping write your mediation agreement. If the mediator encourages the participation of the parties, it's often a good idea to propose the words that should go in each provision of your agreement. One way to accomplish this is to volunteer to take a few minutes and write the first draft of the agreement yourself. Think of it this way; the person who actually picks up the pen and does the work to draft the agreement, or actively helps the mediator draft the language, has a great opportunity to be sure the final version reflects her views. By contrast, it's a lot tougher to end up with exactly the language you want if you let the other person or the mediator do all the drafting work and then try to change the wording later.

B. Nine Guidelines for Writing an Effective Agreement

Following are nine guidelines to keep in mind as you work with the other party and the mediator in drafting your settlement agreement. These are designed to help you produce a document that is understandable, thorough and forward-looking.

1. USE PLAIN ENGLISH

In a mediation agreement, legalese should be kept to a minimum. You simply don't need to use hard-to-comprehend gobbledygook such as "the party of the first part stipulates to heretofore abrogate the prior stipulation of the parties annexed hereto as exhibit A in the attachment to the amended answer." Far better to use plain English, such as this: "John will cancel the agreement that he and Bill had signed earlier. A copy of that agreement is attached."

Here are examples of formal or legalistic terms that can easily be replaced by simpler words that are easier to understand.

INSTEAD OF	USE
abrogate	cancel
afford an opportunity	allow
apprise	inform
cease	stop
commitment	promise
communicate	write, telephone
demonstrate	show
desire	wish
effectuate	bring about
eliminate	remove, strike out
employment	work
endeavor	try
expiration	ending of
heretofore	earlier
locality, location	place
locate	find
objective	aim
prior to	before
remuneration	pay, wages, salary, fee
reside	live
stipulate	agree
terminate	end
utilize	use

2. IDENTIFY PEOPLE BY FULL NAMES

In writing the agreement, always use full names (first and last) rather than using the term "parties" or another legalistic word such as "the Claimant" or "the Respondent." True, in writing this book I have often had to violate this rule and refer to the people who participate in mediation as "the parties," but that's because I have been writing in the abstract, without real people in mind. But when you write your settlement agreement, you will know the actual names of the people involved in the case. Use them. Real names, rather than terms like "the parties," make an agreement much easier to read and understand.

WRONG WAY: *The parties to this dispute have reached an agreement…*

RIGHT WAY: *Marla White and Bonnie Silverman have reached an agreement…*

Similarly, when naming a business corporation, use the business's full name, such as Brannigan's Craft Centers, Inc. If a store has branches, name the specific branch with which you are concerned.

WRONG WAY: *Brannigan's will allow leaflets to be distributed to passersby in front of its main entrance…*

RIGHT WAY: *The Brannigan's Craft Centers store at 1140 Ridgeway Avenue will allow leaflets to be distributed…*

Another advantage to using full names rather than terms like "the parties" or even lots of pronouns like "him," "their," "its," is that using full names makes each part of the agreement understandable if you ever need to discuss it separately from the other parts.

WRONG WAY: *The piano store will let him exchange his piano…*

RIGHT WAY: *The Hilltop Mall branch of Locke's Pianos and Organs, Inc., will allow Richard Goldberg to exchange…*

3. SPECIFY DATES

Be sure your agreement specifies precise dates when things should happen.

WRONG WAY: *The respondent, Mark Rothman, agrees to remove the rusted Chevy from his front lawn as soon as possible.*

RIGHT WAY: *Mark Rothman will remove the rusted Chevy from his front lawn by July 1, 1997.*

Or, as another example:

WRONG WAY: *The bonus to Susan Marshilock will be paid at the end of Southwest Saving's next fiscal year.*

RIGHT WAY: *The bonus to Susan Marshilock will be paid on or before October 30 following the end of Southwest Saving's next fiscal year.*

4. Answer: Who, What, When, Where and How

To do a good job, your mediation agreement needs to cover all the important aspects of your dispute and its resolution, beginning with the most basic issues: Who is involved in this dispute? What is the dispute about? Who is going to do what as part of resolving it? When are they going to do it? How are they going to do it? In short, the agreement should answer the five key questions of "who, what, when, where and how."

EXAMPLE: *[who] Locke's Pianos and Organs, Inc., will allow Richard Goldberg [what] to exchange his Yamaha U-131 model console piano for any piano currently in stock of equal or greater value. The exchange can be made [when] during regular business hours until March 31, 1997, [where] at Locke's main showroom, 1330 Washington Street, Heneson, Pennsylvania. [how] Locke's store manager, Suzannah Locke, will make herself available to help in the exchange.*

5. List Each Key Provision Separately

Your agreement will probably require certain actions of each disputant. To keep the agreement clear and understandable, it's best to state each significant action in a separate, numbered paragraph. An agreement organized in this bite-sized way is far less likely to be misinterpreted than is the same agreement mushed together into several long paragraphs. In addition, using single-subject numbered paragraphs makes it much easier to discuss if questions of interpretation or noncompliance arise.

WRONG WAY: *The Turims agree to keep their dog confined to their house, and the Hershman's agree to instruct their children not to throw things into the dog's enclosed run. The dog will be enrolled in an obedience school and they will keep it confined when they're not home, and their children will not tease the dog.*

RIGHT WAY:

- *Larry and Amy Turim agree to begin immediately keeping their dog, Tammy, confined to the house after 6 p.m. if they are not at home.*

- *Larry and Amy Turim agree to enroll their dog, Tammy, in the Canine Obedience School of the Livingston County Humane Society for the next available program beginning September 1, 1997, and to take the dog to each class of the program.*

- *Jacob and Marie Hershman agree to immediately instruct their children, Sarah and Valerie, not to tease the Turim's dog, Tammy, and particularly not to throw any items into the dog's enclosed run.*

6. SPECIFY METHOD AND DETAILS OF ANY PAYMENT

Many mediation agreements call for one party to pay money to the other. When this occurs, follow a simple rule: Be sure no detail is left vague. Your agreement should state exactly who is to pay how much to whom, when and in what form (check, money order, cash). If more than one payment is involved, it is also wise to say what will happen if a payment is missed. Will there be a late fee and interest on that installment? Will the whole debt now become due, allowing the creditor to immediately sue and get a judgment?

DON'T TAKE A DOUBTFUL CHECK. If you are dealing with an individual or small business and you have reason to doubt their check will be good, insist on payment by money order, certified bank check or, if you are a business, credit card. This is standard business practice and shouldn't be a problem.

WRONG WAY: *Ralph Edwards agrees to pay Frank Richardson the sum of $845.*

RIGHT WAY: *Ralph Edwards will pay to Frank Richardson the sum of $845 by money order or certified bank check sent by U.S. mail to Frank Richardson at 35 Eulalia Way, Coniston, South Dakota 57453, by February 3, 1997.*

On the other hand, if there are good reasons to be confident of the person's or corporation's financial means and the person agrees to pay, chances are excellent their check will be good and insisting on a money order or certified check is a waste of time, and might even be insulting.

7. Do Not Involve Third Parties in Payments

An error sometimes made in drafting mediation agreements is to have one disputant pay money to a third party not involved in the mediation instead of to the other disputant. This can happen because the person making the payment doesn't want to have any personal contact with the other party. Usually, this approach is a mistake. Not only does it involve extra work to verify payment, but if the money isn't paid, the presence of a third party payee may make attempting to enforce it in court more difficult. I recommend that you avoid the possibility of these complications by making sure your mediation agreement calls for any party who owed the other money to deliver it to the other by an appropriate means, such as the mail or personally.

WRONG WAY: *Garden Way Landscape Company agrees to pay the $650 originally paid to it by Gerald Secor to any other landscape company Gerald Secor selects to do the work on his lawn.*

RIGHT WAY: *Garden Way Landscape Company agrees to return to Gerald Secor the sum of $650 paid by Gerald Secor, by August 15, 1997.*

WHAT TO DO IF THE PARTIES REFUSE TO COMMUNICATE: If there is still so much animosity between you and the other party that you suspect he would never actually pay you, one good alternative is to have the agreement state that he should pay the mediation service on your behalf. The mediation service will receive the funds and write a check to you for the same amount.

EXAMPLE: *Garden Way Landscape Co. agrees to pay Gerald Secor the sum of $650. This provision shall be satisfied by issuance of a corporate check, made payable to The Center for Dispute Settlement, Inc., and sent by U.S. mail to the Center, 87 North Clinton Ave., Rochester, N.Y. 14604, by August l5, 1997.*

8. OMIT ANY MENTION OF BLAME, FAULT OR GUILT

One of the nicest things about settling a dispute via mediation is that, unlike court or arbitration procedures, it does away with any need to officially find fault. Echoing this spirit, mediation agreements should never include statements that either party is "guilty," or "has behaved immorally," or "has violated ethical standards." Not only does omitting statements of fault or blame help each party save face, it makes it easier for them to have an ongoing relationship, if necessary. In addition, nonjudgmental wording makes it more likely that each party will keep any promises as to future conduct.

For example, even if it became clear during the mediation that the landlord let the plumbing break down and refused to fix it, the agreement should not state that the landlord was "lazy," "negligent" or even "wrong." Instead, the agreement should spell out what the landlord agrees to do in the future.

WRONG WAY: *"Whereas Francis Riley, manager of the Seneca Tower Apartments, failed to keep the piping to the apartment of Mr. and Mrs. Lester Aggazis adequately insulated against freezing temperatures . . ."*

RIGHT WAY: *"Mr. Francis Riley, manager of the Seneca Tower Apartments, agrees to repair by 5 p.m., March 4, 1997, all piping necessary to the proper functioning of the bathtub, shower, sink and toilet in the master bathroom of Apartment 7-C, occupied by Mr. and Mrs. Lester Aggazis.*

"If plumbing problems recur in the future, Mr. Riley agrees to arrange for repair within 12 hours of being notified of the problem."

IT'S OKAY TO PUT AN APOLOGY IN THE AGREEMENT. Though words of blame do not belong in the agreement, a written apology for past conduct can often be a key part of the settlement, and, if so, must be included. For example, when a respectable middle-aged African-American was falsely arrested for shoplifting, mediation with the store resulted in a cash settlement and a promise of a written apology from the store manager. Since the man would not have made the agreement without the written apology, it had either to be included in the agreement or prepared separately and referred to in the agreement. (For more on apologies, see Chapter 7, Section F6.)

9. GUARD AGAINST CONFLICTS IN INTERPRETING MEDIATION AGREEMENTS

Despite everyone's best efforts to draft a clear mediation agreement, it is always possible that a question will arise in the future about who was supposed to do what, or when. Or, the other party may fail to live up to his or her part of the agreement. How will these new disputes be resolved?.

As you may have guessed, the best way to handle any problems and avoid future lawsuits is to make the final provision of your agreement a "mediation clause" committing all parties to return to mediation if problems or new issues arise. It should clearly detail who will provide the mediation, the timing of the process and how fees will be shared. Usually, it's most efficient to simply name the same mediator or mediation service that handled the original dispute, since it will be relatively easier for them to reopen the file than it will be for another mediator to start from scratch.

> **SAMPLE MEDIATION CLAUSE:** *If any dispute arises out of, or relates to, this agreement or its performance, which Charles Washington and Everett Boyd cannot resolve through negotiation, Mr. Washington and Mr. Boyd agree to try to settle the dispute by mediation through the Minneapolis Mediation Network, Inc., before resorting to arbitration, litigation or any other legal remedy. The costs of the mediation will be shared equally by Mr. Washington and Mr. Boyd.*

You may also want to take the additional step of referring disputes that can't be settled through mediation to binding arbitration. This is done through a clause requiring mediation and arbitration as a two-step process. An advantage of binding arbitration is that one way or another the dispute will be resolved reasonably quickly and privately. The disadvantage is that, unlike mediation where both sides can emerge with a satisfactory result, arbitration is usually a win-lose proposition and you can never be absolutely sure if you will prevail. Arbitration may also not be a good idea if you will want the law strictly followed if a decision by a third party becomes necessary. This is because arbitrators generally have authority to "do justice" as they see it, without being bound by the strict letter of the law. (For more on arbitration, see Chapter 9.)

> **SAMPLE MEDIATION CLAUSE:** *[Step One: Mediation] If a dispute arises out of, or relates to, this agreement or its performance, which Irina Sungren and Susan London cannot resolve through negotiation, then Ms. Sungren and Ms. London agree to try to settle it by mediation at the Minneapolis Mediation Network, Inc., before resorting to arbitration, litigation or other legal remedy.*

[Step Two: Arbitration] If the dispute is not resolved in mediation within 90 days of its referral to the Minneapolis Mediation Network, Inc., Ms. Sungren and Ms. London agree it will be resolved through binding arbitration by the American Arbitration Association, Inc., and that judgment upon the award made by the arbitrator may be entered in any court having jurisdiction.

Fees for mediation and arbitration will be shared equally by Ms.Sungren and Ms. London.

C. Sample Agreements

On the following pages you'll find three agreements reached at actual mediations, with the disputants' names and other identifying information deleted or changed. I've selected these documents both to show what well-drafted agreements look like (although these are not flawless) and also to illustrate the broad range of disputes that can be mediated successfully.

The first two cases were mediated at the Center for Dispute Settlement, Inc., a community mediation center in Rochester, New York, where I was first trained in mediation. The third case is a contract dispute between a manufacturing company and a supplier of machine parts and was handled by a private dispute resolution company with which I am presently associated.

1. LANDLORD/TENANT DISPUTE

This is a dispute where the landlord of a residential apartment building had been threatening to sue a former tenant over property that was missing from the apartment after the tenant moved out. The missing items included doorknobs, curtains and lamps. In mediation, the disputants agreed on a list of items which the tenant either would return by a set date or for which she would compensate the landlord according to a payment schedule. For his part, the landlord agreed to return to the tenant her collection of tapes, records and CDs that she had inadvertently left stored in the basement and which the landlord had impounded. The agreement was drafted with reciprocal promises meant to give it the effect of a legal contract. (For information on how to make a contract legally enforceable, see Section D, below.)

SAMPLE   **THE CENTER FOR DISPUTE SETTLEMENT, INC.**

In the Matter of Mediation Between:
Judith Stevens
vs.   SETTLEMENT AGREEMENT
Seymour Wilson (Wilson Prop. Mangmt, Inc.)
Case Number: C-111-94

Under the Rules and Procedures of The Center for Dispute Settlement, Inc., Judith Stevens and Seymour Wilson (for Wilson Property Management, Inc.) agree that the following provisions fully resolve all the claims they submitted to Mediation on July 3, 199x.

1. Ms. Judith Stevens, formerly a tenant at Bedford Street Apartments owned by Wilson Property Management, Inc., will return no later than July 22, 199x, to Mr. Seymour Wilson of Wilson Property Management, Inc., the following articles: two doorknobs, door plate, kitchen curtains and rod, bath and back bedroom rods, four draw drape rods, one extension cord and two ice trays. Before returning these items, Ms. Stevens will telephone Mr. Wilson at 667-3321 to arrange a convenient time and place for delivery.

2. Ms. Stevens will pay a total of $179 to Wilson Property Management, Inc., for the following items that were broken or are missing from the apartment:

$26.00	Security lock
43.00	Kitchen light fixture
24.00	Bedroom light fixture
66.00	Mini blinds from study
15.00	Smoke alarm
$179.00	Total to be paid

Ms. Stevens will pay the $179 as follows: $40 per month beginning August, 199x by money order mailed by the 10th of the month to: Mr. Wilson, 280 South Hollywood Drive, Apt. 1, Rochester, NY 14620. The fourth and final monthly payment shall be for the amount of $59.00.

3. Mr. Wilson will consider that all possible legal claims which he might have against Ms. Stevens concerning her being a tenant at the Bedford Street Apartments in 199x have been settled if she delivers to him as promised all the items in paragraph 1 and also pays him the amounts in paragraph 2.

4. Upon satisfactory return of all items named above and payment of all amounts due, Mr. Wilson will release the tape, record and CD collection belonging to Ms. Stevens, and arrange with her a date and time when she can collect these items from the offices of Wilson Property Management, Inc.

If any dispute arises out of this agreement or its performance, which Ms. Stevens or Mr. Wilson cannot resolve themselves, they will try to settle the dispute by mediation through the Center for Dispute Settlement, Inc.

Judith Stevens
Judith Stevens

Seymour Wilson
Seymour Wilson

Signature of Mediator
Mediator

2. NEIGHBORHOOD DISPUTE

The next dispute concerns two families, the Bertlesons and the Woos, who are nextdoor neighbors. Each family has small children. At one time the families were quite friendly, but during the course of one summer tension developed between them. Helen and Arthur Woo complained that Melinda Bertleson's three children (she is a single mother) often came into their yard uninvited to use their play equipment, and left clothes, food wrappers, toys and other items in the yard, and also that Ms. Bertleson's house guests would often park in a way to block their driveway. For her part, Ms. Bertleson complained that the Woos had made verbal threats against her and her visitors. When the Woos finally called the police to have parked cars removed from the end of their driveway, the responding officer encouraged both sides to consider mediation at the local community mediation center. They agreed, and in one afternoon worked out the following settlement. The agreement was drafted by the Woos and Ms. Bertleson with the help of the mediator, and signed by them before they left the mediation center.

SAMPLE | THE CENTER FOR DISPUTE SETTLEMENT, INC.

In the Matter of Mediation Between:
Melinda Bertleson
vs   SETTLEMENT AGREEMENT
Helen and Arthur Woo
Case Number: C-352-94

Under the Rules and Procedures of The Center for Dispute Settlement, Inc., Melinda Bertleson and Helen and Arthur Woo agree that the following provisions constitute full satisfaction of all claims submitted to Mediation on July 3, 199x.

I. Helen and Arthur Woo agree that Ms. Bertleson's children and their friends can play on the swing set and other play equipment in the Woo's backyard at any time they wish as long as they are supervised by an adult.

2. Melinda Bertleson agrees that her children and their friends will clean up after themselves when they play in the Woos' yard, and that she will be responsible for seeing that they do.

3. Ms. Bertleson further agrees to tell her visitors not to park in or block the Woos' driveway, and that she will be responsible for seeing that they do not block the driveway.

4. Mr. and Mrs. Woo agree not to make any verbal threats to Ms. Bertleson or her visitors and to contact her directly in person or by phone if they have any complaints about the conduct of guests at her home.

5. Ms. Bertleson and Mr. and Mrs. Woo also agree that if future disputes arise between them they will try to resolve them by talking together, but if they are unable to do so they will return to mediation.

If any dispute arises out of this agreement or its performance, which Melinda Bertleson and Helen and Arthur Woo cannot resolve themselves, they will try to settle the dispute by mediation through the Center for Dispute Settlement, Inc.

Melinda Bertleson
_____
Melinda Bertleson

Helen Woo
_____
Helen Woo

Arthur Woo
_____
Arthur Woo

Signature of Mediator
_____
Mediator

3. CONTRACT DISPUTE

This next dispute arose when a large manufacturing company, Unity Corp., claimed machine parts made for it by a smaller firm, JHL, Inc., were defective and refused further delivery of parts halfway through the contract. JHL, Inc., on the other hand, claimed the parts conformed perfectly to the specifications in the purchase order, and threatened to sue Unity for $2 million ($1.8 million for the actual cost to JHL of making the rejected parts, plus $200,000 in anticipated profits if JHL had been allowed to complete the contract). But JHL was reluctant to file the lawsuit, because Unity was a major customer and winning the lawsuit while losing Unity's business would not be in JHL's long-term interest. The two companies agreed to mediate. Arrangements were made through a private dispute resolution firm.

The mediation took about four days over a period of three weeks. At its conclusion, although Unity would still not accept the disputed parts, it did agree to pay two-thirds of what it cost JHL to manufacture them (about $1.2 million). Half of this amount would be in a lump sum payment and the balance would be in the form of a purchase by Unity of some excess equipment owned by JHL (but virtually worthless to JHL) which Unity could use at one of its own manufacturing sites. In addition, the two companies agreed to try to continue doing business together. Specifically, Unity agreed to give JHL a contract to do additional work; if the new work was done successfully, the profit on it would about equal the $200,000 that JHL had anticipated but not realized on the original job.

A brief outline of the agreement's main points was drafted by the principals of each company and the mediator before the last mediation session concluded; the final version was signed a few weeks later after attorneys for both sides reviewed it and worked out the details.

A noteworthy aspect of this agreement is the total absence of fault-finding in the contract that gave rise to their dispute. The agreement is entirely forward-looking and is designed to preserve the both companies' business relationship to their mutual advantage.

SUMMARY OF AGREEMENT **EMPIRE MEDIATION & ARBITRATION, INC.**

1. The Unity Corp. agrees to award to JHL, Inc., within six months from the signing of a final mediation agreement a contract or contracts for the manufacture of unspecified machine parts with a net profit margin to JHL upon successful completion of not less than $200,000. Counsel for the parties will draft a document further describing the parties' rights and obligations concerning this agreement for future manufacturing work.

2. Unity will pay to JHL, Inc., not later than 30 days from the signing of a final mediation agreement the amount of $600,000 to offset part of the costs incurred by JHL, Inc., to manufacture machine parts under the disputed contract which was the subject of this mediation. Full or partial payments of this amount made after the 30-day period will include interest at the rate of 9% per year.

3. As further offset against JHL's manufacturing costs, Unity will purchase from JHL three Model X7 Impurities Testers for a total price of $600,000. Delivery will be made FOB Unity's East Ridge facility within 60 days following the signing of a final mediation agreement. Unity will pay JHL in full for this equipment within 30 days of satisfactory delivery.

4. JHL agrees that when the steps outlined above in items 1-3 are completed, it will consider all issues concerning the disputed contract to have been settled, and will not in the future bring any legal actions against Unity concerning that contract.

5. The parties will prepare and exchange papers releasing each other from all present legal claims when the steps outlined above in items 1-3 are completed.

JHL, INC.

By *Signature* _____

UNITY CORP.

By *Signature* _____

Signature _____
Mediator

D. Make Your Agreement Legally Enforceable

Experience shows that most mediation agreements are voluntarily upheld by the parties who sign them. Indeed, studies show that people are even more likely to uphold the terms of a mediation agreement than they are to abide by a court order. The reason is as simple as it is logical: when disputants help craft the solution to their own dispute, and then sign an agreement to abide by it in the presence of their mediator, they normally honor it.

Still, since you already know that the other party in your dispute is far from perfect, it makes sense to protect yourself against the chance that she will deviate from the norm and not honor her agreement. The best way to do this is to prepare your agreement in a way that is legally binding. Then, if the other side breaks the agreement, you will have the option of going to court to enforce it or to have the other party compensate you for breaking it (unless you have opted for binding arbitration). The only exceptions would be cases where you would not want to enforce the agreement even if you could (such as in disputes between friends involving personal issues), or cases where the money involved is so small it would not be worth taking it for enforcement even to small claims court.

There are a couple of different ways to make an agreement legally enforceable:

- If a lawsuit is already pending, request a "consent judgment"—a court order that includes the terms of your agreement
- Write the agreement as a legal contract.

Note that some types of agreements, such as those reached at community mediation centers involving neighbors, pose special problems of enforcement. After all, if your neighbor promises to trim a tree in her backyard twice a year to keep it from blocking your view from your back porch, a judge isn't likely to order her to do it, just because she promised in mediation, if the tree isn't legally encroaching on your property. But one way to deal with this type of potential problem is to include in your agreement a monetary fallback if the other side doesn't do what she promises. For example, in this tree case, you could provide in the agreement that if your neighbor didn't trim her tree as promised, you would be entitled to hire a tree service and she would be responsible to pay the fee. Keep this kind of "monetary fallback" provision in mind if your dispute concerns an interpersonal or neighborhood problem.

Now let's look at the two ways to make a mediated agreement legally enforceable.

1. IF LAWSUIT IS PENDING, REQUEST "CONSENT JUDGMENT"

In some instances, a lawsuit may be pending at the time you reach a mediated settlement. This is particularly common if a judge referred the dispute to mediation in the first place. But it also can occur when one party suggests putting the court action on hold while mediation is tried. Either way, you will often have a choice of two options when it comes to making your dispute legal:

- You can ask the judge to dismiss the lawsuit and then write your settlement agreement in the form of a legally binding contract (see below), or
- You can ask the court to approve the agreement and issue a "consent judgment" (or "consent decree"), making your mediated settlement into an official court judgment. An advantage of getting a judgment is that if it's violated, it can be enforced as a court order. By contrast, to enforce a settlement agreement or contract that is not made into a court order

requires filing a new lawsuit and getting a judgment based on breach of contract.

It follows that, if you are concerned about whether the other side will honor the agreement, you will probably want to get a consent judgment. If you do not anticipate a compliance problem, however, you can skip the consent judgment—and avoid some added legal fees, court costs and delay—and rely on the settlement agreement as a legally binding contract. (Some mediation agreements, such as those concerning child custody and visitation, will not be enforceable under federal and state laws unless they are approved by a judge and issued as a court order. For more on this, see Chapter 11, Divorce Mediation.)

GET HELP IF YOUR AGREEMENT MAY BE TOUGH TO ENFORCE. If lots of money or important rights are involved in your lawsuit, it is best to consult with a lawyer who is familiar with contract law and local court rules on how to draft a judgment to be maximally enforceable.

2. WRITE AGREEMENT AS LEGAL CONTRACT

More often than not, a lawsuit will not be pending when you agree to mediate. This means you won't have an opportunity to make it part of a court order and should instead be sure that your settlement agreement takes the form of a binding contract. To accomplish this, at least five, and sometimes six, basic elements of contract law must be met. Though the technicalities of contract law are beyond the scope of this book, the following thumbnail review will probably be adequate:

- *The parties have the legal ability to make a contract.* This is normally an easy requirement to meet, as long as both parties are adults. All mentally competent adults have the power ("capacity," in legalese) to make a contract, so unless the other party is a minor (less than 18 years old in most states) or so mentally impaired that he does not understand he is making a binding agreement, you have no problem.

- *The agreement doesn't call for illegal actions.* The terms of your contract must not call for an illegal act, such as gambling, prostitution or, more likely, a loan of money requiring a person to pay interest above the legal rate, which in many states is in the range of 10% to 12%.

- *The terms of the agreement must be clear enough to be understood.* If your agreement is so vague a reasonable person might have difficulty under-standing it or carrying it out, it does not qualify as a contract. To guard against this, each provision should state clearly who does or pays what to whom, when and how. (See Section B4.) For example, if you want the roof of your house ripped off and replaced with a new asphalt roof with a 20-year guarantee, your agreement should say exactly that. By contrast, an agreement that says nothing more than, "fix the roof," may be too vague to be enforced as a contract.

- *There must be a quid pro quo (lawyers call it "consideration").* A "quid pro quo" is something given or done by one person in return for something given or done by another person. To have a contract, both parties must do, or promise to do, something. Lawyers obscure this simple concept by saying that without a quid pro quo, an agreement "lacks consideration" and therefore isn't a contract. Lack of consideration isn't normally a problem, as long as your agreement reflects either an exchange of services for money ("Rowan will pay Martin 200 dollars; Martin will reseal the driveway") or reciprocal promises ("Smith will keep his dog indoors after 9 p.m.; Jones will call Smith before calling the police"). Similarly, a promise not to file a lawsuit or to badmouth someone is also valid legal consideration. It's really not all that complicated. For example, in an agreement that lacks consideration because only one person has promised to do something, as in: "Betty will turn her pool lights off before 10 p.m.," consideration easily can be inserted by adding: "and Andy will stop calling the City to complain."

- *There is evidence of mutual agreement to the contract terms.* Both parties to the agreement must understand and agree to the terms of the agreement, and there must be evidence of this. The signatures of both parties at the bottom of the agreement will normally satisfy this requirement. But in a few states, including Minnesota and North Carolina, there is the additional requirement for agreements reached at some mediation programs that the mediation agreement explicitly state in writing that the disputants intend it to be binding. Although not technically required in most states, I believe that including this type of statement is always a good practice. If your agreement is written or typed onto a printed form provided by the mediator or mediation service, look to see if it contains a printed statement that the agreement is intended to be legally binding. Usually it will. But if it does not, ask the mediator to insert a statement at the end of the agreement. The following statement should do the job:

"The parties understand and accept the terms stated above and intend this agreement to be a legal contract, binding upon them and enforceable by a court of law."

If your case involves a significant amount of money or property, or important legal rights, you can help ensure it will be enforceable in court by having a competent lawyer review it before you sign.

3. REMEDIES FOR BREACH OF A CONTRACT ARRIVED AT IN MEDIATION

Courts will normally enforce mediated agreements. But how a particular court will enforce a particular mediation agreement will depend on various factors: how well the agreement was drafted, the type of actions called for under the agreement, the facts of the case and the state law the court is applying. Generally, agreements where money damages can be ascertained (such as a promise to pay money or give someone stock) are much more likely to be enforced as contracts than are agreements where the actions called for are more intangible (such as a promise to treat each other civilly, or not call the police or to weed someone's garden). As mentioned earlier, in the latter type of case, it's often easy to draft an agreement so that there is a monetary fallback if someone doesn't do a promised act. For example, if the private mechanic doesn't fix your car as he agrees to do in mediation, you can get the job done at another shop and make the first mechanic liable for the bill.

The following legal remedies are generally available for breach of agreements reached in mediation that were written in the form of binding contracts:

- *Damages:* The court can award you financial compensation for losses due to the other party's breach. This is the most common way for a court to enforce an agreement.
- *Rescission:* If the other party fails to do what she promised to do under the agreement but still expects you to live up to your part, you can ask a judge to void the agreement, releasing both sides from their obligations.
- *Specific performance:* The court can order the other party to do what he ought to have done under the agreement, for example, for a bank to give you a mortgage or another person to sell you a piece of land. Courts generally will not order specific performance of contracts involving personal labor, such as requiring someone to paint your house or put up a building for you.

Note that if your agreement also contains an arbitration clause and a breach occurs, you can get most of the same remedies at arbitration with less expense and delay than would be involved in a lawsuit, although to enforce the arbitrator's award, you would still have to initiate a court proceeding.

E. Providing for a Lawyer's or Other Adviser's Review

If your dispute involves significant amounts of money or property, or may limit important legal or tax rights (for example, your right to a job, or a patent or to receive a big tax refund), you will be wise to consult a lawyer or CPA before signing the agreement. In other situations, it may make sense to have a particular piece of property (for example, land, a painting or a business) involved in a mediation appraised before signing off. After all, you don't want to trade your rights to 50% of a $300,000 asset for 50% of one worth only $200,000. Similarly, if property is to be exchanged under your agreement, particularly if it has gone up in value, you may need to consider the tax basis. In short, if you need expert help, ask the mediator to insert a clause in the agreement making your signature conditional on review by a lawyer or other expert or adviser. The clause could read as follows:

"The terms of this agreement will go into effect five business days after signing unless the attorney (or CPA, appraiser or other adviser) for either party notifies the [mediation service] in writing of objections."

The "adviser's review" clause can also state a longer period for review or it can state that the agreement will not become effective until co-signed by the adviser. Bear in mind, though, that the longer you delay making the agreement effective, the greater chance there is that the other party will find a reason to change his or her mind and decide not to go ahead with the settlement.

Keep in mind, too, that the lawyer or other adviser you ask to review the agreement will read the document without having been at the mediation. In one sense, this is helpful because it lets the person review the settlement objectively as written, uninfluenced by statements made at the session but not put into writing. However, it could also mean that a lawyer might tend to focus on your narrow legal rights, perhaps undervaluing your broader needs that underlie some of the settlement terms. Everyone who participated in the mediation may understand how important these "nonlegal" provisions are, but the lawyer will not know this because she was not there. Therefore, to avoid having a lawyer wrongly dump on an agreement, you need a lawyer who supports and understands how mediation works. (See Chapter 13, Lawyers and Legal Research.) And you need to be able to show how the settlement terms fit together in a package that satisfies many of the "wants" and "needs" of both you and the other party.

F. Signing the Agreement

When you and the other party have read and consented to each provision of your agreement (and if it is necessary, it's been reviewed and approved by your advisers), you are then ready for the last act of the mediation session: the signing.

If the signing occurs at the mediation service, the mediator will likely hand you and the other disputant each a typed copy of the agreement, and read it once more aloud to make sure everyone understands it and that no further changes are needed. If you have had the agreement written in the form of a contract, the mediator may remind you that it is legally binding and potentially enforceable in court, and that the mediation service will be available to help if circumstances change and revisions are needed. (See Chapter 10, What to Do If Your Mediation Agreement Doesn't Work.) The mediator may also remind you of your pledge of confidentiality for everything said or revealed during the session.

The mediator will then ask each of you to sign the agreement. The mediator, too, will probably sign. Sometimes, signatures will be notarized by a notary on staff. Having a signature notarized is a good idea if you anticipate any need to prove in court or arbitration that the signature on the agreement is actually that of the other party.

Be sure to get a copy of the agreement for yourself before you leave the mediation.

(If you signed just an outline or preliminary draft of the agreement in the mediator's presence and saved details to be negotiated by phone later, then the signing of the final mediation agreement will most likely be done by phone or fax.)

SHAKE ON IT?

Exactly what do people who have been engaged in a bitter dispute do when they each sign their names to a paper ending the matter?

Some mediators have experienced cases, such as those involving estranged relatives or friends, where the parties were reconciled through mediation and concluded the session with an embrace. At nonprofit community mediation centers, disputants are sometimes so grateful for the center's help that before they leave they offer a financial contribution, though none is required.

Typically, though, the mediator will end the session simply by shaking hands with each of the parties and congratulate them on the successful result of their hard work. With a nod to one or both of the parties, the mediator may encourage them to shake hands. Some disputants feel enough relief and understanding of each other's positions to take the cue and end the session with a handshake. Others are just glad to have the matter over with, take their copy of the agreement and go home.

If No Agreement Is Reached: Options Available

In the film "Little Big Man," the Native American grandfather decides it is time to die. He climbs a nearby mountain, wraps himself in a blanket and lies down to wait for the Great Spirit to take him away. A little while later, when it begins to rain, he realizes he is still alive. "Sometimes the magic works, and sometimes it doesn't," he says.

The same is true of mediation. The fact that it works far more often than not doesn't help you if your dispute is among those that is not resolved. But even if your attempt to mediate hasn't produced a mutually satisfactory settlement, there is still hope that your dispute can be resolved without a bloody court fight. This chapter examines the range of further options that may be available to you.

A. Three Options Involving the Mediator

There are three ways to continue to make use of the mediator's services even if your mediation did not lead to a settlement:

- Ask mediator to adjourn and reconvene your mediation
- Ask mediator for written recommendation
- Have the mediator return your dispute to the judge, prosecutor or other agency that originally referred it to mediation.

Let's look at each of these options.

1. ASK MEDIATOR TO ADJOURN AND RECONVENE YOUR MEDIATION

If your session ended without agreement, rather than abandoning mediation entirely, you can suggest to the mediator and the other party that the mediation be adjourned and reconvened at a later date. You could propose, for example, that another session be scheduled in three months. By that time, the parties' positions or circumstances may have changed in such a way that settlement is more likely. If you and the other side are willing to reconvene, chances are your mediator will also be willing to give it another try.

DON'T WAIT TO COMMIT TO FUTURE MEDIATION. If you believe another mediation session may produce a settlement, I highly recommend that you set the date while everyone is still together at the first mediation. If you leave the date to be worked out later, by that time the other party may have lost interest—or have decided to take some other action, such as going to court—and be unwilling to reconvene.

2. ASK MEDIATOR FOR WRITTEN RECOMMENDATION

If your mediation ends without a settlement but you and the other party respect and trust the mediator, you can propose that the mediator make a written recommendation as to how the dispute should be resolved. If the other side agrees, the mediator may be willing to do so. Jointly requesting the mediator to do this makes sense, since the mediator is likely to be at least reasonably objective. Even more important, it takes advantage of the fact that if the mediation involved private caucuses, the mediator probably knows more about the dispute than do either of the parties.

But perhaps the biggest advantage of asking the mediator to propose a settlement is that since the mediator isn't a judge, his recommendation is not binding. If you and the other side are both willing to accept it, you have a settlement. If either of you says no, you have lost little.

The main disadvantage of having the mediator recommend a settlement is that it probably forecloses the possibility of using him again in the same dispute. Once he gives his opinion as to how the case should be resolved, his role as a mediator is over, since he can no longer be considered neutral. So, before asking your mediator to recommend a settlement, be sure you will not want to reconvene your mediation at a later date before that same mediator.

ENCOURAGING THE RELUCTANT MEDIATOR. Some mediators may hesitate to give a written recommendation to the parties because they see it as violating their pledge of neutrality. To overcome your mediator's reluctance, it may help to remind him that even if he makes a recommendation, you and the other party will determine for yourselves if you want to follow it. This is consistent with Standard No. 1 of the Standards of Conduct for Mediators (see Appendix B), which states: "Mediation is based on the principal of self-determination by the parties." You can also suggest the mediator formally close the mediation session before making his recommendation. In this way, the mediator need not feel he is violating Standard No. 2, which states: "A mediator shall conduct the mediation in an impartial manner."

If the mediator agrees to make a recommendation, be sure she agrees that nothing she writes will communicate anything said to her in confidence during the caucus stage of your mediation. Also, her recommendation should not contain any statements finding fault or blame with either of the parties. It should simply state her opinion as to what steps both sides should take to create a fair and workable settlement of the dispute. Since the parties will be expected to pay the mediator for the extra time she spent preparing the Recommendation, the amount (or at least an hourly fee) should be agreed to in advance.

The mediator's recommendation, based as it is on information obtained during the mediation, should be considered confidential under most mediation rules. This means neither the mediator nor the parties would be allowed to introduce it as evidence in a later arbitration or court proceeding. Nevertheless, because you and the other party did not have a written recommendation in mind when you signed the agreement to mediate, it is a good idea to sign a separate agreement making it absolutely clear that the mediator's recommendation will be kept confidential. Ask the mediator to draft a brief confidentiality agreement to cover her recommendation, and try to have the mediator and the parties sign it before everyone leaves the session. Here is a sample:

SAMPLE | **CONFIDENTIALITY AGREEMENT**

The undersigned parties have requested ___*name of mediator*___, who acted as mediator on ___*date*___ in regard to their dispute concerning ___*describe nature of dispute*___, to make a written Recommendation to them as to how their dispute might be resolved. The parties and the mediator agree to maintain the confidentiality of the Recommendation and will not rely on it, or seek to introduce it as evidence, in any arbitration, judicial, or other proceeding, nor disclose it to any regulatory agency, prosecutorial authority, or other governmental agency.

A mediator's recommendations would typically be made in writing and mailed to each of the parties within a couple of weeks of the close of the mediation session. The parties are then free to accept the proposals contained in the Recommendation or to use them as a basis for further negotiations.

3. Ask the Mediator to Return Your Dispute to the Judge, Prosecutor or Other Agency that Originally Referred It to Mediation

If your dispute was referred to mediation by a judge or other law enforcement agency, and the mediation fails, one option (and sometimes a legal requirement) is for your dispute to be sent back to the person or organization that referred it to mediation in the first place. The mediator or mediation service can do this for you by sending a letter to the judge or other referral source, noting that mediation was tried but without success.

> **EXAMPLE:** *When Pam's ex-boyfriend Bruce moved out of Pam's home, he took with him several items of her personal property, including a television set and some valuable photography equipment. He refused to return them. Pam called the police and asked that Bruce be arrested.*
>
> *When Pam talked to the officer or assistant district attorney who approves the issuance of arrest warrants, he referred her to the community mediation center. Bruce showed up for mediation, but the session did not result in an agreement to return Pam's property.*
>
> *Either as part of their regular procedures, or at Pam's specific request, the mediation center sent a letter to the law enforcement officer explaining Pam's attempt at mediation and that she still wants to press charges. Now, the law enforcement person in charge of arrest warrants considers whether the facts support issuing a warrant for Bruce's arrest.*

When a judge, police officer or prosecutor sees you have made a good-faith attempt to work out a dispute through mediation, he may be more inclined to exercise his discretion to grant you the legal action you originally requested. In a sense, you may be rewarded for having tried mediation as a first option.

> *"Your Honor, my client made a good faith effort not to burden this Court with this matter by attempting to resolve the dispute through mediation at the Center for Dispute Resolution. A mediation session was held on September 22 at the Center, but after nearly four hours, my client and the defendant were not able to reach a mutually acceptable solution. Now, my client asks this Court to issue the injunction we originally sought to prevent the defendant from unlawfully dumping garbage onto my client's property."*

B. Small Claims Court

If your dispute involves a relatively small amount of money, you can bring your case to small claims court, where it is easy to represent yourself. In most states, the dollar limit for small claims court is between $2,500 and $5,000. To find the dollar limit for small claims court in your area, simply contact the court. If you do not find a listing for small claims court, call the Justice, Municipal, City or District Court and ask for the number of the small claims court clerk. In general, small claims court is so fast and cheap, it can be a better choice than arbitration (see Section C, below) for many cases involving amounts within its monetary limits. In addition, rules in small claims court frequently are more user-friendly to the nonlawyer than those in arbitration; and you're also likely to get a decision faster. For more on small claims court, see Chapter 2, Section B7. If you think small claims court may be right for your case, see *Everybody's Guide to Small Claims Court,* by Ralph Warner (Nolo Press).

THINGS YOU LEARNED IN MEDIATION PROBABLY CAN'T BE USED IN COURT. If you file a case, which you first mediated, in any court, including small claims court, you are bound by the confidentiality rules of mediation not to use in court much of the information disclosed by the other party during mediation. How broad this prohibition is will vary according to state law, but it nearly always prohibits one party in mediation from using statements made by the other party during mediation for the purpose of showing the validity or value of a claim being advanced in the court. But if the same information was separately learned— "discovered" in legal jargon—outside the mediation, then it's okay to use in court. If you are unsure whether a particular statement you heard in mediation can be raised in court, consult with a lawyer or law coach before going to your court hearing.

C. Arbitration

Assuming you've tried mediation and "the magic didn't work," arbitration might be a very good option. At the very least, it will assure you and the other party of a fast, private and, at least as compared to court, reasonably-priced way to resolve your dispute. Arbitration is available to parties in a dispute at any time. The only requirement is that both sides agree, in writing, to arbitrate.

In "binding arbitration," a neutral third party, called the "arbitrator" (sometimes "arbiter"), conducts a hearing between the disputants and then renders a final and legally-binding decision (called an "award"). The arbitrator's award is almost always enforceable in court just like a judge's order.

An arbitrator's power to make a legally-binding award comes from laws passed by the legislatures in each of the 50 states and by Congress. These laws provide, in essence, that if two people agree in writing to have a dispute resolved by a third party, then the decision of the third party—if it meets all of the legal requirements—will have the same force and effect as the order of a judge. As one commentator observed, it is the disputants who "breathe life" into the arbitrator.

Unlike mediation, arbitration requires you to give up control of your dispute to the third-person arbitrator, who takes the place of judge and jury. If you go to binding arbitration, your hearing is, in effect, your "day in court"; you will not get another. For more on the differences between mediation and arbitration, see Chapter 1, Section E.

An arbitrator's decision—except in highly unusual circumstances—will not be overturned in court. Most state laws allow a court to overturn an arbitrator's decision only upon proving there was fraud involved in the hearing, or that the arbitrator was biased against one of the parties, or important procedures were not properly followed (there was no written agreement to arbitrate in the first place) or the arbitrator made an obvious mistake in calculation (he added wrong). A judge almost never overturns an arbitrator's award just because she thinks the arbitrator made a bad decision or misapplied the law. These very restricted appeal rules make sense because the whole point of arbitrating is to let disputants resolve a case once and for all without getting into a court fight.

A full discussion of how to prepare for and present a case in arbitration is beyond the scope of this book. However, to familiarize you with the process, a brief overview of many aspects of arbitration is presented here.

1. WHICH CASES ARE SUITABLE TO ARBITRATE

Arbitration tends to work best with cases that can have a "dollars-and-cents" solution, such as insurance claims, consumer complaints and contract disputes. Cases involving interpersonal disputes, where the parties want to preserve a relationship, often are not well-suited to arbitration. This is because problems with the relationship probably will not be relevant to the legal issues before the arbitrator, and therefore will not be discussed. Also, because one side may win everything and the other lose everything, the result is unlikely to repair a relationship.

Similarly, cases involving relatively small amounts of money—less than a few thousand dollars—are often too small to arbitrate, because the arbitration fees will be too high compared to the amount you hope to gain. However, this isn't always true, as some community mediation centers do offer free or low-cost arbitration. (See Section C4, below)

2. ARBITRATION THROUGH "MED/ARB"

When you first submitted your dispute to mediation, some mediation services may have offered, as an option, the procedure known as "med/arb" (pronounced "meed-arb"). In med/arb, the disputants consent to mediation but with the added provision that if mediation does not produce a settlement, then the mediator (or another neutral party) can act as arbitrator and make a binding decision. Med/arb gives assurance that, one way or the other, the dispute will be resolved: either a settlement will be reached or a decision will be handed down.

Most mediation services that offer med/arb use a system in which the decision-making arbitrator is someone other than the person who acted as mediator. In the jargon of the dispute resolution field, this system is often called by the horrendous title "sequential med/arb." First there is a mediation. Then, if that fails, an arbitration session is scheduled, involving a different person. Separating the two eliminates the problem of a mediator-turned-arbitrator rendering a decision based, in part, on information given to him in confidence during the caucus stage of mediation. (Another, less popular, way around this problem is for two neutrals to attend the mediation session, one to mediate, including caucusing, and the other merely to listen to the joint sessions and then act as arbitrator, if necessary.)

If you submitted your case to med/arb, then at some point in the mediation—after caucuses and negotiation—the mediator may hint she is becoming frustrated and that, if no settlement is reached, she may close the session and direct that the dispute be arbitrated.

> **EXAMPLE:** *Mediator to Disputants: "I have to tell you candidly that I'm not seeing a lot of progress here. The issues have been raised and you've been over them thoroughly several times, both in joint session and in caucus. Some promising settlement options have been put on the table, but I don't see much movement. Let's give it a little longer, but if nothing develops, say in another hour, I will consider declaring the mediation closed and asking that an arbitrator be assigned to conduct a hearing and make an award."*

If you did not submit your case to med/arb and your mediation effort was unsuccessful, you can still ask the mediator to arbitrate a decision. (Also see Section A2, above, for a discussion of instead asking the mediator for a nonbinding recommendation.) Of course, the other side will have to agree to this plan, the mediator will have to be willing to arbitrate and proper agreements and disclosures will have to be signed by the parties.

But again, having your mediator become an arbitrator can raise a problem if, during mediation, either party disclosed information to the mediator that was not also shared with the other side. This would happen, for example, if the parties prepared Pre-Mediation Memoranda for the mediator (see Chapter 6, Section E) but did not exchange them with each other, or if private caucuses were held with the mediator. In either case, you can't be sure the mediator-turned-arbitrator is not influenced by this information when making his arbitrator's award.

If you and the other party did not sign up for med/arb but now agree that you both want the mediator to arbitrate a decision, you will have to sign an Agreement to Arbitrate. (See Section C6, below.) In that Agreement, you should ask the service to add a clause like the following:

We, the undersigned parties to this agreement, affirm that ___[Name of mediator-turned-arbitrator]___ acted as mediator in regard to this dispute in a session held on ___[date]___ at ___[location]___. During the course of the mediation, each of us engaged in private and confidential discussions with the mediator about this dispute. Fully aware that these discussions took place and that they may influence ___[Name of mediator-turned-arbitrator]'s___ decision as arbitrator, we nevertheless request that ___[Name of mediator-turned-arbitrator]___ now arbitrate a decision for us in this case. Further, we agree not to challenge the arbitrator's award based on any claim of bias, partiality or fraud in connection with the arbitrator's prior service to us as a mediator in this dispute.

3. Which Type of Arbitration to Choose?

Assuming you are interested in arbitration, you should know there are many forms from which you can choose. These include "nonbinding arbitration" (similar to mediation, and sometimes called "advisory arbitration") and at least four varieties of binding arbitration, as follows:

- straight arbitration
- high-low arbitration
- "baseball" arbitration
- "night baseball" arbitration.

We'll discuss each of these in more detail below.

In all forms of arbitration, the parties present their points of view to a neutral arbitrator, or sometimes a panel of three arbitrators. Parties may testify, call witnesses and introduce documents and other exhibits as evidence. Rules of evidence apply but are usually applied in a less formal manner than in court. After the hearing, the arbitrator prepares his or her decision in the form of a written Award that is sent to the parties.

A. NONBINDING ARBITRATION

An important first question to consider is whether you want a binding or nonbinding decision. Someone who has already mediated will probably gain little by agreeing to nonbinding arbitration, where neither party is bound by the decision. True, in nonbinding arbitration, unlike most mediations, the arbitrator will render an advisory decision, but you may be able to accomplish the same goal more easily by skipping the nonbinding arbitration hearing and just asking the mediator for a written recommendation. (See Section A2, above.)

B. TYPES OF BINDING ARBITRATION

Among forms of binding arbitration, the "high-low" option has become popular recently, particularly with cases involving personal injury claims against insurance companies. This and other types of binding arbitration are explained below.

- *Straight arbitration:* This is the basic form of binding arbitration. Both sides present their case to the arbitrator and the arbitrator makes a written, binding decision. There are no limitations placed on the arbitrator's authority. Whatever the arbitrator awards is final.
- *High-low arbitration:* This is a binding procedure, but to reduce the risk, the parties agree in advance to high and low limits on the arbitrator's authority. It is most commonly used to resolve monetary claims, such as an individual's claim against an insurance company for compensation for injuries sustained in an auto accident. Usually the arbitrator is not told what these limits are, or even that a "high-low" agreement is in effect. If the arbitrator's award is lower than the low figure, the winning party receives the low figure amount. If the award is higher than the high figure,

the winning party receives only the high figure amount. If the award is between the high and the low, then the winner receives the amount awarded. For example, assume a "high-low" arbitration, where the parties agree in advance to a high of $100,000 and a low of $40,000. If the arbitrator awards $60,000, the winning party will receive that amount. However, if the award is $25,000, the winning party will receive $40,000; and if the award is $150,000, the winning party would receive $100,000.

- *"Baseball" arbitration:* So-called because of its use in recent years to resolve disputes between baseball players and team owners over player salaries. Each party selects, in advance, a figure representing the correct value of the case as they see it and exchanges that figure with the other party. The case is then presented to the arbitrator. After the hearing, the parties show their figures to the arbitrator, who must choose one or the other, with no power to pick an amount in between. This supposedly encourages the parties to be realistic in their evaluation of the case.

- *"Night baseball" arbitration:* As with "baseball" arbitration, before the hearing each side chooses a value for the case and exchanges it with the other side. After the hearing, however, the values are not revealed to the arbitrator. (The term "night baseball" results from the fact that the arbitrator is kept in the dark about the parties' valuations.) Instead, the arbitrator declares his own value for the case and then the parties must accept either the highest or the lowest of their own values, depending on which is closer to the arbitrator's award. This method discourages extreme positions, since the parties are trying to come as close to the arbitrator's figure as possible.

Generally, parties decide among themselves which form of arbitration they want to use before they make an agreement to arbitrate. If they cannot readily agree, the dispute resolution company or other arbitration service can help. Especially for people who have already been through mediation, I generally recommend binding arbitration over nonbinding, for the reasons noted above. Beyond that, the choice of any particular variety of binding arbitration will depend on the facts of the case, the parties' tolerances for risk and the confidence they are willing to place in an arbitrator.

4. WHERE TO GO FOR ARBITRATION

If you used a satisfactory mediation service that also offers arbitration, you and the other party may be able to sign an Agreement to Arbitrate before you leave the mediation session. But if the mediation service does not offer arbitration (many community mediation centers do not), ask the mediator or a staff member to refer you to an organization that does.

Most private dispute resolution companies that provide services to business clients also offer arbitration. For a list of some national and regional private firms, see Appendix C. Private firms offering arbitration in your community may also be listed in your local telephone directory under "arbitration" or "legal services."

THE PROBLEM WITH SOME INDEPENDENT ARBITRATORS. Lawyers, retired judges and other individuals sometimes promote themselves as independent arbitrators, available to hear cases on their own, without your having to go through an arbitration service. This is often less expensive than using a service because you are not paying administrative fees, but I usually don't recommend it, for the following reasons:

- **First, without an administrative agency, there is no independent source of information about the background, skill-level and achievement record of the person who will sit as arbitrator.**
- **Second, there is no buffer between the parties and the arbitrator; the parties must contact the arbitrator directly, which creates the potential for communications in which one side may improperly influence the arbitrator— even inadvertently.**
- **Third, if any problems arise with the arbitration—one side, for example, believes incorrect procedures were followed—there is no one to evaluate or help remedy the problem. In short, the money you might save by cutting out the arbitration service is usually not worth the inconvenience or risk.**

5. Cost of Arbitration

As with mediation, arbitration fees are usually computed by combining the administrative charges of the service with the hourly rates for the arbitrator's time. While these costs will vary somewhat according to region of the country and size of the community, in general you can expect a half-day arbitration hearing conducted by a private dispute resolution company to cost between $500-$1,000 per party.

For cases where the amount in dispute is very small, some organizations assess lower fees. The only way you could have a dispute arbitrated without a fee would be if your local nonprofit community mediation center also offered arbitration as part of its regular tax-supported services. But of the 400-odd community mediation centers around the country, fewer than half offer arbitration. Of those, a few provide arbitration for free; others charge modest fees.

6. Initiating Arbitration

As noted, if you and the other party are still at the mediation session when you agree to arbitrate and the mediation service also handles arbitrations, then you can both just sign an "Agreement to Arbitrate" form supplied by the service. If, however, you have already left the mediation session or the mediation service can't help you with arbitration, then one of you will need to begin the arbitration process much as you did mediation, by going to an arbitration service and completing an intake form, usually called either a "Submission to Arbitration" or, if your dispute is covered by a contract that includes an arbitration clause, a "Demand for Arbitration." Arbitration clauses are commonly found in contracts such as those involving the construction industry, professional sports and sales of stocks and bonds.

But no matter which form you use, it will ask you to describe the nature of your claim, the remedy you seek and the amount of money, if any, you demand.

All arbitration services conduct their hearings in accordance with a set of rules that spell out in detail such things as duties of the arbitrator, use of evidence, confidentiality, fees and expenses and appeals. Be sure to study these rules and ask questions about any provisions you don't understand.

7. CHOOSING AN ARBITRATOR

Most arbitration services maintain rosters or "panels" of arbitrators who have expertise in various fields likely to be the subjects of major disputes, such as business contracts, construction, personal injuries and employment disputes. Staff members of the arbitration service or panel members with more general backgrounds may be made available to disputants involved in smaller cases. When you are ready to choose an arbitrator for your case, the service will send you a list with the names of half a dozen or more arbitrators, sometimes with a brief biographical sketch of each. From this list, you will usually be asked either to cross off the names of anyone you do not want to hear your case, or to rank in order of preference the names of arbitrators whom you would like to hear your case.

The procedures and strategies for investigating and choosing arbitrators from a panel are the same as for choosing a mediator. (See Chapter 5, Selecting Mediation Services and Mediators.) These include reading the arbitrators' qualifications on the material sent from the arbitration firm, looking for someone who is knowledgeable about the subject area of the dispute and getting referrals from friends, businesses, community leaders, lawyers and others.

Although most arbitrations are conducted using one arbitrator, sometimes three arbitrators sitting as a panel are used, either because an arbitration clause in a contract requires it, or because the parties agree to this procedure. For example, some auto insurance policies require three arbitrators to decide a case when a claim is made under the policy. Although cases heard by three arbitrators will obviously be more expensive than those heard by a single arbitrator, there can be reasons why you may want to consider doing this. For example, if a very large monetary award is possible in your case, and you are the party who will be paying out the money, you may prefer the "averaging" effect of having multiple arbitrators, thus eliminating the possibility that a single arbitrator will render too large an award. Similarly, if your dispute is very complex with many facts and witnesses, multiple arbitrators may be better able than a single arbitrator to remember and apply all the evidence in the case.

8. LOCATION OF THE HEARING

Most arbitration services will give you the choice of holding a hearing at their offices, at the arbitrator's office, or, if both parties agree, at the office of either of the disputants. Sometimes it will be helpful to hold the hearing at the site of the dispute. If your dispute involves faulty workmanship, for example, and you want the arbitrator to see the problem firsthand, suggest that the hearing be held at the worksite.

> **EXAMPLE:** *A homeowner hired a general contractor to build an addition to his home. Before construction had gone very far, however, cracks appeared in the newly poured foundation. The homeowner refused to pay the contractor his second payment (draw), and, in response, the contractor walked off the job. The homeowner suggested, and the arbitrator and contractor agreed, that the hearing should be held at the house, so that everyone would be able to inspect the foundation.*

9. DO YOU NEED A LAWYER?

In mediation, the answer to this question of whether you need to hire a lawyer is often "no," there is normally no need for a lawyer. As discussed in Chapter 6, Preparing for Your Mediation, there can be exceptions, as when lots of money or property is at stake, underlying legal issues are complex or one party is a less powerful negotiator than the other. By comparison, in arbitration, the answer will more often be "yes, it's wise to have a lawyer."

As noted, by participating in arbitration, you are giving up your right ever to go to court on this particular dispute, and the decision of the arbitrator will be just as binding and final as that rendered by a judge. If you have a significant amount of money or property in dispute, or the issues are such that if you lose, the result will seriously affect you, then hiring a lawyer or a background law coach to help you prepare for arbitration, and possibly go with you to the hearing is likely to make more sense. Since in most straightforward cases, arbitration hearings seldom last beyond a half day (or at most a full day), the investment in legal fees will not be great compared to what they would be in litigation.

10. THE ARBITRATION AWARD

The length of time after the arbitration hearing in which the arbitrator has to make an award will vary according to which arbitration service you use, but 30 days is typical, unless additional information must be gathered and submitted. The arbitrator has broad authority to make any award that he or she "deems just and equitable and within the scope of the arbitration agreement made by the parties." Nevertheless, a typical arbitration award is one that simply orders one party to pay money to another. A sample Award of this type, for personal injury claims sustained by an employee of a waste disposal company and arbitrated through a private dispute resolution firm, appears on the following page.

D. Start a Lawsuit

Whether or not you come to mediation via a referral from a judge or other law enforcement official, if mediation fails, you retain your rights to file a lawsuit (unless you have already signed a contract to proceed to binding arbitration). To do this, you can bring an action in civil trial court, either by hiring a lawyer to represent you, or by representing yourself. If you should decide to represent yourself, I recommend *Represent Yourself in Court,* by Bergman & Berman-Barrett (Nolo Press), as an excellent resource that will help you at every stage of the process.

THINGS YOU LEARNED IN MEDIATION PROBABLY CAN'T BE USED IN COURT.
As stated in the warning in Section B, most statements or offers of settlement made in mediation by the other party can't be used if you take the same case to court.

S A M P L E | **EMPIRE MEDIATION & ARBITRATION, INC.**

A private forum for dispute resolution.

In the Matter of Arbitration Between:

Thomas and Mary Pat ▮▮▮▮▮▮▮▮▮▮

     vs.   AWARD OF ARBITRATOR

Joseph ▮▮▮▮▮▮▮▮▮▮ and ▮▮▮▮▮ Rubbish Removal, Inc.

EM&A Case No.: ▮▮▮▮▮▮

HAVING BEEN DESIGNATED AS ARBITRATOR in this matter by the Agreement to Arbitrate, signed by the above-named parties or their legal representatives, and having been duly sworn, based upon the testimony of the Parties and their witnesses and presentation of documentation and other evidence at the hearing conducted on April 5, 199x, in accordance with Article 75 of the New York State Civil Practice Laws and Rules, I make the following Award:

I award the Plaintiff the sum of Fifteen Thousand ($15,000) Dollars damages for aggravation of her pre-existing asthmatic condition.

AFFIRMATION AND SIGNATURE OF ARBITRATOR:

I affirm on my Oath as Arbitrator and under penalty of perjury that the foregoing is my Award in this matter.

                                 James P. ▮▮▮▮▮▮▮▮▮

                                 Name: Judge James ▮▮▮▮▮▮▮

Dated: The 29th day of April 199x

Building No. 1 - 000 ▮▮▮▮▮▮▮ — Rochester, NY 14625 — (716) 111-1111 — Fax (716) 222-2222

Regional offices: ▮▮▮▮▮▮▮ , NY — ▮▮▮▮▮▮▮ , NY

IT STILL PAYS TO MEDIATE. Even if you end up suing the other party, you may still get some benefit from having gone to mediation. In their study ("Small Claims Mediation in Maine: An Empirical Assessment," *Maine Law Review*, Vol. 33, 1981, p. 264), Craig McEwen and Richard Maiman found that:

"(T)he fact that defendants [in court] who took part in unsuccessful mediations had a substantially better compliance record than those who had not participated in mediation at all suggests that the negotiation process itself—independent of its outcome—helps to inculcate a sense of responsibility about payments."

What to Do If Your Mediation Agreement Doesn't Work

Your long-term satisfaction with mediation will largely depend on whether your agreement solves your problem more or less permanently:

- Does the contractor who agrees to repaint the hallway do a good job?
- Does your former business partner fully meet the payment schedule she agreed to as part of buying your share of the business?
- Does your neighbor stop harassing your kids?

But although you hope your mediation agreement will put the dispute completely behind you, it's important to recognize that sometimes, despite everyone's best efforts, your mediated agreement will prove to be unworkable or ineffective. This may occur because circumstances have changed since the agreement was made, or because one party has failed to honor the agreement or because the agreement proved to be unworkable in the real world. This chapter examines remedial steps you can take under any of these conditions.

A. If You Need to Change Your Agreement

Even the most thoughtful and well-drafted mediation agreements may need to be modified if subsequent events make the terms irrelevant or impossible to perform. As a general rule, the more an agreement depends on things that haven't happened yet, the more likely it is to unravel. This might occur, for example, with an agreement that was to be performed over a period of years, should one party die, move away or go bankrupt. Consider the following examples.

The first involves an unforeseen event occurring after the mediation, which makes the agreement ineffective.

EXAMPLE: *Marcia, 29, was fired from her job as restaurant manager at a hotel. Believing she had been dismissed for inappropriate reasons, she filed an "unfair termination" lawsuit against the hotel. To try and avoid a full-scale court battle, the hotel's lawyer and Marcia and her lawyer agreed to try to mediate a solution using the local office of a national, private dispute resolution company. After several sessions, an agreement was reached to rehire Marcia at her former position for a trial period of six months after which she would be evaluated and considered for permanent reinstatement. Marcia's lawsuit would remain inactive pending completion of the six-month period.*

But three weeks later, Marcia's husband was notified that he would be transferred to a new job out of state, thus making Marcia's agreement with the hotel unworkable. Though the hotel might have taken the position that it had complied with its end of the agreement and would do no more, it decided instead, for the practical reason of avoiding a likely lawsuit from Marcia, to attend another mediation session. The result was a new agreement in which the hotel agreed to pay Marcia a sum of money to cover most of the time she missed from work and to give her a favorable letter of recommendation.

The second involves a situation in which a mediated solution proves to be unworkable because of incomplete information by one of the parties.

EXAMPLE: *Two teenage boys were arrested and charged with breaking antennas and hood ornaments off of cars at an auto dealer's lot. As part of a mediated agreement arrived at with the help of a community mediation center, the dealer agreed to drop charges if the boys would perform 40 hours of work without pay at his dealership on weekends. The boys agreed and the mediation was closed.*

Soon after, however, the owner called the mediation center and told the staff he just learned that his insurance coverage prevents anyone under 18 from working on the lot. He suggested, as an alternative, that the teens could perform 40 hours of community service by working at a local camp for disabled children where he serves on the board of directors. The boys agreed to the change. The center staff circulated a memo to both sides, obtained their signatures, and the agreement was officially amended.

In the third situation, one party agreed to pay a sum of money but then did not have the cash available.

EXAMPLE: *A general contractor caught a subcontractor stealing lumber. In a mediated agreement, the subcontractor agreed to pay back $2,150, in two monthly payments of $1,150 and $1,000. The subcontractor made the first payment on time, but then received a notice from the Internal Revenue Service demanding immediate payment of a substantial amount of back taxes. If the money wasn't immediately forthcoming, the IRS threatened to padlock the business, with the likely result being that the subcontractor would have to declare personal bank-ruptcy. The subcontractor told the mediator he could not make the second payment on time. After conferring with both sides and obtaining a mutual agreement to an extension of time to pay, the mediator circulated a modified agreement for signature.*

I. Asking the Mediation Service or Mediator to Help

If you believe your agreement needs to be modified, the easiest way to do it is to negotiate the change yourself. For example, if you and the other party orally agree that a payment can be made two months late, you can put it in writing without involving the mediator. But if you do want the mediator's help, don't hesitate to call. While most mediation rules do not require mediators to provide follow-up assistance after a case is closed, in practice, most will be glad to help as they have an interest in your long-term satisfaction with agreements reached through their services. (State laws that require mediation of child custody and visitation, such as those in California, may have specific rules for modifying agreements. See Chapter 11, Divorce Mediation.)

A. FIXING MAJOR PROBLEMS

If you notify your mediation service or independent mediator that you believe a major issue needs to be renegotiated in a face-to-face mediation session, they will normally contact the other party to obtain consent to reopen the mediation. For instance, consider the dispute in the first example, above, where the hotel was going to rehire the restaurant manager but now because she will be leaving town that plan is unworkable. This is the kind of major issue that will almost surely need another face-to-face mediation session. Typically, the case manager at the mediation service, once alerted to the problem, will contact all the parties to arrange another session with the original mediator. The session may not take long, since everyone will be familiar with the facts of the dispute, and can begin working right away on alternative plans for a settlement.

B. FIXING MINOR PROBLEMS

As noted above, the best way to fix minor problems with your mediated agreement is to negotiate them directly with the other side. Even if you need help from the mediator or mediation service, this can often be provided without the need to convene another formal mediation session. Instead, the mediator or staff will conduct "telephone shuttle diplomacy" between you and the other side to work out the needed modification, and will circulate an amendment to the original agreement for both of you to sign. For instance, in the second case example above (concerning the teenage boys who vandalized cars), the parties had agreed that the boys would perform 40 hours of unpaid service at the dealership. When this became impossible, the dealer himself suggested the boys do community service at a camp for disabled children. To agree on this new plan, the parties didn't need another mediation session, since the principle of having the boys perform unpaid labor to compensate for past behavior remained the same. Working out details of where and when the work would now be performed was a relatively minor issue that the center staff could handle by phone and by mailing out a modified agreement for signature.

2. FEES FOR CHANGING AN AGREEMENT

Whether you will be charged an additional fee for help in changing your agreement will depend on which mediator or mediation service you happen to use and how much they do to help you. If the problem is a major one so that a new mediation session is needed, you probably will be charged for the mediator's additional time, but will likely not need to pay another administrative fee. If the problem is a minor one so that a new session is unnecessary, you will probably be charged for the telephone time if a mediator undertakes shuttle telephone diplomacy (unless it is just a few minutes), but may not be charged if the change is negotiated by a staff person. The difference is that the mediation center staff are probably on salary, but the mediator is probably an independent contractor who gets paid by the service only for the hours he or she actually works.

KEEPING THE CUSTOMER SATISFIED. . .

Why should a mediation service help you modify an agreement? For starters, most people who work there will genuinely care about providing a good quality service. But beyond that, private dispute resolution companies, especially, recognize that their business' ability to attract new clients depends on their reputation for helping foster agreements that work. Mediation is well understood to be a business where providers prosper only if their business generates positive word-of-mouth.

Nonprofit community mediation centers, too, have a stake in your long-term satisfaction. Their ability to attract state, loca, and foundation funds depends, in part, on the success or failure rate of their operations as measured by client satisfaction. Some community mediation centers even monitor closed cases to see if agreements are working well. For example, the staff at one community mediation center in New England follows-up on landlord-tenant cases twice: once at 60 days and again at one year.

The staff at court-connected mediation programs should also be willing to help you modify your agreement. Many of these programs are considered pilot projects and statistics on user-satisfaction are monitored by the state agencies that fund them.

B. If the Other Party Reneges

Although rates of compliance with mediated agreements are high—higher even than compliance with court orders—this is cold comfort if your case is one of those in which the other party reneges.

If the other party fails to send you a check when due, fails to fix your water heater, continues to call you at home late at night when he agreed not to do so or otherwise doesn't keep his promise, what action can you take? Step one is to call the person and try to work it out directly. If that fails, or is impractical under the circumstances, consider these other possible remedies.

1. PERSUASIVE AUTHORITY OF THE MEDIATOR OR MEDIATION SERVICE

As noted, the mediator or mediation service will probably be willing to lend a hand if the other side fails to carry out the agreement. To see how this might work, let's assume you used a private dispute resolution company to resolve a dispute about ownership of a small business. Under the agreement, your former partner was to pay you monthly installments towards purchase of your shares in the company. But he has stopped making payments, claiming the deal is too much in your favor and as far as he's concerned he's paid enough. What can you do?

Since further negotiations with your ex-partner appear useless, your next step would be to tell the case manager at the mediation company about the problem. Although he has no obligation to get involved, in all likelihood he will offer to call your ex-partner to discuss the problem.

Case Manager to Reneging Party: "Stan, I understand from Joe there's some problem with the agreement you both reached in mediation last summer. Can you tell me about it?" (The case manager begins simply by offering to listen. He wants to remain neutral until information from both sides convinces him there really is a compliance problem.)

(Later in conversation): "Stan, from what you're telling me it sounds as if you've just flat decided not to honor the agreement. If you and Joe both want, I can see about reopening the mediation. But I have to remind you that you both agreed to have the settlement written as a legal contract. By making the agreement a contract, you both intended that if one of you broke it the other could sue for breach of contract. If Joe did that and won, you might be looking at liability not only for what you still owe him, but also interest, damages, court costs and Joe's legal fees, as well as your own. You'd risk having a judgment issued against you that would be a matter of public record and available to banks, which unless you paid it promptly, in full, could make it difficult for you to get a line of credit for the business. Are you sure it wouldn't be in your best interest just to finish up the payments as you'd agreed?"

Community mediation centers may also have some persuasive authority. In cities and towns where mediation centers are well-established and strongly supported by local government and business, the center often is perceived as representing the "sense of the community." After all, they receive public funds, and prominent judges and community leaders sit on their boards of directors. The staff will try to convey to a noncomplying party that the community at large—as represented by the center—expects both parties to live up to the agreement.

On cases originally referred from the police or a judge, the center will use a more direct approach to encourage compliance, often threatening to send the case back for further legal action. Let's assume, for example, your case involved a criminal harassment charge against a former boyfriend and a city court judge referred you both to mediation. After the mediation, all was calm for a few months, but now your "ex" has started calling and following you again. As a first step, you call the mediation center and alert them to the problem. A person on staff who handles problems of noncompliance will probably contact your ex-boyfriend to discuss the situation and remind him of his obligations under the agreement.

> **EXAMPLE:** *"Hello, Mr. Winters, this is Nancy Hoyer from the Center for Dispute Resolution. I'm calling in regard to your case with Amy Present. Ms. Present tells me there's a problem with the way your agreement is being followed. Is there a problem?" (Discussion follows confirming that there is a compliance problem.)*

"I notice from the file in your case that this case was referred to us by Judge Venditto in City Court. He was willing to adjourn the case for six months if it could be settled through mediation. I need to tell you that if the agreement is not complied with, the Center will send the case back to Judge Venditto with a recommendation that the original charges be reinstated."

2. Asking the Mediator to Intervene

Another approach involves asking the mediator who handled your original case—as opposed to a mediation center's case manager—to call the other party to try to get him to honor the agreement. If you used a mediation center, contact the mediator through them. If you used an independent mediator, call the mediator directly.

If the other party still trusts and respects the mediator, the mediator may be able to persuade her to comply. Many mediators will be willing to help out in this way, although some may decline to do so on the ground that involving themselves in matters of noncompliance is inconsistent with a mediator's neutral role. Mediators who work with private dispute resolution companies tend to be more inclined to help out as a matter of customer service; mediators at public centers are more likely to decline on ethical grounds.

IF YOU ARE THE PARTY WHO RENEGES . . .

If you are the party who does not want to honor the mediation agreement, what can you do? If your agreement was written in the form of a binding contract, you don't have the legal right to change it by yourself. Short of simply ignoring it and hoping the other side will decide it is too expensive or time-consuming to sue you for breaching it, you will have to convince the other side that for some reason it's in their best interest to accommodate you. Reasons might vary from:

- It's in their best interest to do so. Try to persuade the other side that the agreement made in mediation is not maximally beneficial to either of you, and that changing it will benefit not only you but the other party, too.

- It's the only way to avoid more problems. Tell the other side the agreement failed to address important issues (or that new ones have arisen since the agreement was made), and unless the mediation is re-opened to deal with these matters you will not comply and may be forced to take legal action against him in regard to these other issues.

---

3. Suing to Enforce the Agreement

Going to court to enforce a mediation agreement is a last resort. Unless you can make use of small claims court, you will endure at last some of the costs and delays of the adversary system you tried to avoid by going to mediation in the first place. Nevertheless, if the other party reneges on the agreement and ignores all the persuasive efforts of the mediation service or mediator, then court might be the place you have to go.

Fortunately, with a well-drafted, binding mediation agreement in hand, your job (or your lawyer's job) in court can be much easier than it would have been otherwise. Coming into court with the mediation agreement, the question for the judge is: "Is this a valid and enforceable contract?" If it is, the judge can enforce it by entering a judgment in your favor. Had you gone to court without mediation, the questions before the judge would have been far more difficult, such as, What are the facts? Who is right and who is wrong? How much is owed? And of course, there is no assurance you would have come out of court with anything resembling what you wanted. Having a contract should also help speed you through the court process. You may even be eligible, for example, for what is called a "summary judgment." This is an accelerated process available when the facts supporting one party's case are so clear that the judge concludes there are no issues in need of a trial and decides in that party's favor.

In some states—Texas, for example—mediation agreements reached under state-sponsored mediation programs are assumed under law to be enforceable in court. Otherwise, you will need to convince a judge that your agreement satisfies the requirements of a legally binding contract. The other party, for example, may try to argue that the agreement as written lacks reciprocal promises (what the law calls "consideration" or a quid pro quo), or is unclear and open to different interpretations and therefore unenforceable. You or your lawyer will need to counter these kinds of arguments, and your success in doing so will largely depend on how skillfully the agreement was drafted in the first place. You will also want to present evidence that mediation was conducted fairly. (For information on how to write an agreement as a binding, legal contract, see Chapter 8, Section D2.)

A. REPRESENTING YOURSELF IN COURT

If your agreement is mainly concerned with the payment of an amount of money that is less than the small claims court monetary limit in your state, you will probably want to represent yourself in small claims court. If so, be prepared to state your case by telling the judge both that a contract exists and about the process that led up to its writing and signing. Be sure to present a copy of the contract to the judge. Also bring with you a copy of the mediation service's rules, or even a descriptive brochure explaining how mediation is conducted. The judge may be looking for assurance that your session was conducted fairly, that the other party was not coerced into making the agreement and that both of you intended the agreement to be binding. If you take your case to a regular trial court, you or your lawyer will need to offer the same types of proof.

4. ENFORCING THE MEDIATION AWARD

If a judge finds that your agreement was a contract and that the other party breached it, she can issue a judgment in your favor for the full amount due, plus court costs and interest from the date the money was supposed to have been paid. If you have suffered damages because of the other side's failure to live up to the agreement, the judge might award you some money for that, too.

Unfortunately, winning in court does not necessarily resolve your dispute. The same party who reneged on the mediation agreement may balk at paying a court judgment. You may be facing years of collection proceedings before a wage garnishment or seizure of assets yields the money due you. Thus, while court may ultimately be the only way you can collect, you probably made no mistake by trying mediation first.

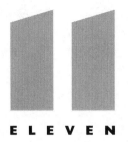

E L E V E N

Divorce Mediation

An increasing number of divorcing couples are going to mediation. Some go by order of a judge to court-sponsored programs— because they live in states that require mediation of issues such as child custody and visitation. Others voluntarily seek out private divorce mediators because they understand mediation to be a civilized and inexpensive alternative to the traditional two-lawyer, adversarial divorce.

This chapter examines both court-sponsored and private divorce mediation, with the intent of helping you mediate divorce-related issues effectively.

THIS CHAPTER APPLIES TO BOTH MARRIED AND UNMARRIED COUPLES. Tens of thousands of couples in the United States never marry. Some are heterosexual and don't choose marriage; others are homosexual and are legally prevented from marrying. Either way, when their relationships end, they often face many of the same issues married couples face when they separate and divorce, that is, division of commonly owned assets and debts and the custody, visitation and support of children they have co-parented. Fortunately, mediation is generally available to unmarried couples as well as those who are married. For example, though courts usually won't order mediation for unmarried couples, court-sponsored mediation programs often are available to help unmarried parents mediate parenting plans for their children, and private mediators are always available to work with unmarried couples. Although the examples in this chapter are written as though a legal marriage had taken place (and the terms "separation" and "divorce" are used), unmarried readers may assume the terms and examples in this chapter also apply to them.

A. What Is Divorce Mediation?

Divorce mediation is a process which can help a couple find a fair and practical way to end their marriage, divide their property and, if minor children are involved, continue to parent them as sensibly as possible.

1. TYPES OF ISSUES THAT MAY BE MEDIATED

In divorce mediation, a mediator works with a couple to help them reach their own agreement on various issues involved in the break-up of their marriage. As in other types of mediation, the mediator has no authority to impose a decision.

Depending on the length of the marriage, the economic situation of the family and whether or not there are minor children, a couple in mediation is likely to focus on the following issues, which are the same issues that lawyers would help a divorcing couple negotiate or fight out in court in an adversarial divorce:

- *Division of property (assets and debts).* How should jointly-owned or marital property (which may include real estate, small business ownership, stocks, automobiles and household and personal items) be divided? Similarly, how should marital debts such as college loans, mortgages and outstanding credit card debt, be divided?
- *Spousal maintenance (also called alimony).* How much money, if any, will one spouse regularly pay to help cover the other's living expenses, and for how long will it be paid?
- *Custody and visitation of children.* Will only one parent have custody of the children, or will custody be shared in some way? How often, for how long and under what circumstances will the children spend time with each parent? How will the parents resolve such major continuing parental issues as education, medical treatment and discipline?
- *Child support.* How much money will one parent regularly pay the other to help cover the cost of raising the children?

2. UNDERSTANDING THE TYPES OF MEDIATION

As mentioned earlier, there are two basic and very different types of divorce mediation offered throughout the country today: court-sponsored mediation and private mediation.

A. COURT-SPONSORED MEDIATION

Court-sponsored mediation occurs in nearly two-thirds of the states, where courts can require couples to mediate issues of child custody and visitation, and, in some states, child support. (See Section D, below.) In some of these states, all couples facing child custody, visitation and support issues are routinely ordered to mediation. In others, judges have the power to order mediation on a case-by-case basis. (And in some states where judges have the power to require mediation, whether they routinely do so varies from one court district to another.)

Court-sponsored mediation is generally of short duration: just one or two sessions are most typical. This is due, in part, to the typically high volume of cases passing through the mediator's office and also because the couple is only mediating child issues; division of property issues are not handled by most of these programs. (There are exceptions. In Maine, for example, couples mediate economic issues, as well.)

Court-sponsored mediation is usually free, or provided at nominal cost. Mediators in these programs are often full-time court employees appointed at random on a case-by-case basis.

B. PRIVATE MEDIATION

In private mediation, couples voluntarily retain the services of a mediator of their own choosing. The couple can choose to make their mediation comprehensive, covering all or most of the issues in their divorce, or to limit it to just some issues, typically custody. A half dozen or more lengthy sessions may be required, depending on the number and complexity of issues being addressed.

Fees vary widely, from about $50 to $300/hour per couple, with $100 per hour being typical in a mid-size city. The mediators tend to be solo or small group practitioners who specialize in divorce and family mediation.

The table below broadly compares the two basic types of divorce mediation.

COURT-SPONSORED VS. PRIVATE DIVORCE MEDIATION

	COURT-SPONSORED	PRIVATE
How cases get to mediation	Parents can be ordered to mediation by the court	Couples agree voluntarily to hire private mediator
Cost	Usually free	Ranges widely from $50-$300/hour per couple, depending on geographical area and other factors; lower fees available at some community dispute centers
Issues addressed	Usually limited to parenting arrangements (custody and visitation), but includes child support and property division in some states	Couple can mediate all issues (custody and economic), or just some
Who are the mediators?	Often full-time court employees with social services or mental health backgrounds	Usually self-employed practitioners or small groups with backgrounds in mental health or law
Confidential?	Yes, unless mediator has power to make recommendation to court, or child abuse is revealed	Yes, unless child abuse is revealed
Length of time	Often just one or two sessions of 1-2 hours each; but some programs offer more sessions plus follow-up	Typically, 4-8 sessions of two hours each spread over 3-4 months; depends on whether couple has minor children or complex financial issues, and their negotiating ability
Involvement of lawyers	Lawyers may, but need not, attend sessions. Spouses can consult a lawyer or other adviser if legal questions arise	Lawyers may, but need not, attend sessions. Spouses can consult a lawyer or other adviser if legal questions arise or significant money or property is involved

3. CONDITIONS FOR SUCCESSFUL MEDIATION

Successful divorce mediation requires that both spouses be able to participate effectively. If either spouse is so impaired psychologically that sustained, rational discussion is impossible, mediation will not work. (A good mediator will usually be able to tell during the first session if a spouse is unsuited for mediation due to depression or otherwise. If so, the mediator will terminate the session and refer the couple to a social service agency or another professional who can help, such as a therapist.)

On the other hand, to mediate does not mean you and your spouse have to like each other, or even be speaking to each other outside the mediation room. It is simply not true, as some divorce lawyers tell their clients, that mediation works only for a small number of couples who remain friendly while they are splitting up. Couples who mediate successfully often are just as dissatisfied with their marriages and just as angry at their spouses as are other couples.

4. WHEN MEDIATION IS SUCCESSFUL

When mediation is successful, the outcome is an agreement written up by the mediator, and approved by both spouses, detailing, in plain language, the terms of their settlement. This can be a brief document of a couple pages covering just the basics—dividing a moderate amount of property (house and cars) and describing the basic child custody and visitation arrangements—or a lengthy one of 40 pages or more specifying, in detail, how the couple will divide a long and complicated list of property and how they will handle a number of parenting issues that are likely to arise. (For a sample court-sponsored agreement, see Section D9; for excerpts from a private agreement, see pages following Section E9.)

In both court-sponsored and private divorce mediation, any agreement a couple reaches must ultimately be submitted to a judge for approval as part of a legal divorce decree.

B. Advantages of a Mediated Divorce

The growing popularity of divorce mediation can be attributed to a number of advantages generally available to couples who use it. These include:

1. Cost Savings: Nearly all studies comparing the costs of a two-lawyer adversarial divorce and mediated divorce show cost-savings through mediation.

Even including the cost of lawyers for each spouse to consult with before and during mediation, and later to review the written agreement and dealing with whatever paperwork is necessary, mediation still costs a fraction (perhaps one-third or less) of what it costs to fight a divorce out in court. A big reason for this is that when a couple works out issues in mediation, it reduces the time that lawyers need to spend on the case, and especially the time lawyers need to be dealing with the case at all in court.

2. Time Savings: In private divorce mediation, a couple could reasonably expect to work out agreements on all major issues—children and economics— after attending five to eight sessions of one to two hours each over a period of three to four months. A couple with no minor children (or no major disputes over custody and visitation) and garden-variety, middle-class property issues might finish in half the time. By comparison, two lawyers negotiating the same range of contested issues on behalf of their clients, while at the same time preparing for a contested court action should negotiations fail, would be likely to take significantly longer—running up hundreds of billable hours between them in the process—to reach a comprehensive settlement.

3. Success and Satisfaction Rates: About three-fourths of couples who mediate—whether in court-sponsored programs or privately—reach agreement on all or some of the issues addressed. For example, in California's mandatory, court-sponsored program, 78.3% of couples reached agreement on custody arrangements either during or soon after mediation. In a Texas program, about 70% reach agreement on custody. Couples who reach agreement—and even many of those who do not—report a high level of satisfaction with the process, noting it gave them a chance to discuss their concerns with a person willing to listen.

4. Post-Divorce Relationship: When compared to similar couples who had an adversarial divorce, couples who mediate have been shown in a number of studies to have more stable agreements (less need to modify), more generous visitation plans for the noncustodial parent, fewer missed payments of child support and a more cordial relationship with their former spouse.

EVEN THOUGH MEDIATION HAS MANY ADVANTAGES, it may also have some disadvantages, especially if there is a power imbalance between the parties. See the sidebar in Section C3, below.

C. Issues Common to Court-Sponsored and Private Mediation

Court-sponsored and private mediation are similar in many ways, but there are also significant differences, such as in how your case gets started and how your mediator is selected or assigned. Read this section first about matters that are common to both types of divorce mediation. Then, in the two sections following, you can read information that applies only to the type of divorce mediation you will be using: Section D for court-sponsored mediation or Section E for private mediation (or read both if you are not yet sure which type you will use). As you work through the specialized information in Sections D and E, refer back to the general points in this section that apply to both types of divorce mediation.

DON'T TRY TO MIX THE TWO TYPES OF MEDIATION. In theory you could mediate custody issues with a court-sponsored program and then mediate economic issues separately with a private mediator, but this would make it difficult to work out an agreement that recognizes the close relationship between custody and economics. If you want to mediate both of these issues, for best results address them together at one type of mediation or the other, and since most court-sponsored programs do not handle economic issues, this means in most instances you will need to use private mediation.

1. THE ROLE OF THE MEDIATOR

The goal of any divorce mediator is to help a couple reach a fair and workable agreement on the various issues involved in the ending of their marriage, including a plan to care for the couple's minor children, if any, as sensibly as possible. The mediator does not function as a lawyer or a therapist (even if the mediator has a professional background in law or counseling), and has no authority to impose a decision.

IN A FEW STATES, A MEDIATOR CAN RECOMMEND A SOLUTION TO THE JUDGE. A partial exception to the general rule that mediators have no power to impose a decision exists in several of the states that have court-sponsored mediation programs. In these states, if the couple does not reach an agreement, the mediator may recommend to the judge how the issues should be decided. For more on mediator recommendations, see Section D11.

It is important to understand that divorce mediators do not try to help a couple reconcile. Helping a couple deal with hurt or anger, and reviewing problems of a marriage, are not relevant to divorce mediation, except to the extent that they help the couple deal with current and future issues, such as dividing property, and deciding who will run a family business or have primary physical custody of the children. Indeed, mediators generally will not consider a couple ready for mediation unless both spouses have accepted the reality that the marriage is ended. (Despite this strong bias against acting as a marriage counselor, some mediators report as many as one in ten mediating couples reconcile because in mediation they are able to communicate in a nonadversarial manner and grow to understand the economic realities of divorce.)

2. ROLE OF LAWYERS

Even if your divorce mediator happens to be a lawyer—or even a judge—by background, he or she is not functioning in this role during the mediation. Although the lawyer-mediator may inform you about the law (some nonlawyer mediators will do this, too), you should not rely on the mediator to evaluate the legal consequences of a particular approach to settlement, or recommend a decision or course of action for you. If you need that kind of advice, you should do your own research and/or ask a lawyer—preferably one acting in the role of self-help law coach. (See Chapter 13, Lawyers and Legal Research.)

As a practical matter, not everyone will want to, or even need to, retain a lawyer. For example, if you and your spouse have no minor children and no significant property to divide up, or your income is such that child support will be at the minimum level required by state law and there will be no spousal support, it would make no sense to pay a hefty hourly fee to have a lawyer advise you as you go through mediation. On the other hand, if you own a thriving business, have major stock and real estate assets and are looking at a potentially big claim for spousal support from your stay-at-home spouse, you really should get good legal advice. (The lawyer should be advising or representing just you—and not both of you—since you and your spouse will not have the same legal interests or rights.)

If you do decide to pay for legal advice, here are some suggestions as to how you can best work with a lawyer at different phases of the mediation process:

Before mediation. Consult with a lawyer or law coach to:

- learn about your legal rights—or be referred to good self-help resources
- learn how a judge might decide your case, and
- plan your negotiation strategy.

During mediation. If you are already informed about the legal rules that affect the disputes in your case, you probably don't need a lawyer present at your mediation, although you always have the right to bring one if you want. As discussed earlier (Chapter 6, Section G), there is seldom much for a lawyer to do during mediation, and occasionally lawyers even disrupt the process by acting in too much of an adversarial manner in what should be a cooperative proceeding. But you may want to consider consulting with your lawyer between sessions to review developments. If your mediation may last only one session (as in many court-sponsored mediation programs), try to arrange for your lawyer to be in his or her office during the session so you can consult by phone if the need arises.

Still, there may be some situations where you do want your lawyer to accompany you to a mediation session. For example, you may expect that a legal issue you don't fully understand will arise during the session and, under the court-sponsored program, a second session will not be available. Or, you may be intimidated by your spouse and want your lawyer there to bolster your confidence and to speak for you (you may be able to achieve the same effect at lower cost by bringing a family member or friend—see Section C4). Or, you may be in a state, such as Maine, where lawyers are encouraged to participate in the sessions.

After mediation. Have your lawyer review the agreement before you sign it to be sure your legal rights are protected.

BE SURE ANY LAWYER YOU CHOOSE SUPPORTS MEDIATION. If you use a lawyer, try to select one who both understands family law and is comfortable with his or her limited role in the mediation process, and who is willing to work with you to make it successful. As one administrator of a court-sponsored program put it, the kind of lawyer you want to work with in mediation is "a guide dog, not a guard dog." For more on finding a lawyer to work with in mediation, see Chapter 6, Section H, and Chapter 13, Section A.

3. Seven Ways to Prepare for Divorce Mediation

The issues you will discuss and the agreement, if any, you reach in divorce mediation will have an important affect on you and your family for many years. It follows that it's worth taking the time necessary to be prepared well. Also, if you prepare for mediation by carefully considering the range of realistic options available for the major custody and financial issues involved in your case and what you want a final plan to look like, you will be much less susceptible to being hurt by a potential power imbalance between you and your spouse. (See sidebar, below.)

Whether you will be using a court-sponsored mediation program or a private divorce mediator, read this section to learn how to prepare. For additional ways to prepare for a mediation that are specific to court-sponsored mediation, see Section D, and for private divorce mediation, see Section E.

A. READ THE PROGRAM LITERATURE AND MEDIATION RULES

You may receive from the court-sponsored mediation program or private divorce mediator a brochure or other written material describing the mediation process. Read it carefully. Once your mediation begins, you don't want to waste time asking questions already covered in a brochure. Look especially for information about the expected length of the session and what to bring. For a court-sponsored program, the brochure may explain what issues you will be allowed to discuss (almost always custody and visitation and less often economic issues), and what will happen if you don't reach a settlement (Can you meet again? Does the mediator make a recommendation to the court? Will someone else be assigned to evaluate your case?).

You may also be sent a list of rules that will govern the procedures to be followed in your mediation. Familiarize yourself with the rules so you understand how the mediation will be conducted. If you have any questions, be prepared to ask them during the initial session. (Some private mediators don't provide a separate set of rules; instead, you will find them included as part of the mediator's Contract for Mediation Services as discussed in Section E3.)

In getting ready for mediation, you may also want to consult other books about separation and divorce, and particularly how to resolve issues of child custody and visitation. Many good works are available, including:

- *Child Custody: Building Agreements That Work,* by Mimi E. Lyster (Nolo Press)
- *Mom's House, Dad's House: Making Shared Custody Work,* by Isolina Ricci, Ph.D. (Macmillan Publishing Co.)
- *Practical Divorce Solutions,* by Charles Sherman (Nolo Press)
- *A Guide to Divorce Mediation,* by Gary J. Friedman (Workman Publishing, 1993). This book includes edited transcripts of actual mediation sessions.

If you are able to mediate economic issues, consider reading *Divorce and Money,* by Woodhouse and Collins (Nolo Press).

B. LEARN WHAT THE LAW SAYS

During mediation, you will be negotiating with your spouse in what mediators often refer to as "the shadow of the law." By this, they mean that how a judge might be expected to apply the law to your case—such as on issues of custody and support—will often serve as a benchmark or at least a starting point for the discussions you and your spouse will have on these issues in mediation.

Because the state claims a major role in trying to guarantee a child will be well cared for, the "shadow of the law" is longer in divorce mediation involving child custody and visitation issues than it usually is in other areas. For example, earlier in this book we pointed out that in most mediations, while it is relevant to understand what a judge would likely do, the parties can still do otherwise. But in divorce mediation involving minor children, you have less leeway.

Let's look at an example. The law in every state requires that the best interests of the child be taken into account when a judge approves or disapproves a proposed child custody and visitation agreement. These rules generally take into consideration such factors as the stability of the parents, the willingness of the parents to co-parent and the wishes of the children (especially older children). If your agreement is very far out of line with these factors, the judge may reject it and require you and your spouse to be more realistic. Of course, these are matters your mediator will be well-versed in, and you can normally expect him or her to discuss these guidelines during your session. But again, the more information you have ahead of time about what's legally required, the better you will be prepared for your session.

Also, you'll likely want to learn how the law would evaluate various other aspects of your case. For example, would the fact that your spouse occasionally used to spank the children cause a judge to give you full legal custody if you asked for it? Would the judge approve an agreement that, in effect, turned your children over to your spouse? If so, this may be a matter you will want to discuss in mediation. If not, you may not want to use up too much time and the mediator's patience harping on it.

IF YOU HAVE QUESTIONS ABOUT LEGAL ISSUES, do your own legal research or consult with your law coach. Start by calling the mediation office or the local family court and ask them to send you any printed materials they have that summarize your state's laws on custody, visitation, child support and valuation and disposition of marital property. You may also want to do some legal research in a law library. (For information on how to do your own legal research in a law library, see Chapter 13, Lawyers and Legal Research.) Most states also have self-help law books on the subject of divorce. They should be available in public libraries or bookstores. The following books may be of particular help:

- *Legal Research: How to Find and Understand the Law,* by Stephen Elias and Susan Levinkind (Nolo Press)
- *Nolo's Pocket Guide to Family Law,* by Robin Leonard and Stephen Elias (Nolo Press), a handy 50-state review of key laws covering marriage, divorce, child custody and visitation. A good place to start.
- *Divorce & Money: How to Make the Best Financial Decisions During Divorce,* by Violet Woodhouse & Victoria F. Collins, with M.C. Blakeman (Nolo Press). A definitive guide to evaluating assets during divorce. If you have a house, business, retirement plan or other significant investments, read this book.
- *Child Custody: Building Agreements That Work,* by Mimi Lyster (Nolo Press). The only book to show separating couples how to make their own excellent, comprehensive child custody agreements, checklists and worksheets.

OVERCOMING A "POWER IMBALANCE" IN DIVORCE MEDIATION

It is not unusual in a marriage for one spouse to be an emotional bully, or for one simply to be stronger than the other in terms of negotiating skill or knowledge about the issues being mediated. The latter situation might occur, for example, where one spouse is a business executive and the other a homemaker. Can the two really sit down in mediation and negotiate a deal that is fair to both? Won't the homemaker always lose out? Mediators refer to this situation as a "power imbalance." It is a question of unequal bargaining strength and it comes up often in the context of divorce mediation. (For a discussion of "power imbalance" generally in mediation, see Chapter 2, Section C.) Should weaker spouses be concerned that in mediation they might strike deals that are not in their best interests or in the best interests of their children?

One way to deal with a power imbalance is to go into mediation well-prepared. If you have considered all the realistic options for handling a particular issue—division of financial assets or your child's education, for example—and know what you want a final plan to look like, you will be less easily swayed in mediation by a more powerful spouse.

Another way to protect yourself is to select a divorce mediator who states in advance a willingness to intervene to block an agreement he or she sees as unfair to one side. (This opportunity would be available when using private divorce mediation, but probably not when using court-sponsored mediation where mediators are usually randomly assigned.) For more on selecting a private divorce mediator, see Section E2.

Finally, you can arrange to consult with a lawyer, law-coach or other adviser during the mediation process, and especially to review the written agreement before you sign it. (See Section C2, "Role of Lawyers," and also Sections D9 and E9.)

C. IDENTIFY YOUR PERSONAL GOALS FOR THE FUTURE

What do you want to do with the next five or ten years of your life? Keep your current job, find a new one in the same field, go back to school or begin a new career? What are your goals in terms of your relationship with your children? Spend more day-to-day time with them? Or spend more time with them on weekends and vacations so you can take them fishing?

Consider how your goals for the foreseeable future can be supported by various possible outcomes in mediation. You might, for instance, want to concentrate on getting higher spousal support payments while going to school and in exchange be more flexible in other areas. For example, if you've been thinking of leaving your current job in a daycare center to study to become a physician's assistant, do a little checking before your mediation on local availability of physician's assistant degree programs. If you find the closest school offering such a program is 70 miles away, that may affect your negotiating position in mediation: you may, for example, be willing to settle for slightly less visitation time during the three years of your academic program in exchange for higher current support payments.

D. IDENTIFY YOUR CHILDREN'S NEEDS

Once again, if you have minor children, the broad legal standard of making custody and visitation decisions based on the "best interests of the child" will serve as a backdrop for the negotiations that occur in your mediation. So, to prepare, it's a good idea to try sincerely to identify your child's "best interests." You'll really know you're on the right track if you can honestly face the possibility that your best interests and those of your child may sometimes differ. Start by asking what your children most need now. Consider financial support, parental supervision, opportunities for study, recreation, access to siblings and friends, relationships with other adults such as teachers, grandparents, other relatives and family friends.

LEARN THE ENTIRE RANGE OF POSSIBLE SOLUTIONS TO YOUR PROBLEM.
There are loads of possible issues in child custody—religion, schooling, step-
parents, moving out of state, worries about the fitness of a parent—but there are
a limited number of possible solutions for each. In her book, *Child Custody:*
Building Agreements That Work **(Nolo Press), Mimi E. Lyster reviews the range of**
possible solutions for dozens of common issues and provides handy worksheets
to help you design a parenting plan. I highly recommend it.

Let's take an example of how Mimi Lyster's book works, by looking at the
question of where the minor children of a divorcing couple will receive their
education. It's a big issue and may seem overwhelming to parents, particularly
when one or both is moving to a new location at the same time each is trying to
cope with the emotional turmoil that surrounds the process of separating.
Fortunately, by breaking the large issue of "education" into smaller parts, and
considering the range of possible choices for each, you can design a solution (or
select one of the options offered by the book) that works for your situation. In
her book, Lyster breaks "education" into these smaller issues:

- Will children attend public, private or home school?
- Who will pay for private or home school?
- How will decisions to change schools be made?
- How will parents participate in the classroom, in parent associations, in
  parent-chaperoned events, in parent-teacher conferences?
- What emergency contact information will be given to the school?
- How will a good or acceptable school performance be defined?
- How will a good or acceptable school performance be encouraged?
- May children attend sex education classes?
- How will post-secondary education be paid for?
- How will decisions about post-secondary education be made?

The following excerpt from the Education section of Lyster's Parenting
Agreement Worksheet offers a range of options from which you and your spouse
can select a solution that works best for your situation.

EXERCISE #1 | **PARENTING AGREEMENT WORKSHEET**

EDUCATION

Our children will attend [choose one]:

☐ public school

☐ private school

☐ home school

We will pay for any private or home school as follows [specify]: _____

Any decision to change schools will be made as follows [choose all that apply]:

☐ If we agree

☐ After consulting our children

☐ After consulting with _____ [parent]

☐ Only _____ [parent] may change
    our children's enrollment in a particular school.

We will participate in parent associations as follows [choose one]:

☐ Either parent may participate

☐ Only one parent may participate at a time.

_____ [parent] will participate.

In short, by using worksheets such as those in Lyster's book, you can sift through lots of alternative solutions to most common divorce-related problems and therefore be prepared to propose in mediation the specifics of a parenting agreement that will work best in your situation. This is the kind of very specific advance preparation that can be especially helpful if your spouse tends to be highly opinionated and often attempts to dominate these decisions. (See sidebar on "power imbalance" at the beginning of this section.)

E. ASSESS YOUR FINANCIAL NEEDS

In order to negotiate effectively in mediation, you will need to understand what your financial needs realistically will be after the divorce. For example, how much will it cost you each month both to pursue the life plan you would like and to support your children? Do you and your ex-spouse earn or own enough to make these goals realistic? One good way to begin thinking about financial issues is to try to list all post-divorce living expenses you reasonably can anticipate. Major categories of monthly expenses are likely to include:

- Residence payments (rent or mortgage, taxes and insurance, maintenance)
- Food at home and household supplies
- Food: eating out
- Utilities
- Telephone
- Laundry and cleaning
- Clothing
- Medical and dental (insurance and out-of-pocket payments)

- Insurance (life and accident)
- Child care
- Education (tuition, continuing education classes)
- Entertainment
- Transportation and auto expenses (insurance, gas, oil and repairs)
- Installment payments (credit cards and loans)
- Incidentals.

If your mediation will include discussion of financial issues such as child support and/or spousal support (also called alimony or spousal maintenance), bring this financial information to the mediation.

DETERMINE WHETHER EITHER SPOUSE IS LIKELY TO RECEIVE SPOUSAL SUPPORT (ALIMONY). In most states, the determination of whether spousal support will be awarded by a court is based on such factors as each spouse's needs and earning capabilities, the age, health and standard of living of each spouse, and the length of the marriage. For example, if a couple was in a very short marriage and both have decent jobs, a court probably will award little or no support to either spouse. But if the marriage has lasted 15 years and one spouse has been out of the job market for a decade or more while spending full-time raising the children, spousal support is likely to be awarded to the nonworking spouse. It is important to find out if spousal support is a realistic option for a couple, because, as emphasized earlier, the mediation will be conducted in the shadow of the law; that is, both parties and the mediator should be negotiating an agreement more or less like what a judge would be likely to impose if the case were fought out in court.

If you are going to a private mediator and will be discussing financial issues, your mediator will probably ask you and your spouse to prepare detailed financial disclosure forms (usually as "homework" in advance of the second or third mediation session—see Section E8). If you suspect your spouse may be inclined to overlook or conceal assets, try quietly, before your mediation begins, to make a list of what you know to be your own and your spouse's assets.

MAKE SURE YOU ARE PROPERLY INFORMED. If you have reason to believe your spouse is a liar and is hiding a pile of assets (stocks, bonds, cash, gold, ownership of real estate), be sure to discuss this with a lawyer. You may want to take legal action in order to do lots of discovery, such as subpoena bank and stock brokerage records, and question your spouse under oath with legal penalties if she is later found to have lied.

F. GATHER EVIDENCE TO BRING TO MEDIATION

There may be issues that you expect will come up during mediation for which you can prepare some supporting evidence. You can probably negotiate more effectively with your spouse if your claims and concerns can be illustrated and supported by documentation and other types of evidence. (For more a more general discussion of the persuasive effect of various kinds of evidence, see Chapter 6, Section D.)

For example, if your child has been seeing a therapist and, at your request, the therapist has made a written report about custody, bring the report with you so you can discuss it with the mediator and your spouse.

G. FOCUS ON THE FUTURE

Mediation is not about problems such as which spouse was right or wrong in a particular dispute or who said what to whom and who was hurt the most. Divorce mediators are not judges and have no power to make a decision (although in a few sates, they sometimes can make a recommendation to the court regarding child custody and visitation issues—see Section D11). Divorce mediation is about creating a plan as to how you and your spouse are going to dissolve your marriage and, if applicable, continue to be parents of your children and give them the best upbringing possible under the circumstances.

In short, to get the most out of mediation, you need to sincerely prepare yourself to use it as a problem-solving process, not as a place to fight old battles. If you can approach mediation looking toward the future, then you will be well-prepared to get the most out of the process.

EIGHT TIPS FOR CONDUCTING YOURSELF IN MEDIATION

As noted earlier (Chapter 7, Section D1), mediators are human beings and may be influenced in their work by the impressions they get of you and your spouse. For example, if the mediator comes to see one spouse as more reasonable and reliable than the other, she may try to move the other spouse's position in that direction. Given the choice, you want to be the one the mediator sees as more reasonable. If you are mediating in a court-sponsored program and the mediator has power to make a recommendation regarding child custody and visitation, this becomes all the more important. See Section D11.

The following tips may help.

1. Realize your mediator is not a judge. Expecting your mediator to function as a judge, therapist, lawyer or marriage counselor just wastes time. The mediator's only job is to help you and your spouse reach agreement on the issues.

2. Don't demonize your spouse. Don't try to prove what a bad person your spouse is and what a great person you are. Deciding who is good and who is bad is not the mediator's job.

3. Don't play the victim. Showing how poorly you have been treated, even if it's true, may appear self-serving and the mediator may not take you seriously. In any case, it's usually not relevant to what will happen in the future. (You are done being a victim, right?)

4. Focus on the future. If your spouse persists in bringing up his or her version of the past, simply say that while you don't necessarily agree, you want to focus on the future and look for a solution that will be good for your children and acceptable to both you and your spouse.

5. Keep in mind the "best interests" of your children. The law says decisions about custody are to be based on the best interests of the child. Develop your arguments around this standard and the mediator will be more likely to help you achieve your goals.

6. Show how you relate to your children. Show what your relationship has been with the child in the past with clear examples (projects, homework, trips, meals, hobbies you share, bedtime rituals, regular time together).

7. Show you can be a good "co-parent." Emphasize you understand that a child needs the support and love of both parents (even imperfect ones) and that you can cooperate with your spouse in co-parenting your child.

8. Raise whatever forward-looking issues are important to you. Raise important issues—even if they are not legal ones—involving children, your extended family, future relations with your spouse, while you have the opportunity.

IF YOU KNOW YOUR SPOUSE WILL MAKE ANGRY FALSE CHARGES.
Although it can be tough to keep your cool, your best approach is not to respond
to your spouse's anger. Just politely say and repeat that you are present to work
out what's best for your children in the future. You can count on the mediator
supporting this view and helping to calm down your spouse.

4. WHO MAY ATTEND MEDIATION?

Usually, just the spouses attend mediation sessions, but if you and your spouse both want, and the mediator agrees, you can invite others to participate when their presence would be helpful. For example, when you are negotiating visitation plans, you may want to include one or more of the children's grandparents or other relatives who have a significant stake in the future of your children. You can also invite people who have been involved in an important way in your marriage and family life, such as relatives or friends living in your home. (Your new partner may be welcomed, but not if his or her presence would make it more difficult for your spouse to participate effectively in the mediation.)

Or you may simply want to bring someone with you for emotional support, or to assist in describing your family situation, or to help you consider settlement options as they arise during the session. (This would be more typical in court-sponsored mediation when you may have only one session to get everything on the table and decided.) You also have the right to bring a lawyer to mediation, although this is generally not done. See Section C2.

As for children attending, some mediators like to devote part of a session to meeting with children, usually those above the age of eight to ten. This occurs after the parents have completed negotiating their parenting plan. The mediator, meeting alone with the children, will review the plan, ask for the children's reaction, and assure them their parents love them and have worked hard to create a good plan for the future. If the children have questions or problems with the plan, the mediator will review these with the parents. Other mediators prefer not to involve children. Whether your children will be able to participate will depend in part on their ages and the rules followed by the particular court-sponsored program or private mediator.

If you have children, relatives or other friends who you think should attend the mediation, check the mediation brochure, printed rules, or call the mediation office or private mediator to see if this will be allowed.

5. CONFIDENTIALITY

As a general rule, your mediator will be required by law and/or court rule to keep confidential everything that is said during mediation. This means if you do not reach a settlement and your case ends up in court, you cannot call the mediator as a witness to tell the judge what your spouse said during mediation. There are some important exceptions to this general rule, however:

- *In many states, mediators are required to report any reasonable suspicions of child neglect or abuse.* This means, for example, if you tell the mediator— even in private caucus—that you or your spouse has physically abused your children, if the mediator believes what you are saying may be true, he may be required under law to report it to a social service agency for investigation.
- *Mediators may have a duty to report anyone who, in the mediator's opinion, makes a specific and believable threat against another person.* For example, you might say to the mediator in caucus, "I don't care what happens at this mediation because next Saturday night I'm going to deal with this problem once and for all." If the mediator concludes that this is a threat, he may be required under law to report it to the police or other authority.

DON'T MAKE REMARKS THAT CAN BE MISCONSTRUED AS THREATS.
Realize that every year people who work in areas relating to child custody and support, including judges, lawyers, social workers and even occasionally mediators, are attacked and sometimes killed. As a result, everyone in this field is extremely sensitive to threatening behavior. Just as you wouldn't tell a joke about bombing an airplane while walking through an airport metal detector because it is illegal to do so, do not make remarks as part of your mediation session that could possibly be interpreted as threats to the mediator, your spouse or anyone else.

D. Court-Sponsored Divorce Mediation

Lawmakers are becoming convinced that mediation really is a better way to negotiate issues affecting the custody and visitation of children. Accordingly, in many states, judges can order couples to mediate before they can argue about these issues in court. As one observer put it, "It's got to be better to give a couple two hours with a mediator to talk about who is going to have custody of their kids, than five minutes in front of a judge."

The state with the largest program of mandated, court-sponsored mediation is California. Since 1981, California law has required parents to try mediating child custody and visitation issues before proceeding to a court hearing. Today, court-based mediators in California conduct about 65,000 mediation sessions per year. Other states with court-sponsored programs are listed in the table below.

As noted, three aspects of court-sponsored divorce mediation that distinguish it from private mediation are:

1. It is generally free,

2. The discussions usually are limited to parenting issues, such as child custody and visitation, and

3. The process is shorter, usually lasting just one or two sessions.

STATES WITH COURT-SPONSORED PROGRAMS WHERE PARENTS CAN BE ORDERED TO PARTICIPATE IN MEDIATION BEFORE BRINGING A CUSTODY OR VISITATION DISPUTE TO COURT

Alabama	Indiana	Missouri	Rhode Island
Alaska	Iowa	Montana	South Carolina
Arizona	Kansas	Nevada	South Dakota
California	Kentucky	New Jersey	Texas
Colorado	Louisiana	New Mexico	Utah
Connecticut	Maine	North Carolina	Virginia
Delaware	Maryland	North Dakota	Washington
Florida	Michigan	Ohio	West Virginia
Idaho	Minnesota	Oregon	Wisconsin
Illinois	Mississippi	Pennsylvania	

Table adapted from *Nolo's Pocket Guide to Family Law,* by Leonard and Elias (Nolo Press).

I. HOW YOUR CASE GETS STARTED

The trigger that usually kicks a case into a court-sponsored mediation program is parents with minor children filing a divorce action in court. (For unmarried couples, cases can come into a court-sponsored program in various ways, such as when a child's father who is no longer living with the mother petitions the court for the right to spend more time with the child, or the mother asks the court to determine paternity or for help in securing financial support from the father.) An officer within the court system typically will automatically notify you in writing that you are required to participate in the mediation program, if you are unable to settle matters among yourselves.

The written notice may tell you the date and time when you should report for mediation, or may instruct you to contact the office to schedule a time. For example, here is a notice you would receive if you lived in Oakland, California, and filed a divorce action in the Superior Court of Alameda County:

EXERCISE #2 **FAMILY COURT SERVICES**

The Superior Court of Alameda County encourages parents to settle matters of how their children will be raised after their separation between themselves. If you are unable to agree with the other parent about what should happen with your children, you must discuss these matters before your court hearing with a Family Court Services counselor who will assist you in developing a plan for your children.

YOU ARE ORDERED TO CALL FAMILY COURT SERVICES IMMEDIATELY,
IF YOU DO NOT HAVE A PARENTAL AGREEMENT.

CALL AT LEAST FIFTEEN (15) WORKING DAYS PRIOR TO YOUR
COURT DATE TO ALLOW FOR THE SCHEDULING OF THE MEDIATION

For an action filed in OAKLAND call: (510) 272-6030

For an action filed in HAYWARD call: (510) 670-6350

For an action filed in PLEASANTON call: (510) 551-6892

DISREGARD THIS NOTICE IF THERE IS NO DISAGREEMENT REGARDING THE
CHILDREN BETWEEN THE PARENTS.

2. Can You Avoid Mandatory Mediation?

There may be good reasons why you do not want to mediate, or you may be willing to mediate but do not want to do it through the court-sponsored program. Perhaps your spouse has been physically violent toward you and under no circumstances are you willing to sit in the same room with her, or maybe you know of and can afford an excellent private divorce mediator and prefer to use him instead of the mediators available through the court program. Following are several ways you may be able to "opt-out" of a court-sponsored program:

A. REACH AGREEMENT BEFORE MEDIATION

If you and your spouse can agree on your own about parenting before the scheduled date of your mediation, you do not need to mediate. The mediation office will probably require you to file a written statement, signed by you and your spouse, affirming you are in full agreement on issues of custody and visitation.

B. CHOOSING A PRIVATE MEDIATOR

In many states, you can opt out of the court-sponsored mediation program by instead using a private mediator. (See Section E, below.) In Wisconsin, for example, parents "may, at their own expense, receive mediation services from a mediator other than one who provides services under [the court-sponsored program]." To do so, both parents have to sign and file with the court a written notice giving the private mediator's name and the date of the first scheduled session. (Wisc. Stat. Section 767.11(7).)

For couples who can afford private mediator fees (see Section E2, below), private mediation offers several advantages:

- the opportunity to pursue a comprehensive agreement on all issues, not just those involving co-parenting
- the ability to choose your own mediator rather than having one appointed
- the flexibility of scheduling sessions after business hours and in convenient locations and
- generally, more time to explore the issues.

It's worth noting that not everyone who can afford to do so opts out of the court-sponsored programs in favor of private mediation. "It's true that many couples at the upper socio-economic levels go to private mediators," notes Doneldon Dennis, a supervisor at Hennepin County (Minnesota) Family Court Services, "but we also handle cases where couples report annual gross income of one-quarter to one-half million dollars."

Even if you cannot afford a private mediator, you may still be able to opt out of the court-sponsored program by going to your local community mediation center. As discussed earlier (see Chapter 3, Section B1), nonprofit community mediation centers usually provide mediation services free or at nominal cost, and about half of the 400-plus centers nationally handle divorce cases. As with private mediation, at a community center you would probably not be restricted to mediating parenting issues but could pursue a comprehensive settlement of all issues. However, the quality of volunteer mediators handling divorce cases at community centers may be uneven, so if you choose this option you need to assure yourself that the mediator assigned has the training and skills you require. (See Section E2.)

If you think you might prefer private or community-center mediation to a court-sponsored program, ask the staff at the court-sponsored program if these alternatives are available to you under the law.

C. HISTORY OF DOMESTIC VIOLENCE

In some states, you may be excused from mandatory mediation if you can show you have been the victim of abuse or violence within your marriage. The concern is that an abused spouse would suffer emotionally from being forced to mediate or would be unable to mediate effectively. For example, Oregon law lets the court exempt a person from mediation if mediating would "subject the party to severe emotional distress." (Oregon Revised Statutes, Section 107.179(3).) States with similar provisions include Florida, Maryland, Minnesota and Wisconsin. Other states may allow victims of domestic abuse to refuse joint sessions; spouses can remain in separate rooms while the mediator shuttles between them. If you have been a victim of abuse and do not want to mediate, call the media-tion office and ask if state law or local court rules will allow you to be excused.

D. HISTORY OF CHILD ABUSE

Some states will excuse a couple from mediation if the court determines through past conviction or current presentation of evidence that one of the parents has engaged in child abuse. The purpose of this exemption seems to be to avoid a mediation session that would be too stressful for the nonabusive parent, and to allow the court itself to oversee issues of custody and visitation to be sure children are adequately protected. For example, Washington State exempts parents from mediation if the court finds a parent has engaged in "physical, sexual, or a pattern of emotional abuse of a child." (Wash. Rev. Code Section 26.09.191(1).) Typically, these exemptions are triggered when a parent raises the objection as part of the divorce proceeding, and the court determines there has, in fact, been a history of child abuse. It may not make sense to try to raise this type of claim to avoid mandatory mediation unless you can really back it up.

E. MEDIATION WOULD BE "INAPPROPRIATE" OR AN "UNDUE HARDSHIP"

In some states, the court may waive the requirement to mediate if you can show that mediation would be "inappropriate" or an "undue hardship" under the circumstances. What qualifies for this catch-all type of exemption will vary from state to state. But in general, you would need to show that the particular facts of your case make it extremely unlikely that mediation would succeed, or that mediating itself would be overly burdensome. In North Carolina, for example, you can be excused from mediation based on "allegations of alcoholism, drug abuse, or spouse abuse; or allegations of severe psychological, psychiatric, or emotional problems," but also simply because you happen to live "more than fifty miles from the court." (North Carolina Gen. Stat. Section 50-13.1(c).) (For couples who do live in different cities—or in the same city but cannot get away from work—some court-sponsored programs may offer telephone mediation as an alternative.)

F. DOING THE MINIMUM REQUIRED

If for whatever reason you do not want to participate in court-mandated mediation (but have no grounds for opting out), the question arises: what is the least you must do to comply with the law? States differ on this question but, as a general rule, showing up for one session will fulfill your legal obligations. "It's rare," comments one mediator, "but occasionally someone shows up, crosses his arms, and says, 'My attorney says I have to be here but I'm not agreeing to anything.' In that case, we give it a try, but it may be just twenty minutes and out."

Some states make their minimum requirements explicit: in Wisconsin, for example, parties must "attend at least one session with a mediator." (Wisc. Stat. Section 767.11(8).) By contrast, Utah requires attendance at two sessions. (Utah Code Ann. Section 30-3-24(1)(a).)

A few states, such as Maine, are more vague and require parties "to make a good faith effort" to mediate. (Maine Rev. Stat. Ann. Section 752.) Most mediation offices interpret "good faith" to mean showing up for one session at the scheduled time and acting polite towards the mediator, your spouse and any others present. You don't have to be enthusiastic about mediation and you don't have to agree to anything. As one mediator put it, "What is mandatory is that you be exposed to the process. If you don't want to take advantage of it, that's your business."

To find what the minimum requirements are for your court-sponsored mediation program, call the mediation office (you may need to speak with a supervisor to get the correct answer to this question) or ask a lawyer or law coach.

3. WHO ARE THE DIVORCE MEDIATORS AND WHAT DO THEY DO?

What type of background and training is your mediator likely to have? Do you have any control over the specific mediator assigned to your case? In Chapter 3, we examined the backgrounds and training of mediators at various types of mediation providers. In this section, we will look more closely at these issues as they concern mediators in court-sponsored divorce mediation programs.

A. QUALIFICATIONS AND BACKGROUND

When court-sponsored divorce mediation began more than a decade ago, mediators were often volunteers or part-time court employees. These programs have grown in use and sophistication, however, and it is increasingly common to find mediators who are full-time, paid employees of the court system. As full-time mediators, they are likely to conduct between three and five mediations daily.

In large cities, full-time mediators are likely to be well-educated, often with master's degrees in the social sciences and professional backgrounds in mental health or family counseling. Many states set fairly stiff qualifications that typically include a minimum educational level and/or training and experience. In Oregon, for example, court-sponsored mediators must have a master's or law degree; about 60 hours of mediation training additional course work in areas such as child development, substance abuse and domestic violence; and two years' work experience in mediation, counseling or law.

Some states continue to use part-time employees or volunteers as mediators. Maine, for example, uses part-time mediators who work as independent contractors (some of whom may also work part-time as private divorce mediators). In selecting mediators, Maine emphasizes skills and experience rather than academic background. Still, two-thirds of Maine's family mediators—which include lawyers, therapists, social workers, college professors and homemakers—hold post-graduate degrees.

B. ROLE OF THE MEDIATOR

For a discussion of the role of divorce mediators generally, see Section C1. In addition, note that mediators in court-sponsored programs in some states are required by law to protect the interests of the children, in effect to act as advocates for the children. As such, a mediator would be obligated to raise questions about your children's welfare even if you and your spouse did not. Similarly, the mediator may block an agreement if he or she thinks it does not protect your children's interests. (Ultimately, of course, a court will have to approve any child-related decisions, but some court-sponsored mediators will be active monitors of child welfare issues even as the mediation takes place.)

THE STAKES ARE HIGHER IF THE MEDIATOR CAN MAKE A RECOMMENDATION TO THE JUDGE. In a few states, mediators have the power to make a recommendation to the judge if you and your spouse cannot reach an agreement. This power changes the mediator's role from one of neutral facilitator to one of evaluator or arbitrator and means you'll want to work hard to get a favorable recommendation. For more on mediators with power to recommend, see Section D11, below.

To better understand who court-sponsored mediators are and how they experience their work, consider the following profile of one mediator who works in a California program. Note the relatively heavy case load which is typical of court-sponsored mediators.

MEDIATOR PROFILE

Name: Brian Johnson

Profession: Family Court Services Counselor and Mediator

Employed: Superior Court, Alameda County, California

Educational Background: Master's in Clinical Psychology, California State University

Years in Practice: 14

Professional Affiliations: Member, American Association of Conciliation Courts

Number of Cases Handled in Career: 3,500

Current Case Load: 5 new and 10-15 returning families per week

Most Memorable Mediation Moment: "When I asked a husband how to spell his new girlfriend's name (in the presence of his estranged wife), he unbuttoned his shirt and checked his chest for the spelling."

Notable Features of My Conference Room: "A comfortably cluttered room in a county office building, including two framed photographic enlargements of a market square and a fountain from my last trip to Italy."

Favorite Expression Related to Conflict: "It's not the visitation schedule that makes an agreement work, its how the parents feel about the schedule."

Philosophy of Divorce Mediation: "I'm only there for a couple until they have the courage to exclude me. By that, I mean couples come to us at a time when they feel their world is falling apart. They need me to validate them as people and parents. But during mediation, people can grow in confidence and self-knowledge, and a time comes when they have the courage not to need me. That is when my job is done."

C. HOW A MEDIATOR IS ASSIGNED TO YOUR CASE

At most court-sponsored mediation programs, your mediator will be randomly assigned from a pool of mediators, although occasionally the assignment may be made based at least somewhat on the facts of a case. For example, if a couple has a child whose physical disabilities may affect decisions on custody and visitation, a mediator with special training in this area may be assigned. Similarly, a California mediator, skilled in dealing with men who are very upset about their divorce, reports he often is assigned the "angry man" cases; that is, those where the husband has acted violently either with his wife or with the staff at the mediation office.

MAKE YOUR NEEDS KNOWN IF YOUR MEDIATION INVOLVES SPECIAL ISSUES. If you think your case needs a mediator with special training, education or language ability, make this request to the staff. They will probably accommodate you if they are able.

D. CHECKING ON THE ASSIGNED MEDIATOR

Before your mediation, it is a good idea to do some checking to be sure the mediator assigned to your case does not have a conflict of interest that would prevent him or her from being neutral as between you and your spouse. (See Chapter 5, Selecting Mediation Services and Mediators, for more on how to do this.)

4. ROLE OF LAWYERS

For a discussion of this issue, see Section C2. For a general discussion about finding a lawyer to work with in mediation, see Chapter 6, Section G, and Chapter 13, Lawyers and Legal Research.

5. PREPARING FOR YOUR COURT-SPONSORED MEDIATION

To get ready for your court-sponsored mediation, review Section C3. Also, note the following issues special to court-sponsored mediation.

A. ATTEND THE ORIENTATION

The notice you received with the date of your mediation will probably tell you if an orientation session is available. If it is, try to attend. Some programs schedule orientations a week or more before the date of your mediation, others offer it the morning of the day of your mediation, and others offer them at regular times (for example, Wednesday mornings), and leave it up to the parties to attend if they choose.

Orientations, usually provided to groups of 10-20 people at a time, are often conducted like a classroom. Social workers or administrators usually lead the sessions, which last from one to two hours; your mediator probably will not be there. Typically, you will be informed about the mediation process, state laws on child custody and support, and receive some "parenting education" about the developmental needs of children. You may be shown a video about parenting education and/or mediation procedures. In some orientations, judges make an appearance to encourage couples to work together in the best interests of their children. If you missed your orientation, some offices may have a film or video of the class you can borrow.

B. CHECK IF THE MEDIATOR HAS POWER TO RECOMMEND OR EVALUATE

As noted earlier, mediators in some states have authority to recommend how your case should be decided if you and your spouse cannot reach an agreement. These states include California, Alaska and Delaware, but even in these areas, not all local courts give mediators the power to recommend. In other states— including Michigan, Minnesota, Ohio, New Jersey and Pennsylvania—the court can order a custody evaluation to help it make a decision. In some states, the "evaluator" could be the same person who was your mediator.

AS MENTIONED EARLIER, IT IS ESSENTIAL THAT YOU FIND OUT IF YOUR
mediator will have power to make a recommendation or evaluation if you and
your spouse do not agree on a parenting plan. Frankly, where this is true, it
means that you will be under more pressure to settle and therefore not risk a
possibly negative recommendation, and should plan your strategy accordingly. It
also means you will want to avoid any conduct that could turn the mediator
against you. (See Section D11, below.)

6. WHO MAY ATTEND THE MEDIATION?

For a discussion of this issue, see Section C4.

7. CONFIDENTIALITY

For a discussion of this issue, see Section C5. Note that the confidentiality of
your session may be jeopardized if you do not reach an agreement and your
mediator has the power to make a recommendation to the court.

8. INSIDE THE MEDIATION ROOM

Court-sponsored programs often are located in a government building attached
to, or nearby, the courthouse where divorces are heard. Mediation sessions,
however, do not take place in a courtroom or judge's chamber. Instead, you can
expect your session to be held in a small conference room or, if your mediator is
a full-time court mediator, in his private office. The big rectangular table typically used in other types of mediation is usually avoided in family mediation in
favor of a less formal, less imposing arrangement of comfortable armchairs set
about in a semicircle, with the mediator occupying the middle chair. Flip charts,
blackboards and tissue boxes often adorn the room.

As noted earlier, sessions often last from one to two hours. If no settlement is reached, how many additional sessions will be held depends on the rules of the program. Most offer at least two or three sessions if the couple needs them, but a few programs limit each case to a single session. Multiple sessions would usually be spread over several weeks.

Use of private caucuses where the mediator meets with one spouse at a time to talk informally and candidly about the case also varies among programs. (For more on private caucuses, see Chapter 7, Section F1.) Some court-sponsored programs always use a caucus, others never do. If you want the chance to speak privately with the mediator, ask for a caucus; if it is not prohibited under the rules of the program, the mediator probably will agree unless your spouse strongly objects.

HOW TO CONDUCT YOURSELF IN THE MEDIATION

For tips on how to conduct yourself in a court-sponsored mediation session, review the information in the sidebar following Section C3.

---

9. WHEN YOU REACH AN AGREEMENT

The result of a successful mediation will be a written document setting out the terms of your agreement on custody, visitation and any other issues you covered. The mediator likely will draft this document for you, and forward it to the court for approval. (A sample agreement reached at a California court-sponsored mediation program with the names of the parties and attorneys changed appears on the facing page.) Following are some points to keep in mind when you reach this stage of the process.

SAMPLE AGREEMENT

Date prepared: ███████████, 1995
MEMO TO: The Honorable ███████████████████████
Judge of the Superior Court
Dept. ████
FROM: ████████████████████████████
Family Court Counselor
COURT DATE: ███████████████, 1995
RE: XXXXXXXXXXXXXX
XXXXXXXXXXXXXX
FATHER'S NAME: Mr. A
ATTORNEY: B
MOTHER'S NAME: Mrs. CC
ATTORNEY: D
CHILDREN/DOB: Child 1, 2/26/8x; Child 2, 11/18/8x;

CURRENT SITUATION:

The parents met with the Mediator and agreed to the following custody/visitation plan:

1. The order for physical and legal custody with Mrs. C to stand.

2. Mr. A will see Child 1 and Child 2 every 3rd weekend of each month beginning March 24th, 1995, from Friday 6:00 p.m. to Sunday 6:00 p.m.

3. Mr. A agrees to arrange to get Child 1 and Child 2 to their sports activities when they are visiting in his home.

4. Mr. A agrees to not drink 24 hours prior to a visit and/or during a visit with Child 2 and Child 1.

5. Mr. A agrees to give not less than a 72-hour notice if he plans to change a visit.

6. Parents agree to maintain direct communications regarding Child 1 and Child 2, and not use other family members.

7. Mr. A will see Child 1 and Child 2 after school to 8:30 p.m. on each of their birthdays.

8. Mr. A will see Child 2 and Child 1 from August 21st to August 30th, 1995, for summer vacation time.

9. Mr. A agrees to not take Child 1 and Child 2 in the company of any relatives or friends who actively consume alcohol in their presence.

10. Parents agree to submit vacation dates by April 30th, each year.

11. Mrs. C will see Child 1 and Child 2 for the Easter Holidays, 1995, and Mr. A will share in 1996.

12. Mr. A will see Child 1 and Child 2 for Thanksgiving, 1995, and Mrs. C will share same in 1996.

13. Mr. A will see Child 1 and Child 2 the week leading into 4:00 p.m. Xmas Day and Mrs. C will see them from 4:00 p.m. Xmas Day to 4:00 p.m. New Year's Day, alternating times every other year.

RECOMMENDATION:

The parents were not in total agreement regarding a common definition of "no drinking." The following recommendation is submitted:

1. Supervised visitations shall be initiated if drinking becomes a problem and/or an issue affecting visitation.

A. CONSIDER HAVING A LAWYER REVIEW YOUR AGREEMENT

If your agreement involves important legal rights, consider having a lawyer or law coach review the agreement before you sign it. Some mediators will give you a draft of the agreement with instructions to take it to your lawyers to review within a set number of days. If no objections are raised, they will then forward it to the court. If the mediator does not make this proposal, you can make it yourself and offer the following "lawyer review" provision:

PROCEDURE FOR LAWYER REVIEW

The above-stated terms may be deemed to reflect the agreement of the parties unless the attorney for either party notifies the [mediation program] in writing of objections within five business days.

B. INCLUDE A DISPUTE RESOLUTION CLAUSE

Request that a dispute resolution clause be included in the agreement so you and your spouse have a process in place to handle future disputes. Indeed, some states, such as Washington, now require by law that all custody and visitation agreements produced by court-sponsored mediation include a process other than court action for resolving future disputes. (Wash. Rev. Code Sec. 26.09.184(3).)

Many court-sponsored programs will allow couples to return for follow-up mediation if disputes later arise. As children grow, for example, changing circumstances involving their education, health and relationship with parents can raise difficult issues that can best be resolved through further mediation. One California mediation office reports a couple who returned 45 times over nine years.

In many states, such as California and Oregon, you can return for additional mediation simply by calling the mediation office and setting up an appointment; in other states you may need to file a motion in court to modify your agreement in order to get back into the mediator's office. Call the court-sponsored mediation office to find out the rule in your state.

If you do return for follow-up mediation, the mediator who originally handled your case will be assigned if you and your spouse both want that mediator and the mediator is willing to serve. Currently, most programs offer follow-up mediation at no charge, although modest user-fees may be added in the future.

Following is a sample dispute resolution clause you can ask the mediator to include in your agreement:

PROCEDURE FOR RESOLVING FUTURE DISPUTES

*The parties agree to return to [Name of Court-sponsored Mediation Program]
if they are unable to resolve any proposed changes, disputes or alleged
breaches relating to this agreement.*

10. IF NO AGREEMENT IS REACHED

If you cannot reach an agreement in mediation, you can:
- continue discussions on your own
- hire a private mediator and try again (see Section E, below)
- ask the court to appoint an independent evaluator to make a recommendation (available in some communities)
- submit the case to arbitration. Both parties go before an arbitrator (often a
  retired judge from the family court) and present their case with or without
  their own attorneys. The arbitrator then renders a final and legally-binding
  decision. Arbitration is most appropriate when a couple is unable to agree
  on some critical point, such as the amount of spousal support (alimony).
  Some states prohibit arbitration of child custody and support, although
  the trend seems to favor increased use of arbitration. In Michigan, for
  example, an appeals court recently upheld the right of a couple to submit
  their divorce dispute, including custody issues, to binding arbitration.
- litigate the issues in court.

11. IF THE MEDIATOR HAS POWER TO RECOMMEND

**SKIP THIS SECTION if you are in a state where the court-sponsored mediation
program has no power to recommend a result if the parties fail to agree.**

In a handful of states, including most of California, mediators in court-sponsored programs have the power to recommend to a judge how a case involving disagreements over child custody and visitation should be decided, if a couple is unable to reach an agreement. In this section, we will look at how this power of the mediator—even if it is not exercised—affects the process of mediation and how your strategy for the session should change in response.

A. HOW IT WORKS

Since California is by far the most populous state to allow mediators to recommend a solution in contested child custody and visitation cases, let's take a quick look at how it's done in that state. There, local courts in each county have the option of allowing their mediators make child custody and visitation recommendations; about two-thirds of the counties do so. At mediation programs in those counties, the majority of cases are settled by the parties arriving at their own agreement. But in the cases where this doesn't occur, the mediator recommends what the judge should decide. Judges almost always follow a mediator's recommendation.

A sample Mediator Recommendation from one California program appears below.

SAMPLE RECOMMENDATION

Date prepared: ██████████████, 1995

MEMO TO: The Honorable ██████████████████████████
              Judge of the Superior Court
              Dept.█████

FROM: ██████████████████████████
              Family Court Counselor

COURT DATE: ██████████████, 1995

RE: XXXXXXXXXXXXXX
              ACTION NO.:XXXXXXXXX
              FATHER'S NAME: Mr. E
              ATTORNEY:F
              MOTHER'S NAME: Mrs. E
              ATTORNEY:H
              CHILDREN/DOB: J (6/18/86)

CURRENT SITUATION:

The parents met with the Mediator and agreed to the following custody/visitation plan:

The parties have been married for ten years. Since their separation last year, their child J has lived primarily with her mother and older sister, K. She has seen her father Mr. E every weekend, during the week, and for two weeks during the summer. Both J and Mr. E report that their communication has been generally good.

J's teacher recently called Mr. E to inform him that J had missed a great deal of school, and that Mrs. E had not responded to the school's concerns about this. Mr. E felt that Mrs. E had been drinking, and was unable to get up in the morning to get her to school. Mrs. E stated that the children had been sick. She stated that she did drink 3 or 4 glasses of wine on some nights, but did not feel she had a drinking problem.

Two weeks ago, Mr. E requested and obtained temporary custody of J. Last week, Mrs. E came to Mr. E's home and got into a physical fight with his cousin in front of J. She stated that she felt the cousin had prevented her from talking to J on the phone. She stated that she had not been drinking, although Mr. E believed that she had. He noted that she had come to his home in 1993 and broken some windows when drunk, and feels she is drinking again.

J was seen twice, once right after the fight she witnessed, and once a week later. She stated at the first session that she wanted to stay with her father. She stated at the second session that she wanted to give her mother a second chance, because her mother had promised to stop drinking. Therefore, J wanted to go back to her mother for six months, to see if she really did stop drinking.

J obviously loves both of her parents. She is torn about what she wants, and feels some pressure to make a decision. However, she was very consistent in stating that her greatest wish is that her mother would stop drinking.

Mrs. E stated that she has promised her daughter that she would stop drinking, and she is willing to seek treatment for herself and family counseling with her daughters. She stated that she did not realize her drinking was such a problem for J, and feels she will have to win back her trust. She stated that she wants the chance to prove to J that she will keep her word, and wants custody while she is doing so.

It seems that Mrs. E does have a drinking problem which has created significant anxiety for her daughter. I believe that she has very strong intentions to address the issue of drinking, and to meet J's needs. However, it does not make sense to have J return to her mother's care until Mrs. E has established herself in a sober lifestyle, which would include regular attendance in AA and a treatment program. I recommend the following:

1. Joint legal custody.

2. J should remain in her father's primary care for the next six months.

3. J may see her mother at least twice each week after school. There will be no alcohol use during or 12 hours before these visits. Visits will not be overnight until Mrs. E has been in treatment and sober for at least two months.

4. Mrs. E shall begin treatment immediately, and shall attend AA. I suggest 90 meetings in 90 days. Since she is on Medi-Cal, she may be eligible for services through the ▮▮▮▮▮▮ Substance Abuse Program (123-4567) or the ▮▮▮▮▮▮▮▮▮ Clinic (765-4321). These agencies also offer family counseling…

Note that the sample case involves a married couple who are parents of a nine-year-old girl. As noted in the beginning of this chapter, court-sponsored mediation programs often provide services to unmarried parents. To find out if the court-sponsored mediation program where you live provides services to unmarried couples, call the mediation program office.

In several areas of the country, variations on the California mediator recommendation approach are practiced. In Oregon, for example, mediators can make recommendations only with "the written consent of the parties or their counsel." (Oregon Revised Statutes Section 107.765.) In Dallas County, Texas, if a couple does not reach agreement on custody, the mediator can recommend to a judge that a written custody evaluation be done by someone else. As in most states other than California, any evaluation or recommendation that is forwarded to the judge is done by a person other than the mediator. In Minnesota, however, couples are given the choice of having the evaluation done by another person or by the mediator. Most couples choose to have the mediator do the evaluation to avoid having to go through another session with a new person (and perhaps because they've come to trust the mediator).

The next few pages focus on how you should approach a mediation where a mediator has the power to recommend a solution if parties can't agree. Or put another way, if you face this type of mediation instead of the normal type, where the mediator has no power to recommend (or ask that someone else make a recommendation), what should you do differently?

B. STRATEGY TO FOLLOW

Even if your mediator has the power to recommend, your best strategy is still to try to settle with your spouse. A voluntary agreement is almost always the best way to get a result you can live with, with the least risk of an adverse decision. Nevertheless, knowing the mediator has at least considerable power to determine how your case may be decided, it makes sense to regard this person as a judge and consider how to influence her to decide in your favor.

Following are a few tips to keep in mind:

i. *Base your presentation (arguments) on the legal standard the mediator/ recommender is required to follow.* If you and your spouse are not able to reach an agreement, the mediator/recommender will have to make her recommendation based on specific legal standards, and if you can base your presentation on those standards, it will make it easier for the mediator to recommend in your favor. In most states, the standard for determining custody is "the best interests of the child," which includes such factors as:

- the child's health, safety, and welfare
- any history of abuse against the child
- the nature and quality of contact between the parents (that is, each spouse's willingness to be a co-parent with the other spouse).

For example, if you are seeking liberal visitation with your child, do so not because you think it's best for you personally, but because you genuinely believe it will be best for your child in terms of her health, safety and general welfare. And be ready to back this up with objective information (not just opinions).

ii. *Show you can get along with your spouse.* The mediator will be impressed by your ability to act civilly toward your spouse. It suggests maturity, emotional stability and reliability—all traits a mediator would want to see in someone asking for custody or liberal visitation. On the other hand, if you cannot control yourself in the presence of your spouse, it may discourage the mediator from granting you custody, and if the mediator writes in his recommendation, "I had to ask Mr. Smith to leave the session because he was threatening and hostile toward his wife," the judge will probably assume there is good reason to follow the mediator's recommendation that Mrs. Smith be granted custody of the children.

REMEMBER THAT THE MEDIATOR IS SICK OF ARGUMENTS. Just like a bus driver who has totally lost patience with people who want him to change a $20 bill, your mediator is probably fed up with angry finger-pointing spouses who lose sight of what their kids really need (almost always, two parents at least willing to co-exist civilly). In short, even if you would love to explain just what a louse your spouse is, doing so is likely to be counterproductive.

iii. *Treat the mediator politely.* Mediators—especially those who are full-time employees of the court-sponsored program—are trusted co-workers of the family court judges. If you act disrespectfully to your mediator or otherwise make a poor impression, the judge will often be told in person or in a written report.

C. CHALLENGING THE RECOMMENDATION

In many states, if you do not agree with the judge's decision (based on the mediator's recommendation), you can challenge the decision in court. Typically, you would cross-examine the mediator to show some important fact was omitted, misstated or misinterpreted in the recommendation the mediator prepared for the judge. You might show, for example, that the recommendation failed to mention that your spouse was, until recently, a heavy cocaine user. In California, of all the cases where the mediator makes a recommendation, only about 5%-10% are challenged in court, and of these, few appeals are successful.

CONFIDENTIALITY CAN BE JEOPARDIZED WHEN A RECOMMENDATION IS CHALLENGED

The confidentiality of your session may be jeopardized if you do not reach an agreement and your mediator has the power to make a recommendation to the court. While it is only in parts of a few states that mediators have this power in these areas, it does weaken the normal rules of confidentiality. That's because mediators who make recommendations are usually required to be available for cross-examination in open court if a party wants to challenge the recommendation. During cross-examination, the mediator may be forced to reveal what was said during mediation—even what was said during private caucus. Therefore, if your mediator has the power to recommend, you may want to avoid discussing sensitive information about aspects of your marriage, financial dealings or personal life.

GET HELP IF YOU PLAN TO CHALLENGE A MEDIATOR'S RECOMMENDATION. Face it, it's a tough job to overcome a mediator's recommendation. If you plan to try, consult with an experienced family lawyer or law coach and consider the advisability of having the lawyer represent you at the court hearing.

E. Private Divorce Mediation

Private divorce mediation has grown in popularity since it first became widely available in the 1970s. Today, it is used by many couples who understand that a good divorce is almost as valuable as a good marriage. These couples look at what the divorce process is as offered by the courts and conclude that it is not thorough or patient enough, costs too much, and at times can be brutalizing for themselves and their children. Instead, they are willing to put the time and energy into mediation as an investment in the future for themselves and, especially, for their children.

Today in some large cities, 10%-15% of divorcing couples use private mediators. For a discussion of the financial and child issues a couple can address in private mediation, and a brief overview of the process, see Sections A through C, above.

1. How to Start Your Case

Either spouse can initiate divorce mediation. Questions of timing and strategy are discussed in this section.

A. WHEN SHOULD YOU BEGIN MEDIATION?

The best time to propose mediation to your spouse is after both of you have accepted the reality that your marriage is ending (because until then mediation will not be productive) but before either of you has initiated a legal action for divorce. This is because filing of court papers can cause emotional trauma, and once lawyers get involved, it can be much more difficult to get an agreement to mediate. However, you do not need to be living apart in order to mediate; many divorcing couples, for example, start mediation while still living together but planning to separate (perhaps they are waiting for their house to sell).

If divorce papers have already been filed in your case, you can still propose mediation, particularly if the matter is still at an early stage and the lawyer or lawyers involved are supportive of mediation. In the early stages of a contested divorce proceeding, positions have usually not hardened as often occurs later when the very nature of the adversary process propels at least one side to go for the jugular (and by so doing, convinces the other to respond in the same way).

You can also use mediation even if you and your spouse have not decided to divorce, but only to separate temporarily. You could, for example, agree to a trial separation and mediate how to divide household bills and parenting responsibilities during the period you are living apart.

B. HOW TO PROPOSE MEDIATION TO YOUR SPOUSE

Rather than trying to "sell" your spouse on mediation (remember the saying: "In a dispute, when one party proposes, the other opposes"), it's usually best to just provide some information about the process and advantages of mediation, with the suggestion that you both consider exploring it as an option. If you are on speaking terms, you can raise the idea during a regular conversation and offer to send some literature for him or her to review. If you are not speaking, you can do the same in a brief letter. Whether in person or by letter, following are some of the points to make:

- We can both save money on legal fees and avoid a possibly nasty public court fight.
- Mediation offers us a cooperative, nonadversarial approach to problem-solving—if we both agree to a settlement, nothing can be imposed on us.

- In mediation we can both think through what we really want rather than engaging in a legal "tug of war."
- Mediation will benefit our children by reducing conflict between us now and in the future.
- Our discussions will be confidential so we can avoid public disclosure of our personal problems.
- In mediation, we can complete our agreements more quickly, so we can move ahead with our lives.
- Neither of us will be risking anything legally because we can each have our own lawyers review the agreement before we sign anything.
- If we don't go to private mediation we'll be required to go to the court-sponsored program anyway (if you and your spouse have minor children and if your state has a mandatory court-sponsored program), so we might as well go private and take advantage of choosing our own mediator, discussing all issues, scheduling the sessions at our convenience, etc.

You can also offer to call several divorce mediators in your area and have them send printed material to you and your spouse, and then get back in touch later to see if you can both agree on one to use.

C. HOW TO DEAL WITH A RELUCTANT SPOUSE

If you have proposed mediation to your spouse but your spouse is reluctant to participate, try the following tactics:

- *Have materials sent about mediation.* If you have not already done so, have a local divorce mediator or mediation service send printed materials to your spouse. Some state and national organizations that promote use of mediation also will send materials upon request. The leading organization nationally in divorce mediation is the Academy of Family Mediators. Upon request, they will send a general brochure, called "Mediation." The Academy also has a 20-minute videotape, "Mediation: It's Up to You" available for $59.95. The tape simulates a mediation between a couple who have one small child and also own a business together. If divorce is being contemplated, this tape could be the best deal going if it helps convince your spouse to try mediation, because $59.95 is a drop in the ocean compared to the potential cost of a contested, adversarial divorce.

The Academy of Family Mediators
4 Militia Drive
Lexington, MA 02173
(617) 674-2663
FAX (617) 674-2690
afmoffice@igc.apc.org

- *Have your spouse talk to a mediator.* Suggest your spouse have a private phone conversation with one of the mediators you would be willing to use. While most mediators would not call your spouse because it would make them appear to be advocating for mediation rather than remaining neutral, most would accept a call from your spouse to answer questions about mediation.
- *Offer to pay for first session.* Many mediators will offer an initial session of one-half to one hour during which the mediator can assess whether mediation is appropriate for a couple and the couple can consider whether they want to go ahead with the mediation. To encourage your spouse to participate, you can offer to pay the full fee for this session.

2. HOW TO FIND AND SELECT A PRIVATE DIVORCE MEDIATOR

In Chapters 3 and 5 we examined the backgrounds, education and skill levels of mediators generally and the types of disputes they commonly handle. In this section, we will look specifically at private divorce mediators and how to select one for your case.

A. HOW TO FIND A MEDIATOR

There are many thousands of mediators in the United States today who specialize in divorce and family cases. The majority are in solo practice; most of the rest work at community mediation centers or in small group practices. The easiest way to find a list of divorce mediators is to look in the telephone directory under "mediation" or "divorce." Other resources in your community who may be able to give you the names of divorce mediators include:

- the staff of your community mediation center
- matrimonial lawyers
- the staff at a family services office (some are connected to a local court; others are independent, nonprofit agencies)
- clergy
- therapists
- employee assistance personnel at large corporations
- friends and relatives who have used a mediator.

In addition, the following national organizations maintain lists of private divorce mediators and can provide names of practitioners in your community:

The Academy of Family Mediators
4 Militia Drive
Lexington, MA 02173
(617) 674-2663
FAX (617) 674-2690
afmoffice@igc.apc.org

The Association of Family and Conciliation Courts
329 West Wilson Street
Madison, WI 53703
(608) 251-4001
(608) 251-2231

B. MEDIATOR FEES

This issue was discussed earlier in this chapter in Section A. In addition, note that many private divorce mediators will work with couples on a sliding fee scale; if you can't afford the full rate, discuss your financial situation with the mediator. You may be able to get a better deal. For example, one mediator whose standard fee is $120/hour, reduces it to $60/hour for couples with combined gross income of less than $30,000, and to $50/hour for families on public assistance.

Even in large cities, you may be able to find low rates by using a divorce mediator who works on the staff of, or as an independent contractor with, a nonprofit, community mediation center. About half the centers nationwide provide this service. (For more on community mediation centers, see Chapter 3, Section B1.)

IF YOUR SPOUSE HAS PROPOSED MEDIATION...

You are under no obligation to go to a private mediator merely because your spouse has proposed it. If your spouse has suggested you use a particular mediator, investigate the mediator to be sure he or she is someone with whom you will be comfortable working. Does this mediator have the background, skill level, and accreditation you want? (See Section E2, below, and Chapter 5, Selecting Mediation Services and Mediators, where the issue of how to choose mediators is discussed in depth.).

Before agreeing to even an initial session with the mediator your spouse has selected, call the mediator and have a private conversation with him or her about your case and his or her credentials and approach to mediation. If the mediator does not do private caucusing, this may be the only time you have to have a private conversation with him or her. Ask about the mediator's background, credentials, fees and other factors discussed below.

Finally, are there other mediators in your community you would prefer to use? Check out the alternatives to the mediator your spouse has chosen. (See Section E2, below.) Even if you don't find anyone else better suited to handle your case, it is important that you do the search yourself so you feel comfortable that the choice to use that mediator was equally your own.

MEDIATION IS ALMOST ALWAYS CHEAPER THAN GOING TO COURT.
A mediated divorce should cost you and your spouse a fraction (perhaps one-third or less) of what a two-lawyer adversarial divorce would cost in the same community. (See Section B for more on why this is true.)

C. NINE QUESTIONS TO ASK A PROSPECTIVE MEDIATOR

Once you get a list of possible names, you need to check the person out. Here is how to do it. The mediator you select should not only be professionally competent, but his or her style and approach to mediation should be broadly compatible with your own. For example, if you are a practical down-to-earth person, you probably don't want a mediator who fills every sentence with what you see as New Age psychobabble. On the other hand, if you feel that your inability to maximize your potential as human beings is precisely what has been wrong with your marriage, you may find that a mediator who focuses only on practical issues to be jarring.

When you find a mediator you think you would like to work with, there are a number of ways to evaluate his or her suitability for your case. For example, ask for names of lawyers who have reviewed agreements the mediator has drafted for other couples; the lawyers can give you an opinion on the mediator's technical competence. You can also ask the mediator for references from former clients. The mediator will not give you another client's name, but may be willing to take your name and have a former client call you.

Of course, you will want to ask prospective mediators about fees, but beyond that, there are other issues of qualification, philosophy and style you should review with them, either on the phone or during an initial consultation. Following are nine issues you may want to explore.

I.   WHAT IS THE MEDIATOR'S PROFESSIONAL BACKGROUND?

Because the field is relatively new and there is still very little formal college or graduate level training available, most divorce mediators have a professional background in some other discipline, such as law, social work, mental health, education, or the clergy. You may feel more comfortable with a mediator from one of these backgrounds than from another.

WHO ARE THE MEDIATORS?

The Academy of Family Mediators, the nation's largest accrediting organization of divorce and family mediators, completed a demographic survey of its members in 1995. Of 1,776 mediators who responded, approximately:

- 40% have backgrounds in law; 30% in therapy or social work
- 80% hold master's degrees, Ph.D.s, or law degrees
- 70% are between the ages of 40 and 59
- 60% are female
- 70% are in solo practice.

II.   WHAT TRAINING AND QUALIFICATIONS DOES THE MEDIATOR HAVE?

There are no state laws that set minimum qualifications or training requirements for divorce mediators who practice privately (although in some states, such as Florida, private mediators must meet minimum standards in order to receive case referrals from the courts). In theory, anyone can open an office and call himself a divorce mediator. It is important, therefore, to ask prospective mediators about their training. Most competent mediators should have completed at least a 40-hour training program offered by a private training service, a court agency or a community mediation center. The training should have been specific for people practicing divorce mediation (as opposed to general community or commercial mediation) and should have covered, among other topics, conflict resolution theory, your state's divorce laws, laws and issues of custody, support, asset distribution, taxation and the psychological issues of separation, divorce and child development. Some training programs also include supervised observation of actual mediation sessions.

The Academy of Family Mediators maintains a list of "approved" training courses based on course content and trainer qualifications. Ask the prospective mediator if the training he or she took was approved by the Academy. If so, it is some indication that the mediator was well-trained. However, if the mediator's training was not approved by the Academy, you cannot really draw a negative conclusion about its quality, because there are a number of good trainers who have not sought Academy approval.

III. HOW MUCH EXPERIENCE DOES THE MEDIATOR HAVE?

Divorce mediation is a relatively young field, and mediator experience varies widely. The majority of mediators working today probably have practiced less than five years and some may have handled only a few dozen cases. The most experienced mediators may have practiced for 10 or 15 years and have handled hundreds of cases. Ask how long a mediator has been practicing and how many cases he or she has handled. Find out if they handle just a few cases a year, indicating they are probably part-time practitioners (maybe a lawyer who mediates on the side), or whether they have a full-time practice with dozens of active clients.

IV. DOES THE MEDIATOR HAVE ANY PROFESSIONAL ACCREDITATION?

State agencies do not license or certify mediators as they do physicians, psychiatrists or lawyers. However, in the absence of state licensing requirements, your mediator's membership in, or accreditation by, various professional organizations may be some indication of his or her qualifications.

Membership in the Academy of Family Mediators does not guarantee the quality of a mediator's work, but if a mediator is a practitioner member, it does indicate he has fulfilled certain requirements for training and experience. The Academy currently maintains two membership classes:

General Member: Anyone may become a general member; there are no formal requirements.

Practitioner Member: Practitioner members are required to:

1. Complete 60 hours of Academy-approved mediation training;

2. Have 100 hours of face-to-face mediation experience in at least ten mediation cases;

3. Submit six sample memoranda, case reports or other documentation from the required ten mediation cases;

4. Complete 20 hours of continuing education every two years.

The Academy has just over 3,000 members, only about 700 of whom are practitioner members. While there probably are some excellent divorce mediators who for various reasons choose not to join the Academy (they are just not "joiners" or don't want to pay the $95-$130 annual fee, for example), it's also true that many of the best-trained, experienced private divorce mediators in the country are likely to be found among the Academy's 700 practitioner members.

The Academy publishes a directory, organized by state, containing the names, addresses and telephone numbers of all of its members. It is available without charge to anyone who requests a copy. Telephone: (617) 674-2663.

In the following profile of a practitioner member of the Academy, note the mediator's educational background and experience level, which is probably typical of private divorce mediators at this level of accreditation and practice.

MEDIATOR PROFILE

Name: Vicki Lewin

Profession: Divorce and Family Mediator

Name of Practice: Goodman Associates, Rochester, New York

Educational Background: Master's in Education, Hunter College, City University of New York

Years in Practice: Six

Professional Affiliations: Practitioner Member, Academy of Family Mediators; Board of Directors, New York State Council on Divorce Mediation

Number of Cases Handled in Career: 300+

Number of Cases Now Open: 20

Most Memorable Mediation Moment:

"She said, 'I want you to stay away from me! I never want to see you again! Ever!'
'Does this mean you're going to stop doing my laundry?' he replied."

Notable Features of My Conference Room: The fireplace and the easy chairs.

Favorite Expression Related to Conflict: "Attack the problem, not the person."

Philosophy of Divorce Mediation: "Divorce is like buying a house: it's a legal event, but it's more than that. When you buy a house you don't ask the attorney what kind of house, which neighborhood to live in and how much to spend. You make those choices on your own. When you divorce, you can ask your attorney for advice, but it's your life and your family and you need to work through those decisions yourself. Mediation can help you do that."

V. CAN THE MEDIATOR GIVE YOU REFERRALS TO ATTORNEYS AND OTHER ADVISORS?

During the course of your mediation you may need to consult with an attorney, accountant or other adviser to get expert advice on legal, financial or other issues. A good mediator will encourage you to seek expert advice from others, and will also have a list of skilled local professionals for you to contact.

A good mediator should also recognize that in some cases—particularly where significant money, property or legal rights are involved—a couple can benefit by each having their own lawyer available to consult with before mediation, during the mediation process and afterwards to review the agreement before signing. For more on the role of lawyers in divorce mediation, see Section C2.

VI. IS THE MEDIATOR WILLING TO INTERVENE?

Ask prospective mediators to describe under what circumstances, if any, they would intervene to protect the "weaker" spouse or if they would reject a proposed agreement they personally believed to be unfair. As noted, a "power imbalance" between mediating spouses creates the risk that one spouse may strike a deal that is not in his or her best interests, or in the best interests of the

children. (See sidebar in Section C3.) If you think during the course of mediation you might find yourself in this situation, select a mediator willing to intervene to prevent an unfair agreement.

WILL A MEDIATOR BLOCK AN UNBALANCED AGREEMENT?

Professors Joseph P. Folger and Sydney E. Bernard have studied
mediators' willingness to intervene and found that:

- 25% of mediators are "highly interventionist": very
  likely to block agreements that do not protect children
  or a weaker spouse
- 10% of mediators are "highly non-interventionist":
  unlikely to block any agreement a couple reaches after
  being fully informed
- 65% of mediators are "interventionist as facts warrant":
  most likely to intervene when agreements involve
  children or weaker spouses

Joseph P. Folger and Sydney E. Bernard, "Divorce Mediation: When
Mediations Challenge the Divorcing Parties," *Mediation Quarterly*,
No. 10, 1985, p.19.

GOOD PREPARATION CAN HELP DEFEAT A POTENTIAL POWER IMBALANCE.
If you prepare for mediation by carefully considering the range of realistic
options available for the major parenting and financial issues involved in your
case and what you want a final plan to look like, you will be much less susceptible
to being hurt by a potential power imbalance. See Section C3 of this chapter and
***Child Custody: Building Agreements That Work,* by Mimi Lyster (Nolo Press).**

VII. DOES THE MEDIATOR USE PRIVATE CAUCUSES?

As discussed earlier, some divorce mediators use caucusing and some do not. Consider your position on this and then ask prospective mediators if they use the caucus.(For a discussion of caucusing in general, see Chapter 7, Section F.)

VIII. WILL THE MEDIATOR MEET WITH YOUR CHILDREN?

For a discussion of this issue, see Section C4. Find out if a prospective mediator's position on this issue is compatible with your own.

IX. WHAT IS THE MEDIATOR'S WORK PRODUCT: A MEMORANDUM OR FINAL LEGAL PAPERS?

Assuming the couple reaches an agreement, mediators traditionally conclude their work by drafting a written agreement, called a Memorandum of Understanding, that lays out in clear language all the terms to which the couple has agreed. One or both spouses then take the Memorandum to their lawyer who must "translate" it into legal terms for presentation to the court as part of the divorce decree.

Some mediators—particular those trained in the law—may skip the Memorandum, and instead simply draft the final legal papers the couple will need to apply for their divorce, incorporating in them the agreements they have reached in mediation. Except in the few states where mediators are prohibited by law from preparing the final legal papers, this practice can save you time and money, because it eliminates the need for an outside lawyer to re-draft your agreements into legal terms. And it allows you the possibility of saving even more money by bypassing a lawyer altogether and filling out the necessary papers to get your own divorce.

3. THE CONTRACT FOR MEDIATION SERVICES

Your mediator will probably require you and your spouse each to sign a contract for mediation services. The purposes of the contract are to clarify in writing the procedures that will be followed in the mediation, and to be sure you pay the mediator.

The contract will probably set out the mediator's fees and schedule of payments, recite the goals of mediation, your right to have an attorney, rules of confidentiality, disclosure of financial information and the ability of third parties to participate. It will express the willingness of both spouses to make a good-faith effort to work toward a settlement, and may commit you not to pursue litigation, arbitration or other remedies during the course of the mediation. (Of course, if mediation does not result in a full settlement of the issues in dispute, you will be free to pursue litigation or any other remedies you wish. See Section 9, below).

DON'T SIGN A LONG-TERM CONTRACT UNTIL YOU ARE SURE YOU HAVE FOUND THE RIGHT MEDIATOR. If the mediator sends you a contract that obligates you to more than one session if an agreement isn't reached, call the mediator and explain that, while you are willing to pay for the first session up-front, you prefer to wait until its conclusion before making a longer-term commitment. This will give you time during the first session to decide if you really want to use this mediator.

4. ROLE OF LAWYERS

For a general discussion of this issue, see Section C2. For other suggestions on finding a lawyer to work with in mediation, see Chapter 6, Section G, and Chapter 13, Lawyers and Legal Research.

5. HOW TO PREPARE FOR YOUR MEDIATION

Refer to the general tips on preparation in Section C3. For private divorce mediation in particular, you don't need to bring anything to the first session other than what the mediator may specifically request. For example, the mediator may send you an Intake Form with instructions to complete it and bring it to the first session. The Form asks for general biographical information about you and your family. Once the sessions begin, your mediator will guide you through the process, giving you "homework" to do in between sessions. (See Section 8, below.)

6. WHO MAY ATTEND THE MEDIATION

For a general discussion of this issue, see Section C4.

7. CONFIDENTIALITY

For a general discussion of this issue, see Section C5.

HOW TO CONDUCT YOURSELF IN PRIVATE MEDIATION

For tips on how to conduct yourself in the mediation sessions, review the information in the sidebar following Section C3.

8. STAGES OF THE MEDIATION

As with other types of mediation, private divorce mediation proceeds through stages. Of course, procedures used by individual mediators may vary. The number of sessions and the topics discussed at each session will also vary depending on the number and complexity of issues involved and the negotiating skill of the couple.

Private divorce mediation tends to be much slower than court-sponsored mediation and cover more issues. Indeed, it's different enough from court-sponsored mediation and from general mediation as discussed elsewhere in this book, that it's worth going through the process step-by-step.

YOU MAY WANT TO READ A MEDIATION TRANSCRIPT. For an interesting inside look at couples going through private divorce mediation, including edited transcripts of actual mediation sessions, see *A Guide to Divorce Mediation*, by Gary J. Friedman (Workman Publishing, 1993).

A. STAGE ONE: INTAKE AND COMMITMENT

In the first session, the mediator will review with you the procedures, rules and goals of mediation. This is the time to ask questions, and to decide whether you can trust and feel comfortable with this mediator and want him or her to mediate your divorce. If you and your spouse have not previously signed a Contract for Services with the mediator, you will likely be asked to sign it now. If you want, you can take it with you to have your lawyer or law coach review it and then bring it to the next session either signed or with specific questions about it to discuss with the mediator.

B. STAGE TWO: FINANCIAL DISCLOSURE AND FACT-FINDING

At the end of your first session, the mediator may give you financial worksheets on which you will need to list all your assets, such as bank accounts, stocks, bonds, real estate, partnerships, pension funds and business interests. (If your mediation is limited to matters of child custody and visitation, it may not be necessary to make detailed financial disclosures.) In some states, the information requested on the forms is dictated by state law, and each spouse will later need to affirm to the court that complete disclosure of assets was made. You may also be asked to turn over to each other payroll records, checkbooks, pension plan summaries and three years' worth of past federal and state tax returns.

If substantial assets are involved, such as a family business or a company pension plan, you may want to have a lawyer, or an accountant, review your spouse's financial records to interpret financial data and be sure everything has been disclosed. If you believe assets are being hidden, a lawyer can issue a subpoena for additional records. But consult with the mediator before asking a lawyer to do this; the mediator will want to remain in control of the process and not let adversarial actions such as a subpoena interfere unless necessary.

Review and analysis of this information typically occupies the second and part of the third mediation sessions.

INSIDE THE PRIVATE MEDIATOR'S OFFICE

As noted, private divorce mediators most often work as solo practitioners. Their offices may be located in downtown office buildings, suburban office parks or in their own homes.

The meeting room, and the arrangement of furniture and people in it, is designed to give couples a private and secure feeling. For example, rather than being "squared off" across a conference table as would be typical in a business mediation, a couple typically will be seated on a sofa, or in armchairs arranged around a coffee-table.

To illustrate, one mediator in a mid-sized eastern city works in a 1930-era, Art Deco home now converted into professional offices. It is located on a quiet street off a downtown artery. In a small waiting area, a "white noise" machine hums quietly, adding extra privacy for the couple mediating inside.

In the conference room, three upholstered armchairs are arranged around a coffee-table near a fireplace. On the table is a box of tissues and a glass bowl filled with hard candies. Nearby, a book-shelf holds books and journals on parenting, self-esteem and personal finance. All are available for clients to borrow.

As the session begins, the mediator offers the couple tea or coffee, and takes the armchair facing into the office. The couple is invited to sit facing the windows, a position affording a view of the world outside.

C. STAGE THREE: IDENTIFYING THE ISSUES

After all the financial cards have been laid on the table, the mediator will begin discussions of the various issues in dispute. This likely would occur late in the second or early in the third session. On some issues—who will have primary custody of the children, for example—you may already be in agreement. But as to others—for example, the details of visitation and amount of child support— you may be far apart. Some property issues may also emerge that are going to need a lot of negotiation: Should the cost of one spouse's professional degree be considered marital property, some of which is owed to the nonprofessional spouse? Who should get the home computer?

Once all the issues in dispute are identified, the mediator may help the couple list and number them according to the order in which they will be discussed.

D. STAGE FOUR: NEGOTIATION

For the next several sessions, you and your spouse will address—in sequence— the issues in dispute. As each issue is discussed, the mediator will help you think of ways to resolve it that you may not have thought of on your own. Often, due to anger and emotional fatigue, couples are unable to see options for settling disputes beyond a few obvious choices. The mediator will help you take a fresh look at the issues in order to think of all options for settlement.

On custody issues, for example, the mediator will help you consider all the possible solutions for each issue that is identified. As noted earlier, if you have already consulted *Child Custody: Building Agreements That Work,* by Mimi Lyster (Nolo Press), you will already understand the range of available solutions your mediator will be trying to help you achieve.

As your mediation proceeds and you have considered most or all issues on your list, you'll likely see that trying to resolve each one separately (sequentially) does not work well. This is because most couples view their settlement plan as a package, so that while you may begin by discussing one issue at a time, by the fourth or fifth session, you are probably considering several issues at once, trading off one thing for another in order to arrive at a fair settlement package. For more information on understanding financial assets and how to negotiate a fair package, see *Divorce & Money: How to Make the Best Financial Decisions During Divorce,* by Violet P. Woodhouse and Victoria F. Collins, with M.C. Blakeman (Nolo Press).

If your mediator uses caucusing, it is during the negotiation stage that you are most likely to caucus.

E. STAGE FIVE: AGREEMENT, DRAFTING THE MEMO, LAWYER REVIEW, CLOSING

When negotiations have concluded, and assuming an agreement as to some or all of the issues has been reached, the mediator will draft the proposed agreement, often referred to as a "Memorandum of Understanding." The mediator will review each part with you in session to be sure the wording accurately reflects your agreement.

At this point, mediators who are willing to include children in the process may invite you to have your older children come in for part of a session so the mediator can explain the process you have gone through and the decisions that have been made. See the earlier discussion of this in Section C4.

You and your spouse will each be given copies of the draft Memorandum for your lawyers or other advisers separately to review, if you wish. If you have any doubts about the wisdom of having agreed to any parts of your settlement plan, be sure to tell your lawyer or adviser. If, on the other hand, you are well-satisfied with it, don't let a lawyer start unraveling it for trivial reasons as some lawyers by their training may be inclined to do. Also, you may find that your lawyer is especially troubled about discrepancies between the terms of your agreement and what she believes the law would award. You can accept your lawyer's point of view and seek to modify your agreement, or you can explain to the lawyer that the law's solution isn't always the best solution, and also that fighting in court might lose you in court costs, lawyer's fees and the goodwill of the other parent what you gain in vindicating your legal rights.

Most mediators will hold one session in reserve in case you need to come back to discuss questions raised on review.

Typically, one or both parties will take the final Memorandum to their lawyer to be drafted into appropriate legal form (sometimes called a "separation agreement" or "marital settlement") and presented to the court for approval and issuance of a legal divorce decree, or the mediator will draft the court papers for you directly.

9. IF NO AGREEMENT IS REACHED

If you cannot reach an agreement through private mediation, you can:
- continue discussions on your own or through attorneys
- initiate a legal action (if you or your spouse have not already done so) and try again through a court-sponsored mediation program, if available (see Section D) or ask the court to appoint an independent evaluator to make a recommendation (available in some communities)
- submit the issues to arbitration (see Section D10)
- litigate the issues in court.

TWELVE

Mediating Business Disputes

Owners and managers of large businesses are extremely sensitive to the high costs of litigation in terms of legal fees, executive time, customer relationships and public image. For this reason, more than 800 major companies (including most of the "Fortune 500") have pledged in writing to consider mediation and other alternatives before pursuing lawsuits. (See below for more on the "Corporate ADR Pledge.")

Use of mediation by smaller businesses has lagged somewhat, but this seems more due to lack of awareness of its great benefits than a deliberate business strategy. Indeed, because small businesses often have less comprehensive insurance coverage and therefore are at increased risk of being wiped out by even one outsized court or arbitration award, mediation offers a far safer way to settle disputes.

It's important to realize that mediation of business disputes, unlike mediating a simple neighborhood squabble or a straightforward damage claim against an insurance company, will usually take considerable time and may be exhausting. For example, a mediation between two partners about the division of a $3 million business might take a week of daily sessions. The partners might need to invite financial experts to participate as part of creating and refining various buy-out scenarios. And even when everything is supposedly settled, writing a final agreement can be difficult, since success often depends on careful drafting and redrafting, so that all details are correctly accounted for.

The decision as to whether to mediate any particular business dispute will largely depend on the facts of the case. For a discussion of how various factors line up either favoring mediation or opposing mediation, see Chapter 2, Selecting Disputes for Mediation.

Mediation's ability to accommodate disputes with multiple parties is especially important in regard to business disputes, as cases often can involve three, four, five or sometimes even more parties. For example, even a relatively simple mediation arising out of the construction of a small retail store can involve not only the store owner and prime contractor, but also an architect, soils engineer and a slew of sub-contractors. (See Section B3 for more on mediation of construction disputes.) Mediation is the one forum where all parties involved in the dispute can come together efficiently, quickly and privately, to try to work out a timely settlement. If the terms of settlement are creative and fair, the process can even forge a stronger business relationship between some of the parties.

Other advantages offered by mediation to the business owner include:

- *Control of the outcome:* The terms of settlement, if any, will be decided by the parties, not imposed by a judge, jury or arbitrator. This greatly reduces the fear that is especially likely to occur when the dispute is large enough to threaten the solvency of the business or its owners.

- *Control of the process:* The parties will select the mediator and decide which issues will be addressed, when sessions will be scheduled and how fees will be apportioned. In short, the process of mediation is far more defined and predictable than is trying to cope with the free-for-all of court.

- *Save on legal fees:* In mediation, lawyers are usually used only in a consultative role, with executives normally participating directly in the mediation. In contrast, full-blown business disputes in court result in lawyers taking over important decision-making and in the process running up tremendous legal fees—$100,000 is cheap in many business disputes.

- *Address real issues:* Parties can discuss the true problems and issues in dispute, including personalities, rather than arguing about and probably exaggerating each side's best legal points, as normally occurs in court. The result often is that a better, more honest solution is reached, which leaves participants feeling better, not worse.

- *Intelligently discuss technical issues:* Issues too complex for judge or jury to grasp in the hurly-burly of the courtroom can be handled in mediation, particularly if the mediator is knowledgeable about the subject matter.

- *Time is of the essence:* Mediation can be scheduled and likely concluded as quickly as the parties need.

- *No unwanted publicity:* Mediation avoids public exposure of business mistakes, internal problems and trade secrets. This is no small matter. For all sorts of sensitive issues, a prominent local or national company has a huge interest in preserving its reputation and goodwill, and not becoming media fodder. Sometimes, as in a case involving a claim of racial discrimination, sexual harassment or unfair treatment of the disabled, the negative costs of going public with a dispute can be huge.

- *Preserve relationships:* Nonadversarial mediation can allow the relationship between disputing businesses to outlast the dispute. The very process of arriving at a consensus decision can be the foundation for the parties to continue to do business together. By contrast, going to court destroys relationships almost every time. Many businesses are also realizing the value of using mediation as part of an overall strategy to build and keep good customer relationships. (See sidebar on The Toro Company's mediation policy for personal injury claims, in Section B.) The same is true as far as disputes with employees are concerned: why create an enemy in court who may hound your company and badmouth you for years when you have a chance to resolve the problem through mediation?

- *Plan for future:* Parties can devise a plan for a future working relationship rather than limit discussion only to the dispute at hand.

Against this positive background, this chapter is designed to help business owners and managers successfully mediate disputes that arise out of the ownership and operation of their businesses. In so doing, it deals with several important considerations not generally a part of other types of mediation, such as:

- where to look for and how to find a business mediator, and
- which types of business disputes are typically mediated, and
- how to get the other company to agree to mediate.

READ THIS CHAPTER ALONG WITH THE REST OF THIS BOOK. This chapter does not repeat the essential information covered in Chapters 1-10. Instead it builds on this information to discuss mediation in the context of small business disputes. For a full understanding of how to mediate business disputes, be sure to refer to Chapters 1 through 10.

A. Selecting a Business Mediator

In selecting a mediator for your business dispute, you should consider a few special factors regarding the skill level and style of the mediator you choose. This section briefly examines these factors, as well as where to find mediators who can handle business disputes.

1. Particular Skills Desired

As discussed in Chapter 5, Selecting Mediation Services and Mediators, mediators may bring to their work a combination of what are called "process skills" (knowledge of how to conduct a mediation) and "subject-matter knowledge" (understanding of the subject area in dispute). Mediators with good process skills can handle a wide array of cases, even if they start with very limited knowledge of the dispute's subject matter.

A. CHOOSING A MEDIATOR WITH SUBJECT-MATTER SKILLS

In some business mediations, however, having a mediator with subject-matter knowledge can be especially useful. Some business disputes (partners breaking up, for example) involve the need for financial savvy. Sure, the parties are the ones who have to agree, but a mediator who knows how to structure a buy-out over five years with adequate security to be sure installment payments are made at the same time that tax considerations are sensibly juggled might be a huge help as opposed to a similarly skilled mediator from a community mediation center who has trouble balancing his own checkbook. Similarly, if your business dispute involves technical issues—such as manufacturing processes, patents or construction law—it will likely be advantageous to use a mediator who, either due to his or her professional background, or experience mediating similar cases, starts with an understanding of these issues.

Using such a mediator has at least two advantages: you won't have to spend time at the beginning of the mediation educating the mediator about the issues, and the mediator may be better able to generate creative settlement proposals that involve the technical aspects of the dispute.

B. CHOOSING A CO-MEDIATION TEAM

An alternative is to use a co-mediation team. Typically, this would consist of a skilled, general mediator paired with a second person who serves as a technical adviser to the mediator. The advisor can be a nonmediator or a mediator who does not have good enough process skills to handle the case by himself. Putting together a co-mediation team would be the responsibility of the case manager at a private dispute resolution company. For more on using a co-mediation team or one mediator aided by a technical expert, see Chapter 5, Section C2.

C. CHOOSING A FACILITATIVE OR EVALUATIVE MEDIATOR

Another consideration in selecting a business mediator is whether you want someone whose style is more "facilitative" or "evaluative." (See Chapter 5, Section C3, for a discussion of these different styles.) The "facilitative" mediator sees his role primarily as a neutral listener, helper and message carrier. The "evaluative" mediator is more inclined, after listening to everyone's point of view, to help the parties develop a concrete settlement proposal. Many business people prefer "evaluative" mediators because their input tends to speed up the process and put executives in the familiar role of weighing options rather than having to start from scratch and work cooperatively with an opponent to create a solution to the problem.

2. WHERE TO FIND BUSINESS MEDIATORS

Usually the best place to find a capable mediator to handle most business disputes is through a private dispute resolution company. (See Chapter 3, Where to Take Your Dispute for Mediation.) Today, there are several large firms capable of providing mediation for business clients anywhere in the country. Many private firms also operate regionally, within a particular state or area of the country. (List of firms and contact information for some leading national and regional mediation companies appears in Appendix C.) You may also have in your city a small, private firm that just operates locally. To find a local firm, or the local office of a national or regional company, check the Yellow Pages under "Mediation Services," "Arbitration" or "Dispute Resolution."

Some highly skilled mediators who specialize in business cases work as independents, unaffiliated with any private firm. Their case referrals tend to come from a national network of professionals who specialize in a given area of law or business, such as construction, civil engineering or business termination disputes. To locate independent mediators who specialize in your type of business dispute, try the following:

- Ask a partner in a local law firm who specializes in that subject area—for example, patent law, securities or construction.
- Call the national office of a professional association involved in the subject area, such as the American Consulting Engineers Council or the American Medical Association.
- Contact the national office of the Society of Professionals in Dispute Resolution, or other mediator associations. (See Appendix C.)

Nonprofit, community mediation centers generally do not handle cases between businesses. If your business is small and your dispute reasonably uncomplicated, however, your local community mediation center may be able to accommodate it. If so, this would be the least expensive place to take your case. And even if they can't help you, they may be able to suggest a good local mediator who can.

3. FEES

Fees will vary with the number of parties involved, how long the mediation lasts, whether the mediation service or independent mediator operates nationally, regionally or locally and the particular mediator selected. Typically, fees will be quoted as a combination of administrative charges plus an hourly or daily rate based on the mediator's time. In general, for a relatively straightforward two-party mediation lasting one full day, using a mediator from a national firm, the cost per party will be in the range of $1,500 to $2,500. If the mediator is provided by a regional or local company, the daily cost per party would probably be more like $1,200-$1,500. For more on fees, see Chapter 3, Where to Take Your Dispute for Mediation.

How long do most business mediations take? As a rough generalization, business mediations tend to occupy from two days to a week of a mediator's time. At least several hours of that time will involve the mediator reviewing documents submitted by the parties; the rest will be actual time spent in session.

HOW TO MAKE A ROUGH CALCULATION OF HOW MUCH A BUSINESS MEDIATION WILL COST: Take the average daily rate for the type of mediator you're considering (for example, $1,500 a day per party for a mediator provided by a regional, private dispute resolution company) and multiply by the number of days you expect it may last (unless your dispute is either extremely simple or extremely complicated, I would figure on three or four days). For four days, your total would be about $6,000 (the other side would pay the same). That's a real bargain as compared with litigating your dispute in court.

B. Types of Business Disputes That Can Be Mediated

Many disputes typically faced by businesses are good candidates for mediation. Examples are discussed below.

1. Contract Disputes

Contract disputes include those based on written or oral contracts your business may have with suppliers or customers. These disputes can be about quality of goods or services, responsibilities of the parties, late delivery or payments due.

EXAMPLE: *The owner of a pizza franchise rented space in a shopping plaza for a new restaurant. Unfortunately, the discovery of asbestos in the ceiling and the need for its removal meant the space couldn't be used for a year. As a result of the delay, the restaurant owner demanded $70,000 in damages from the plaza, based on his estimates of lost profits. The plaza manager refused, saying the space had been rented "as is," and that, in any case, it was unlikely that a new restaurant would have cleared a $70,000 profit. As a complicating factor, the restaurant owner also had a contract with the franchiser requiring the restaurant to be open by a certain date and to pay a monthly fee regardless of income.*

After weeks of acrimonious negotiation left the restaurant owner and the plaza manager far from a settlement, the restaurant owner suggested they try mediation as an alternative to his filing a lawsuit. Both the plaza owner and the franchiser, whose contract with the franchisee included a clause obligating him to mediate, agreed to participate.

The mediation lasted two full days. On the afternoon of the second day, during private sessions ("caucuses") between the mediator and each party, the general outline of a three-way agreement took shape. Under this plan, the plaza agreed to pay the restaurant $20,000 for lost profits and to pay directly to the franchiser one-third of the restaurant's franchise fee for the months during which opening was delayed. The franchiser agreed to forego one-third of the fee, and to look to the restaurant owner for the balance. But instead of paying this in cash, the restaurant owner agreed to reduce the size of his exclusive franchise territory, allowing the franchiser to make up the lost income by selling another franchise in a nearby town, which the restaurant owner never really planned to serve anyway. In addition, once the restaurant finally opened, the restaurant owner agreed to issue to the plaza $10,000 in gift certificates for distribution to other tenants and their customers to build good will and help insure the restaurant would succeed.

2. CUSTOMER COMPLAINTS

Some of the most expensive and publicly embarrassing lawsuits businesses face are those brought by irate customers. These can include allegations of defective products or substandard services, misleading advertising and/or illegal collection practices. Sometimes the grievance is relatively small, while in others, it's much more serious, as might be the case if an organized group of customers claims your advertising has intentionally misled or defrauded them. Either way, mediation gives your customer a confidential way to vent his anger and lets your company settle privately without risking an adverse court decision that might encourage similar claims. Hopefully, it also results in a happier customer—one who won't badmouth your business until the end of time.

> **EXAMPLE:** *A married couple who had requested a smoke-free hotel room complained that the room they were given was instead contaminated by chemical cleaning agents. They demanded their money back, plus an unspecified amount for what they claimed was false advertising (the hotel emphasized "clean smoke-free air"), and unspecified damages for inhalation of the chemicals. When they threatened to get a lawyer and bring a class action on behalf of themselves and other former hotel guests who had experienced the same problem, the hotel invited them to mediate, offering to pay all fees.*
>
> *In mediation, the health risks claimed by the couple were discussed at length in the presence of both parties and in private caucuses between the couple and the mediator. Although the couple continued to claim that they had both gotten headaches and felt nauseated during their stay, they reluctantly concluded their likelihood of being able to prove significant long-term injuries from inhaling the cleaning agents was small. After a long day of mediation, at which the hotel manager was able to explain that, on the day in question, her assistant manager had quit, and a small business meeting had suddenly demanded 20 additional rooms, they settled with the hotel for an apology, plus a cash payment equaling three times the cost of one room, and free passes to several restaurants and movie theaters owned by the hotel's parent corporation. In addition, the couple agreed in writing not to bring any lawsuit on their own behalf or on the behalf of other former hotel guests.*

3. CONSTRUCTION DISPUTES

Construction disputes are particularly well-suited to mediation. Not only do they often involve many parties (owner-developer, architect, engineer, primary contractor and sub-contractors), but almost always involve technical issues which might be difficult to explain to a judge or jury. In addition, because construction often halts while a dispute is being resolved, time is often a critical factor. In fact, it sometimes can cost more to have a job shut down than the underlying dispute is worth.

> **EXAMPLE:** *The construction of a retail "warehouse" store had been interrupted in upstate New York when cracks appeared in the 100,000-square-foot concrete slab floor. The owner, who had been forced to pay to have the floor ripped out and re-done, brought suit against seven parties seeking $2 million in money damages on claims of breach of contract, negligence and breach of warranty. The defendants included the architecture firm that designed the building, the engineering firm that supervised construction, the primary contractor, the concrete manufacturer, the sub-contractor who mixed and poured the concrete and the sub-contractor who finished the concrete floor. After initial depositions in the case had been completed, the owner contacted a private dispute resolution company with instructions to see if all parties would agree to mediate. Everyone agreed to participate. The mediation service arranged for a co-mediation team consisting of an attorney-mediator experienced as both a construction litigator and a mediator of multi-party disputes, and a second mediator with a background in civil engineering and a specialty in soils, foundations and concrete technology. During the first full day of mediation, much of the discussion concerned proper and improper ways to pour concrete. Three hours into the second day of mediation, when the parties were still obsessing about concrete, the co-mediators threatened to end the mediation unless progress was made toward a settlement. The defendants met privately among themselves and proposed to pay the owner $1.2 million, to be split among them according to a formula they themselves had worked out. By the end of the day, the owner accepted the offer and the case resolved.*

4. EMPLOYMENT DISPUTES

Union grievance procedures have long included mediation, but many companies today use mediation with nonunion employees, too. These include claims involving discrimination, harassment and wrongful termination. Similarly, where groups of employees are involved in interpersonal disputes that impair productivity, mediation can help the whole group resolve a conflict.

> **EXAMPLE:** *Six employees, including the executive director and program director, of a local theater group became so entangled in personality disputes that absenteeism was high and the quality of the organization's dramatic work had begun to suffer. Lack of communication, stress due to unrealistic deadlines and wrong assumptions about what everybody was doing or should be doing contributed to an atmosphere where misperceptions, hurt feelings and bad communication were endemic. At the suggestion of the board of directors, the organization retained a local community mediation center to meet with all members of the group in two successive weekend sessions. The mediator conducted private caucuses with each of the employees, as well as several lengthy joint sessions with all present. The idea was to have the group develop on its own a detailed step-by-step plan for resolving the issues, improving communication and establishing procedures for dealing with future conflicts. This included setting a fixed time each week for all employees to*

meet, with a rule that no one would be allowed to be "too busy" to attend. It also established several ways to improve internal communication, both face-to-face as well as written. Finally, it provided for follow-up conflict management training for individual staff members. The mediator formalized these in a report on "Findings of Fact and Recommendations" which he submitted to the organization's board of directors.

EMPLOYEES INVOLVED IN JOB-RELATED DISPUTES SHOULD CHECK OUT THEIR LEGAL RIGHTS IN PREPARATION FOR MEDIATION. Various federal and state statutes are designed to protect workers facing harassment, discrimination, unsafe working conditions and other job-related problems. Under any of these laws, an employee's work-related dispute could involve significant legal rights which he or she should learn about in preparing for mediation. These statutes (and how they relate to one another) are often complicated and some expert advice is often needed to understand one's rights under them. Employees should see a lawyer or law coach to check out their rights or consult legal guides such as *Your Rights in the Workplace, Sexual Harassment on the Job* and *The Employer's Legal Handbook,* all published by Nolo Press.

5. Disputes Involving Partners and Owners

Disputes among business owners—whether partners, stockholders or family members—can destroy a business and, in the case of family-owned businesses, sometimes tear a family apart. For these disputes, mediation offers a protected forum where the parties can safely work out a private settlement. In fact, business ownership and termination mediation is becoming a big business, especially in areas such as California's Silicon Valley, where businesses are routinely opened, financed and taken public (or sometimes abandoned) all in a matter of a few years. But whether we are talking high tech or low tech, California or Maine, one thing is sure—everyone benefits if disputes among business owners stay out of court and are settled promptly and fairly.

MOWING COMPANY TRIMS LEGAL COSTS

The Toro Company, the Minnesota-based maker of lawnmowers, snow blowers, hedge trimmers and other power equipment, receives about 100 personal injury claims each year. "We get our share of people claiming injury as a result of using our products," acknowledges Andrew Byers, Corporate Product Integrity Manager.

For years, Toro routinely referred these claims to outside counsel who, says Byers, posed a "vigorous and aggressive" defense. "But typically we'd end up settling on the courthouse steps for $20,000 after incurring an $80,000-$100,000 defense bill and a bitter experience that didn't do much for our customers."

Beginning in 1990, Toro tried a new approach. "Our goal was to take control," recalls Byers, "control of our time, our money, our documents and our relationships with our customers."

Toro employees, who are not lawyers, now investigate all claims themselves. They meet with customers and bring an engineer to inspect the allegedly defective product. If a settlement is not reached in direct talks, the company proposes mediation. Mediations usually are held where the customer lives or in a nearby city. Toro uses private dispute resolution firms as well as retired judges acting as independent mediators. Fees are split with the customer, or sometimes Toro pays all the fees.

The results? "We settle 90%-95% of claims in mediation or within a couple of weeks as a direct result of the mediation," reports Byers. "Legal fees and insurance premiums have declined."

EXAMPLE: *The widows of two brothers who, before World War II, had founded what eventually became a large chain of auto service centers in New England, were shocked when a nephew revealed that one of the brothers had used corporate funds to develop a private real estate business on the side. This disclosure, coupled with a demand to repay the money, at a time when the real estate market was bad and it would be hard to raise additional money, threatened to tear apart the extended family of siblings and cousins, all of whom owned shares in the auto business. To avoid a wrenching, public battle, the two women retained a private dispute resolution firm in Boston. After several months of mediation, the family agreed on a restructuring plan that satisfied all the family interests under its terms. The children of the brother who had set up the real estate* *venture agreed to offer each child of the other brother shares in the real estate business or to agree to pay them over ten years the present-day value of the approximate amount their father had siphoned from the company. They all agreed to take the money instead of the stock, thus keeping the real estate business on one side of the family at the same time the improper cash diversion from the business was dealt with.*

C. Getting Your Case to the Table

Overcoming the other party's reluctance to mediate is an occasional problem in business disputes as it is in other types of disputes. Below are some techniques to consider in getting your case into mediation. (See Chapter 4, Section F.)

1. CONTRACT PROVISION

The easiest way to get a business dispute into mediation is if the dispute arises out of a contract that requires the parties to mediate. So if a contract is involved, start by reading it to see if there is such a clause. Mediation clauses usually appear near the end, under a heading such as "Mediation," "Dispute Resolution" or, sometimes mistakenly, "Arbitration." Even if the contract calls for arbitration rather than mediation, you can propose to the other party that you mediate first to see if you can mutually arrive at a solution, thus avoiding the risk that an arbitrator will impose a result one or both of you doesn't like. (See Chapter 1, Section E, for a discussion of differences between mediation and arbitration.)

For two sample mediation contract clauses, see the sidebar below. Samples of other pre-dispute clauses that can be used in standard business contracts and more detailed clauses with drafting guidance are available on a 3.5" inch diskette for PC ($8.00 shipping and handling charge) from:

CPR Institute for Dispute Resolution
366 Madison Avenue
New York, NY 10017
(212) 949-6490

SAMPLE MEDIATION CONTRACT CLAUSE

For those in a position to think ahead, the best way to get your business' disputes to mediation is by adding a contract clause requiring the parties to mediate before going to court. Below is a sample mediation clause:

If a dispute arises out of or relates to this contract, and if the dispute cannot be settled through direct negotiation, the parties agree to try in good faith to settle the dispute by mediation before resorting to arbitration or litigation.

You can make your mediation clause more detailed by specifying the mediation service which the parties must use, the minimum amount of time the parties must spend in mediation and how fees will be apportioned. This kind of clause is generally best if you do have a strong preference for using a particular mediation service. For example:

If a dispute arises out of or relates to this contract, and if the dispute cannot be settled through direct negotiation, the parties agree to try in good faith to settle the dispute by mediation before resorting to arbitration or litigation. To fulfill the requirements of this provision, the parties agree to participate in at least four hours of mediation provided by the ABC Mediation Co., Inc., of Grand Rapids, Michigan, and to split equally the mediation fees.

2. INVOKE THE OTHER PARTY'S ADR PLEDGE OR POLICY

Hundreds of major American companies (including thousands of their subsidiaries) have pledged in writing to try mediation as a first resort when disputes arise. This pledge, called the Corporate Policy Statement on Alternatives to Litigation, is circulated by a nonprofit group based in New York City called CPR Institute for Dispute Resolution. It reads, in part:

We recognize that for many disputes there is a less expensive, more effective method of resolution than the traditional lawsuit. . . . In the event of a business dispute between our company and another company which has made, or will then make, a similar statement, we are prepared to explore with that other party resolution of the dispute through negotiation or ADR ("alternative dispute resolution") techniques before pursuing full-scale litigation.

If another party in your dispute has signed this pledge, you can remind them of this with the expectation they will honor the pledge and agree to mediate.

EXAMPLE: *A small machine tool company and a major copier manufacturer had a contract dispute that looked like it was headed for court. The president of the tool company suggested that mediation be given a try. At first, the copier manufacturer said no. But when the lawyer for the machine tool company discovered that the copier company had signed an ADR pledge and reminded it's general counsel of this, the copier maker agreed to mediate.*

To find out if a company involved in your dispute has signed the pledge, ask the person you are dealing with or, if he or she doesn't know, ask the head of the company's law department. If you can't reach anyone who knows the answer (or if you don't trust the answer they give you), you can investigate further by contacting the CPR Institute for Dispute Resolution at the address listed above or by calling (212) 949-6490. There is no fee for this information and they usually can provide it to you on the phone.

Businesses in a few locales have developed their own "ADR Pledges," sometimes at the urging of a local chamber of commerce or another business organization. For example, in Colorado, nearly 1,000 businesses have signed "The Colorado Pledge" committing them to explore use of mediation. To find out if a party to your dispute has signed a similar local or statewide pledge, try contacting the Chamber of Commerce or the bar association where the other party has its principal place of business. If the other company is located in a small town where there is no chamber of commerce or the chamber does not have the information, check to see if there is a state chamber, probably with offices located in the state capital. Another source for this information might be a statewide mediation office (see Chapter 3, Section C2) if the other party is located in one of the nearly two dozen states that have one. These offices are usually not governmental agencies but are quasi-governmental programs, paid for in part with tax dollars, that track and coordinate mediation programs within a given state for the purpose of encouraging development and use of mediation. Contact information for these offices appears in Appendix D.

IF YOU DON'T WANT TO MEDIATE...

What if another party in a dispute has come to you demanding mediation based on a mediation clause in a contract you have signed, but for some reason you don't want to mediate? Do you have to go to mediation? The answer is yes, but that's not a major commitment. Most mediation clauses, including the samples offered here, commit the parties to participate in a "good faith" effort to mediate. In reality, all that means is you agree to go to the mediation, behave pleasantly and at least go through the motions of giving it a fair try. It does not obligate you to agree to pay for the most expensive mediator; it does not require you to prepare an exhaustive pre-mediation memorandum; it does not mean you must confide to the mediator all your hidden agendas and business secrets to help the mediator invent proposals for settlement.

3. INVOKE THE OTHER PARTY'S ATTORNEY'S LAW FIRM PLEDGE

Not to be outdone by their business clients, more than 1,500 of the nation's law firms have pledged to discuss with their clients the availability of mediation and other forms of dispute resolution. Called the "Law Firm Policy Statement on Alternatives to Litigation," the pledge is circulated by the CPR Institute for Dispute Resolution (see above). It states, in part:

> (W)here appropriate, the responsible attorney will discuss with the client the availability of ADR [Alternative Dispute Resolution] procedures so the client can make an informed choice concerning resolution of the dispute.

If you are unable to get the other party even to consider mediation, ask your lawyer to find out if the other party's law firm has signed this pledge. If so, your attorney can remind the opposing lawyer of the firm's pledge at least to consider the use of mediation. To find out if the other party's law firm has signed the pledge, write the CPR Institute at the address above, or call them at (212) 949-6490. There is no fee for getting the information.

4. INVOKE GOVERNMENT POLICY FAVORING MEDIATION

If your dispute concerns a contract to supply goods or services to the federal government, you can encourage a federal agency to mediate by invoking government-wide policies favoring alternative dispute resolution. Under the Alternative Dispute Resolution Act, federal agencies must appoint a "dispute resolution specialist" to develop policies for the use of mediation and other dispute resolution methods. More than two dozen agencies, including all branches of the military, have gone further and signed a government "ADR Pledge." The Pledge says the agencies will use mediation and related techniques to try to prevent and resolve disputes arising from outside procurement contracts.

To find out more about the mediation policy of the government agency with which you have a dispute, call the agency's main number and ask to be connected with the "dispute resolution specialist." If the main switchboard does not show anyone listed with that job title, ask to be connected to the Law Department or General Counsel's Office. Someone within that office may be designated as dispute resolution specialist or should be able to refer you to another office within the agency where the specialist is located.

5. Persuading Other Parties to Mediate

As we have noted previously in this book, in most cases the best way to persuade a reluctant party to mediate is to have the mediation service contact him or her to discuss the process. For a full discussion of why and how it works so well to have a neutral party issue the "invitation to mediate," see Chapter 4, Section D.

D. Preparing for Your Business Mediation

The steps involved in preparing for mediation of a business dispute are essentially the same as those discussed for regular mediation in Chapter 6. As you read Chapter 6, note especially Section B2, which covers the value of expert consultants in helping prepare for mediation. If you are involved in the break-up of a small business, for example, consultation with an accountant, business broker or business valuation expert can help you define your goals and consider various options—including some you may not have thought of—for carving up or selling the business, or buying out your partner's share.

E. Inside the Mediation Session

Business mediation sessions will generally follow the six-stage process described in Chapter 7. Pay particular attention to Section G4 on the value of being able to consult with expert advisers during the mediation. As your mediation moves toward a conclusion, proposals and counterproposals are likely to fly back and forth fairly quickly. This is when consultation with the right experts can be vitally important. Unfortunately, this will be difficult or impossible unless you have had the foresight to line up the experts you are likely to need in advance. For example, suppose your case involves a business break-up, and you start proposing to buy all of your partner's shares for cash. But your partner counters by saying she wants all patents and copyrights, and will pay for them in a complicated formula of a down payment and a percentage of profits over five years, with various additions and subtractions depending on market conditions. Surely someone on your side of the table will have to crunch the numbers, as well as consider the tax consequences of various break-up and payment scenarios. Obviously, to get this to happen efficiently, you'll want to have skilled help at the ready.

Typically, both parties will want to consult privately with their own experts and use that information to develop their own negotiating positions. But sometimes this approach will lead to an impasse, as when one or both side's experts stake out too extreme a position. For example, your accountant may say your partner's shares are worth $50,000, but your partner's accountant may insist they are worth $500,000. That doesn't advance your negotiations very far, even though both sides are paying their experts chunky fees for their opinions.

In certain circumstances, a good way to avoid or break this expensive stalemate is to agree to abide by the opinion of just one expert. Since no one is bound to accept the single expert's opinion, this is less radical than it might at first seem. But how to agree on who the expert will be? One approach is to ask the mediator to select an expert. Mediators who handle a lot of business break-ups, for example, are experienced in consulting with business valuation experts and probably can locate a good one on short notice. Another way to choose an impartial expert is to have your accountant and the other party's accountant mutually select a third accountant.

F. Writing the Agreement

The many detailed steps recommended in Chapter 8 for writing an effective settlement apply to business mediations, as well. But because business issues tend to be more complicated, and business people are prone to rely on the literal language of contracts should there be a future dispute, it's doubly important that your agreement be clear and complete.

Typically, you will reach a settlement after a long day of mediation and leave the room with only an outline or rough draft of the agreement initialed by both parties and the mediator. If so, be ready for a number of days or possibly weeks of phone calls and faxes back and forth as lawyers or other advisers for both sides help work out the final language. You may even need to reconvene the mediation for a follow-up session to have the mediator help iron out the final wording. As the saying goes, "the devil is in the details."

It is also common for an agreement to start to unravel during the final drafting stage as one or both parties is influenced by others who were not at the mediation, or simply has legitimate second-thoughts about some aspect of the pending settlement. Don't despair. This kind of "backsliding" is fairly typical and does not mean all your hard work has been for naught. Go back and mediate some more. After all, fighting over details may even be good if it forces both parties to get the final settlement agreement exactly right.

G. Other Dispute Resolution Procedures for Business Cases

If mediation does not work in your case or you do not think it is suitable, one of the following variants on mediation sometimes used by businesses may be of help.

1. Mediation With Settlement Proposal

If your case does not settle during the mediation, but you believe the mediator has a good understanding of the dispute and is fair, you can propose that the mediator prepare a settlement proposal (also referred to as a "written recommendation"), for consideration by the parties. For more on this, including how to encourage a reluctant mediator to do it, see Chapter 9, Section A2.

TIMING IS IMPORTANT IN SUGGESTING A SETTLEMENT PROPOSAL.
It is best not to raise the possibility of the mediator making a settlement
proposal before or during the mediation itself, since doing this is likely to result
in the parties trying to curry favor with the mediator, thereby skewing the
mediator's neutral role. (See Chapter 6, Section C2.) Far better to wait until the
mediator declares the mediation effort ended before raising the possibility of
asking the mediator for a settlement proposal.

2. MINI-TRIALS

Despite its name, a mini-trial is not a court trial at all, but rather an innovative
dispute resolution technique designed to allow top managers from both disputing companies to quickly hear the guts of each other's positions, often taking less
than one day. Mini-trials have been used successfully by major corporations and
government agencies. The U.S. Army Corps of Engineers, for example, has used
the device to resolve claims of tens of millions of dollars.

Mini-trials are usually arranged through a private dispute resolution company. Participants include a top manager from each side who has authority to
settle, each side's lawyers and a neutral advisor supplied by the dispute resolution company. The neutral advisor—companies often like to use retired judges—
should be someone who is extremely knowledgeable in both the subject matter
and legal issues in dispute. It's key that both sides highly respect this person.

As the mini-trial opens, lawyers for each side are given the chance within strict time limits—usually half a day—to present their best arguments before executives from both companies and the neutral advisor. This is a unique opportunity for the executives to hear—unfiltered by their own legal staffs—the best legal arguments of the other side. The advisor then tells the executives what he believes are the strengths and weaknesses of each side's case and gives his opinion as to how a judge might decide it. Then, the executives meet in private, away from their lawyers, to try to negotiate a settlement

The best type of dispute for a mini-trial is one that concerns a factual, not a legal, matter. If the law is fairly clear and only the facts are in dispute, then it is easier for the neutral advisor and executives to form an opinion on how a real court might decide the case.

Mini-trials typically cost more than mediation or arbitration. Lawyers for both sides must prepare for and make formal presentations, and the fee for the highly knowledgeable and respected neutral advisor is likely to be substantial as compared to a typical mediator. Still, even if the cost for a one- or two-day mini-trial is as high as $10,000 per side, that is still a bargain compared with conducting a full-blown trial in a complicated business dispute.

If you want to set up a mini-trial to resolve a dispute involving your company, ask one of the national or regional dispute resolution firms listed in Appendix C to send you information about how they would conduct this type of proceeding.

3. IN-HOUSE MEDIATION PROGRAMS

Some companies with large numbers of employees have found it advantageous to establish in-house dispute resolution programs to resolve conflicts between and among employees and managers. Typically, in these programs, selected staff members (managers and employees of different ages, ethnic backgrounds and job descriptions) are trained to act as mediators. Training is typically provided by an outside firm, usually a private dispute resolution or training company, but sometimes by trainers from the local community mediation center. Then, when disputes arise between or among employees, the disputants are invited (or sometimes required) to go to mediation conducted by one of the staff-mediators. Your company can establish whatever rules and procedures you want for how the program will work (but if union grievance procedures apply to some of your employees, rules for the mediation program will have to be designed so they don't conflict with the union rules). The mediation company or center that helps you set up the mediation program can customize a set of rules that meet your company's particular needs.

AS AN EMPLOYEE, YOU STILL HAVE THE RIGHT TO FILE DISCRIMINATION OR HARASSMENT CLAIMS. The availability of an in-house mediation program may dissuade a company's employees from filing discrimination claims with appropriate state or federal agencies. But employees retain the right to file these claims if they want to, and the existence of an in-house mediation program cannot prevent them from doing so.

One company that recently began an in-house mediation program is Bally's in Las Vegas. The resort, which has 4,000 employees, established the mediation program for several reasons, including improving communications among staff, improving customer service and reducing the likelihood of workplace violence. Twenty-four staff members, representing a wide cross-section of employees from senior management to support staff and including union members, were trained by mediators from the local community mediation center. Their training included techniques for handling employee disputes, inter-departmental conflicts and supervisor-employee disputes. Bally's employee relations manager, Patricia Hogan, says the program is working well and has had the added benefit of reducing management time spent dealing with internal company conflicts.

For more information on setting up an in-house mediation program for your company, I would start by asking the local nonprofit community mediation center (if you have one) whether they can help your company establish such a program and train your employees to be mediators. If not, inquire with one of the national or regional dispute resolution firms listed in Appendix C.

Lawyers and Legal Research

This book provides enough information to help most readers prepare for and bring their dispute to mediation by themselves. Nevertheless, depending on the nature of your case, you may require more advice or information about the law or the probable result of taking a dispute to court. Particularly in preparing for cases involving complex legal issues or substantial amounts of money or property, you may want to consult with a lawyer before mediation, or in between mediation sessions, or after mediation to review the settlement agreement before you sign it.

Although it's a mistake to try to achieve in mediation exactly what you think you would get in court, it nevertheless can be a good idea to use such a result as a guideline or benchmark for your mediation goals. For example, if you are mediating with an insurance company about how much they should pay you for a broken leg, knowing what juries in your area have lately been awarding for similar injuries can be a big help as you evaluate offers made in mediation by the insurance company. (See Chapter 6, Section B1.)

If your case is a relatively simple one and you are unclear about who is legally in the right, you might want to do some legal research on your own instead of, or in addition to, consulting a lawyer. For example, if your dispute involves a neighbor who claims your apple tree drops leaves, blossoms and fruit into his pool and hot tub, some research in the law library would tell you that the tree legally may belong to both of you because a small part of it now touches the property line. This information could easily change the discussion and outcome of mediation. (Note that the law on this question isn't the same in all states. For more on this and similar issues, see *Neighbor Law: Fences, Trees, Boundaries & Noise,* by Cora Jordan (Nolo Press)

This chapter provides information to help you find a lawyer or law coach as well as to do some legal research on your own.

A. Using Lawyers to Help You in Mediation

Whether you should retain a lawyer or law coach to help you with your case will depend on the nature of your dispute, your own time and ability to research the law on your own and the availability of other nonlawyer advisers, such as accountants, business valuation experts, etc. Certainly if your case concerns a multi-million dollar contract dispute potentially involving the solvency of your manufacturing company, having one or more lawyers to provide you with information and advice on contract law, taxes, patents and trademarks probably would be advisable, and the cost would not be out of line with the amount of money in dispute. On the other hand, if your case concerns a dispute of just a few hundred dollars with a home remodeling contractor, you probably won't want to pay a lawyer $150 an hour to help you prepare for mediation.

CONSIDER USING A SELF-HELP LAW COACH

As discussed several times throughout this book, a law coach is a lawyer who does not represent you in your case but who is willing to provide you legal advice as you handle the case on your own. The coach will charge you a fee only for the time you consult with him and should help you educate yourself so as to do as much as possible on your own. Hiring a coach can be a sensible and affordable compromise between going it totally alone and hiring and paying a lawyer to be involved in every aspect of your mediation.

If you need more information about some legal aspect of your case, your best bet will be to look it up yourself in a law library. Here too, of course, the time it takes you to do your own legal research may not be worth the amount in dispute.

WHEN AND HOW YOU MAY WANT TO USE A LAWYER OR LAW COACH
in mediation has been discussed in various chapters throughout this book and
won't be repeated here. These include:

- For advice on whether the law might provide any remedy for your dispute, see
  Chapter 2, Section A1.
- For help in identifying the legal issues in your dispute and what result a judge
  or jury might award if you took your case to court, see Chapter 6, Section H.
- For advice during a mediation session or between sessions on the legal
  consequences of settlement options under consideration, see Chapter 7,
  Section G4.
- To review the mediated agreement before you sign it to be sure it does not
  impair any of your legal rights in ways you did not intend, see Chapter 8,
  Section E.
- For help preparing your case for arbitration if you choose to arbitrate after an
  unsuccessful mediation, see Chapter 9, Section C.

1. WHAT TO LOOK FOR IN A LAWYER

In trying to find the right lawyer or law coach to support your mediation effort,
consider the following factors:

A. IS SPECIALIZED EXPERTISE REQUIRED?

Some lawyers are experienced in handling a variety of legal issues, such as wills,
divorces, business contracts and injury claims. If your case involves a relatively
small amount of money or property, a generalist may be just fine.

But these days the law is potentially so complex and changes so fast that
more complicated issues are usually handled by people who specialize in the
particular area of concern. Specialists often charge a little more, but if they know
the subject area better are probably worth it, for two reasons: First, they probably won't need to do as much time-consuming research, and second, you are
likely to get a more specific answer from the specialist for the time he or she
expends on the issue.

For example, if you believe you have been the victim of sexual harassment by your boss, you really should use a lawyer with special knowledge in employment law generally and sexual harassment in particular, since the opinion you get from the specialist is more likely to be accurate. Similarly, if your case concerns a dispute with your partner in a small business, you should use a lawyer who specializes in the issues of small business ownership. And even in areas where generalists have traditionally held sway—preparing a will, for example—more and more of the work is being done by specialists in estate planning.

B. DOES THE LAWYER UNDERSTAND AND SUPPORT MEDIATION?

To some extent, the type of lawyer you choose will depend on whether you want the lawyer to counsel you throughout the mediation or are only interested in an initial consultation. The lawyer's personality and attitude towards self-help law doesn't make much difference when it comes to legal advice, but it can mean a world of difference if you are primarily interested in having the lawyer coach you on a continuous basis.

If you do need a law coach, you should make it very clear from the first interview that you want to work with a lawyer who understands and supports mediation. This means a lawyer who accepts that mediation sometimes involves compromise and that what you settle for in mediation can be influenced by, but should not be determined only by, what the lawyer believes a judge or jury might give. For example, you might tell the lawyer you are interviewing that you will want him to help you prepare for your mediation, but you do not anticipate the need for him to attend the actual sessions. And you might also ask that he be available to review the anticipated written settlement agreement before you sign it.

In an age when many lawyers are under-employed, there is always the risk that a lawyer who wants your business will say that "of course'" she supports mediation, when in fact her attitude is fairly negative. To probe a little deeper to try to root out any hidden bias, ask the following questions:

- *Has the lawyer ever worked with clients going through mediation?* If so, what did the lawyer think of the process? Was it successful for the client? The way lawyers talk about their prior experiences in mediation often reveals whether they really support and respect the process, or think it's a waste of time. For example, some lawyers who have had handled one or two cases in mediation that did not settle may gloat about the result ("I told my client it wouldn't work, but he wouldn't listen"). Fortunately, many other lawyers come out of mediation with an understanding and respect for the process, regardless of whether a particular case happened to settle.

- *Has the lawyer ever been trained in mediation?* There are two types of "mediation training" that many lawyers take these days. One is training to be an actual mediator; the other is training in how to represent clients effectively in the course of a mediation. Both show an interest in mediation but, of the two, I'd probably be more interested in a lawyer who had taken the second type because it suggests a more serious professional desire to help clients through the mediation process. This is particularly true if the training to be a mediator was very limited and the lawyer didn't have to pay for it.

If a lawyer tells you he's been trained as a mediator, ask for specifics. There's a big difference between a lawyer who has paid a professional training company $500 to $1,500 for a serious training program lasting 25-40 hours, and a lawyer who spent a single afternoon attending a free training seminar put on by the local bar association. The lawyer who paid for the serious training may have been hoping to develop enough skills to be a paid mediator for a private dispute resolution company, meaning this person probably does understand and respect the mediation process. But the lawyer who took the free, half-day training may have done so merely to be a volunteer mediator once a year for a court-sponsored mediation program. That training's okay for what it is, but the investment in time and money is so minimal it doesn't tell you much about the lawyer's attitude, or understanding of mediation.

C. FEES

When you hire a lawyer to help you with a mediation, be sure you have a clear understanding about how fees will be computed. Don't expect any special price break because you are mediating; most lawyers will charge you their normal hourly rate. The key is to define, in advance, when and how the lawyer will help you. For example, if the lawyer says it will take three hours to advise you on the legal aspects of your case in advance and another three hours to review and discuss any proposed written settlement, you'll know that your bill will be six times the lawyer's hourly fee, unless, of course, you call the lawyer during the mediation and ask for additional advice.

2. HOW TO LOCATE THE RIGHT LAWYER

Don't expect to locate a good lawyer just by looking in the phone book, consulting a law directory or reading an advertisement. There's not enough information in these sources to help you make an informed choice. Also mostly useless are lawyer referral services operated by bar associations. Generally, these services make little attempt to evaluate a lawyer's skill and experience. They simply supply the names of lawyers who have listed with the service, often accepting the lawyer's own word of what types of skills he or she has.

The best approach is to talk to people you know who may have used the kind of lawyer you are seeking. This includes your personal network of friends, relatives, co-workers and other members of your church, synagogue, book group or bowling league. If someone you know and respect for having good judgment can recommend a lawyer based on a type of legal problem that's similar to yours, you are probably on the right track.

For example, if your case involves an injury you sustained in a car crash, ask around the office, gym and among friends to find other people who have had injuries and were satisfied with the legal work done by the lawyers who helped them. Of course, that a friend or colleague was satisfied with the work of a particular lawyer is no guarantee that you will also be satisfied, but it's a lot more to go on than a flashy advertisement on the back cover of the local phone book.

Other good resources are people in your community involved in the type of activity of your dispute. For example, if you seek a lawyer who specializes in small business ownership disputes, call the director of the local small business council and ask for names of three or four lawyers who do that kind of work. If you do not have a business council or similar group in your town, then pick five of the most successful small local businesses and ask the owners or managers who they use as their lawyers.

It makes sense to talk with professional people in your community who have frequent contact with lawyers and can make informed judgments about the quality of their work. For example, by speaking to your banker, accountant, insurance agent or real estate agent, you can probably develop a short list of lawyers known for their work in these areas.

Once you have the names of several lawyers, a source of more information about them is the *Martindale-Hubbell Law Directory*, available at most law libraries and some local public libraries. This resource contains biographical sketches of most practicing lawyers and information about their experience, specialties, education and the professional organizations to which they belong. Many firms also list their major clients in this directory—a good indicator of the types of practice in which the firm is engaged.

With the names of several good prospects, you can begin by meeting and interviewing some lawyers. If you tell lawyers in advance you are shopping around, most will be willing to speak to you for a half hour or so at no charge so you can size them up and make an informed decision. Of course, this will be far more appropriate if yours is a large complicated mediation for which you need considerable help than if it's a much smaller dispute with a neighbor for which you want an hour's legal help. In this situation, most local lawyers will do fine, and you should expect to pay for their time.

LOOK FOR A LAWYER YOU LIKE. In addition to looking for a lawyer with experience representing clients in mediation and who knows about your type of legal problem, look also for personal rapport and accessibility. As with most other relationships in life, you'll be happier in both the short and long run if you find a lawyer whose personality is compatible with your own.

B. Researching the Law

References to federal and state laws that affect mediation are scattered throughout this book. Some of these require or allow judges to refer disputes to mediation; others establish rules and procedures for government-run mediation programs. You can find these statutes yourself and read more about them. You can also research the specific laws involved in your dispute—for example, laws about noise limits in your neighborhood, how contracts should be interpreted and about protecting the environment.

Doing a little legal research on your own to prepare for your mediation should not be difficult once you understand a few basics about law libraries, statute books, court opinions and the general reference books that lawyers themselves use when they want to learn about an issue.

More Nolo Resources

Legal Research: How to Find and Understand the Law

Attorneys Stephen Elias & Susan Levinkind

Excellent for law students, paralegals, legal assistants, journalists and anyone who wants to find information in the law library this book shows, step-by-step, how to conduct legal research. Includes instructions, examples and library exercises.

Law on the Net

James Evans

For anyone who wants to take advantage of the thousands of legal resources available on the Internet, commercial services and bulletin boards worldwide. A detailed directory of what's available, what's valuable & how to get to it at little or no cost. Easy access to:
• federal and state government agencies, court opinions, legislation and codes
• international treaties, agreements and constitutions
• law school & law library catalogs
• legal issue discussion groups & more.

You can also get a year's subscription to *Law on the Net* on CDROM.

Legal Research Made Easy:
A Roadmap Through the Law Library Maze (Video)

From statutes to court cases and agency regulations, University of California law professor Bob Berring explains how to use all the basic legal research tools in the law library. Berring comes armed with an easy-to-follow six-step research plan and a sense of humor.

See the back of this book for details.

I. FINDING A LAW LIBRARY

In some states, finding a well-stocked law library that is open to the public is no problem; at least one library will be at a principal courthouse in every metropolitan area. But in other states, courthouse libraries are nonexistent or inadequate, and the only decent law libraries open to the public are located at a publicly funded law school, such as at a state university. Some private law schools also open their law libraries to the public, at least for limited hours.

For simple legal research tasks, a public library can be a fine place to start. The main branch of your public library may have a small but helpful legal section where you can find your state's statutes as well as county and local ordinances. Another possibility is to ask permission to use your lawyer's law office library—if, of course, you are hooked up with a lawyer.

2. LAW LIBRARIANS

All sorts of legal information, including legal forms, reference books explaining areas of law, rules of evidence and procedure, court cases, statutes and much more are available at law libraries. Law librarians, who increasingly have experience with large numbers of nonlawyers who need to look up the laws that affect their lives are usually most helpful in pointing you to the appropriate resources and legal research tools. But do not ask or expect a law librarian to do your research for you, or provide legal advice. Librarians can't and won't provide these types of services.

3. PRIMARY AND SECONDARY SOURCES

In doing legal research, you'll refer to both primary and secondary sources. Primary sources are statements of the law itself, including:
* Constitutions (federal and state)
* Legislation (laws—also called statutes or ordinances—passed by Congress, your state legislature and local governments)

- Administrative Rules and Regulations (issued by federal and state administrative agencies charged with implementing statutes)
- Case Law (decisions of federal and state courts interpreting statutes—and sometimes making law, known as "common law," if the subject isn't covered by a statute).

In the mediation of most disputes, you are unlikely to get involved in questions of constitutional law. You're far more likely to be concerned with law created by a federal or state statute, or by an administrative rule or regulation. At the federal level, for example, if your case involves environmental issues, you may be interested in regulations designed to protect wetlands issued by the Environmental Protection Agency; if you believe you were fired from a job because of your race or sex, you will want to check equal opportunity statutes such as Title VII of the Civil Rights Act administered by the Justice Department and the Equal Employment Opportunities Commission. At the state level, depending on your dispute, you may be interested in statutes dealing with partnership law, corporate law, domestic relations (marriage and family) and employment matters. If your dispute involves neighborhood issues, then you would probably want to check local ordinances dealing with issues such as zoning, noise, recreation and pets.

A. LAW BOOKS FOR NONLAWYERS, TREATISES, LEGAL ENCYCLOPEDIAS, ETC.

Obviously, primary sources—statements of the "raw law"—are important. But most legal research begins with secondary sources—books that comment on, organize or describe primary materials. This makes sense, since you get to take advantage of a great deal of preliminary work done by the person who gathered and explained the primary sources.

It often makes sense to start with law books written for nonlawyers. The better books of this type are comprehensive, well-organized and written in plain English to help you easily find and understand the particular points of law you are seeking. For example, if your dispute involves a neighborhood issue, you might want to start with *Neighbor Law,* by Cora Jordan, or, more specifically, *Dog Law,* by Mary Randolph, both from Nolo Press. Many other publishers also provide law books written for nonlawyers.

It's also helpful if you can find a treatise on the subject you're researching. A treatise is simply a book (or series of books) written for lawyers that covers a specific area of law. For example, the Nutshell Series published by the West Publishing Company offers several fine volumes, such as *Contracts in a Nutshell*, by Gordon A. Schaber and Claude D. Rohwer, and *Corporations in a Nutshell*, by Robert W. Hamilton. In a few hundred pages, each of these books does a good job of simplifying and organizing important legal areas.

The next place to do your research might be in either of two national legal encyclopedias, *American Jurisprudence 2d* (cited as AMJur2d) or *Corpus Juris Secundum* (cited as CJS). If your state has its own encyclopedia, check that, too. These encyclopedias organize the case law and some statutes into narrative statements organized alphabetically by subject. Through references in footnotes, you can locate the court decisions and laws for your state.

Law reviews published by law schools and other legal periodicals may also contain useful summaries of the law.

B. STATUTES AND CASES

When you go to look up a statute, try to use what is called an "annotated" version of the statutes. Annotated statutes include not only the text of the statutes themselves, but also brief summaries of court cases and legal articles that have discussed each statute. After you look up a statute, you may want to read the cases listed, too, to see how judges have interpreted the language of the statute.

Federal statutes: Federal statutes are organized by subject in a set of books called the United States Code (U.S.C.), which is available in probably every law library. Libraries often have one or both annotated versions of the U.S.C.—either United States Code Service (U.S.C.S.) or United States Code Annotated (U.S.C.A.). If you know the statute's common name or its citation, you should be able to find it easily.

> **EXAMPLE:** *You have a dispute with a federal agency and want to read the federal Administrative Dispute Resolution Act, 5 U.S.C. 571, to see what that agency's obligations might be about using mediation. You would look in Title 5 of the U.S.C., U.S.C.S. or U.S.C.A. (the numbers are on the spine of the book) and find section 571. The statute begins with section 571 and includes many sections.*

State statutes: State statutes, which fill many volumes, are often organized into "codes." Each code covers a separate area of law, such as Business Law, Domestic Relations (marriage and divorce) or Taxes. You can look up the subject of the law you want to read in the index to the code or statutes. For example, if your dispute is with a local cemetery over how it is maintaining a relative's grave, look in the index under "Cemetery" and you should find the laws in your state that regulate cemeteries.

You can also find a state statute if you have a section number of the particular law. For example, if want to read the Wisconsin law that allows a divorcing couple to choose a private mediator instead of using the court-sponsored mediation program, the statute citation is Wisc. Stat. Section 767.11(7). To find this statute, just get the volume corresponding to Section 767.

Once you have found the right statute, here are some suggestions for reading and making sense of it:

Make sure you understand all the terms. Refer to a legal dictionary to look up unfamiliar terms. In longer statutes, the first parts often define terms used in the later parts.

Make sure you have the most recent version. Each year, Congress and state legislatures pass hundreds of new laws and change (amend) lots of existing ones. When you look up a statute or ordinance, it's crucial that you get the most recent version.

To do that, look for a pamphlet that is inserted in the back of the hard cover volume of statutes. It's called a pocket part, and it contains any changes made to the statute in the hardcover book since the hardcover was printed. Pocket parts are updated and replaced every year—it's much cheaper than producing a whole new hardcover volume each year.

Look up the statute again in the pocket part. If there's no entry, that means the statute hasn't been changed as of the date the pocket part was printed. If there is an entry, it will tell you what language in the statute has been changed.

To check for changes that are even more recent—made since the pocket part was printed—you can check something called the Advance Legislative Service. It's a series of paperback pamphlets that contain the very latest statutory changes. The law librarian should be able to point you to it.

Local Ordinances. Cities and counties pass a wide variety of ordinances— rules which, subject to state and federal laws, have the force and effect of law.

They can have a great impact on your daily life and business. Among other things, they can affect:
- parking and driving
- health and safety standards in rental properties
- new building requirements, and
- zoning (restrictions on how land can be used).

Local governments vary as to how they organize and publish their ordinances, so you may have to check with a law librarian to find what you need. Public libraries often have local ordinances, too. Sometimes you can obtain copies of local ordinances from a city office, such as a police or motor vehicles department for traffic concerns or a planning department for zoning and building rules. If you know the specific subject of the ordinance you are looking for, you can probably get a copy by just calling the City or County Clerk's Office, or the City or County Attorney. They will usually send you a copy, free or for a small photocopying fee.

C. FINDING CASES

If you want to look up a case (court decision) and have the citation, all you need to do is decipher those strange numbers and abbreviations.

EXAMPLE: *The proper citation for the case holding that arbitration agreements are enforceable in employment contracts is* Gilmer v. Interstate/Johnson Lane Corp., *500 U.S. 20, (1991).*

The name of the case includes the name of the plaintiff (Gilmer) followed by a *v.* (meaning versus) followed by the defendant's name (Interstate/Johnson Lane Corp.); 500 is the volume number where the case is found in the series of books called United States Reports (abbreviated U.S.) at page 20. The case was decided in 1991.

Only cases decided by the U.S. Supreme Court are published in the United States Reports. (They are also published in the Supreme Court Reports.) Most of the cases you'll want to read will have been decided by courts within your state, and published in volumes entitled something like:

- [name of your state] Reports, or
- [name of your state] Appellate Reports, or
- possibly in a reporter for a region of the U.S., such as the Atlantic Reporter.

A law librarian can help you figure out exactly which series of books (reports) contains the case you are looking for.

D. MAKE SURE THE CASE IS STILL GOOD LAW

Judges don't go back and change the words of earlier decisions, like legislatures amend old statutes, but cases can still be profoundly affected by later court decisions. For example, any state's highest court, usually called the State Supreme Court, has the power to overrule a decision of a trial court or an appellate court. If it does, the trial court or appellate court's written decision no longer has any legal effect.

There are several ways to check to make sure a case you're relying on still represents valid law. The most common is to use a collection of books called "Shepard's," which lets you compile a list of all later cases that mention the case in which you are interested. Unfortunately, the Shepard's system is too complicated to explain here. If it is important to you, consult one of the tools for more legal research mentioned below, such as *Legal Research: How to Find and Understand the Law,* by Stephen Elias and Susan Levinkind (Nolo Press).

HOW MUCH IS A BROKEN ARM WORTH?

If you have been injured in a car crash or other accident and will be mediating with an insurance company about how much they will pay you for the accident, a little research in the law library can help you learn what a judge or jury might give you for the same type of injury. You can use this information as a benchmark to evaluate whatever offers may be made to you in mediation.

In many states, you can find in the law library a weekly or monthly publication called a "jury verdict reporter." Ask the law librarian if one is published in your state. In the index to these reporters, you can look up whatever type of injury you have, such as "abdominal injuries, ankle injuries, arm injuries," etc., and then find recent awards for those types of cases. If your state does not have a jury verdict reporter, look for an easy-to-use book called *What's It Worth? An Annual Guide to Current P.I. Awards and Settlements.* This book, published by Michie Company, lists injury-related awards for the whole country.

For more on evaluating personal injuries, see the chapter entitled "How Much is Your Claim Worth" in *How to Win Your Personal Injury Claim*, by Joseph Matthews (Nolo Press).

E. WHAT YOU MAY WANT TO RESEARCH

Here are a some typical disputes often brought to mediation and the kinds of legal information you may want to locate in a law library in the various books, encyclopedias, journals and other materials we discussed above:

Neighborhood Disputes. These cases often involve local ordinances concerning noise, light, property maintenance, land-use, etc. Ordinances are available at law libraries, many public libraries, or from city or town clerks. Sometimes ordinances are organized or well-indexed by subject matter. But often you need to spend a little time sifting through material that is poorly organized and will definitely want to check your conclusions by calling a knowledgeable person in the relevant municipal department.

Contract Disputes. How are contracts interpreted in your state and what are the penalties for breaking them? Contract law doesn't vary much from state to state. Start with a book for nonlawyers such as *Contracts in a Nutshell* (see Section B3) or a national encyclopedia like *Am Jur*, or *Corpus Juris Secundum*. Look up "contracts" in the index and then use the leads to pinpoint the particular type of contract issue in which you are interested, such as "employment contract" or "mistakes in contracts" or "modifying or changing a contract."

Personal Injury Claims. Is the driver who hit your car legally responsible for the accident? If so, how much should his insurance company pay you for the permanent, visible scar on your cheek? General discussions of negligence laws can be found in legal encyclopedias and in treatises on negligence. To find how local juries have valued your type of injury in recent years, refer to a "jury verdict reporter" for your state (see sidebar).

Environmental Disputes. How can your conservation group help protect the local marsh, or glen or creek from plans to erect a new office park? Much environmental law is governed by federal statutes, and many states—New York and California, for example—have passed many of their own environmental laws. Check encyclopedias or treatises specifically dealing with the environment.

Business Ownership Disputes. To see what options the law in your state allows for dissolving or reorganizing business corporations and partnerships, check the annotated statutes under "Business Organizations" or "Partnerships," as well as encyclopedias or treatises on business law written specifically for your state. An easy-to-use national treatise is Robert W. Hamilton's *Corporations in a Nutshell* (West Publishing Co.). See also *The Legal Guide for Starting & Running a Small Business,* by Fred S. Steingold (Nolo Press).

Divorce and Family Disputes. Laws of separation and divorce are governed by state law. In the annotated version of your state's statutes, check under "Domestic Relations," "Marriage and Divorce" or "Family Law." There should also be plenty of treatises on family law available for your state, as well as other books written for nonlawyers. For an overview of the field, check *Pocket Guide to Family Law,* by Robin Leonard and Stephen Elias (Nolo Press), and other Nolo Press books on legal, financial and parenting aspects of divorce, listed in the back of this book; *A Guide to Divorce Mediation,* by Gary J. Friedman (Workman Publishing, 1993), is also helpful in understanding divorce mediation.

4. MORE INFORMATION ON MEDIATION AND DISPUTE RESOLUTION

If you need to do additional research specifically about the laws relating to mediation, an excellent legal research tool is a two-volume treatise called *Mediation: Law, Policy, and Practice,* by Nancy H. Rogers and Craig A. McEwen (Clark, Boardman Callaghan; Rochester, NY, 1995). In addition to discussing many of the substantive legal issues that can arise in mediation, the book includes tables listing mediation laws by subject matter in all 50 states and the federal government, as well as lengthy excerpts from many of these laws. Although it's written for use by lawyers, the organization and writing is generally clear enough so that much of it should be useful to nonlawyers, too. It should be available at many of the better law libraries.

I can also recommend three journals about dispute resolution which may be available in the law library that you use. In these publications, you can find articles on issues involving mediation, such as how courts interpret mediation clauses in contracts, how major companies and government agencies administer mediation programs, and changes in state and federal laws that set up mediation programs.

- *Dispute Resolution Journal,* published by the American Arbitration Association. This journal is widely available in law libraries and is especially strong on issues involving mediation of employment and business disputes.
- *World Arbitration & Mediation Report,* published by Transnational Juris Publications, Inc. This publication does a good job of reporting on major federal laws and court decisions affecting mediation and arbitration. Because it is rather expensive, only the largest law libraries are likely to carry it. If necessary, you can contact the publisher directly at: One Bridge Street, Irvington-on-Hudson, NY 10533 (914) 591-4288).
- *Dispute Resolution Magazine,* published by the American Bar Association Section of Dispute Resolution. This is a magazine that lawyers read who are especially interested in mediation and arbitration. It includes well-written articles on a variety of issues, such as divorce and family mediation, new state laws affecting mediation and the lawyer's role in preparing clients for mediation.

- *Dispute Resolution Journal* and *World Arbitration & Mediation Report* are indexed by subject matter every year, so to find an article on a particular subject, check the annual index in the December volumes. *Dispute Resolution Magazine*, which appears quarterly, is not currently indexed.

5. LEGAL RESEARCH ONLINE

Until recently, doing legal research meant visiting a law library. No longer. Daily, tons of legal information is being posted on computer bulletin boards, commercial services such as America Online and, most importantly, the Internet. If you have a reasonably new computer (with at least eight megabytes of memory), a reasonably fast device for communicating over the telephone (a modem that can communicate at the speed or baud rate of at least 14,400) and the means to subscribe to a commercial service or an internet provider (at a cost ranging from $10 to $30 a month), you can do a lot of legal research without leaving your home or office.

Probably the easiest way to get started is to sign up with America Online or CompuServe. These services not only offer you lots of information available only to members, but also provide a relatively trouble-free way for you to get onto the internet, including the World Wide Web. Since these services charge you by the hour of use (around $3 an hour) as well as a monthly charge, they may be a little more expensive to use than is the case with a direct Internet provider, but you will have the benefit of the information and services they provide only to their members.

The best way to discover what's "out there" and how to get to it is to acquire a copy of *Law on the Net,* by James Evans (Nolo Press). The best place to start your online searching is the Nolo Press online site at either America Online (keyword "Nolo") or the World Wide Web *(http:///www.nolo.com),* a part of the internet. Here you will find informative articles, chapters from Nolo's books, schedules for Nolo's interactive chats and forums, Nolo's catalog and updates to Nolo products, including this book. See the front inside cover for more about what Nolo offers online.

Once you learn how to navigate the World Wide Web, consider visiting the following sites to find interesting and relevant legal materials:

- Conflictnet at the following address (called a URL, or Uniform Resource Locator): *(http://www.igc.apc.org/conflictnet/).* Conflictnet is subscribed to by hundreds of mediators for the purpose of communicating with each other and keeping up to date on developments in the mediation field. While only subscribing members have full access to these communications, the Conflictnet web page (where you end up if you use the URL described above) provides lots of useful information about the mediation profession, mediators and scheduled training events.

- Yahoo, an online subject-matter catalog that lists a number of sites containing mediation-related materials, at the following URL: *(http://www.yahoo.com/Business_and_Economy/Companies/Law/Arbitration_and_Mediation/).*

- The Better Business Bureau at the following URL: *(http://www.bbb.org/adr/medrule.html).* This site is especially appropriate for people interesting in mediating consumer or small business disputes. It provides information about the BBB's mediation programs and also contains some general information about mediation and what it can accomplish.

- Findlaw, an online searching service dedicated to legal topics, at the following URL: *(http://www.findlaw.com/01topics/index.html).* This site groups legal subjects by topic and points you to other sites that contain related legal materials.

- LawGroup Network, another dedicated law searching service that excels in helping the user find state and federal legal materials such as statutes and recent court decisions, at the following URL: *(http://www.llr.com/).*

- Magellan, an excellent searching tool that lets you search by legal topic or key word, at the following URL: *(http://www.mckinley.com/)*.
- The Law Source, yet another means of searching law on the Internet, at the following URL: *(http://thelawsource.com)*.

6. FURTHER LEGAL RESEARCH

Legal research is a subject that can (and does) easily fill a whole book of its own. Here are some good resources if you want to delve further into the subject:

- *Legal Research: How to Find and Understand the Law,* by Stephen Elias and Susan Levinkind (Nolo Press). A thorough, how-to approach to finding answers to your legal questions written for the average person in nontechnical language. The book explains how to use all major legal research tools and helps you frame your research questions.
- *Legal Research Made Easy: A Roadmap Through the Law Library Maze,* by Robert C. Berring (Legal Star/Nolo Press). This is an entertaining videotape with a six-step strategy for legal research. If you really plan to do your own legal research, this is a must-see. It's available from many public and law library video collections.
- *The Plain-Language Law Dictionary for Home and Office,* edited by Robert S. Rothenberg (Penguin Books). The more familiar *Black's Law Dictionary* frequently uses jargon to define jargon. Rothenberg's book is far better for your uses.
- *Nolo's Pocket Guide to Family Law,* by Stephen Elias and Robin Leonard (Nolo Press). Explains family law terms in plain English.

Sample Mediation Rules

This set of mediation rules is used by a private dispute resolution company with which I am associated, Empire Mediation & Arbitration, Inc., based in Rochester, New York. These rules are typical and should be similar to most you will encounter with mediators or mediation services handling a general variety of cases.

1. MEDIATION DEFINED/ROLE OF THE MEDIATOR: Mediation is a voluntary process in which the parties to the dispute meet together confidentially with a neutral third party called a "mediator." The mediator does not take sides and has no authority to make a decision, but works with the parties to help them evaluate their goals and options in order to find a solution to the dispute satisfactory to all sides.

2. INITIATING THE PROCESS: Any party to a dispute may begin mediation by sending to Empire Mediation & Arbitration, Inc. ("Empire") a completed Submission Form.

3. AGREEMENT TO MEDIATE: Empire will contact all parties to a dispute to determine their willingness to participate in mediation. If the parties agree to participate, each will sign an "Agreement to Mediate" before the commencement of the first mediation session.

4. APPOINTMENT OF MEDIATOR: From its panel of mediators, Empire will propose to the parties the names of one or more mediators qualified and available to mediate their case. The panelist will be chosen by agreement of all the parties.

5. SCHEDULING/NOTICE OF MEDIATION: Empire will schedule the mediation at a time and place convenient to all parties, and notify the parties in writing of the date, time and location of the session. The mediation may be rescheduled upon a party's request but a rescheduling fee will be assessed against the requesting party.

6. REPRESENTATION AT SESSION: Each party must be represented at the mediation by a person with authority to settle the dispute. Individuals may be represented by legal counsel, and counsel are encouraged to have their clients participate. Insurance companies may be represented by claims staff or defense counsel. Other business corporations may be represented by executive staff or counsel. It is not necessary for witnesses to attend the mediation, but if they do, their testimony will be heard at the mediator's discretion.

7. RULES OF EVIDENCE: The rules of evidence common to judicial and arbitral proceedings do not apply in mediation. Any statement, document or other record offered by the parties will be admissible unless the mediator, in his or her sole discretion, finds it to be irrelevant or otherwise inappropriate in the session.

8. SESSION PROCEDURE—OPENING STATEMENTS: The mediator will commence the session with an Opening Statement in which he or she will explain the purposes and procedures of the session. The parties will then make their opening statements, explaining their positions on the issues in dispute, including the presentation of any documents, photographs and oral or written summaries of witness testimony that would be helpful to the mediator in understanding the case.

9. SESSION PROCEDURE—PRIVATE CAUCUSES: During the mediation, the mediator may meet in private caucus with each of the parties and counsel, to explore positions and settlement options. Any information disclosed to the mediator in the caucus will be kept confidential unless the party expressly tells the mediator it may be disclosed to the other parties.

10. CONFIDENTIALITY: The mediation session constitutes a settlement negotiation and statements made during the mediation by the parties are inadmissible, to the extent allowed by law, in subsequent judicial or arbitral proceedings relating to the dispute. The parties will maintain the confidentiality of the mediation and not introduce as evidence in any future arbitral or judicial proceeding statements made by the mediator or by any other party or subpoena a mediator to testify or produce records in any such proceeding. Evidence otherwise discoverable or admissible is not made inadmissible or non-discoverable because of its use in mediation.

11. NO RECORD: No stenographic or other record of the mediation will be made.

12. CONCLUSION OF THE MEDIATION: The mediation will conclude when the parties have reached a settlement agreement, or upon the oral or written request of the parties or at the discretion of the mediator.

13. SETTLEMENT DOCUMENTS: If a settlement agreement is reached during the mediation, the parties will make their own arrangements for the drafting and later execution of settlement documents.

14. EXCLUSION OF LIABILITY: Mediators conducting sessions for Empire act as independent contractors; they are not employees of the company. Neither mediators nor the company act as legal counsel for any of the parties in the dispute. Parties have the right to legal counsel and are encouraged to obtain legal advice in connection with a dispute. Parties not represented by counsel at a mediation may condition a settlement agreement upon review by their attorney. Neither mediators nor the company are necessary parties in judicial proceedings relating to mediation, and neither the mediator nor the company will be liable to any party for an act or omission in connection with a mediation conducted under these rules.

Standards of Conduct for Mediators

These standards were developed by three professional groups: the American Arbitration Association, the American Bar Association and the Society of Professionals in Dispute Resolution, and appear here by permission of those organizations.

The three organizations intend these Standards to apply to all types of mediation, but recognize that in some cases the application of these Standards may be affected by laws or contractual agreements.

I. SELF-DETERMINATION: A MEDIATOR SHALL RECOGNIZE THAT MEDIATION IS BASED ON THE PRINCIPLE OF SELF-DETERMINATION BY THE PARTIES.

Self-determination is the fundamental principle of mediation. It requires that the mediation process rely upon the ability of the parties to reach a voluntary, uncoerced agreement. Any party may withdraw from mediation at any time.

COMMENTS: The mediator may provide information about the process, raise issues, and help parties explore options. The primary role of the mediator is to facilitate a voluntary resolution of a dispute. Parties shall be given the opportunity to consider all proposed options.

A mediator cannot personally ensure that each party has made a fully informed choice to reach a particular agreement, but it is a good practice for the mediator to make the parties aware of the importance of consulting other professionals, where appropriate, to help them make informed decisions.

II. IMPARTIALITY: A MEDIATOR SHALL CONDUCT THE MEDIATION IN AN IMPARTIAL MANNER.

The concept of mediator impartiality is central to the mediation process. A mediator shall mediate only those matters in which she or he can remain impartial and evenhanded. If at any time the mediator is unable to conduct the process in an impartial manner, the mediator is obligated to withdraw.

COMMENTS: A mediator shall avoid conduct that gives the appearance of partiality toward one of the parties. The quality of the mediation process is enhanced when the parties have confidence in the impartiality of the mediator.

When mediators are appointed by a court or institution, the appointing agency shall make reasonable efforts to ensure that mediators serve impartially.

A mediator should guard against partiality or prejudice based on the parties' personal characteristics, background or performance at the mediation.

III. CONFLICTS OF INTEREST: A MEDIATOR SHALL DISCLOSE ALL ACTUAL AND POTENTIAL CONFLICTS OF INTEREST REASONABLY KNOWN TO THE MEDIATOR. AFTER DISCLOSURE, THE MEDIATOR SHALL DECLINE TO MEDIATE UNLESS ALL PARTIES CHOOSE TO RETAIN THE MEDIATOR. THE NEED TO PROTECT AGAINST CONFLICTS OF INTEREST ALSO GOVERNS CONDUCT THAT OCCURS DURING AND AFTER THE MEDIATION.

A conflict of interest is a dealing or relationship that might create an impression of possible bias. The basic approach to questions of conflict of interest is consistent with the concept of self-determination. The mediator has a responsibility to disclose all actual and potential conflicts that are reasonably known to the mediator and could reasonably be seen as raising a question about impartiality. If all parties agree to mediate after being informed of conflicts, the mediator may proceed with the mediation. If, however, the conflict of interest casts serious doubt on the integrity of the process, the mediator shall decline to proceed.

A mediator must avoid the appearance of conflict of interest both during and after the mediation. Without the consent of all parties, a mediator shall not subsequently establish a professional relationship with one of the parties in a related matter, or in an unrelated matter under circumstances which would raise legitimate questions about the integrity of the mediation process.

COMMENTS: A mediator shall avoid conflicts of interest in recommending the services of other professionals. A mediator may make reference to professional referral services or associations which maintain rosters of qualified professionals.

Potential conflicts of interest may arise between administrators of mediation programs and mediators and there may be strong pressures on the mediator to settle a particular case or cases. The mediator's commitment must be to the parties and the process. Pressures from outside of the mediation process should never influence the mediator to coerce parties to settle.

IV. COMPETENCE: A MEDIATOR SHALL MEDIATE ONLY WHEN THE MEDIATOR HAS THE NECESSARY QUALIFICATIONS TO SATISFY THE REASONABLE EXPECTATIONS OF THE PARTIES.

Any person may be selected as a mediator, provided that the parties are satisfied with the mediator's qualifications. Training and experience in mediation, however, are often necessary for effective mediation. A person who offers herself or himself as available to serve as a mediator gives parties and the public the expectation that she or he has the competency to mediate effectively. In court-connected or other forms of mandated mediation, it is essential that mediators assigned to the parties have the requisite training and experience.

COMMENTS: Mediators should have available for the parties information regarding their relevant training, education and experience.

The requirements for appearing on a list of mediators must be made public and available to interested persons.

When mediators are appointed by a court or institution, the appointing agency shall make reasonable efforts to ensure that each mediator is qualified for the particular mediation.

V. CONFIDENTIALITY: A MEDIATOR SHALL MAINTAIN THE REASONABLE EXPECTATIONS OF THE PARTIES WITH REGARD TO CONFIDENTIALITY.

The reasonable expectations of the parties with regard to confidentiality shall be met by the mediator. The parties' expectations of confidentiality depend on the circumstances of the mediation and any agreements they may make. A mediator shall not disclose any matter that a party expects to be confidential unless given permission by all parties or unless required by law or other public policy.

COMMENTS: The parties may make their own rules with respect to confidentiality, or the accepted practice of an individual mediator or institution may dictate a particular set of expectations. Since the parties' expectations regarding confidentiality are important, the mediator should discuss these expectations with the parties.

If the mediator holds private sessions with a party, the nature of these sessions with regard to confidentiality should be discussed prior to undertaking such sessions.

In order to protect the integrity of the mediation, a mediator should avoid communicating information about how the parties acted in the mediation process, the merits of the case, or settlement offers. The mediator may report, if required, whether parties appeared at a scheduled mediation.

Where the parties have agreed that all or a portion of the information disclosed during a mediation is confidential, the parties' agreement should be respected by the mediator.

Confidentiality should not be construed to limit or prohibit the effective monitoring, research, or evaluation of mediation programs by responsible persons. Under appropriate circumstances, researchers may be permitted to obtain access to statistical data and, with the permission of the parties, to individual case files, observations of live mediations, and interviews with participants.

VI. QUALITY OF THE PROCESS: A MEDIATOR SHALL CONDUCT THE MEDIATION FAIRLY, DILIGENTLY, AND IN A MANNER CONSISTENT WITH THE PRINCIPLE OF SELF-DETERMINATION BY THE PARTIES.

A mediator shall work to ensure a quality process and to encourage mutual respect among the parties. A quality process requires a commitment by the mediator to diligence and procedural fairness. There should be adequate opportunity for each party in the mediation to participate in the discussions. The parties decide when and under what conditions they will reach an agreement or terminate a mediation.

COMMENTS: A mediator may agree to mediate only when he or she is prepared to commit the attention essential to an effective mediation.

Mediators should only accept cases when they can satisfy the reasonable expectations of the parties concerning the timing of the process. A mediator should not allow a mediation to be unduly delayed by the parties or their representatives.

The presence or absence of persons at a mediation depends on the agreement of the parties and mediator. The parties and mediator may agree that others may be excluded from particular sessions or from the entire mediation process.

The primary purpose of a mediator is to facilitate the parties' voluntary agreement. This role differs substantially from other professional-client relationships. Mixing the role of a mediator and the role of a professional advising a client is problematic, and mediators must strive to distinguish between the roles. A mediator should therefore refrain from providing professional advice. Where appropriate, a mediator should recommend that parties seek outside professional advice, or consider resolving their dispute through arbitration, counseling, neutral evaluation, or other processes. A mediator who undertakes, at the request of the parties, an additional dispute resolution role in the same matter assumes increased responsibilities and obligations that may be governed by the standards of other professions.

A mediator shall withdraw from a mediation when incapable of serving or when unable to remain impartial.

A mediator shall withdraw from the mediation or postpone a session if the mediation is being used to further illegal conduct, or if a party is unable to participate due to drug, alcohol, or other physical or mental incapacity.

Mediators should not permit their behavior in the mediation process to be guided by a desire for a high settlement rate.

VII. ADVERTISING AND SOLICITATION: A MEDIATOR SHALL BE TRUTHFUL IN ADVERTISING AND SOLICITATION FOR MEDIATION.

Advertising or any other communication with the public concerning services offered or regarding the education, training, and expertise of the mediator shall be truthful. Mediators shall refrain from promises and guarantees of results.

COMMENTS: It is imperative that communication with the public educate and instill confidence in the process.

In an advertisement or other communication to the public. a mediator may make reference to meeting state, national, or private organization qualifications only if the entity referred to has a procedure for qualifying mediators' and the mediator has been duly granted the requisite status.

VIII. FEES: A MEDIATOR SHALL FULLY DISCLOSE AND EXPLAIN THE BASIS OF COMPENSATION, FEES AND CHARGES TO THE PARTIES.

The parties should be provided sufficient information about fees at the outset of a mediation to determine if they wish to retain the services of a mediator. If a mediator charges fees, the fees shall be reasonable considering, among other things, the mediation service, the type and complexity of the matter, the expertise of the mediator, the time required, and the rates customary in the community. The better practice in reaching an understanding about fees is to set down the arrangements in a written agreement.

COMMENTS: A mediator who withdraws from a mediation should return any unearned fee to the parties.

A mediator should not enter into a fee agreement which is contingent upon the result of the mediation or amount of the settlement.

Co-mediators who share a fee should hold to standards of reasonableness in determining the allocation of fees.

A mediator should not accept a fee for referral of a matter to another mediator or to any other person.

IX. Obligations to the Mediation Process.

Mediators have a duty to improve the practice of mediation.

COMMENTS: Mediators are regarded as knowledgeable in the process of mediation. They have an obligation to use their knowledge to help educate the public about mediation; to make mediation accessible to those who would like to use it; to correct abuses; and to improve their professional skills and abilities.

National and Regional Mediation Organizations and Services

Organizations listed below can be contacted for more information about the mediation field in general, such as career and training opportunities, state and federal legislation, and references to specific mediators or mediation services in your area.

The mediation services listed include private dispute resolution companies as well as nonprofit associations that provide mediation, arbitration, and other dispute resolution services for actual cases.

MEDIATION ORGANIZATIONS

Academy of Family Mediators
4 Militia Drive
Lexington, MA 02173
(617) 674-2663
Provides support, training and guidance for practicing divorce and family mediators, and information for the public including a list of approved training programs and mediators who have met requirements for Academy membership.

American Bar Association
Section on Dispute Resolution
740 15th St., NW, 8th Floor
Washington, DC 20005
(202) 662-1680
Monitors and provides information on dispute resolution and the courts, and dispute resolution legislation pending and enacted.

Association of Family and Conciliation Courts
329 West Wilson Street
Madison, WI 53703
(608) 251-4001
Monitors and provides information on court-sponsored divorce and family mediation and arbitration programs.

Conflict Resolution Center International
2205 East Carson St.
Pittsburgh, PA 15203
(412) 481-5559
Provides information to individuals and communities working to resolve neighborhood disputes, and racial, ethnic and religious conflicts.

CPR Institute for Dispute Resolution
366 Madison Avenue, 14th Floor
New York, NY 10017
(212) 949-6490
Encourages large businesses and law firms to use mediation and other dispute resolution techniques ("ADR Pledge") as a first resort to settle disputes.

National Association for Community Mediation
1726 M St., Suite 500
Washington, DC 20036
(202) 467-6226
Supports the growth of nonprofit, community mediation centers. Can provide contact information for hundreds of centers nationally.

National Center for State Courts
300 Newport Avenue
Williamsburg, VA 23187
(804) 253-2000
Compiles and analyses statistics on court-connected ADR programs around the country.

National Institute for Dispute Resolution
1726 M St., NW, Suite 500
Washington, DC 20036
(202) 466-4764
Information clearinghouse for dispute resolution and conflict education programs nationally.

Society of Professionals in Dispute Resolution
815 15th Street, NW, Suite 500
Washington, DC 20005
(202) 783-7277
Provides information on dispute resolution field, and can make recommendations to practitioners nationwide.

MEDIATION SERVICES

American Arbitration Association
140 West 51st Street
New York, NY 10020
(212) 484-4000
Nonprofit organization provides information and maintains extensive library on all forms of dispute resolution; sponsors training programs and administers mediation and arbitration programs through offices across the country.

Arbitration Forums, Inc.
3350 Buschwood Park Drive, Suite 295
Tampa, FL 33688
(813) 931-4004
(800) 967-8889
Nonprofit organization arbitrates and mediates commercial disputes, particularly those involving the insurance industry, through offices nationwide.

Asian Pacific American Dispute Resolution Center
1010 South Flower Street, Suite 301
Los Angeles, CA 90015
(213) 747-9943
Provides mediation and conciliation services in Asian Pacific languages. Handles cases involving ethnic disputes and race relations, and domestic, housing, neighborhood, employment and business conflicts.

CDR Associates
100 Arapahoe, Suite 12
Boulder, CO 80302
(303) 442-7367
(800) MEDIATE
Provides extensive training programs in mediation and conflict management, and mediates major disputes involving corporations, governments, and communities nationally.

Center for Dispute Settlement
1666 Connecticut Ave., NW
Washington, DC 20009
(202) 265-9572
Provides general mediation and arbitrations services, and training.

Dispute Resolution, Inc.
179 Allyn Street, Suite 508
Hartford, CT 06103
(860) 724-0861
(800) 726-2393
Private dispute resolution company offers mediation and arbitration of wide range of commercial disputes.

Empire Mediation & Arbitration, Inc.
Building No. 1
625 Panorama Trail
Rochester, NY 14625
(716) 381-6830
Private dispute resolution firm mediates and arbitrates wide range of commercial disputes.

Federal Mediation and Conciliation Service
2100 K Street, NW
Washington, DC 20427
(202) 606-8080
Government agency provides information
and services in connection with the
resolution of labor disputes.

Institute for Christian Conciliation
1537 Avenue D, Suite 352
Billings, MT 59102
(406) 256-1583
Mediates disputes based on Christian
biblical principles of conflict resolution, and
provides conflict resolution training.

Jewish Conciliation Board of America
120 West 57th Street
New York, NY 10019
(212) 425-5051, ext. 3202
Provides dispute resolution services to the
Jewish community on cases involving
parents and children, financial matters,
marital conflicts and other issues.

Judicial Arbitration & Mediation Services,
Inc./Endispute
1920 Main St., Suite 300
Irvine, CA 92714
(714) 224-1810   (800) 352-JAMS
Largest private dispute resolution company
with offices nationwide; mediates and
arbitrates wide range of commercial disputes.

The Keystone Center
PO Box 8606
Keystone, CO 80435
(303) 468-5822
Resolves public policy conflicts associated
with science, technology, energy, health
and the environment.

Lesbian and Gay Community Services
Center Mediation Program
208 West 13th St.
New York, NY 10011
(212) 620-7310, ext. 321
Program helps gay men and lesbians
resolve conflicts outside the court system
including relationship breakups, child
custody and visitation issues, and
organizational disputes.

Resolute Systems, Inc.
15710 West Greenfield Ave., Suite 301
Brookfield, WI 53005
(414) 784-1595
(800) 776-6060
Private dispute resolution company with
five offices nationally; mediates and
arbitrates wide range of commercial
disputes.

Resolve, Inc.
2828 Pennsylvania Ave., NW
Washington, DC 20007
(202) 944-230
Specializes in resolving environmental
disputes.

Settlement Consultants International Inc.
14330 Midway Road, Suite 108
Dallas, TX 75244
(214) 661-3771
(800) 574-4744
Private dispute resolution company
provides mediation and arbitration of
commercial disputes, and extensive conflict
resolution training.

U.S. Arbitration & Mediation, Inc.
National Administrative Office
2100 Westown Parkway, Suite 210
West Des Moines, IA 50265
(800) 318-2700
Network of national offices providing
general mediation and arbitration of
commercial disputes.

Western Network
616 Don Gaspar
Santa Fe, NM 87501
(505) 982-9805
Specializes in public policy disputes
involving natural resources and
environmental regulation and which affect
relations between communities, organized
interest groups and government.

Statewide Mediation Offices

Many states now have, or are in the process of forming, special offices to coordinate mediation services within the state. Some offices are sponsored or partly funded by state governments; others are independent non-profit organizations that assume this role themselves. These offices specialize in mediating disputes involving public policy issues, and many can also provide information on mediators and mediation services located within their states.

The following list is provided by the National Council of State Dispute Resolution Programs, of which the National Institute of Dispute Resolution serves as secretariat. For more information on any of the offices listed, contact the National Institute for Dispute Resolution, 1726 M Street, NW Suite 500, Washington, DC 20036, (202) 466-4764, ext. 312.

ALABAMA
Alabama Center for Dispute Resolution
415 Dexter Avenue
PO BOX 671
Montgomery, AL 36101
(205) 269-0409

CALIFORNIA
Common Ground
Law & Public Policy Programs
University of California, Davis
Research Park
Davis, CA 95616
(916) 757-8569

California Center for Public Dispute
Resolution Joint Program of CA State
Univ., Sacramento &
McGeorge School of Law
980 Ninth Street, Suite 300
Sacramento, CA 95814
(916) 445-2079

COLORADO
Office of Dispute Resolution
Colorado Judicial Department
1301 Pennsylvania Street, Suite 300
Denver, CO 80203-2416
(303) 837-3667

FLORIDA
Florida Conflict Resolution Consortium
325 John Knox Road, Suite G-100
Tallahassee, FL 32303-4161
(904) 921-9069

Florida Dispute Resolution Center
Supreme Court Building
500 South Duvall Street
Tallahassee, FL 32399-1905
(904) 921-2910

GEORGIA
Georgia Office of Dispute Resolution
Supreme Court of Georgia
800 The Hurt Building
50 Hurt Plaza
Atlanta, GA 30303
(404) 527-8789

HAWAII
Center for Alternative Dispute Resolution
Office of the Admin. Dir. of the Courts
The Judiciary - State of Hawaii
P.O. Box 2560
Honolulu, HI 96804
(808) 539-4980

MAINE
Public Sector Dispute Resolution Project
University of Maine School of Law
246 Deering Avenue
Portland, ME 04102
(207) 780-4566

MASSACHUSETTS
Office of Dispute Resolution
Commonwealth of Massachsetts
Saltonstall Building, 14th FL
100 Cambridge Street
Boston, MA 02202
(617) 727-2224

MINNESOTA
MInnesota Office of Dispute Resolution
Department of Administration
304 Centennial Office Building
St. Paul, MN 55155
(612) 296-2633

MONTANA
Montana Consensus Council
Office of the Governor
State Capital Building
Helena, MT 59620
(406) 144-2075

NEBRASKA
Office of Dispute Resolution
Supreme Court of Nebraska
Adm. Off. of the Courts/Probation
PO Box 98910
Lincoln, NE 68509-8910
(402) 471-3730

NEW HAMPSHIRE
New England Center Program on
Consensus and Conflict Resolution
University of New Hampshire
11 Brookway, Rm 207
Durham, NH 03824
(603) 862-2232

NEW JERSEY
Office of Dispute Settlement
Department of the Sec. of State Advocate
CN 850, 25 Market Street
Trenton, NJ 08625
(609) 292-1773

NEW YORK
New York State Forum on Conflict &
Consensus, Inc.
244 Hudson Avenue
Albany, NY 12210
(518) 465-2500

NORTH DAKOTA
North Dakota Consensus Council, Inc.
1003 Interstate Avenue, Suite 7
Bismarck, ND 58501-0500
(701) 2244588

OHIO
Ohio Commission on Dispute
Resolution and Conflict Management
77 South High Street
Columbus, OH 43266-0124
(614) 752-9595

OREGON
Oregon Dispute Resolution Commission
1174 Chemeketa Street, NE
Salem, OR 97310
(503) 378-2877

TEXAS
Center for Public Policy Dispute Resolution
School of Law, Univ. of Texas at Austin
727 East 26th Street
Austin, TX 78705
(512) 471-3507

VERMONT
The Governor's Commission on
Dispute Resolution
109 State Street, 4th Floor
Montpelier, VT 05609
(802) 828-3217

VIRGINIA
Dispute Resolution Services
Supreme Court of Virginia
100 North Ninth Street
Richmond, VA 23219
(804) 786-6455

WASHINGTON
Washington Dispute Resolution Project
Office of Financial Management
Insurance Bldg., PO Box 43113
Olympia, WA 98504-3113
(360) 586-8629

A

B

C

E

F

G

H

 I

 J

L

M

P

Q

R

S

CATALOG

...more from Nolo Press

	EDITION	PRICE	CODE
BUSINESS			
Business Plans to Game Plans	1st	$29.95	GAME
Helping Employees Achieve Retirement Security	1st	$16.95	HEAR
⌨ Hiring Indepedent Contractors: The Employer's Legal Guide	1st	$29.95	HICI
How to Finance a Growing Business	4th	$24.95	GROW
⌨ How to Form a CA Nonprofit Corp.—w/Corp. Records Binder & PC Disk	1st	$49.95	CNP
⌨ How to Form a Nonprofit Corp., Book w/Disk (PC)—National Edition	3rd	$39.95	NNP
⌨ How to Form Your Own Calif. Corp.—w/Corp. Records Binder & Disk—PC	1st	$39.95	CACI
How to Form Your Own California Corporation	8th	$29.95	CCOR
⌨ How to Form Your Own Florida Corporation, (Book w/Disk—PC)	3rd	$39.95	FLCO
⌨ How to Form Your Own New York Corporation, (Book w/Disk—PC)	3rd	$39.95	NYCO
⌨ How to Form Your Own Texas Corporation, (Book w/Disk—PC)	4th	$39.95	TCI
How to Handle Your Workers' Compensation Claim (California Edition)	1st	$29.95	WORK
How to Market a Product for Under $500	1st	$29.95	UN500
How to Write a Business Plan	4th	$21.95	SBS
Make Up Your Mind: Entrepreneurs Talk About Decision Making	1st	$19.95	MIND
Managing Generation X: How to Bring Out the Best in Young Talent	1st	$19.95	MANX
Marketing Without Advertising	1st	$14.00	MWAD
Mastering Diversity: Managing for Success Under ADA and Other Anti-Discrimination Laws	1st	$29.95	MAST
⌨ OSHA in the Real World: (Book w/Disk—PC)	1st	$29.95	OSHA
⌨ Taking Care of Your Corporation, Vol. 1, (Book w/Disk—PC)	1st	$26.95	CORK
⌨ Taking Care of Your Corporation, Vol. 2, (Book w/Disk—PC)	1st	$39.95	CORK2
Tax Savvy for Small Business	1st	$26.95	SAVVY
The California Nonprofit Corporation Handbook	7th	$29.95	NON
The California Professional Corporation Handbook	5th	$34.95	PROF
The Employer's Legal Handbook	1st	$29.95	EMPL
The Independent Paralegal's Handbook	3rd	$29.95	PARA
The Legal Guide for Starting & Running a Small Business	2nd	$24.95	RUNS
The Partnership Book: How to Write a Partnership Agreement	4th	$24.95	PART
Rightful Termination	1st	$29.95	RITE
Sexual Harassment on the Job	2nd	$18.95	HARS
Trademark: How to Name Your Business & Product	2nd	$29.95	TRD
Workers' Comp for Employers	2nd	$29.95	CNTRL
Your Rights in the Workplace	2nd	$15.95	YRW
CONSUMER			
Fed Up With the Legal System: What's Wrong & How to Fix It	2nd	$9.95	LEG
Glossary of Insurance Terms	5th	$14.95	GLINT
How to Insure Your Car	1st	$12.95	INCAR
How to Win Your Personal Injury Claim	1st	$24.95	PICL
Nolo's Pocket Guide to California Law	4th	$10.95	CLAW
Nolo's Pocket Guide to Consumer Rights	2nd	$12.95	CAG
The Over 50 Insurance Survival Guide	1st	$16.95	OVER50
True Odds: How Risk Affects Your Everyday Life	1st	$19.95	TROD
What Do You Mean It's Not Covered?	1st	$19.95	COVER

⌨ Book with disk

	EDITION	PRICE	CODE
ESTATE PLANNING & PROBATE			
How to Probate an Estate (California Edition)	8th	$34.95	PAE
Make Your Own Living Trust	2nd	$19.95	LITR
Nolo's Simple Will Book	2nd	$17.95	SWIL
Plan Your Estate	3rd	$24.95	NEST
The Quick and Legal Will Book	1st	$15.95	QUIC
Nolo's Law Form Kit: Wills	1st	$14.95	KWL
FAMILY MATTERS			
A Legal Guide for Lesbian and Gay Couples	8th	$24.95	LG
Child Custody: Building Agreements That Work	1st	$24.95	CUST
Divorce & Money: How to Make the Best Financial Decisions During Divorce	2nd	$21.95	DIMO
How to Adopt Your Stepchild in California	4th	$22.95	ADOP
How to Do Your Own Divorce in California	21st	$21.95	CDIV
How to Do Your Own Divorce in Texas	6th	$19.95	TDIV
How to Raise or Lower Child Support in California	3rd	$18.95	CHLD
Nolo's Pocket Guide to Family Law	4th	$14.95	FLD
Practical Divorce Solutions	1st	$14.95	PDS
The Guardianship Book (California Edition)	2nd	$24.95	GB
The Living Together Kit	7th	$24.95	LTK
GOING TO COURT			
Collect Your Court Judgment (California Edition	2nd	$19.95	JUDG
Everybody's Guide to Municipal Court (California Edition)	1st	$29.95	MUNI
Everybody's Guide to Small Claims Court (California Edition)	12th	$18.95	CSCC
Everybody's Guide to Small Claims Court (National Edition)	6th	$18.95	NSCC
Fight Your Ticket ... and Win! (California Edition)	6th	$19.95	FYT
How to Change Your Name (California Edition)	6th	$24.95	NAME
Represent Yourself in Court: How to Prepare & Try a Winning Case	1st	$29.95	RYC
The Criminal Records Book (California Edition)	5th	$21.95	CRIM
HOMEOWNERS, LANDLORDS & TENANTS			
Dog Law	2nd	$12.95	DOG
⌐ Every Landlord's Legal Guide (National Edition)	1st	$29.95	ELLI
For Sale by Owner (California Edition)	2nd	$24.95	FSBO
Homestead Your House (California Edition)	8th	$9.95	HOME
How to Buy a House in California	3rd	$24.95	BHCA
Neighbor Law: Fences, Trees, Boundaries & Noise	2nd	$16.95	NEI
Safe Homes, Safe Neighborhoods: Stopping Crime Where You Live	1st	$14.95	SAFE
Tenants' Rights (California Edition)	12th	$18.95	CTEN
The Deeds Book (California Edition)	3rd	$16.95	DEED
The Landlord's Law Book, Vol. 1: Rights & Responsibilities (California Edition)	5th	$34.95	LBRT
The Landlord's Law Book, Vol. 2: Evictions (California Edition)	5th	$34.95	LBEV
HUMOR			
29 Reasons Not to Go to Law School	1st	$9.95	29R
Poetic Justice	1st	$9.95	PJ
IMMIGRATION			
How to Become a United States Citizen	5th	$14.95	CIT
How to Get a Green Card: Legal Ways to Stay in the U.S.A.	2nd	$24.95	GRN
U.S. Immigration Made Easy	5th	$39.95	IMEZ

⌐ Book with disk

CALL 800-992-6656 OR USE THE ORDER FORM IN THE BACK OF THE BOOK

	EDITION	PRICE	CODE
MONEY MATTERS			
Building Your Nest Egg With Your 401(k)	1st	$16.95	EGG
Chapter 13 Bankruptcy: Repay Your Debts	2nd	$29.95	CH13
How to File for Bankruptcy	6th	$26.95	HFB
Money Troubles: Legal Strategies to Cope With Your Debts	4th	$19.95	MT
Nolo's Law Form Kit: Personal Bankruptcy	1st	$14.95	KBNK
Nolo's Law Form Kit: Rebuild Your Credit	1st	$14.95	KCRD
Simple Contracts for Personal Use	2nd	$16.95	CONT
Smart Ways to Save Money During and After Divorce	1st	$14.95	SAVMO
Stand Up to the IRS	2nd	$21.95	SIRS
PATENTS AND COPYRIGHTS			
Copyright Your Software	1st	$39.95	CYS
Patent, Copyright & Trademark: A Desk Reference to Intellectual Property Law	1st	$24.95	PCTM
Patent It Yourself	4th	$39.95	PAT
Software Development: A Legal Guide (Book with disk—PC)	1st	$44.95	SFT
The Copyright Handbook: How to Protect and Use Written Works	2nd	$24.95	COHA
The Inventor's Notebook	1st	$19.95	INOT
RESEARCH & REFERENCE			
Law on the Net	1st	$39.95	LAWN
Legal Research: How to Find & Understand the Law	4th	$19.95	LRES
Legal Research Made Easy (Video)	1st	$89.95	LRME
SENIORS			
Beat the Nursing Home Trap: A Consumer's Guide	2nd	$18.95	ELD
Social Security, Medicare & Pensions	6th	$19.95	SOA
The Conservatorship Book (California Edition)	2nd	$29.95	CNSV
SOFTWARE			
California Incorporator 2.0—DOS	2.0	$47.97	INCI2
Living Trust Maker 2.0—Macintosh	2.0	$47.97	LTM2
Living Trust Maker 2.0—Windows	2.0	$47.97	LTWI2
Small Business Legal Pro—Macintosh	2.0	$39.95	SBM2
Small Business Legal Pro—Windows	2.0	$39.95	SBW2
Nolo's Partnership Maker 1.0—DOS	1.0	$47.97	PAGI1
Nolo's Personal RecordKeeper 3.0—Macintosh	3.0	$29.97	FRM3
Patent It Yourself 1.0—Windows	1.0	$149.97	PYWI
WillMaker 6.0—Macintosh	6.0	$41.97	WM6
WillMaker 6.0—Windows	6.0	$41.97	WIW6

ORDER FORM

Name

Address (UPS to street address, Priority Mail to P.O. boxes)

Catalog Code	Quantity	Item	Unit Price	Total

Subtotal	
In California add appropriate Sales Tax	
Shipping & Handling: $5 for 1 item, $6 for 2-3 items $7 for 4 or more.	
UPS RUSH delivery $7-any size order*	
TOTAL	

UPS to street address, Priority mail to P.O. boxes

* Delivered in 3 business days from receipt of order.
S.F. Bay area use regular shipping.

METHOD OF PAYMENT

☐ Check enclosed   ☐ VISA   ☐ Mastercard   ☐ Discover Card   ☐ American Express

Account #   Expiration Date

Signature   Phone

FOR FASTER SERVICE, USE YOUR CREDIT CARD and OUR TOLL-FREE NUMBERS

ORDER 24 HOURS A DAY	1-800-992-6656
FAX US YOUR ORDER	1-800-645-0895
e-MAIL	NoloInfo@nolopress.com
GENERAL INFORMATION	1-510-549-1976
CUSTOMER SERVICE	1-800-728-3555,
	Mon.-Sat. 9am-5pm, PST

Or mail your order with a check or money order made payable to:
Nolo Press, 950 Parker St., Berkeley, CA 94710

PRICES SUBJECT TO CHANGE.

CALL 800-992-6656 OR USE THE ORDER FORM IN THE BACK OF THE BOOK